My Heavenly Hockey Club

1

Ai Morinaga

Translated and adapted by Athena and Alethea Nibley

Lettered by North Market Street Graphics

DEL
REY

BALLANTINE BOOKS • NEW YORK

My Heavenly Hockey Club volume 1 is a work of fiction. Names, characters, places, and incidents are the products of the author's imagination or are used fictitiously. Any resemblance to actual events, locales, or persons, living or dead, is entirely coincidental.

A Del Rey Trade Paperback Original

Published in the United States by Del Rey Books, an imprint of The Random House Publishing Group, a division of Random House, Inc., New York.

Del Rey is a registered trademark and the Del Rey colophon is a trademark of Random House, Inc.

Publication rights arranged through Kodansha Ltd.

First published in Japan in 2005 by Kodansha Ltd., Tokyo as *Gokuraku Seishun Hockeybu*.

ISBN 978-0-345-49904-2

Printed in the United States of America

www.delreymanga.com

9 8 7 6 5 4 3 2 1

Translator/Adapter—Athena and Alethea Nibley
Lettering—North Market Street Graphics

Contents

When I was in high school, my friend in the hockey club would always ask me to join, saying, "You have a nice build. Would you be our goalie?" As ever, it would seem there was only one school in the prefecture that had enough members.—Morinaga

*The picture has no relation to the comment (lol)

Honorifics Explained

Throughout the Del Rey Manga books, you will find Japanese honorifics left intact in the translations. For those not familiar with how the Japanese use honorifics and, more important, how they differ from American honorifics, we present this brief overview.

Politeness has always been a critical facet of Japanese culture. Ever since the feudal era, when Japan was a highly stratified society, use of honorifics—which can be defined as polite speech that indicates relationship or status—has played an essential role in the Japanese language. When addressing someone in Japanese, an honorific usually takes the form of a suffix attached to one's name (example: "Asuna-san"), is used as a title at the end of one's name, or appears in place of the name itself (example: "Negi-sensei," or simply "Sensei!").

Honorifics can be expressions of respect or endearment. In the context of manga and anime, honorifics give insight into the nature of the relationship between characters. Many English translations leave out these important honorifics and therefore distort the feel of the original Japanese. Because Japanese honorifics contain nuances that English honorifics lack, it is our policy at Del Rey not to translate them. Here, instead, is a guide to some of the honorifics you may encounter in Del Rey Manga.

-san: This is the most common honorific and is equivalent to Mr., Miss, Ms., Mrs. It is the all-purpose honorific and can be used in any situation where politeness is required.

-sama: This is one level higher than "-san" and is used to confer great respect.

-dono: This comes from the word "tono," which means "lord." It is an even higher level than "-sama" and confers utmost respect.

-kun: This suffix is used at the end of boys' names to express familiarity or endearment. It is also sometimes used by men among friends, or when addressing someone younger or of a lower station.

-chan: This is used to express endearment, mostly toward girls. It is also used for little boys, pets, and even among lovers. It gives a sense of childish cuteness.

Bozu: This is an informal way to refer to a boy, similar to the English terms "kid" and "squirt."

Sempai/Senpai: This title suggests that the addressee is one's senior in a group or organization. It is most often used in a school setting, where underclassmen refer to their upperclassmen as "sempai." It can also be used in the workplace, such as when a newer employee addresses an employee who has seniority in the company.

Kohai: This is the opposite of "sempai" and is used toward underclassmen in school or newcomers in the workplace. It connotes that the addressee is of a lower station.

Sensei: Literally meaning "one who has come before," this title is used for teachers, doctors, or masters of any profession or art.

-[blank]: This is usually forgotten in these lists, but it is perhaps the most significant difference between Japanese and English. The lack of honorific means that the speaker has permission to address the person in a very intimate way. Usually, only family, spouses, or very close friends have this kind of permission. Known as *yobisute*, it can be gratifying when someone who has earned the intimacy starts to call one by one's name without an honorific. But when that intimacy hasn't been earned, it can be very insulting.

My Heavenly Hockey Club

I

Ai Morinaga

Contents

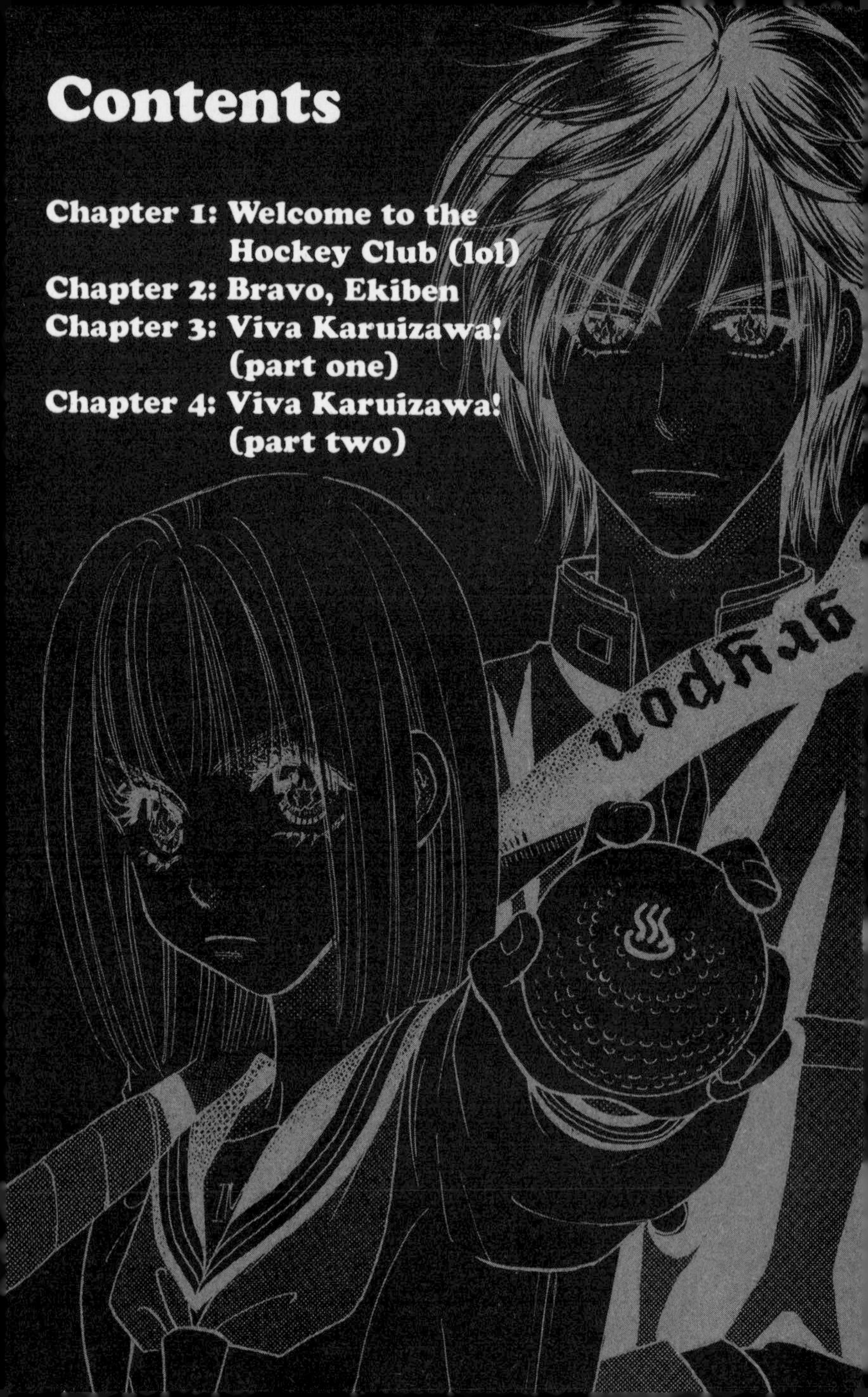

Chapter 1: Welcome to the Hockey Club (lol)

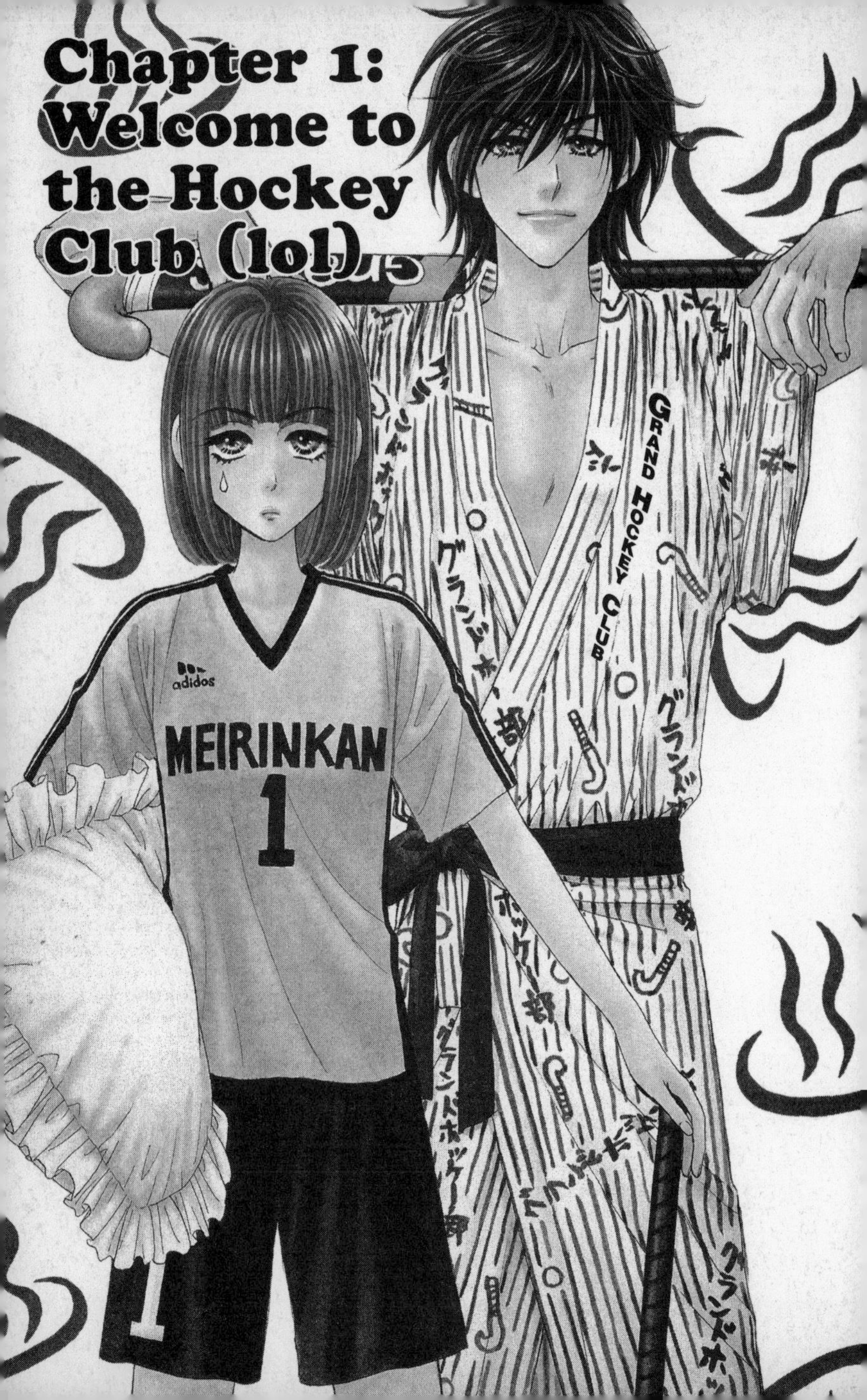
GRAND HOCKEY CLUB
adidos
MEIRINKAN
1

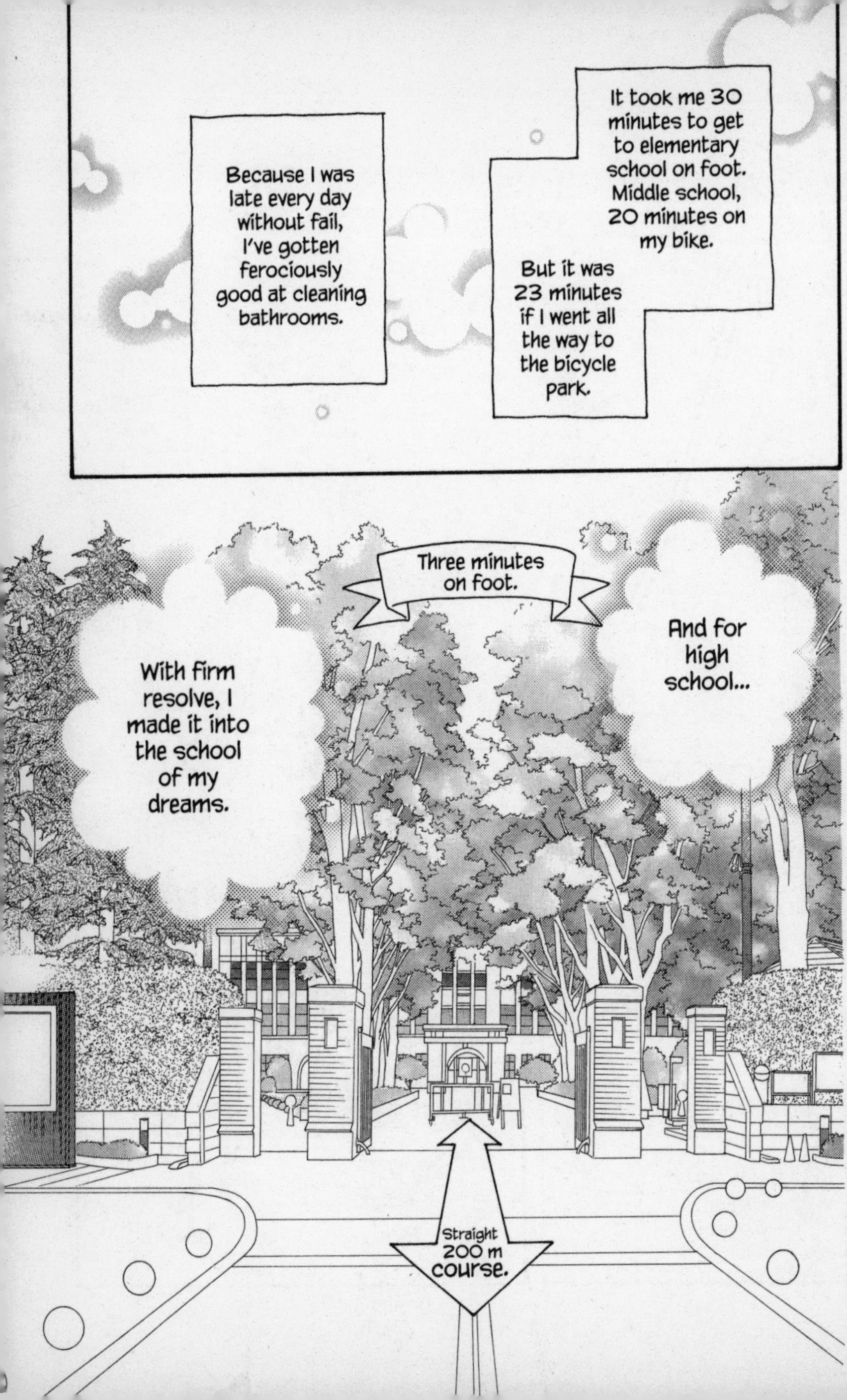
It took me 30 minutes to get to elementary school on foot. Middle school, 20 minutes on my bike.
But it was 23 minutes if I went all the way to the bicycle park.
Because I was late every day without fail, I've gotten ferociously good at cleaning bathrooms.
And for high school...
Three minutes on foot.
With firm resolve, I made it into the school of my dreams.
Straight 200 m course.

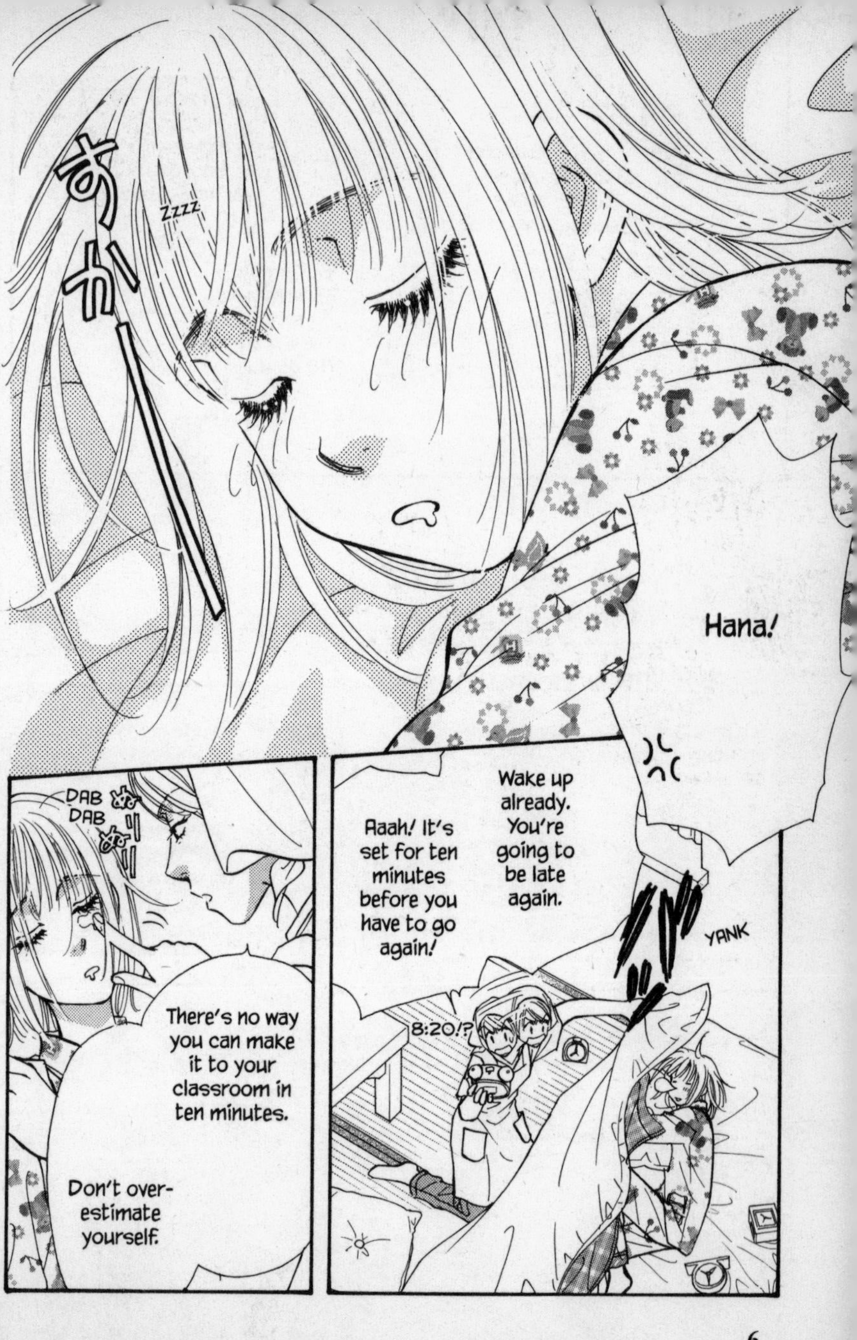
ZZZZ
Hana!
Wake up already. You're going to be late again.
YANK
Aaah! It's set for ten minutes before you have to go again!
8:20!?
DAB DAB
There's no way you can make it to your classroom in ten minutes.
Don't over-estimate yourself.

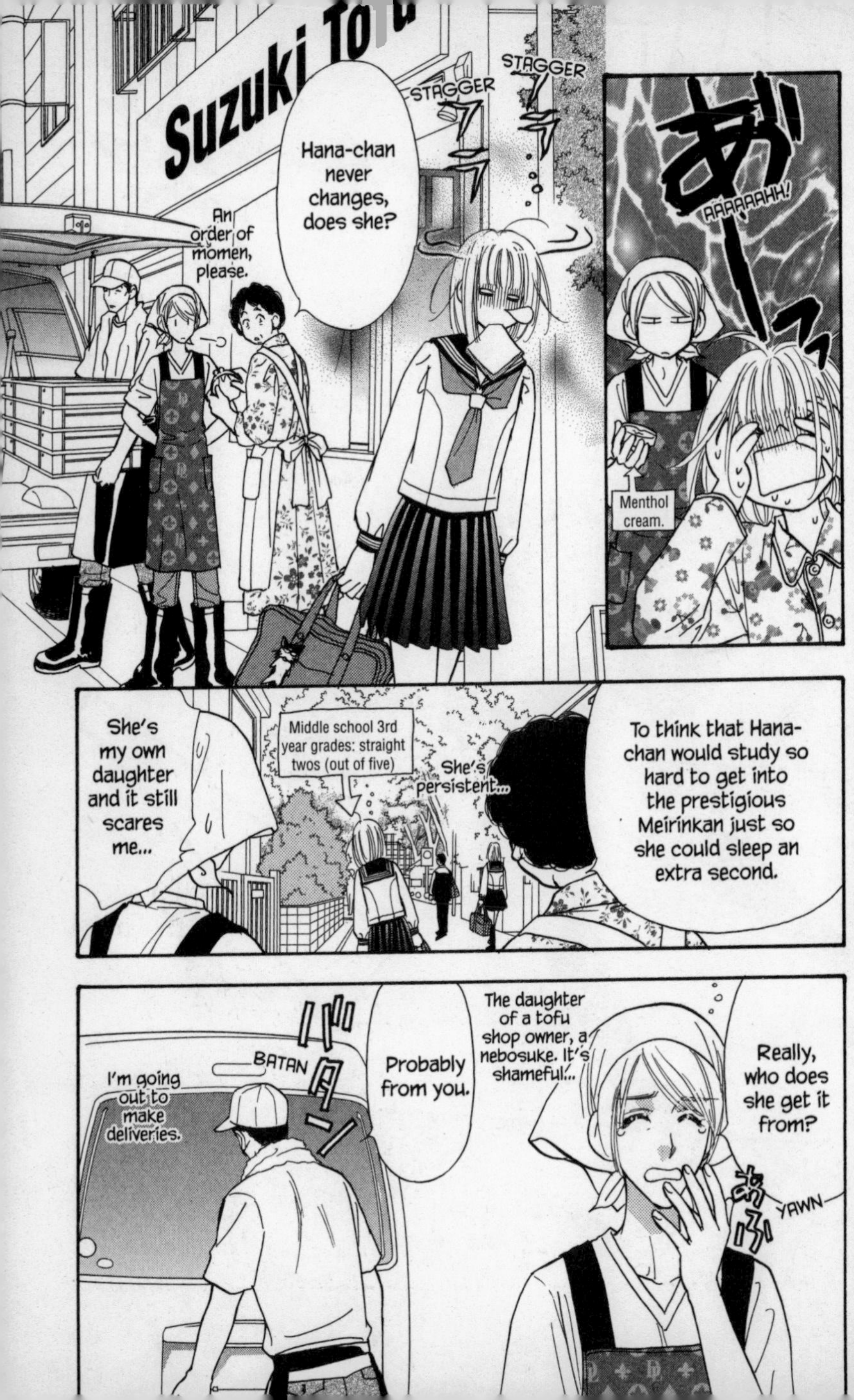
AAAAAAHH!
Menthol cream.
STAGGER
STAGGER
Hana-chan never changes, does she?
An order of momen, please.
Suzuki To
To think that Hana-chan would study so hard to get into the prestigious Meirinkan just so she could sleep an extra second.
She's persistent...
Middle school 3rd year grades: straight twos (out of five)
She's my own daughter and it still scares me...
Really, who does she get it from?
YAWN
The daughter of a tofu shop owner, a nebosuke. It's shameful...
Probably from you.
BATAN
I'm going out to make deliveries.

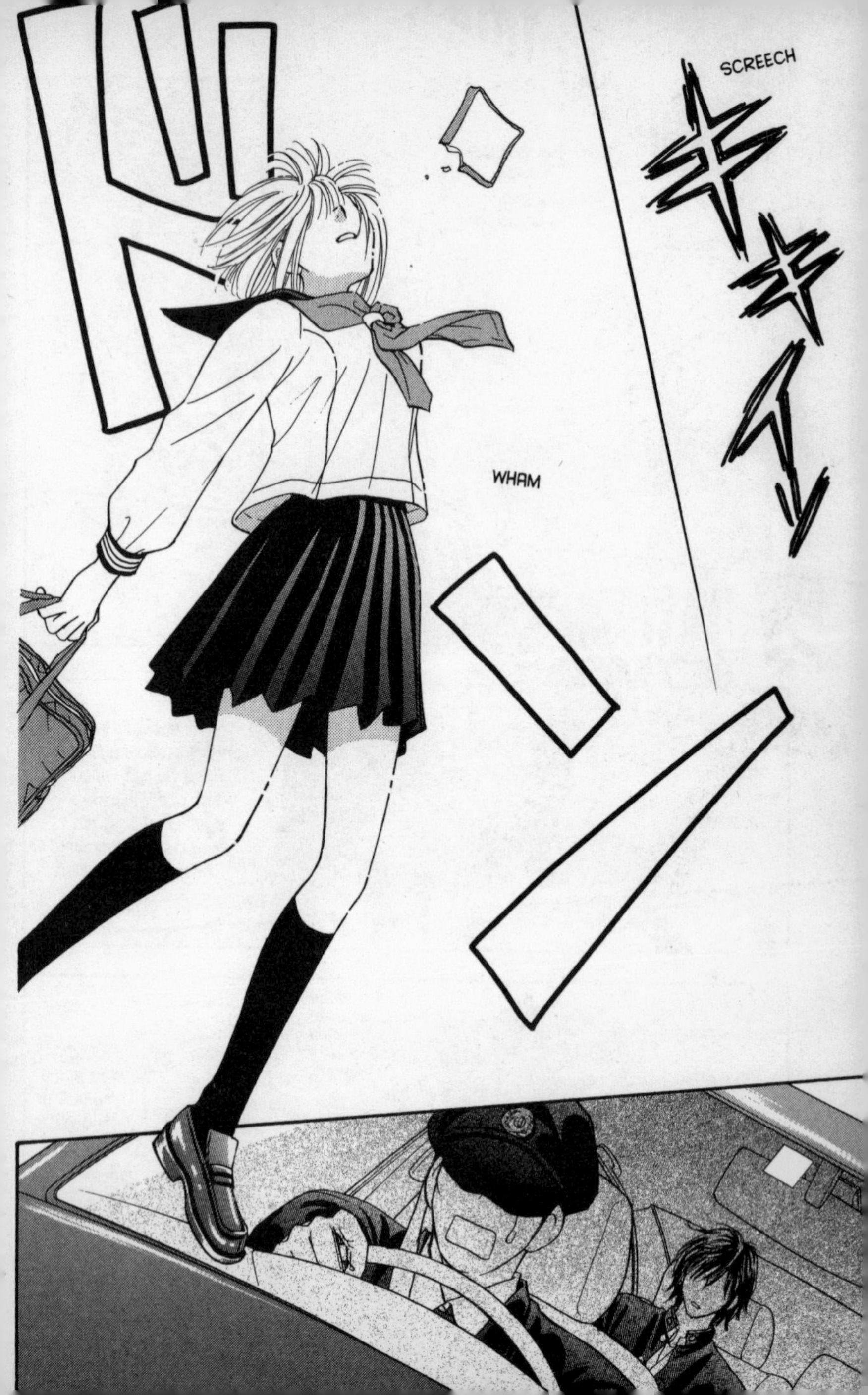
SCREECH
WHAM

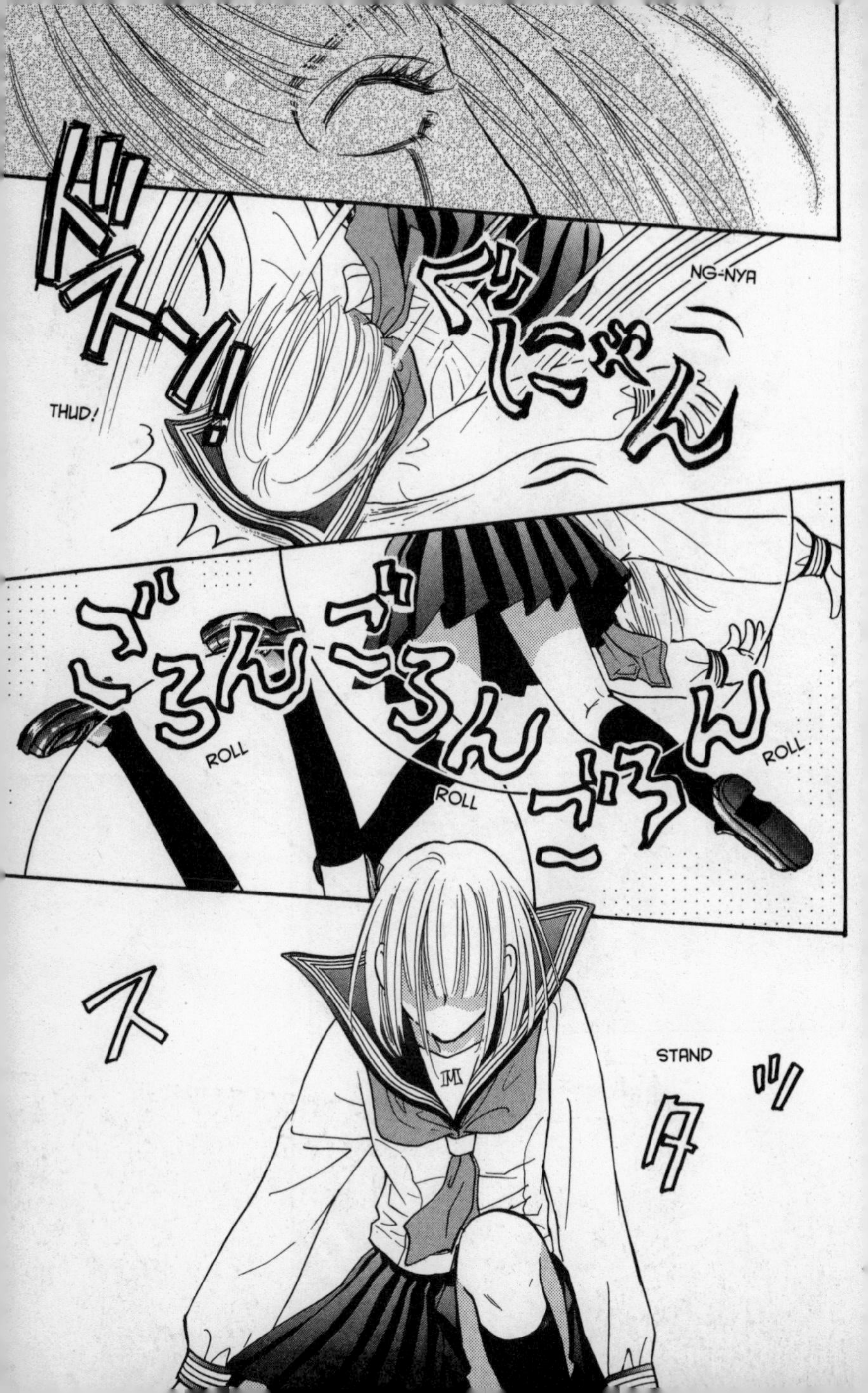

ぐにゃん
NG-NYA
ドスーン!
THUD!
ごろんごろんごろん~
ROLL
ROLL
ROLL
ス
STAND

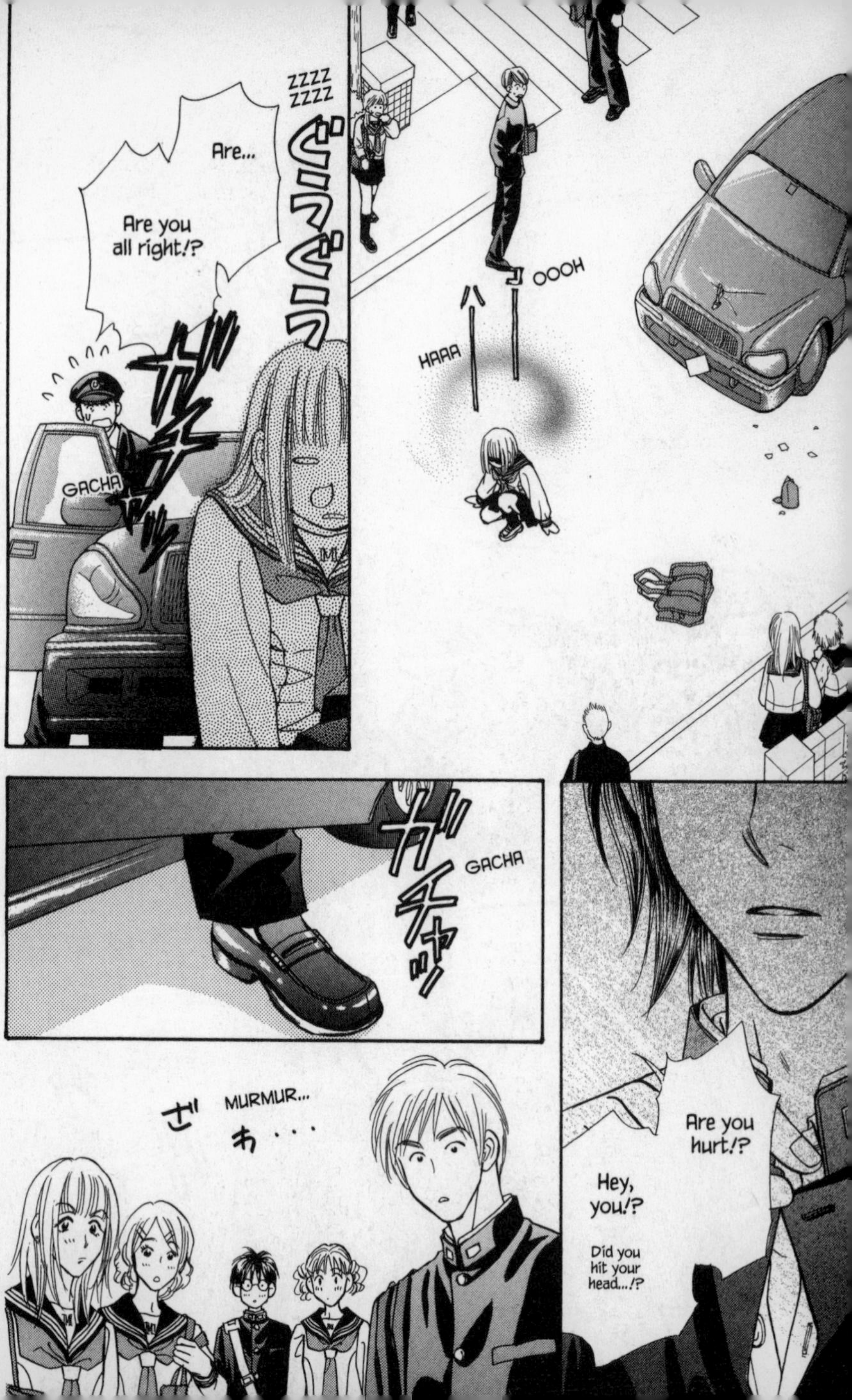

OOOH
HAAA
ZZZZ
ZZZZ
Are...
Are you all right!?
GACHA
Are you hurt!?
Hey, you!?
Did you hit your head...!?
GACHA
MURMUR...

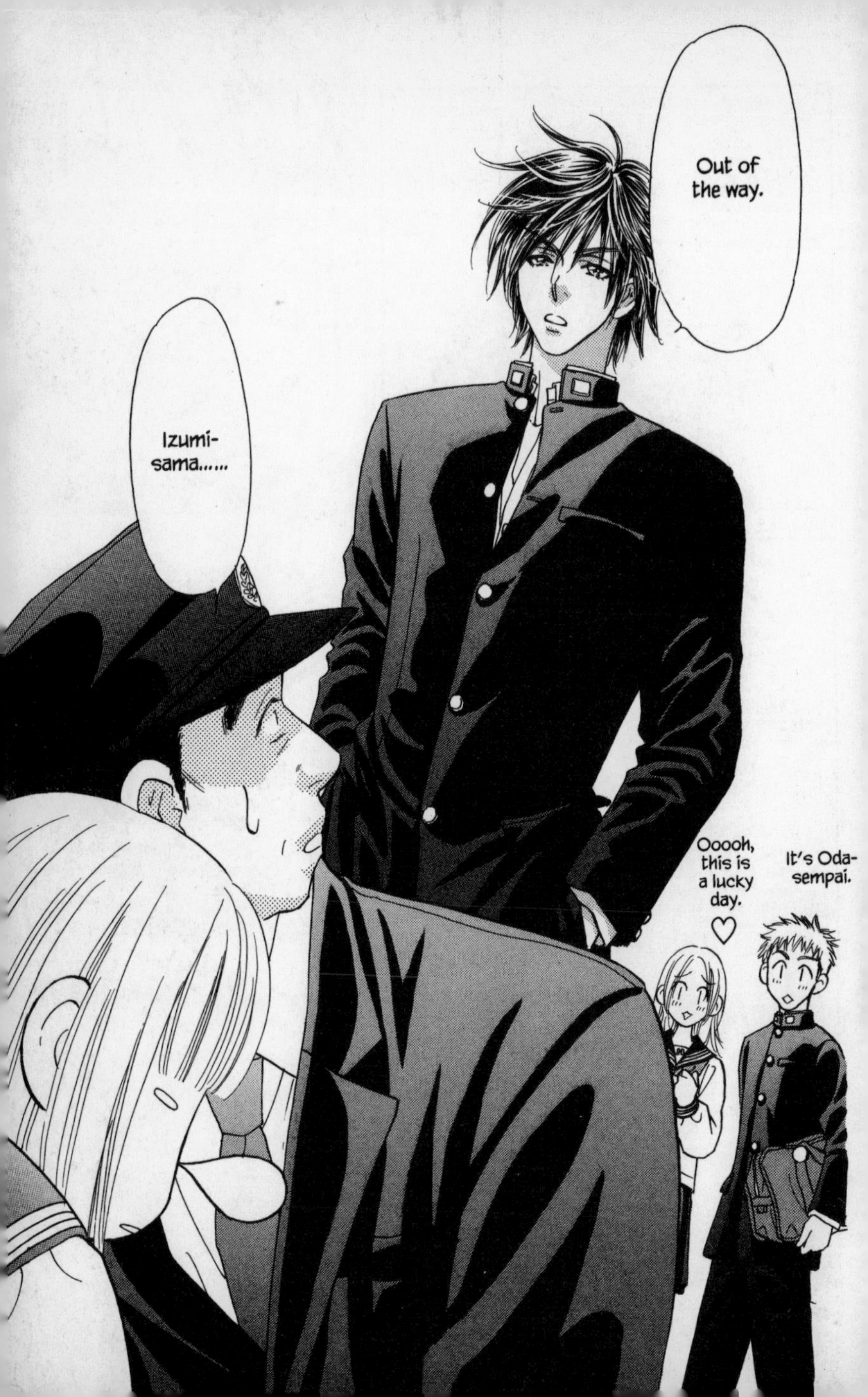
Out of the way.
Izumi-sama......
It's Oda-sempai.
Ooooh, this is a lucky day. ♡

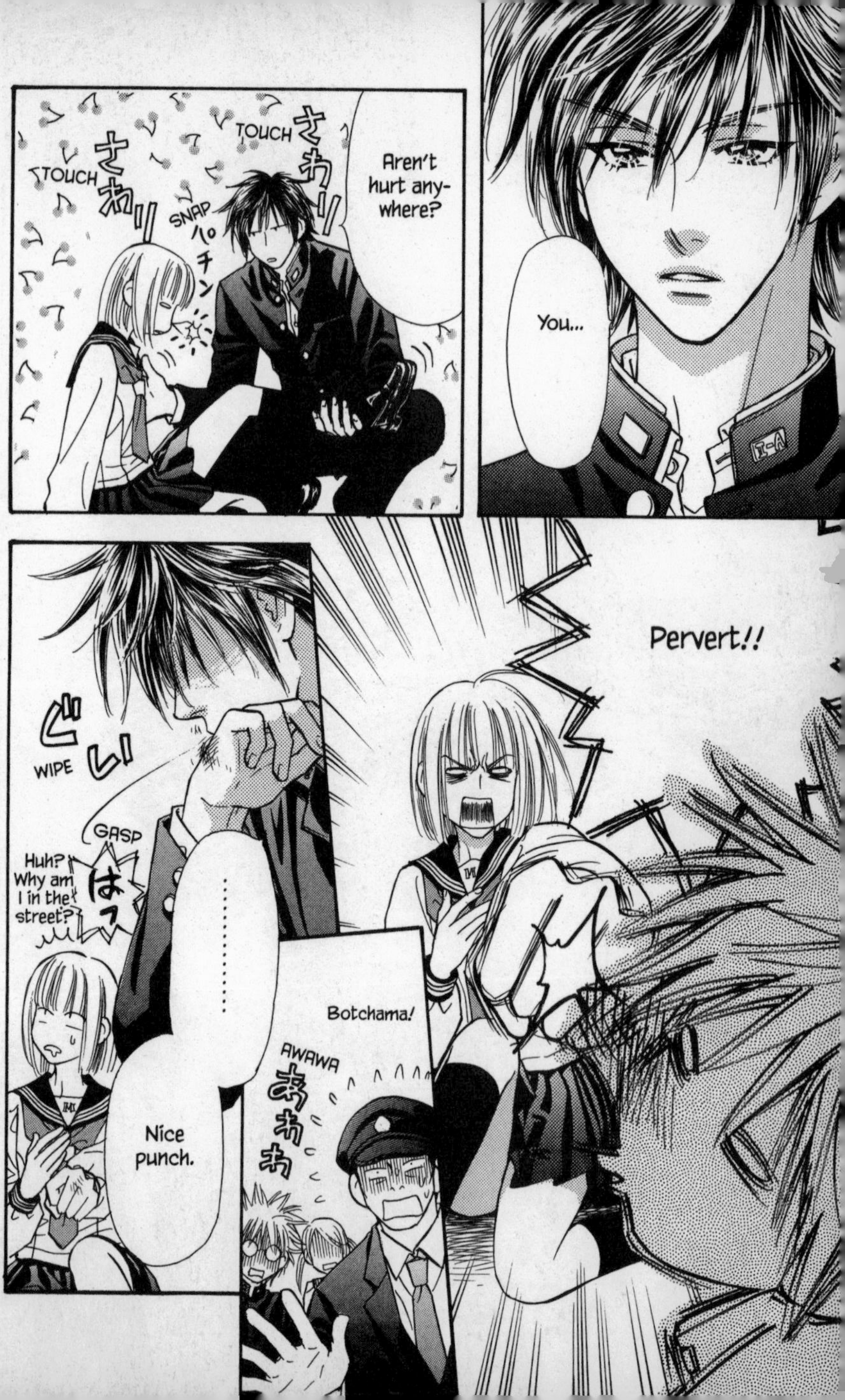
You...
Aren't hurt anywhere?
TOUCH さわ
TOUCH さわ
SNAP パチン
Pervert!!
WIPE ぐい
......
GASP はっ
Huh? Why am I in the street?
Nice punch.
Botchama!
AWAWA あわわ

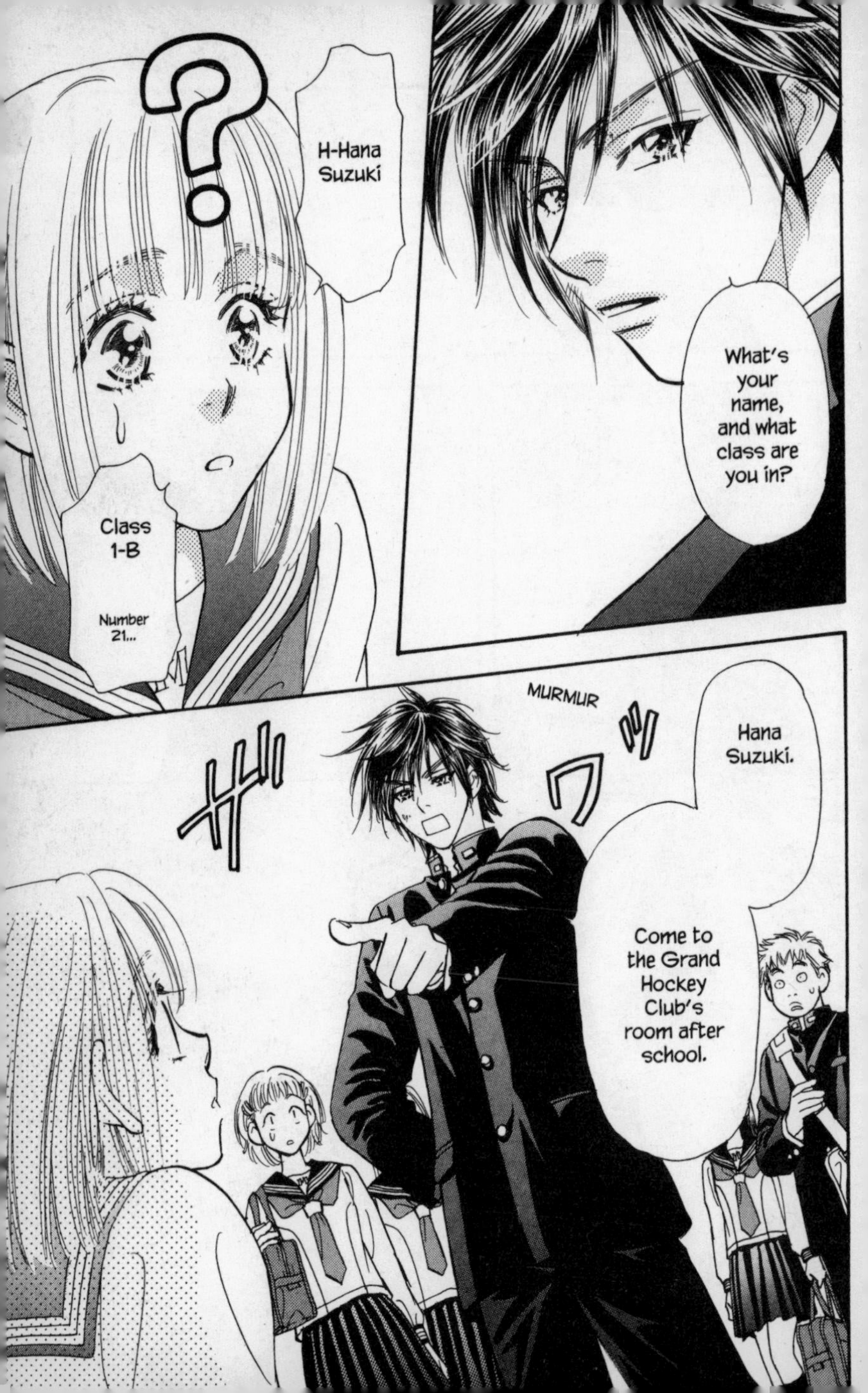
What's your name, and what class are you in?
H-Hana Suzuki
Class 1-B
Number 21...
Hana Suzuki.
Come to the Grand Hockey Club's room after school.
MURMUR

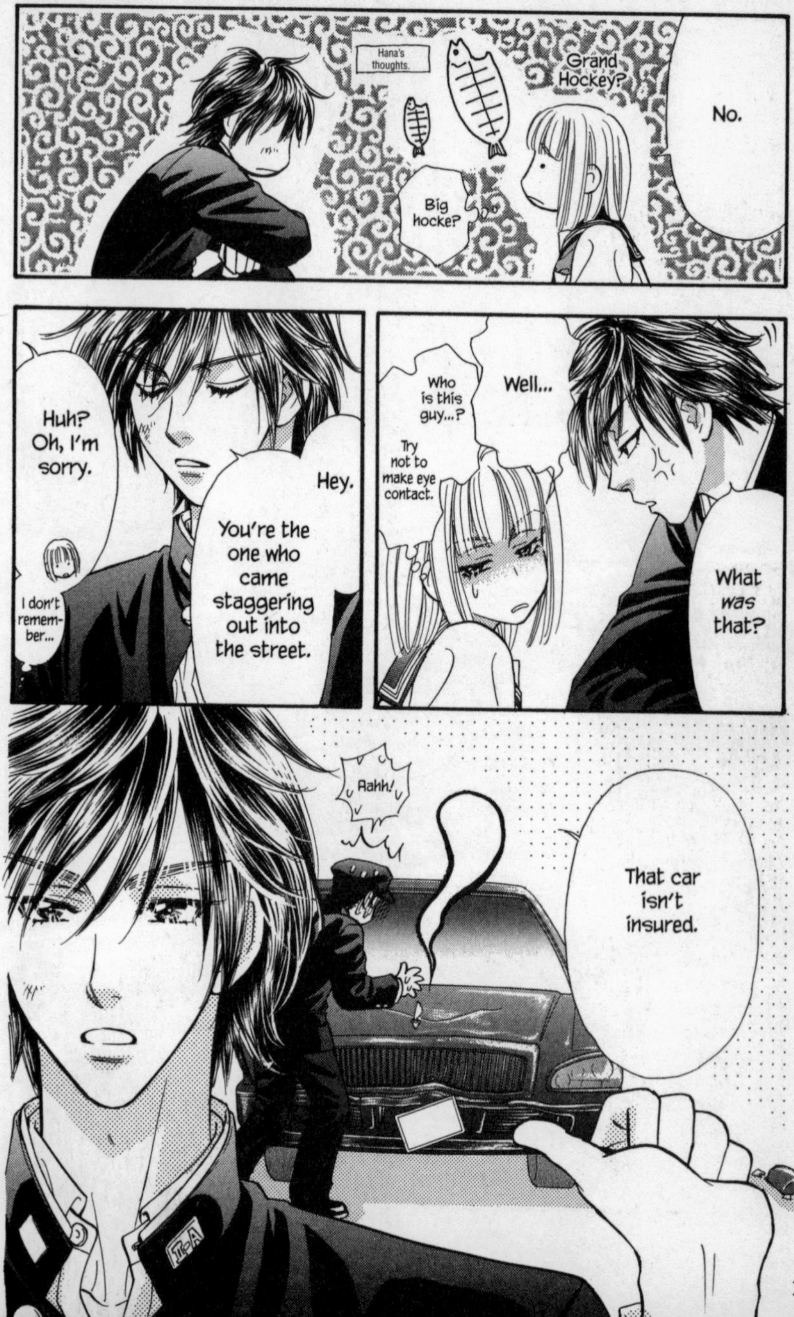
No.
Grand Hockey?
Hana's thoughts.
Big hocke?
Well...
Who is this guy...?
Try not to make eye contact.
What was that?
Hey.
You're the one who came staggering out into the street.
Huh? Oh, I'm sorry.
I don't remember...
That car isn't insured.
Aahh!

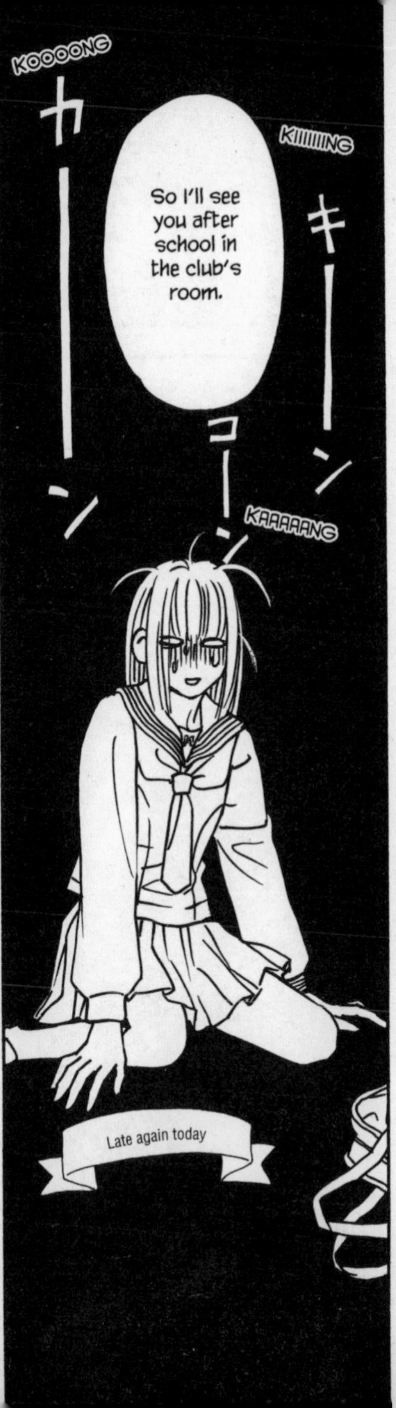
KOOOONG
カーン
KIIIIIING
キーン
So I'll see you after school in the club's room.
コーン
KAAAAANG
Late again today

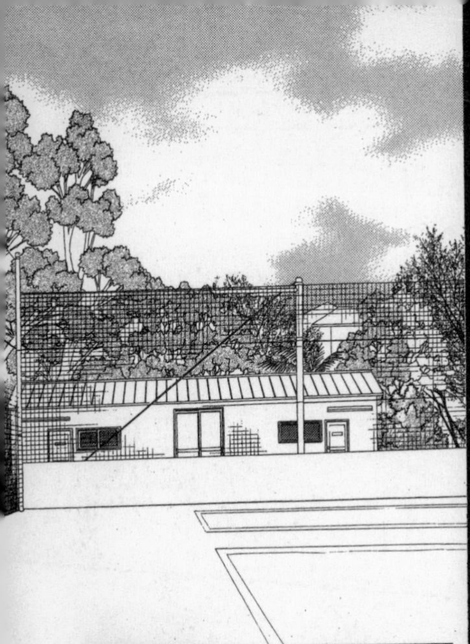

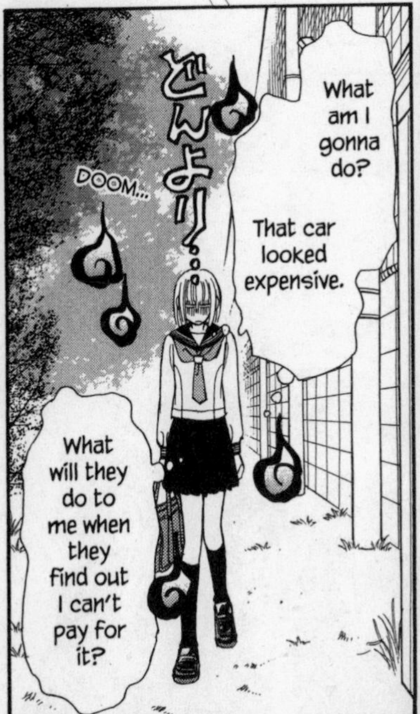
What am I gonna do?
That car looked expensive.
どんより…
DOOM...
What will they do to me when they find out I can't pay for it?

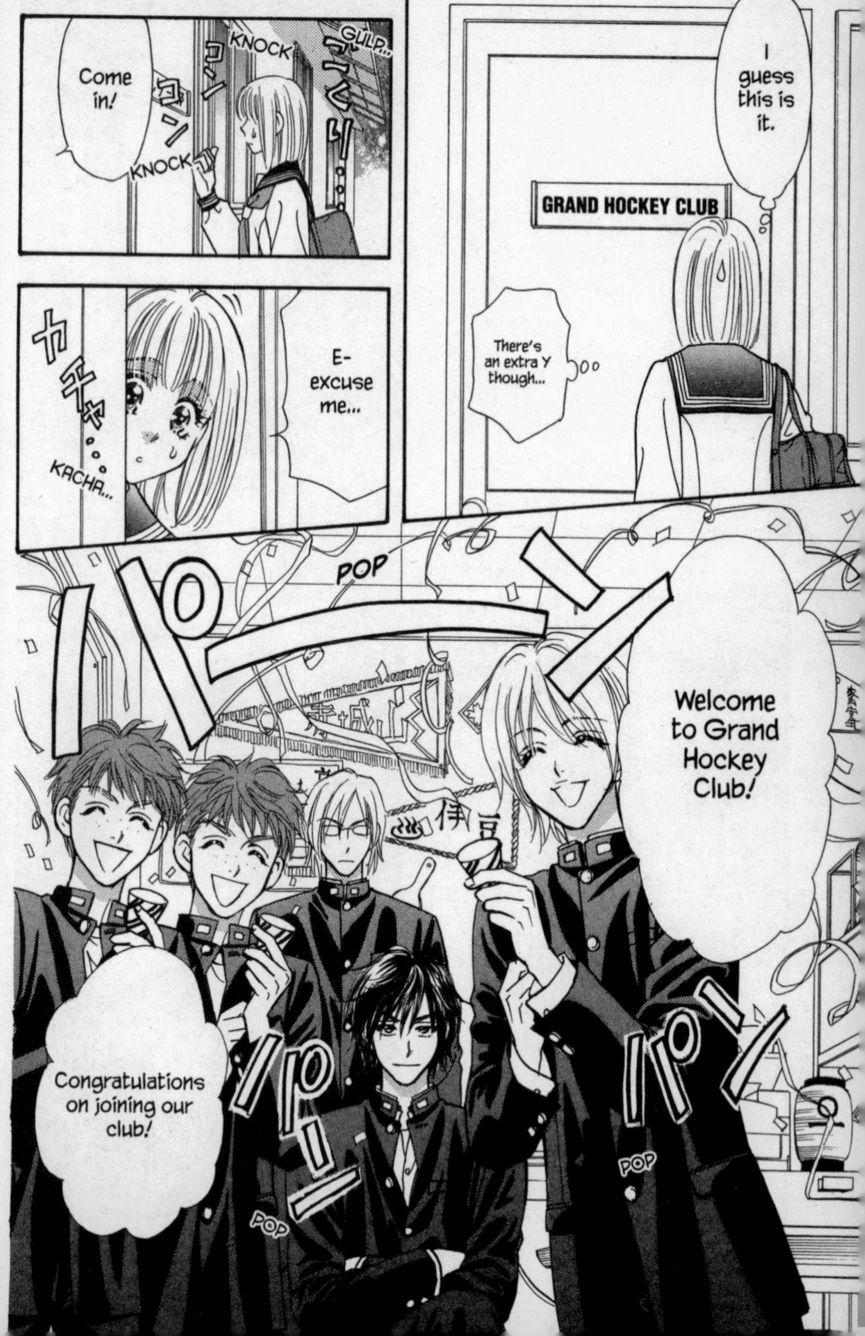
I guess this is it.
GRAND HOCKEY CLUB
There's an extra Y though...
GULP...
KNOCK
KNOCK
Come in!
E-excuse me...
KACHA...
POP
Welcome to Grand Hockey Club!
POP
Congratulations on joining our club!
POP

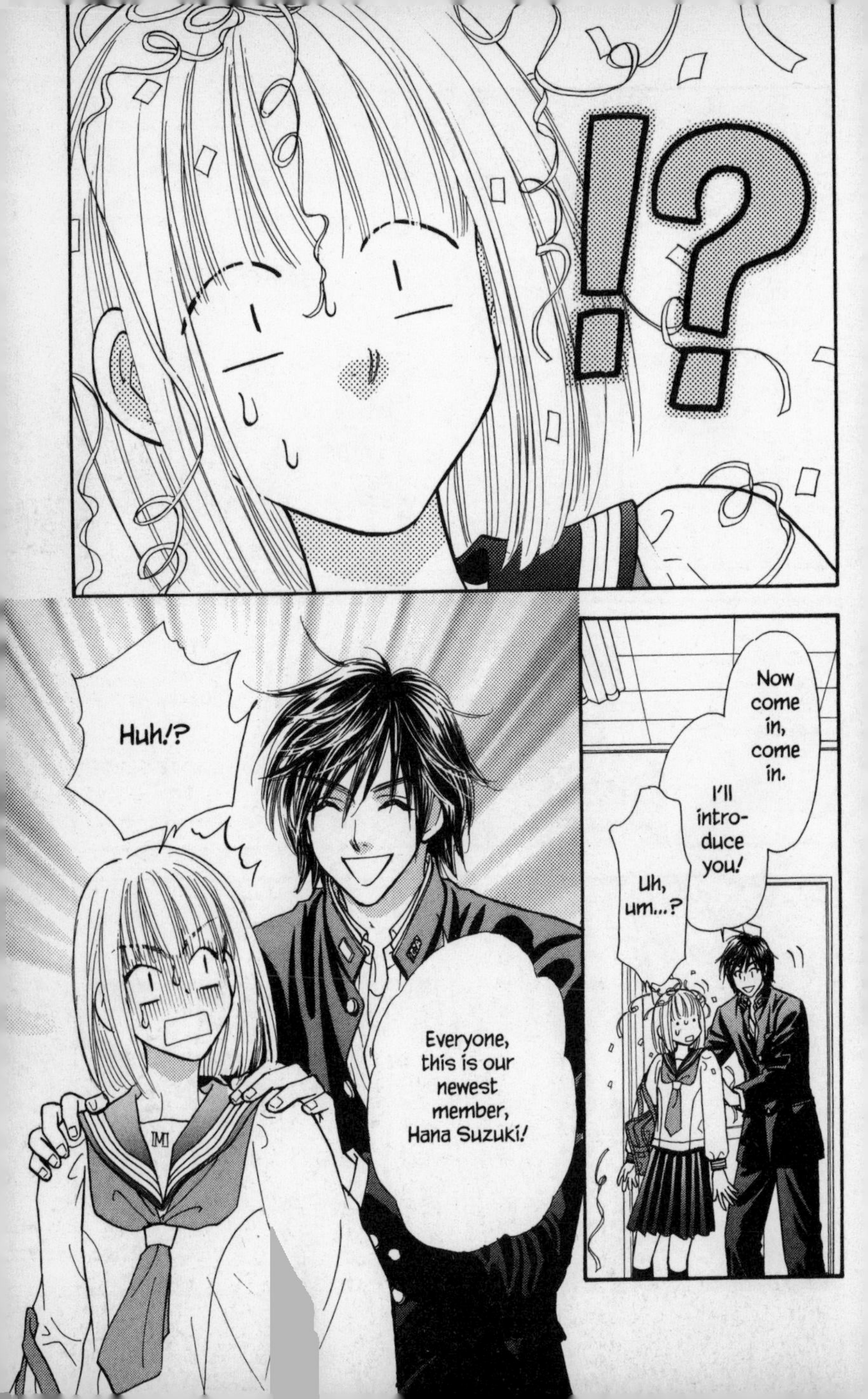
!?
Now come in, come in.
I'll intro-duce you!
Uh, um...?
Everyone, this is our newest member, Hana Suzuki!
Huh!?

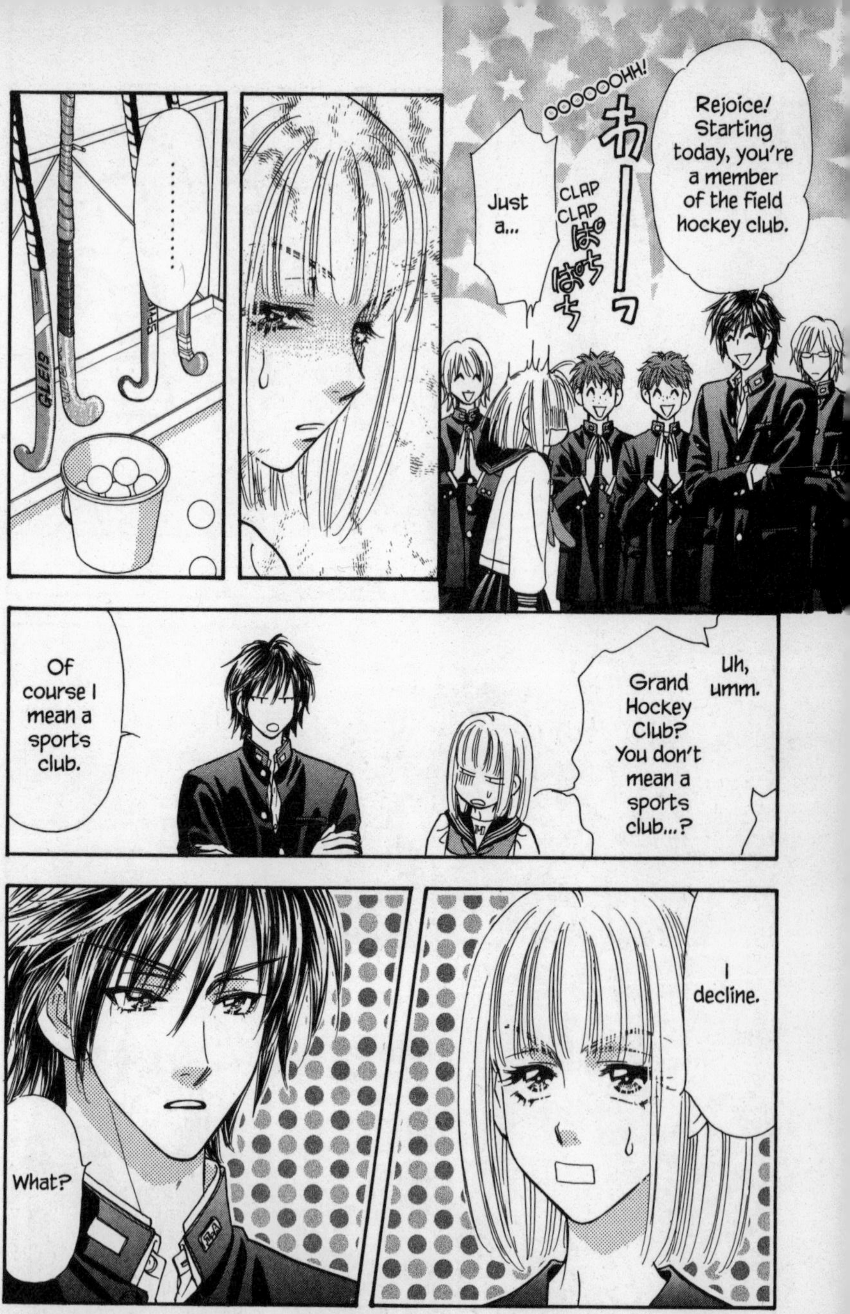
Rejoice! Starting today, you're a member of the field hockey club.
OOOOOOOHH!
わーっ
CLAP CLAP
ぱちぱち
Just a...
......
Uh, umm.
Grand Hockey Club? You don't mean a sports club...?
Of course I mean a sports club.
I decline.
What?

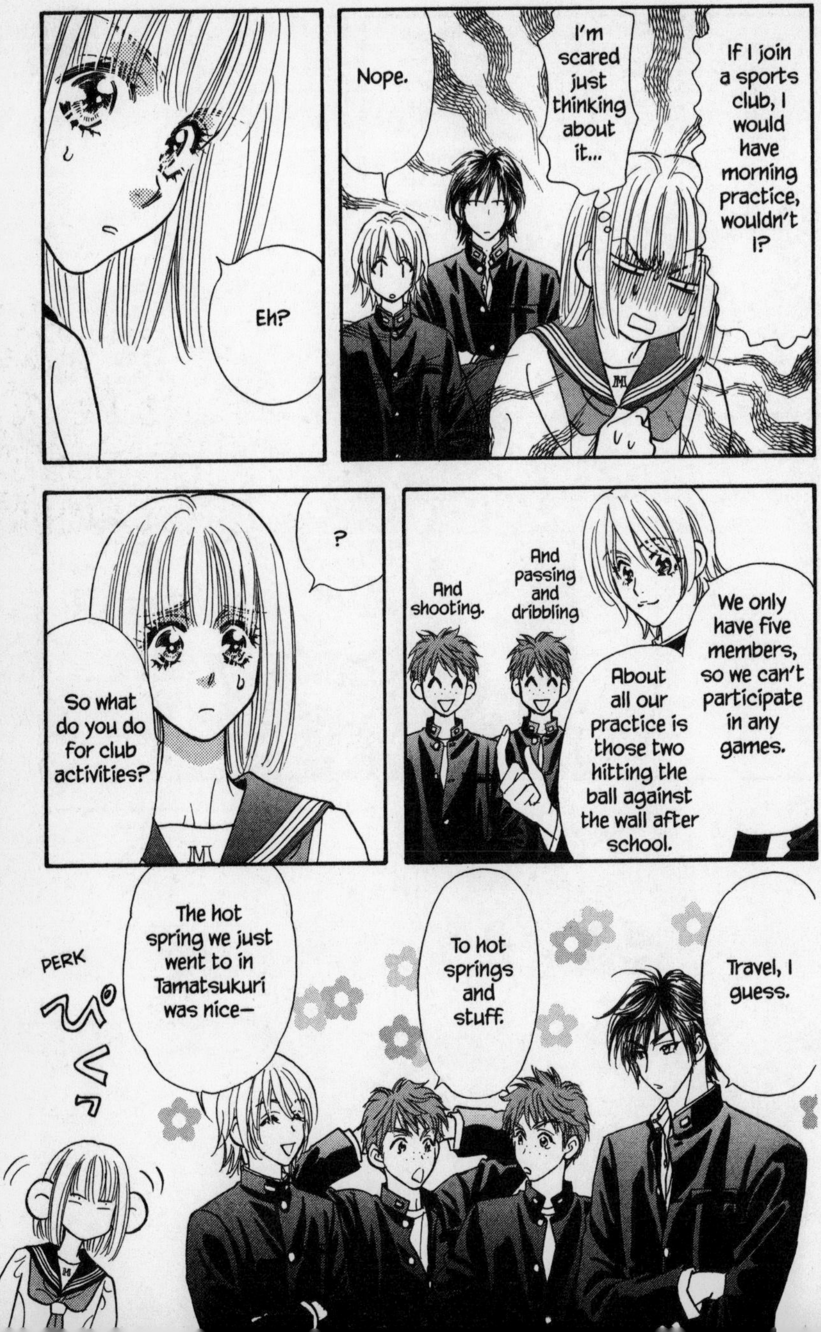
If I join a sports club, I would have morning practice, wouldn't I?
I'm scared just thinking about it...
Nope.
Eh?
We only have five members, so we can't participate in any games.
About all our practice is those two hitting the ball against the wall after school.
And passing and dribbling
And shooting.
?
So what do you do for club activities?
Travel, I guess.
To hot springs and stuff.
The hot spring we just went to in Tamatsukuri was nice—
PERK

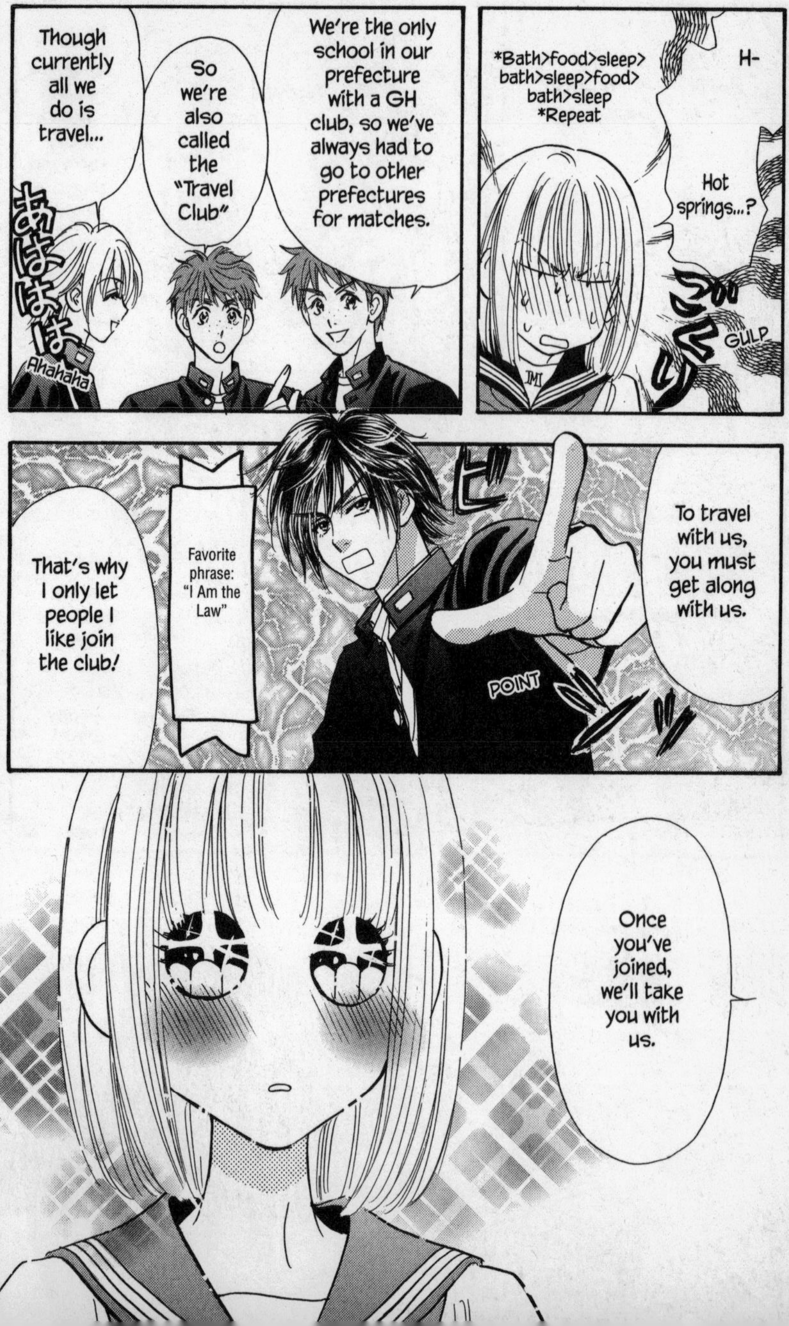
H-
Hot springs...?
*Bath>food>sleep> bath>sleep>food> bath>sleep *Repeat
GULP
We're the only school in our prefecture with a GH club, so we've always had to go to other prefectures for matches.
So we're also called the "Travel Club"
Though currently all we do is travel...
Ahahaha
To travel with us, you must get along with us.
POINT
Favorite phrase: "I Am the Law"
That's why I only let people I like join the club!
Once you've joined, we'll take you with us.

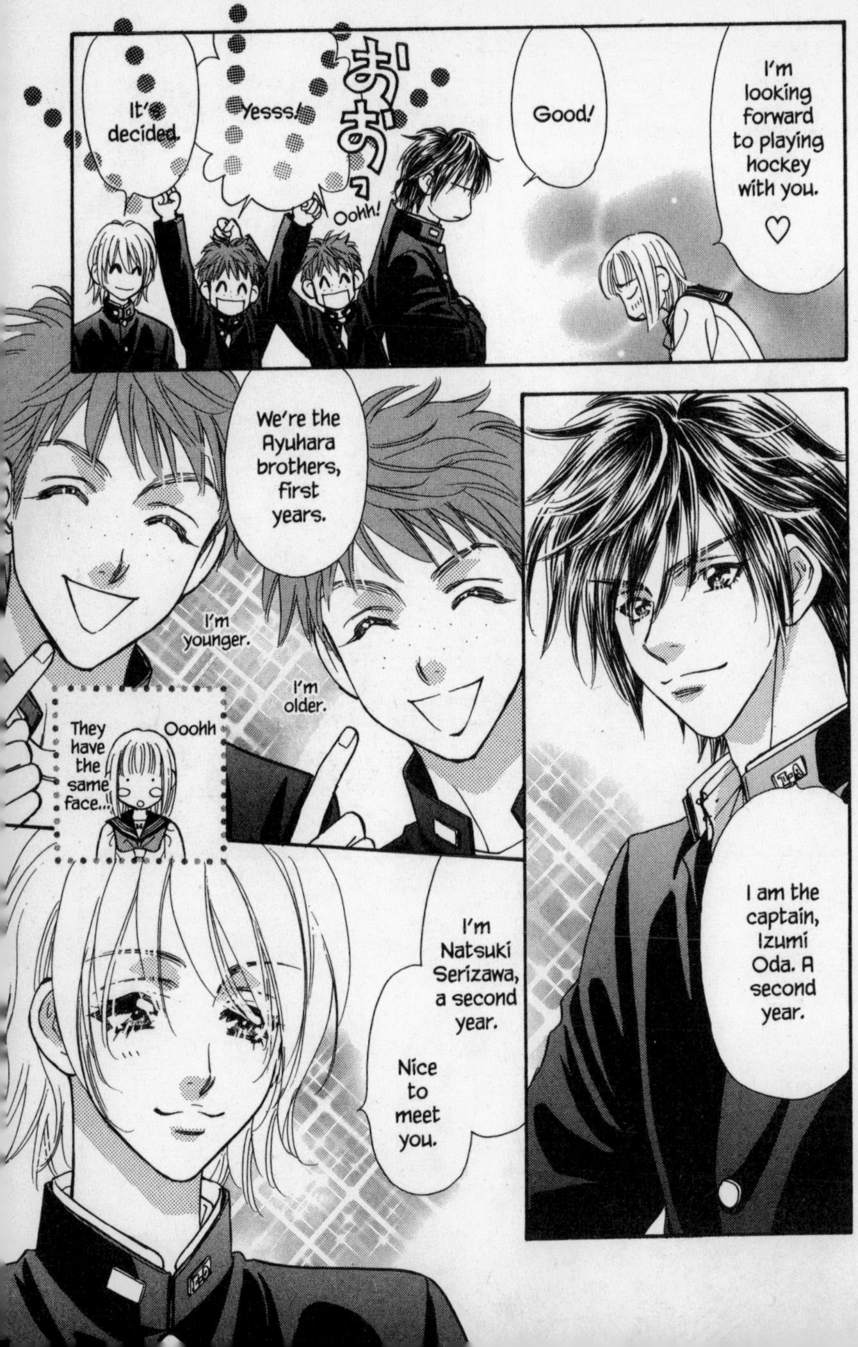
I'm looking forward to playing hockey with you. ♡
Good!
おおっ
Oohh!
Yesss!
It's decided.
I am the captain, Izumi Oda. A second year.
We're the Ayuhara brothers, first years.
I'm older.
I'm younger.
Ooohh
They have the same face...!
I'm Natsuki Serizawa, a second year.
Nice to meet you.

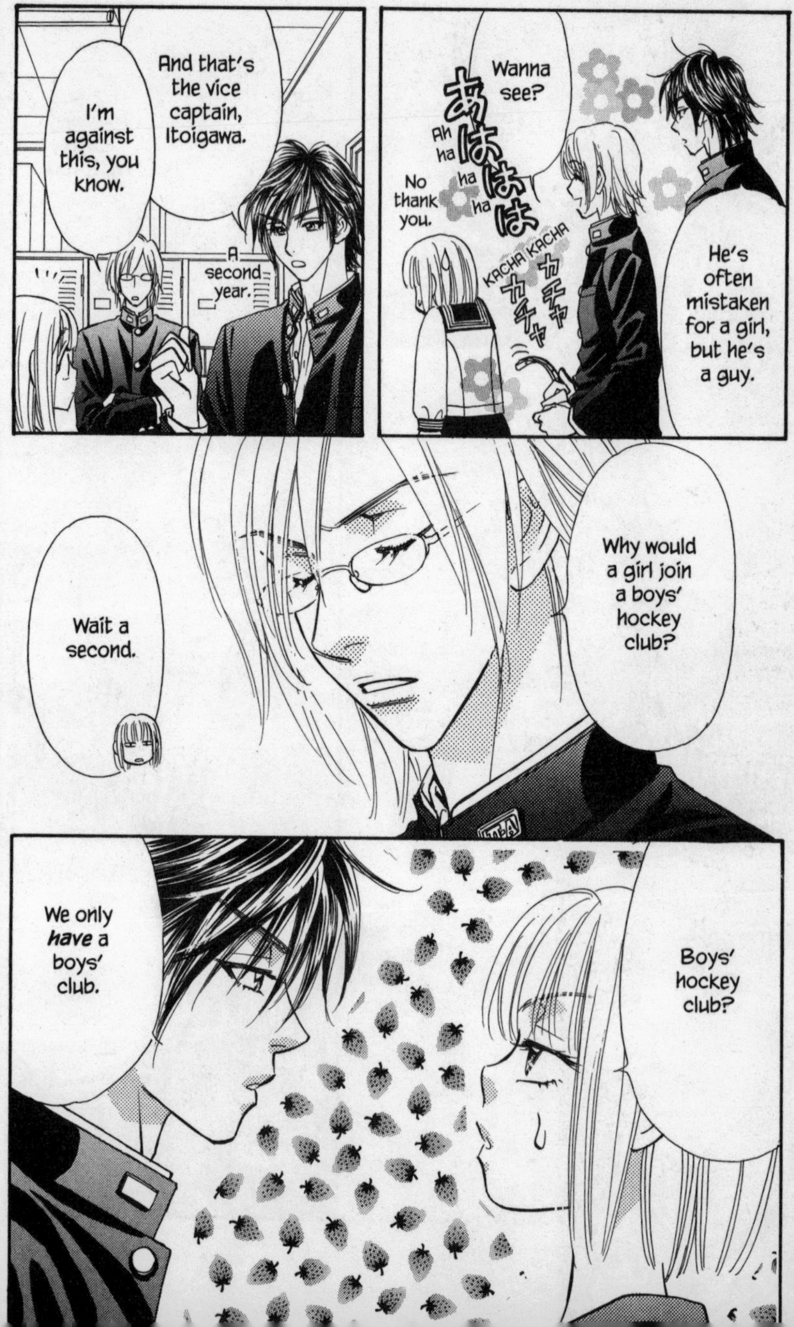
He's often mistaken for a girl, but he's a guy.
Wanna see?
Ah ha ha ha
あははは
No thank you.
KACHA KACHA
カチャカチャ
And that's the vice captain, Itoigawa.
I'm against this, you know.
A second year.
Why would a girl join a boys' hockey club?
Wait a second.
Boys' hockey club?
We only *have* a boys' club.

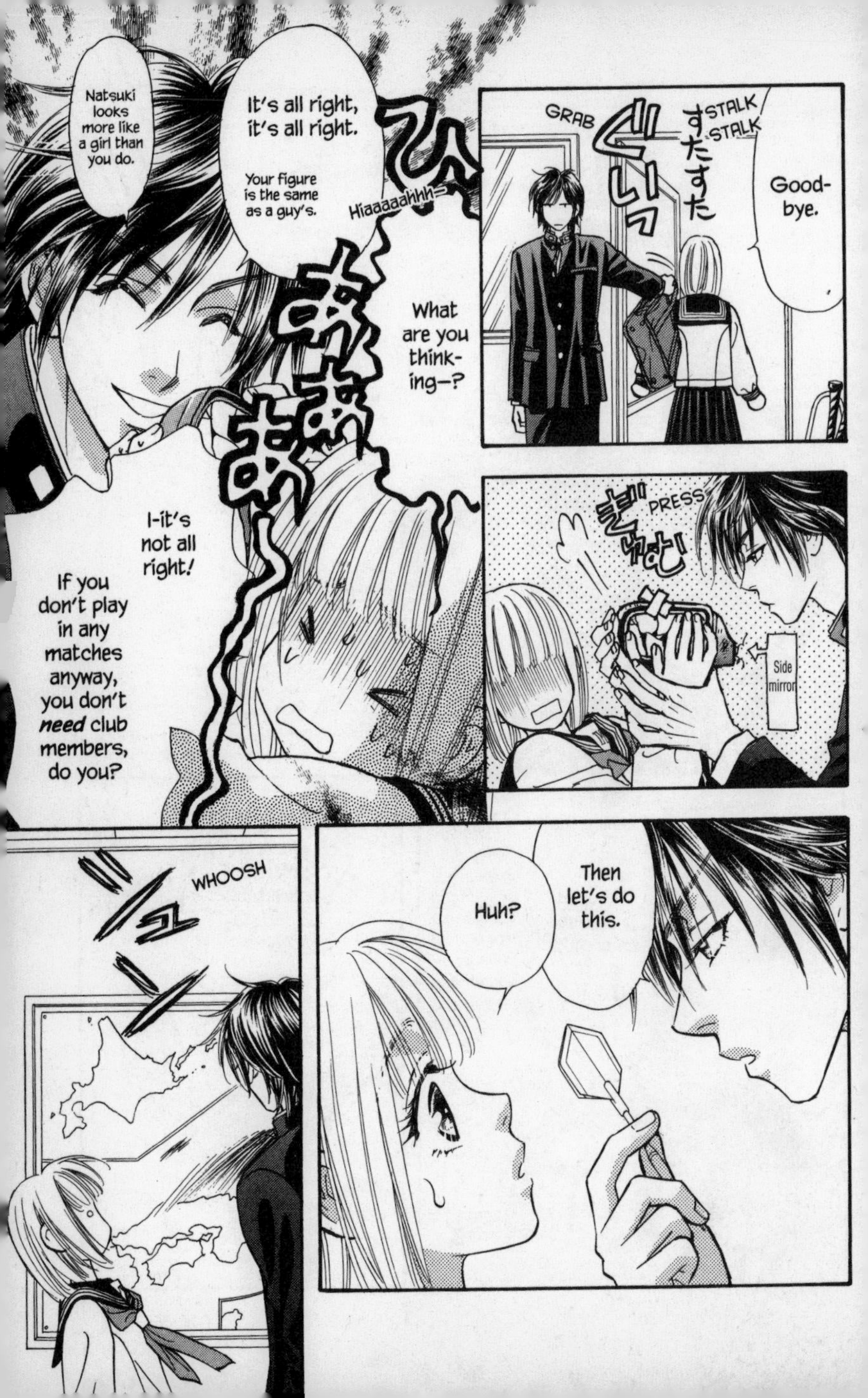
Good-bye.
GRAB
すたすた
STALK STALK
PRESS
Side mirror
It's all right, it's all right.
Your figure is the same as a guy's.
Natsuki looks more like a girl than you do.
Hiaaaaahhh—
What are you think-ing—?
I-it's not all right!
If you don't play in any matches anyway, you don't *need* club members, do you?
Then let's do this.
Huh?
WHOOSH

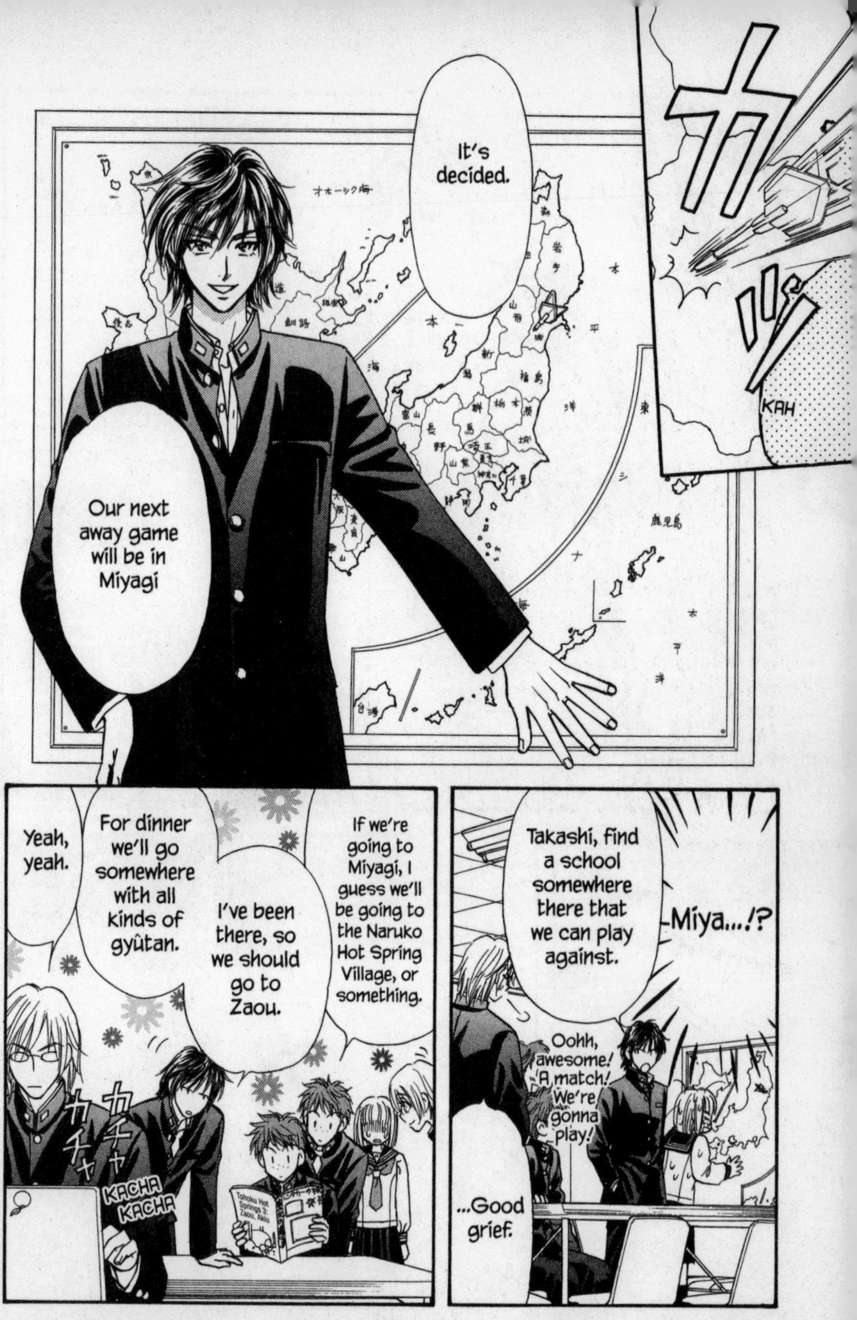
KAH
It's decided.
Our next away game will be in Miyagi
Takashi, find a school somewhere there that we can play against.
Miya...!?
Oohh, awesome! A match! We're gonna play!
...Good grief.
If we're going to Miyagi, I guess we'll be going to the Naruko Hot Spring Village, or something.
I've been there, so we should go to Zaou.
For dinner we'll go somewhere with all kinds of gyûtan.
Yeah, yeah.
KACHA KACHA
Tohoku Hot Springs 3: Zaou, Akiu

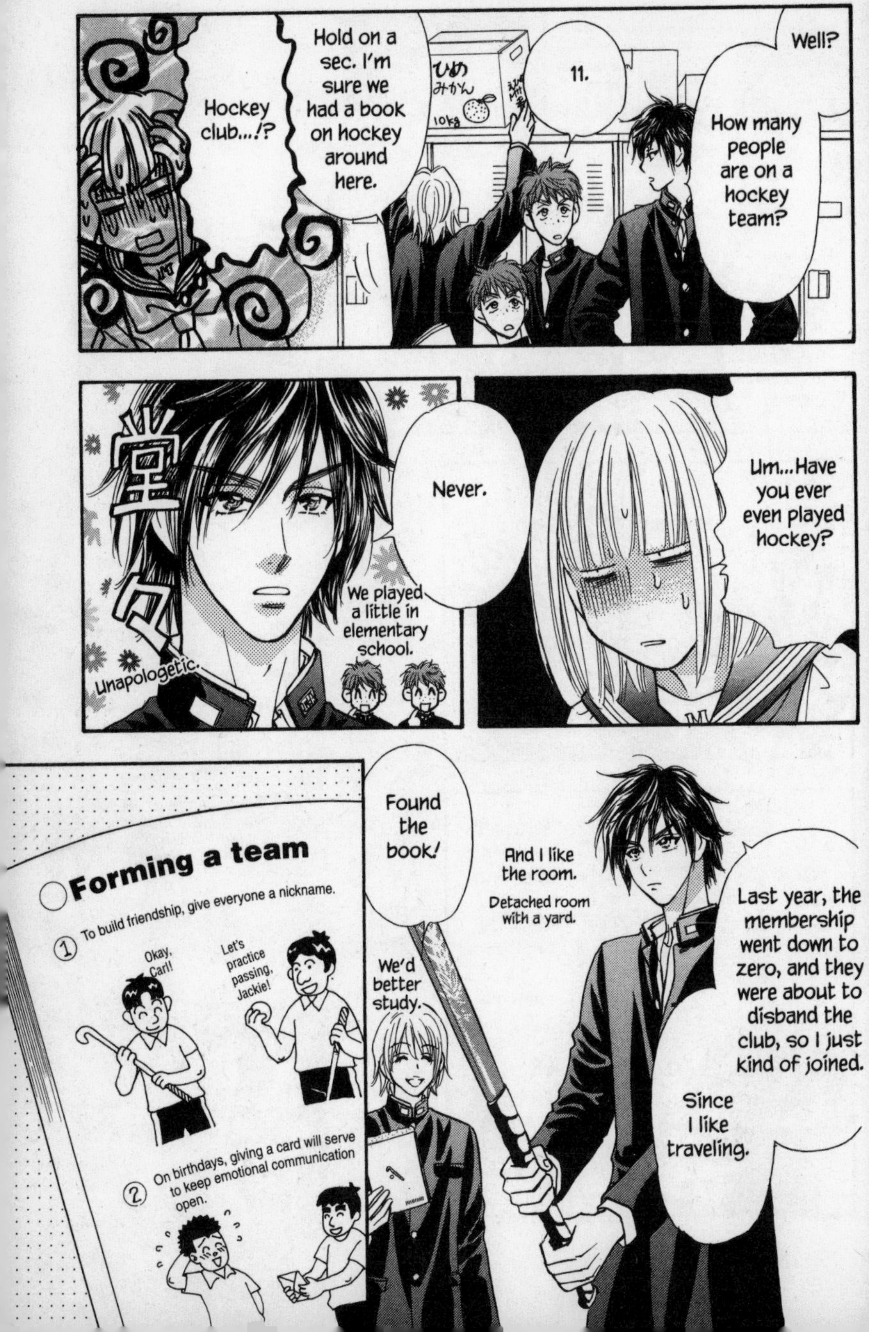
Well?
How many people are on a hockey team?
11.
ひめ
みかん
10kg
Hold on a sec. I'm sure we had a book on hockey around here.
Hockey club...!?
Um...Have you ever even played hockey?
Never.
堂々
Unapologetic.
We played a little in elementary school.
Last year, the membership went down to zero, and they were about to disband the club, so I just kind of joined.
Since I like traveling.
And I like the room.
Detached room with a yard.
Found the book!
We'd better study.
Forming a team
To build friendship, give everyone a nickname.
Okay, Carl!
Let's practice passing, Jackie!
On birthdays, giving a card will serve to keep emotional communication open.

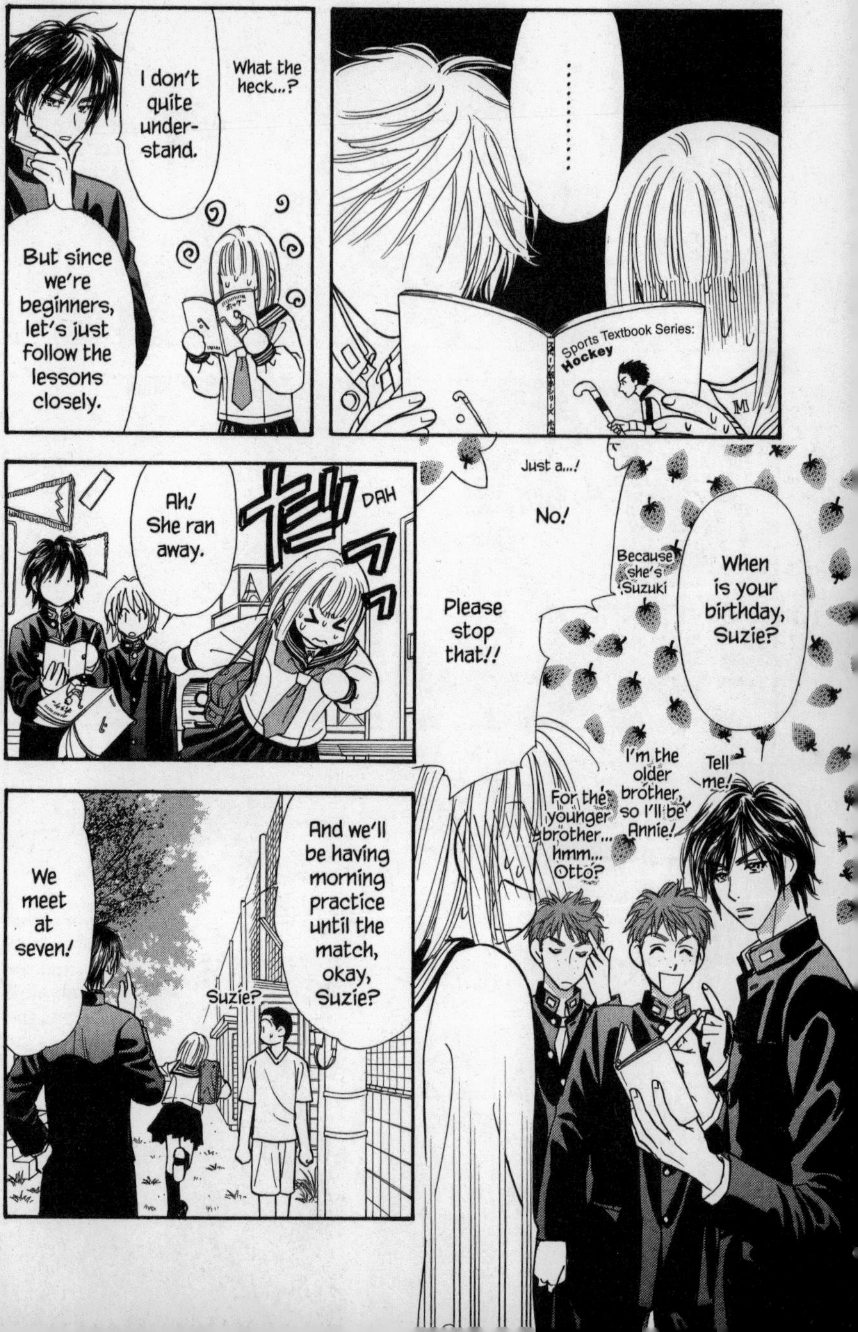
....
Sports Textbook Series: Hockey
What the heck...?
I don't quite understand.
But since we're beginners, let's just follow the lessons closely.
When is your birthday, Suzie?
Because she's Suzuki
Tell me!
I'm the older brother, so I'll be Annie!
For the younger brother... hmm... Otto?
No!
Just a...!
Please stop that!!
DAH
Ah! She ran away.
And we'll be having morning practice until the match, okay, Suzie?
Suzie?
We meet at seven!

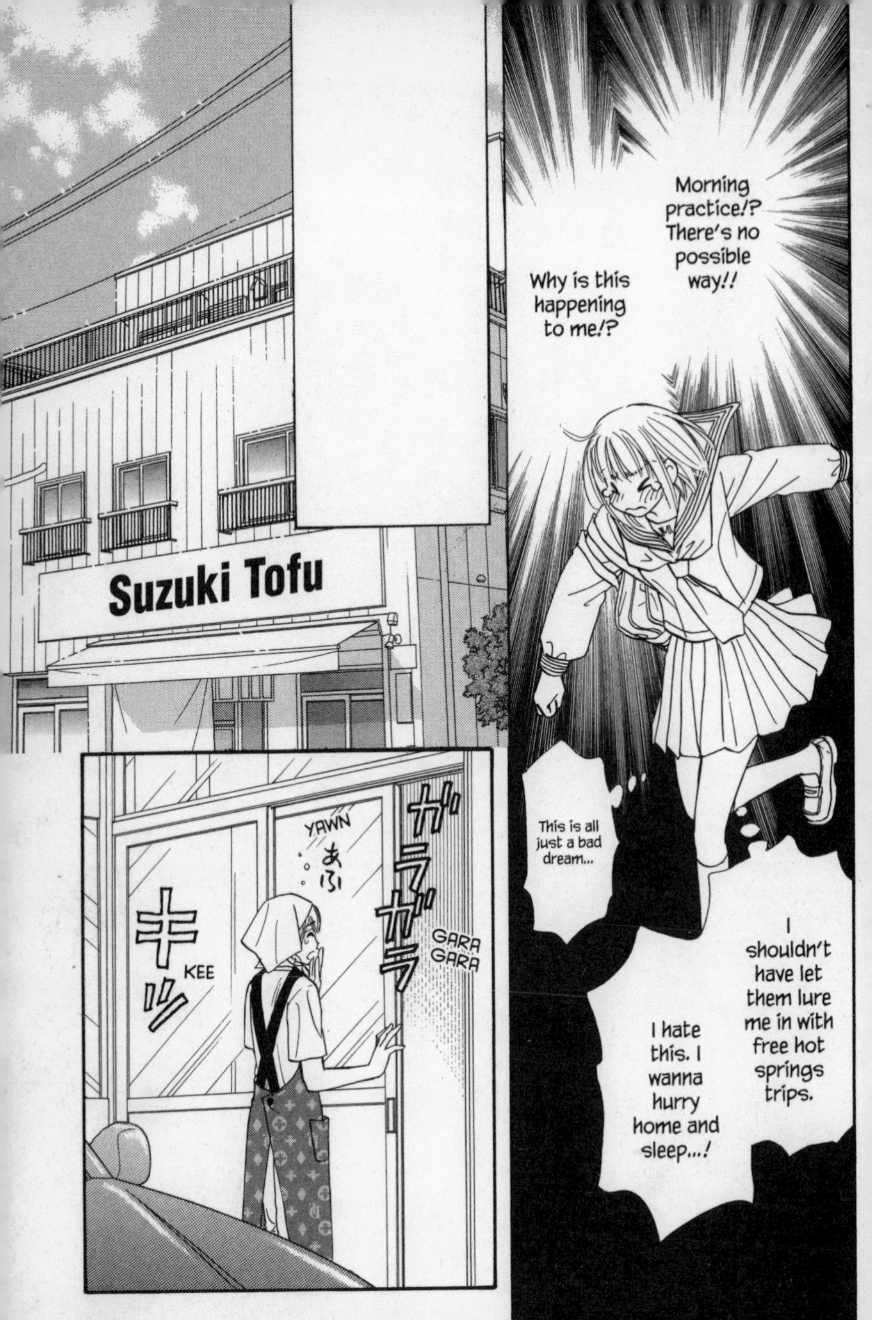
Morning practice!? There's no possible way!!
Why is this happening to me!?
This is all just a bad dream...
I shouldn't have let them lure me in with free hot springs trips.
I hate this. I wanna hurry home and sleep...!
Suzuki Tofu
ガラガラ
GARA GARA
あふ
YAWN
キッ
KEE

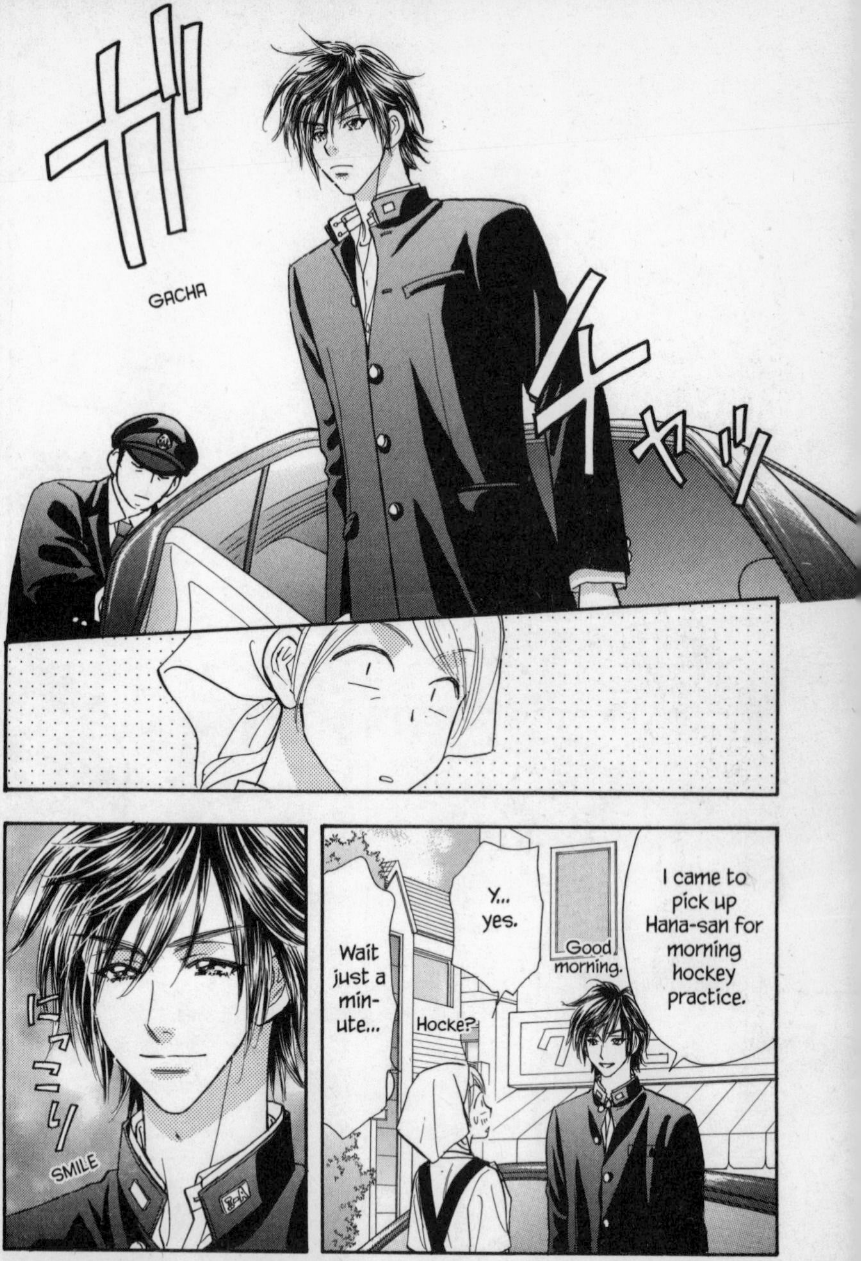

GACHA
I came to pick up Hana-san for morning hockey practice.
Good morning.
Y... yes.
Hocke?
Wait just a minute...
SMILE

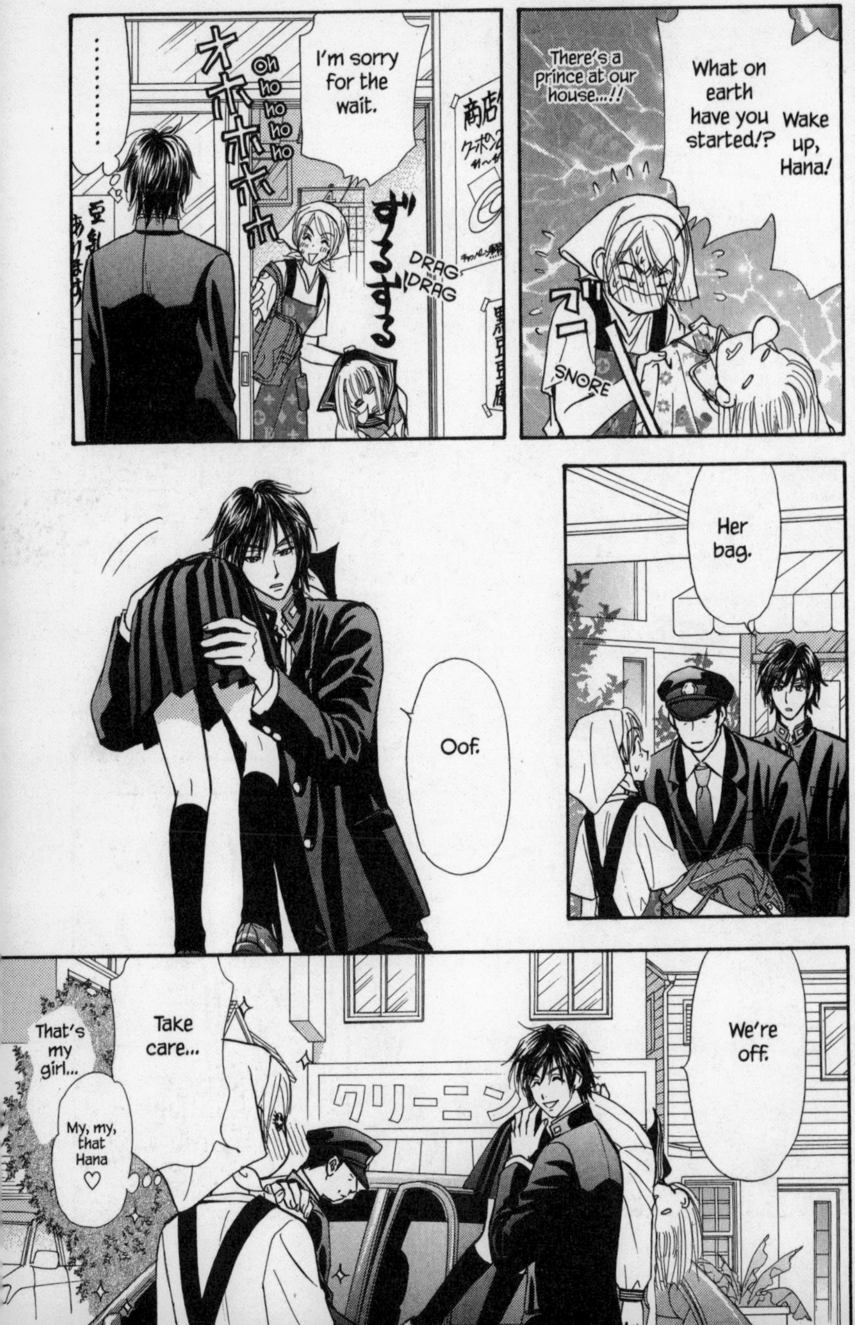
Wake up, Hana!
What on earth have you started!?
There's a prince at our house...!!
ブー
SNORE
I'm sorry for the wait.
ずるずる
DRAG DRAG
オホホホホ
Oh ho ho ho ho
……
Her bag.
Oof.
We're off.
クリーニン
Take care...
That's my girl...
My, my, that Hana ♡

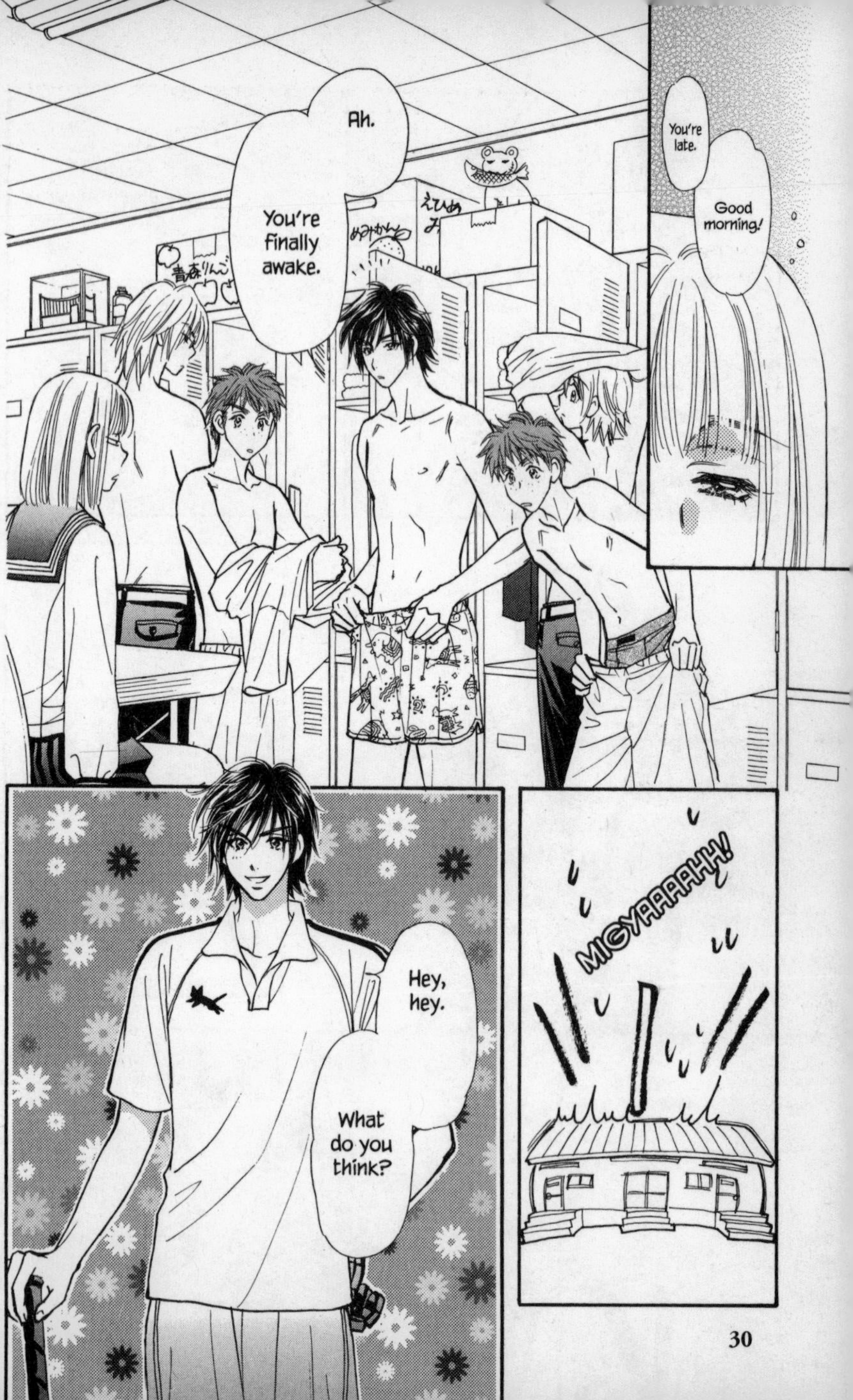
You're late.
Good morning!
Ah.
You're finally awake.
MIGYAAAAHH!
Hey, hey.
What do you think?

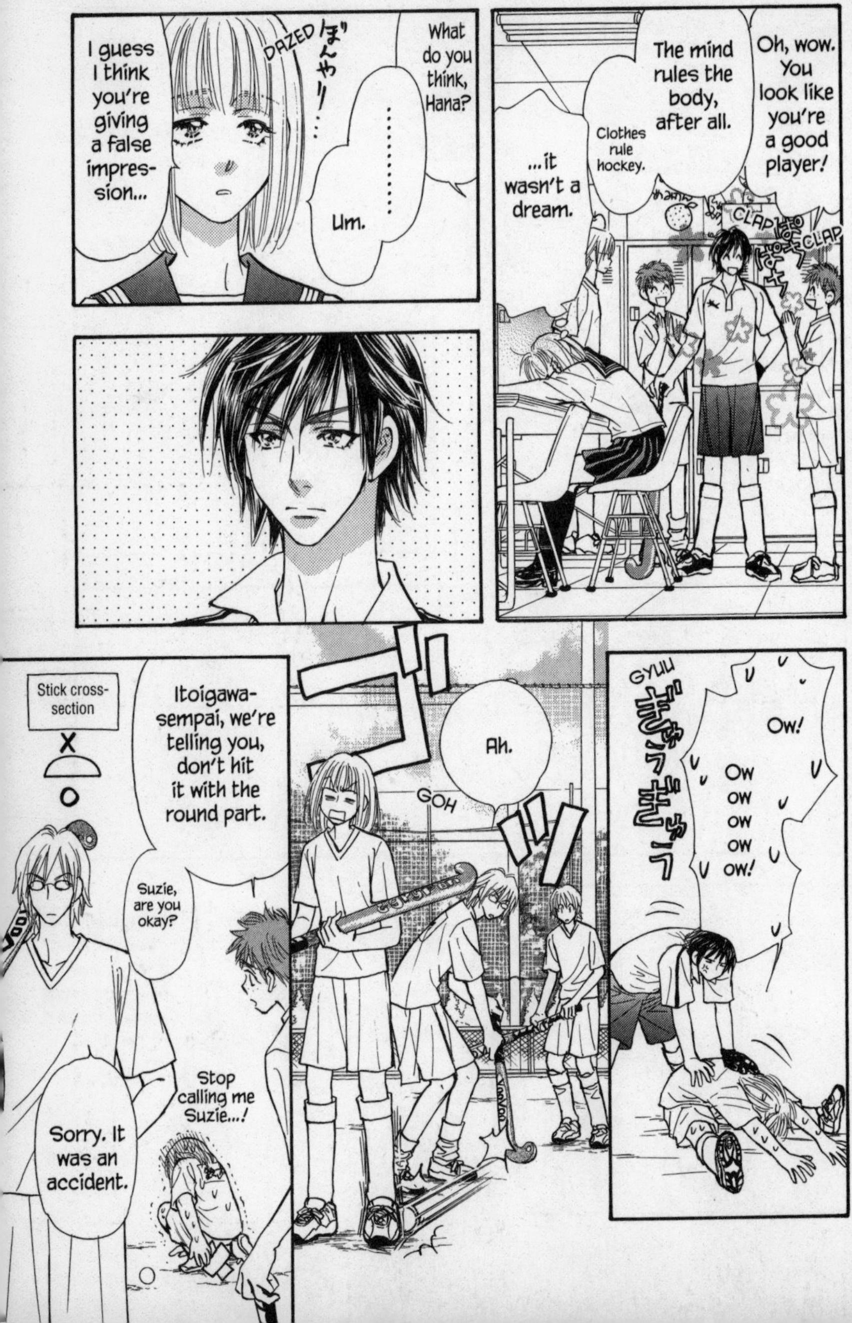
Oh, wow. You look like you're a good player!
The mind rules the body, after all.
Clothes rule hockey.
...it wasn't a dream.
CLAP CLAP
What do you think, Hana?
DAZED ぼんやり…
……
Um.
I guess I think you're giving a false impression...
GYUU ぎゅうぎゅう
Ow!
Ow ow ow ow ow!
Ah.
GOH
Itoigawa-sempai, we're telling you, don't hit it with the round part.
Stick cross-section
Suzie, are you okay?
Stop calling me Suzie...!
Sorry. It was an accident.

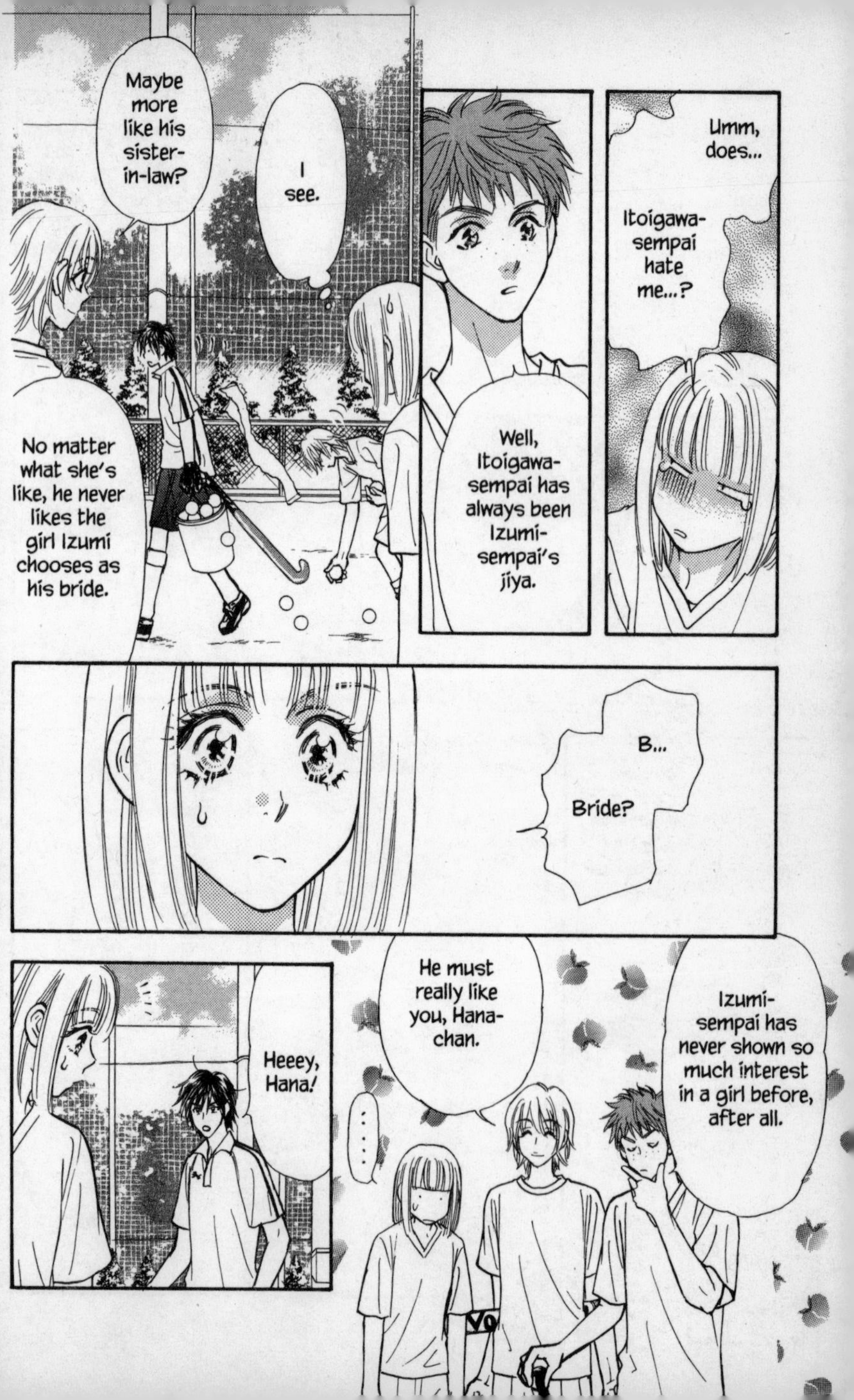
Umm, does...
Itoigawa-sempai hate me...?
Well, Itoigawa-sempai has always been Izumi-sempai's jiya.
Maybe more like his sister-in-law?
I see.
No matter what she's like, he never likes the girl Izumi chooses as his bride.
B...
Bride?
Izumi-sempai has never shown so much interest in a girl before, after all.
He must really like you, Hana-chan.
......
Heeey, Hana!

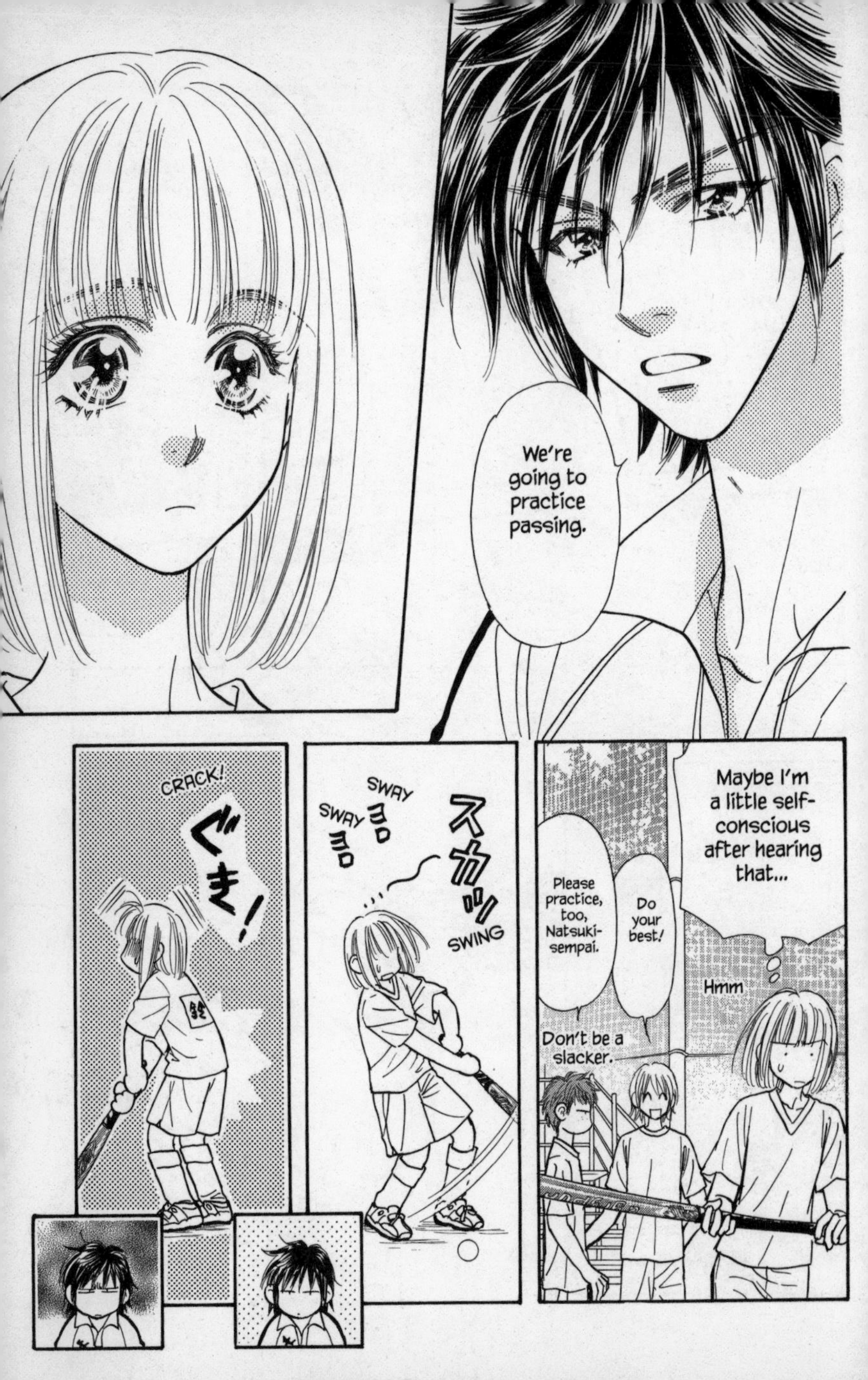
We're going to practice passing.
Maybe I'm a little self-conscious after hearing that...
Hmm
Do your best!
Please practice, too, Natsuki-sempai.
Don't be a slacker.
スカッ
SWING
SWAY
ヨロ
SWAY
ヨロ
CRACK!
ぐき!

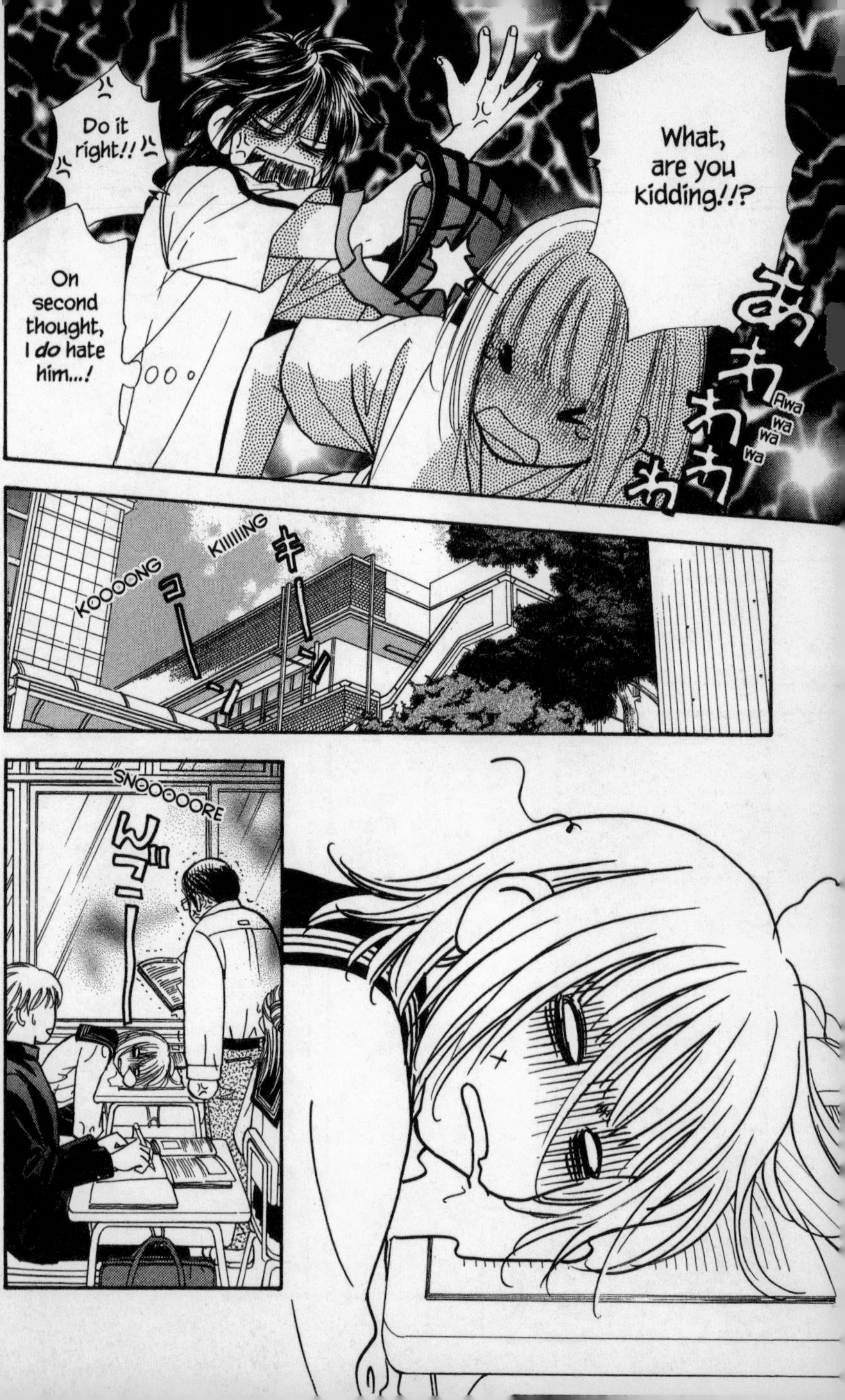
What, are you kidding!!?
Do it right!!
あわわわ
Awa wa wa wa
On second thought, I do hate him...!
キーン
KIIIIING
コーン
KOOOONG
SNOOOOORE
んゴー

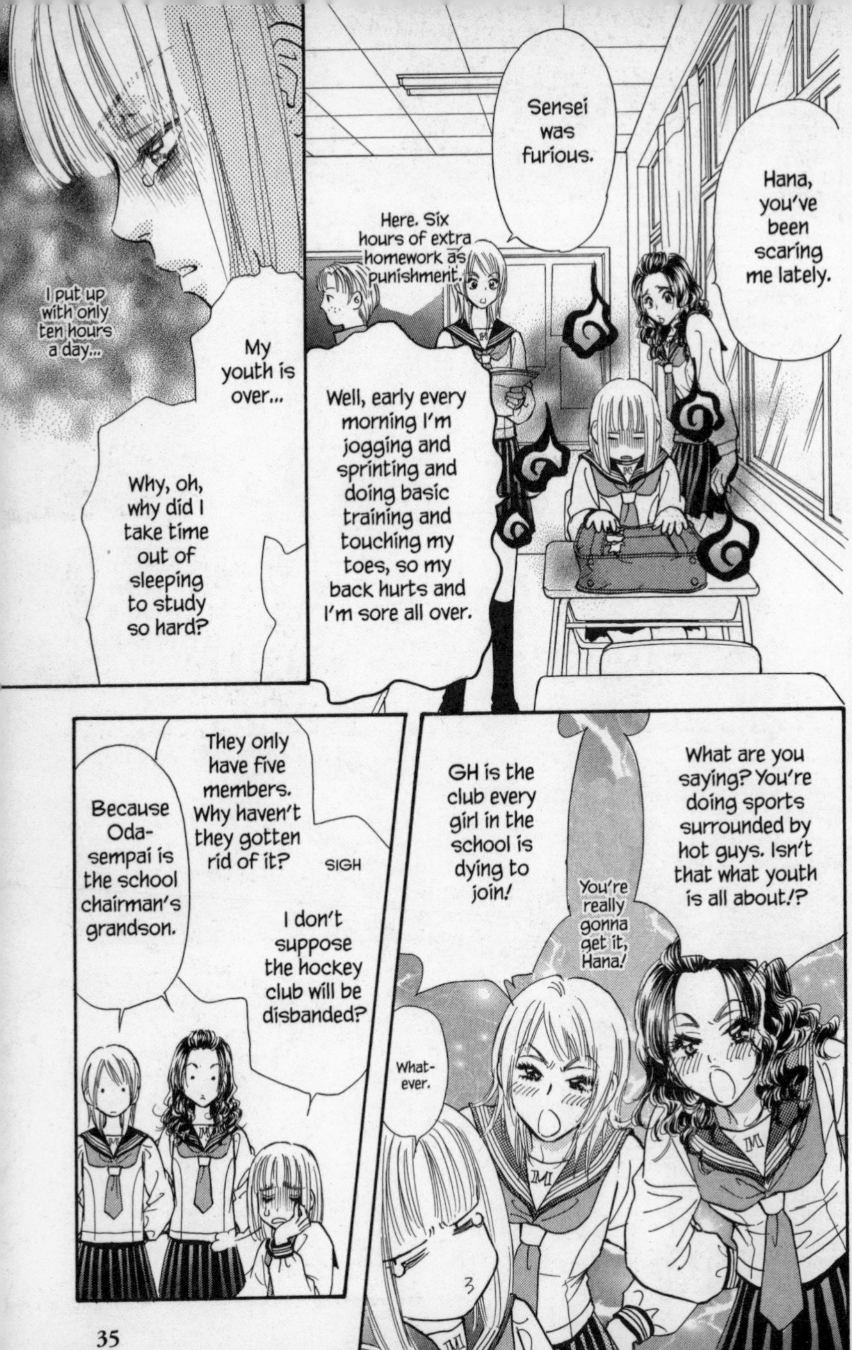
Hana, you've been scaring me lately.
Sensei was furious.
Here. Six hours of extra homework as punishment.
Well, early every morning I'm jogging and sprinting and doing basic training and touching my toes, so my back hurts and I'm sore all over.
My youth is over...
I put up with only ten hours a day...
Why, oh, why did I take time out of sleeping to study so hard?
What are you saying? You're doing sports surrounded by hot guys. Isn't that what youth is all about!?
You're really gonna get it, Hana!
GH is the club every girl in the school is dying to join!
What-ever.
They only have five members. Why haven't they gotten rid of it?
Because Oda-sempai is the school chairman's grandson.
SIGH
I don't suppose the hockey club will be disbanded?

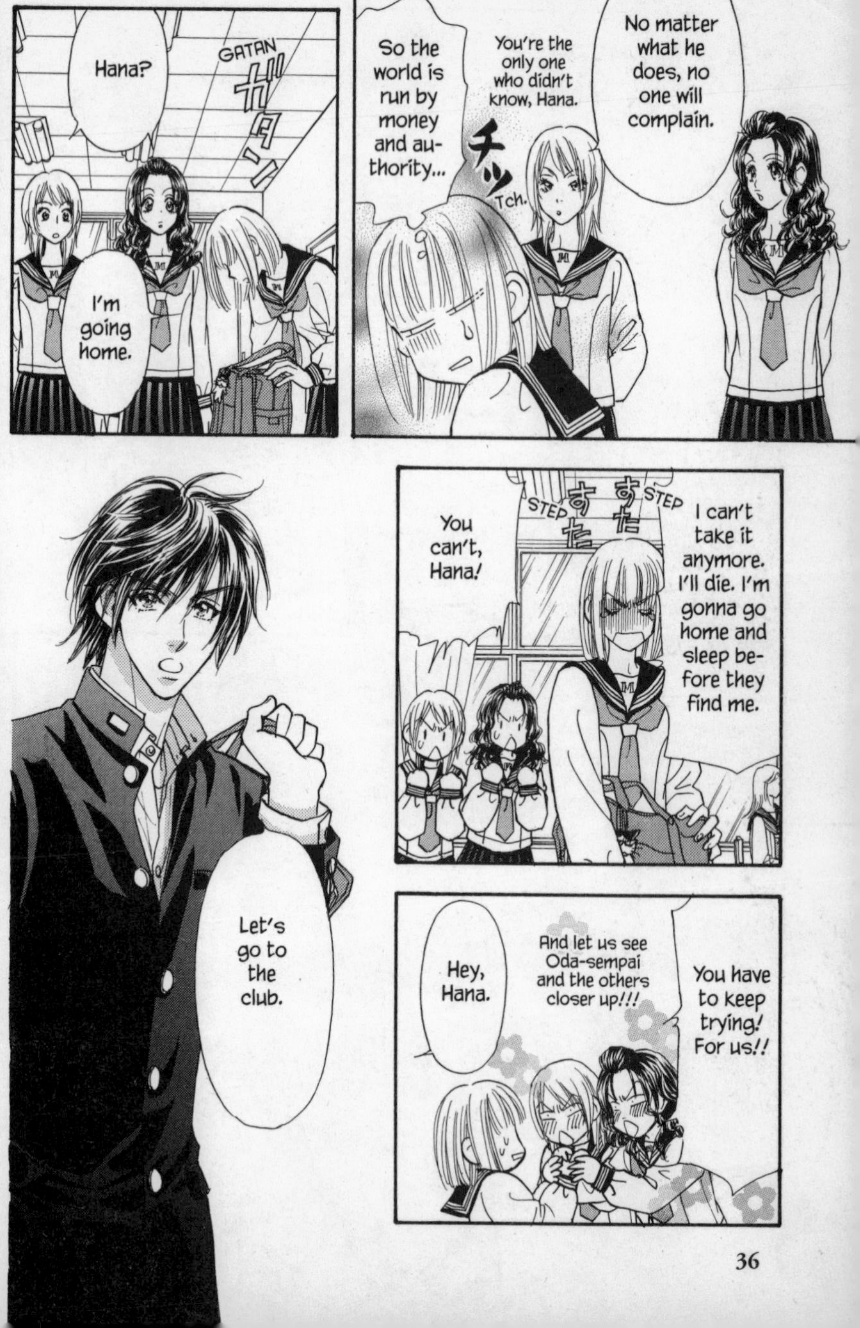
No matter what he does, no one will complain.
You're the only one who didn't know, Hana.
So the world is run by money and authority...
チッ
Tch.
GATAN
ガタン
Hana?
I'm going home.
STEP
すた
STEP
すた
I can't take it anymore. I'll die. I'm gonna go home and sleep before they find me.
You can't, Hana!
You have to keep trying! For us!!
And let us see Oda-sempai and the others closer up!!!
Hey, Hana.
Let's go to the club.

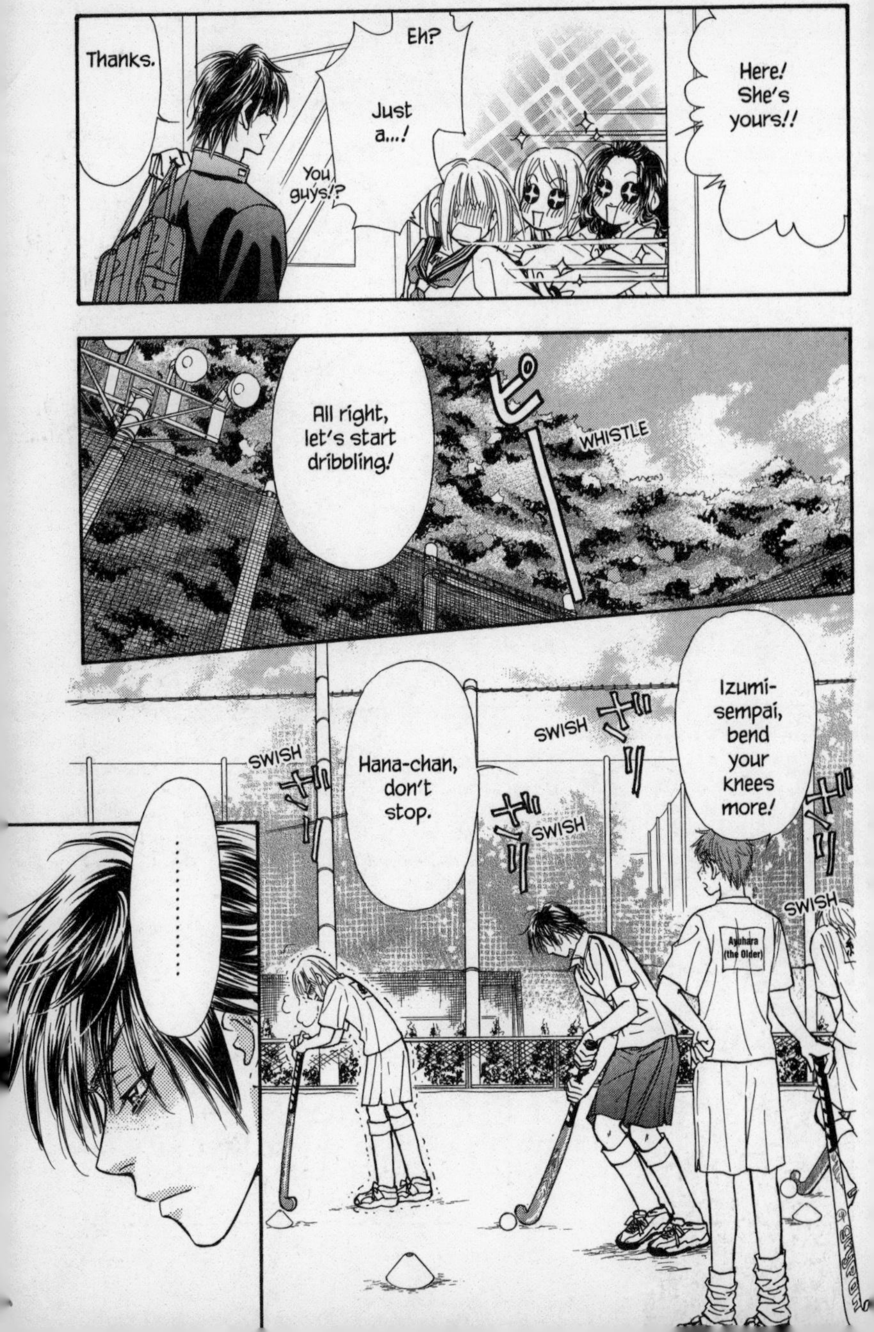
Here! She's yours!!
Eh?
Just a...!
You guys!?
Thanks.
All right, let's start dribbling!
WHISTLE
SWISH
Izumi-sempai, bend your knees more!
SWISH
SWISH
Ayuhara (the Older)
Hana-chan, don't stop.
SWISH
......

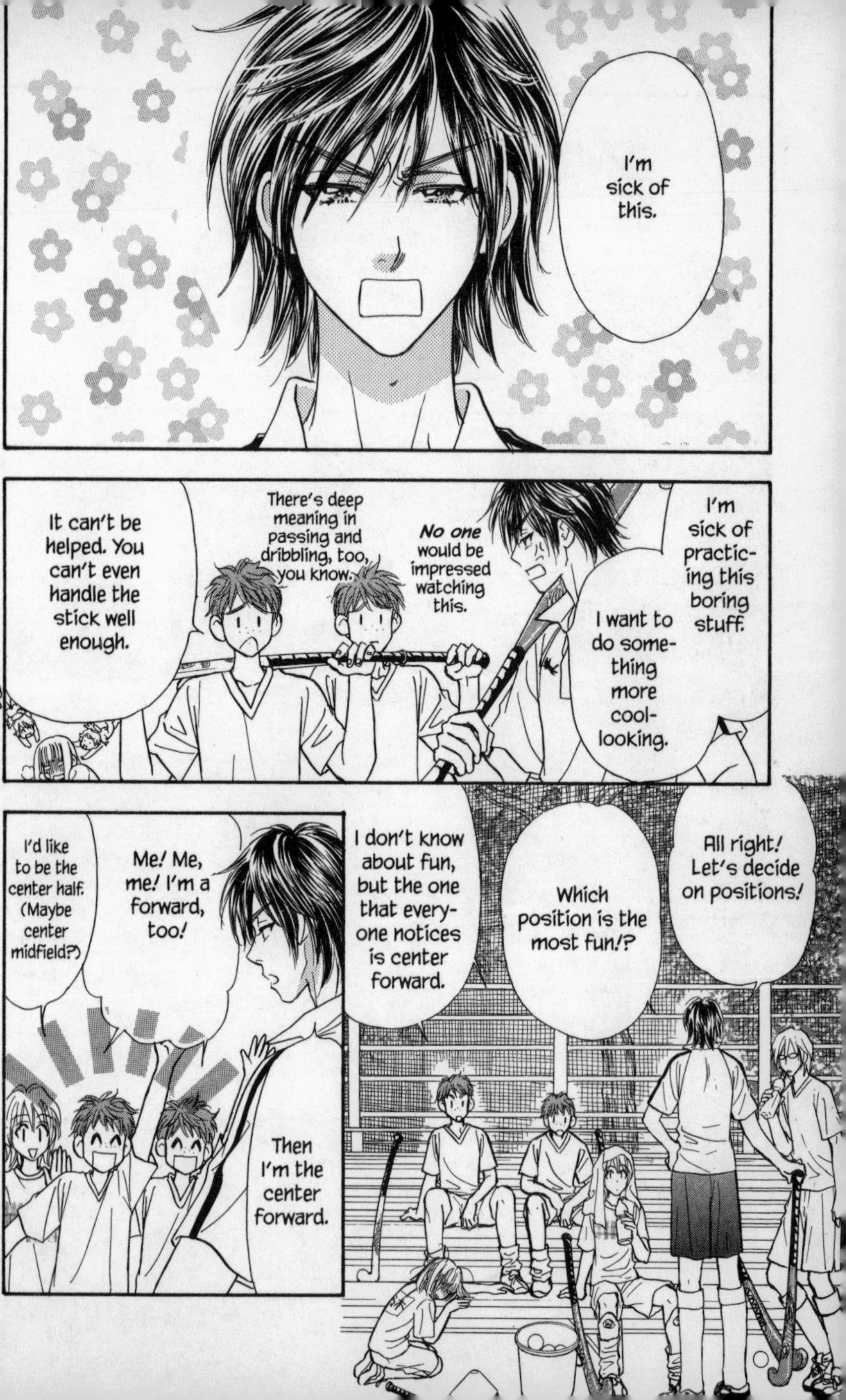
I'm sick of this.
I'm sick of practicing this boring stuff.
I want to do something more cool-looking.
No one would be impressed watching this.
There's deep meaning in passing and dribbling, too, you know.
It can't be helped. You can't even handle the stick well enough.
All right! Let's decide on positions!
Which position is the most fun!?
I don't know about fun, but the one that everyone notices is center forward.
Then I'm the center forward.
Me! Me, me! I'm a forward, too!
I'd like to be the center half. (Maybe center midfield?)

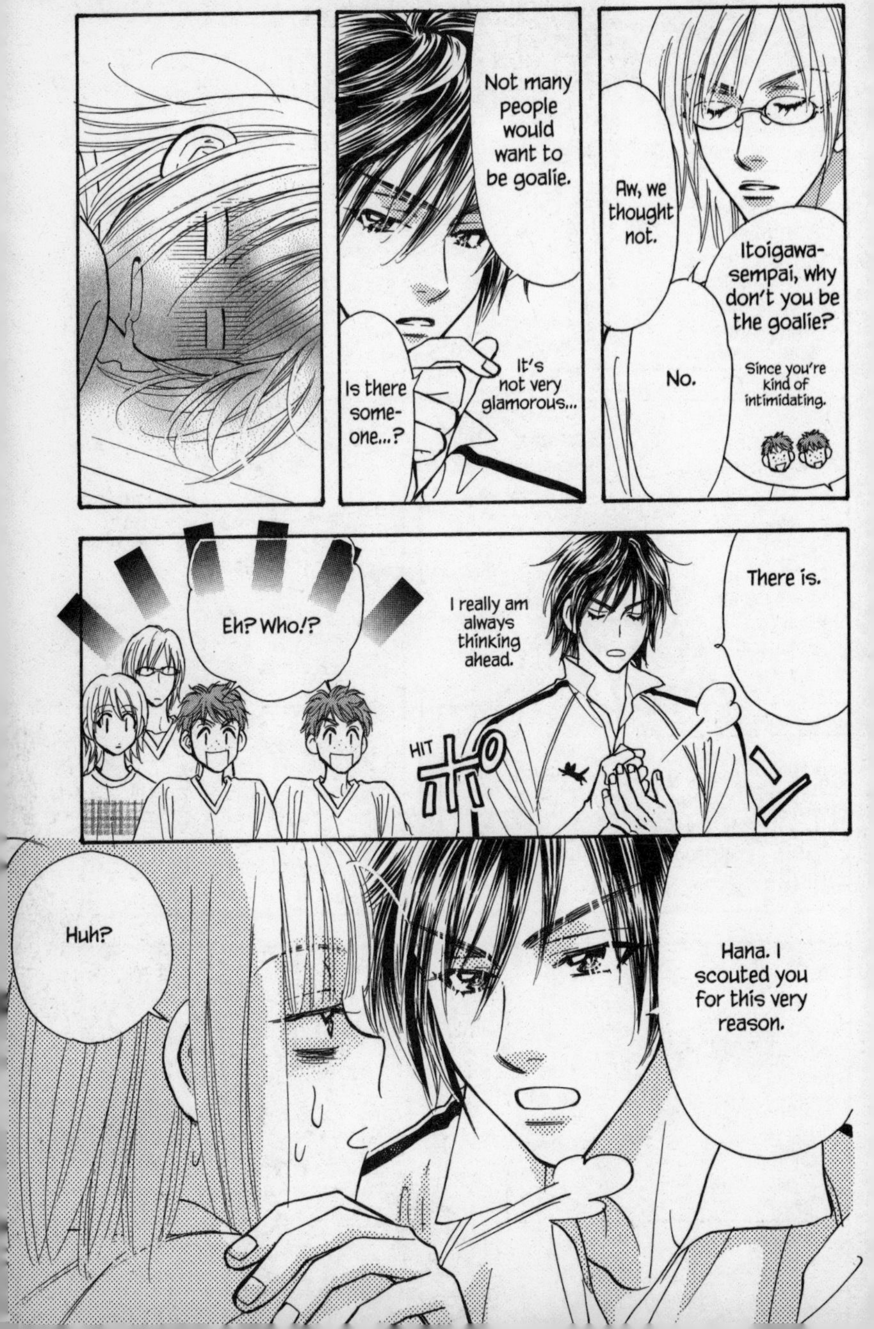
Itoigawa-sempai, why don't you be the goalie?
Since you're kind of intimidating.
No.
Aw, we thought not.
Not many people would want to be goalie.
It's not very glamorous...
Is there someone...?
There is.
I really am always thinking ahead.
ポ
HIT
Eh? Who!?
Hana. I scouted you for this very reason.
Huh?

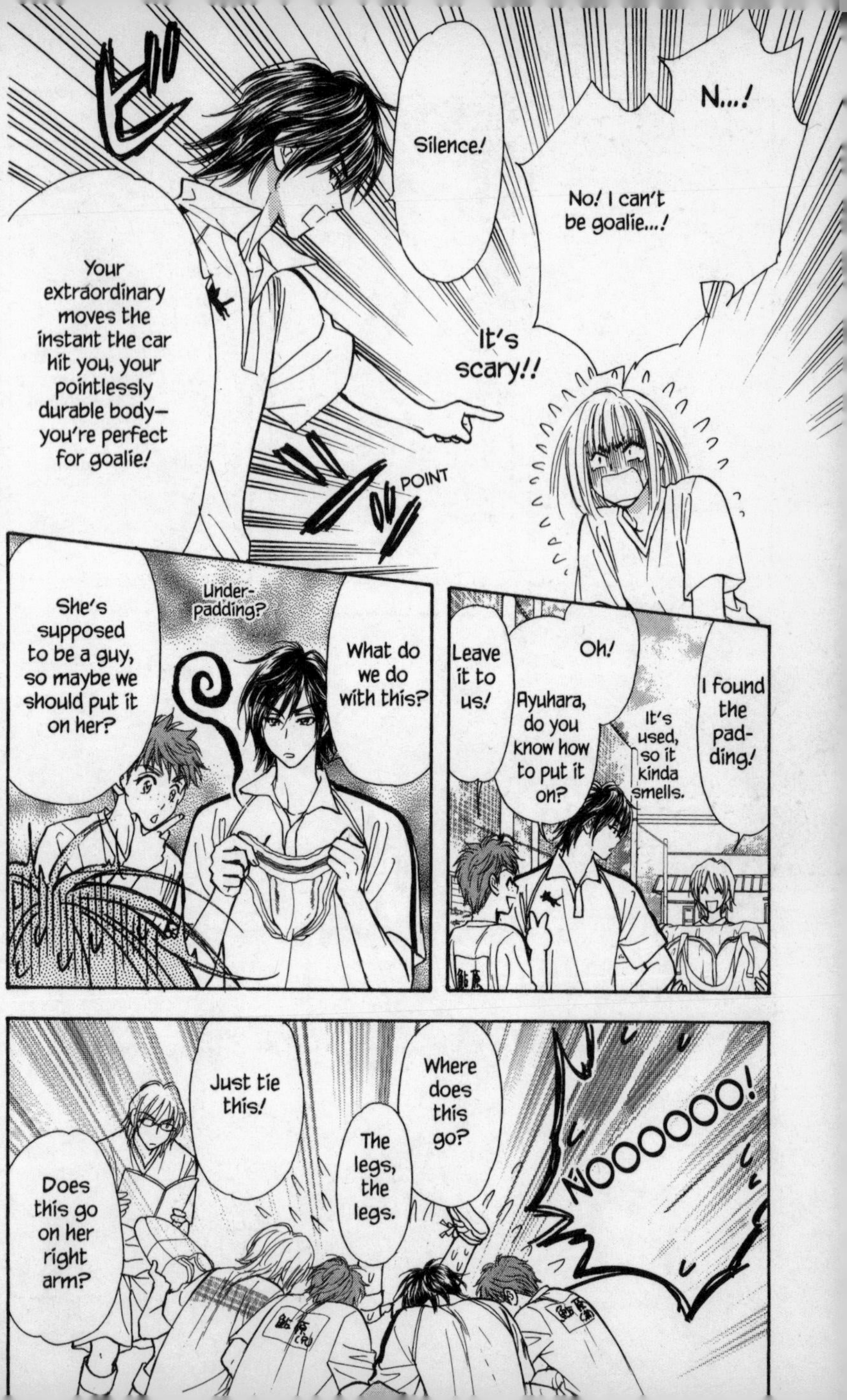

N...!
No! I can't be goalie...!
It's scary!!
Silence!
Your extraordinary moves the instant the car hit you, your pointlessly durable body—you're perfect for goalie!
POINT
I found the padding!
It's used, so it kinda smells.
Oh!
Ayuhara, do you know how to put it on?
Leave it to us!
What do we do with this?
Under-padding?
She's supposed to be a guy, so maybe we should put it on her?
NOOOOOOO!
Where does this go?
The legs, the legs.
Just tie this!
Does this go on her right arm?

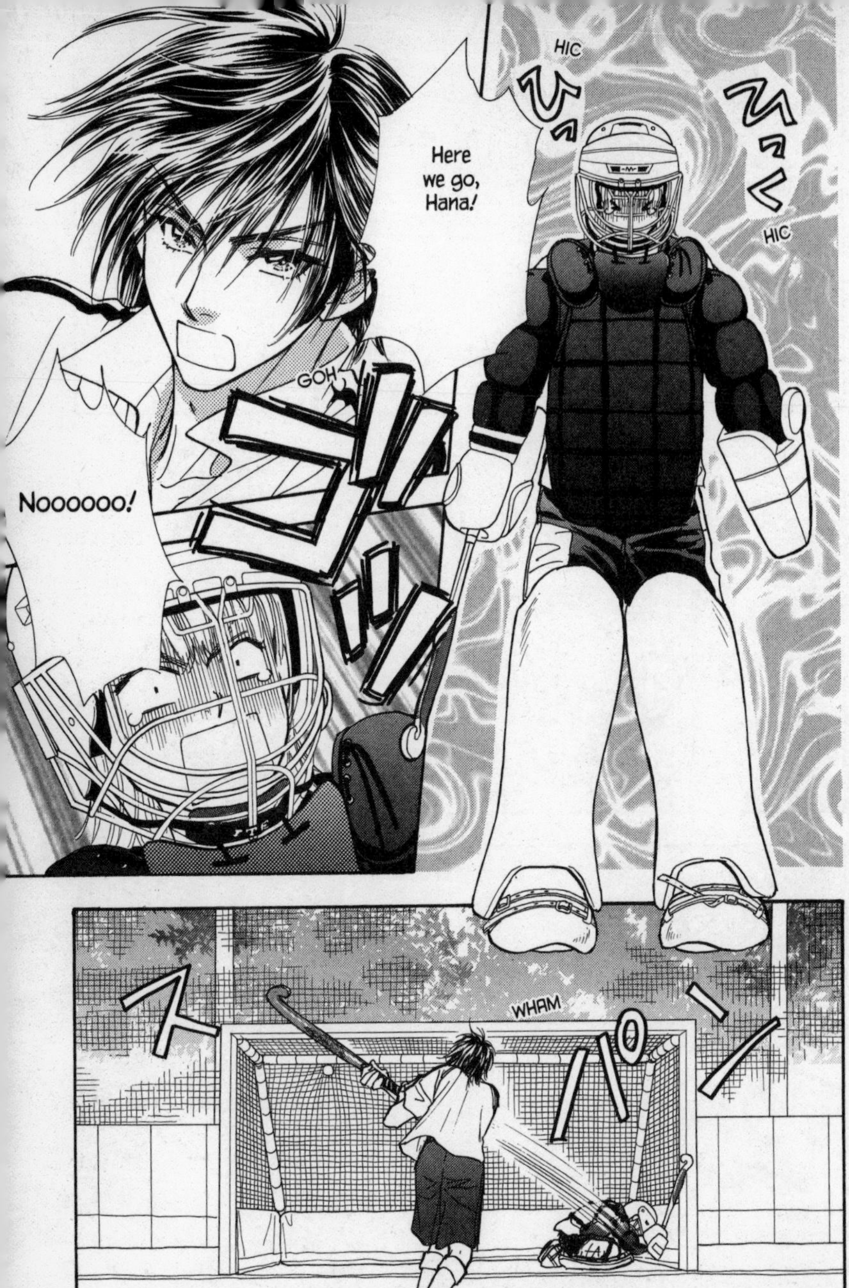
HIC
HIC
Here we go, Hana!
GOH
Noooooo!
WHAM

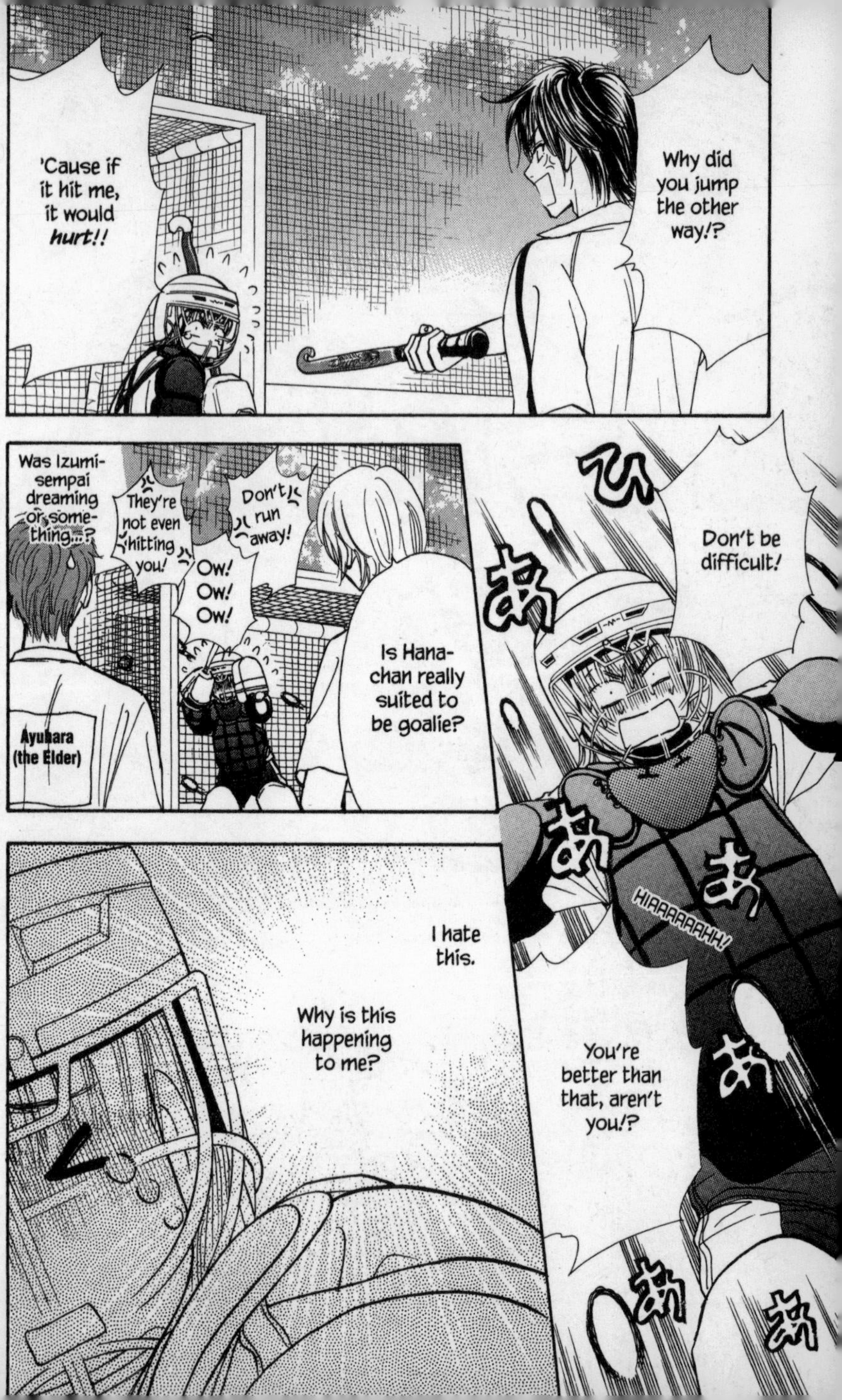

Why did you jump the other way!?
'Cause if it hit me, it would *hurt!!*
ひ
あ
Don't be difficult!
あ
あ
HIAAAAAAAHH!
あ
You're better than that, aren't you!?
あ
あ
Don't run away!
They're not even hitting you!
Was Izumi-sempai dreaming or some-thing...?
Ow! Ow! Ow!
Is Hana-chan really suited to be goalie?
Ayuhara (the Elder)
I hate this.
Why is this happening to me?

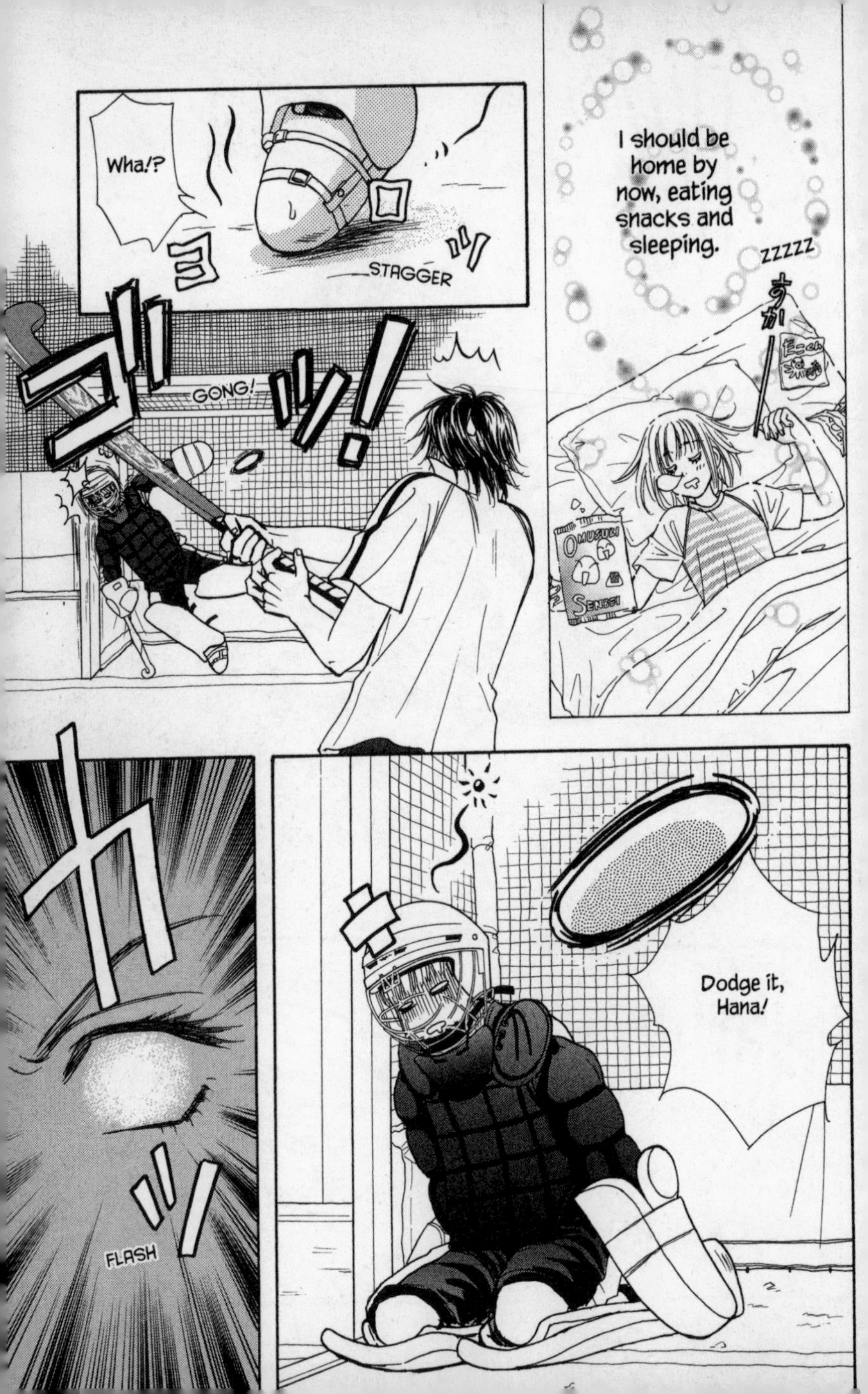
I should be home by now, eating snacks and sleeping.
ZZZZZ
OMUSUBI SENBEI
Wha!?
STAGGER
GONG!
Dodge it, Hana!
FLASH

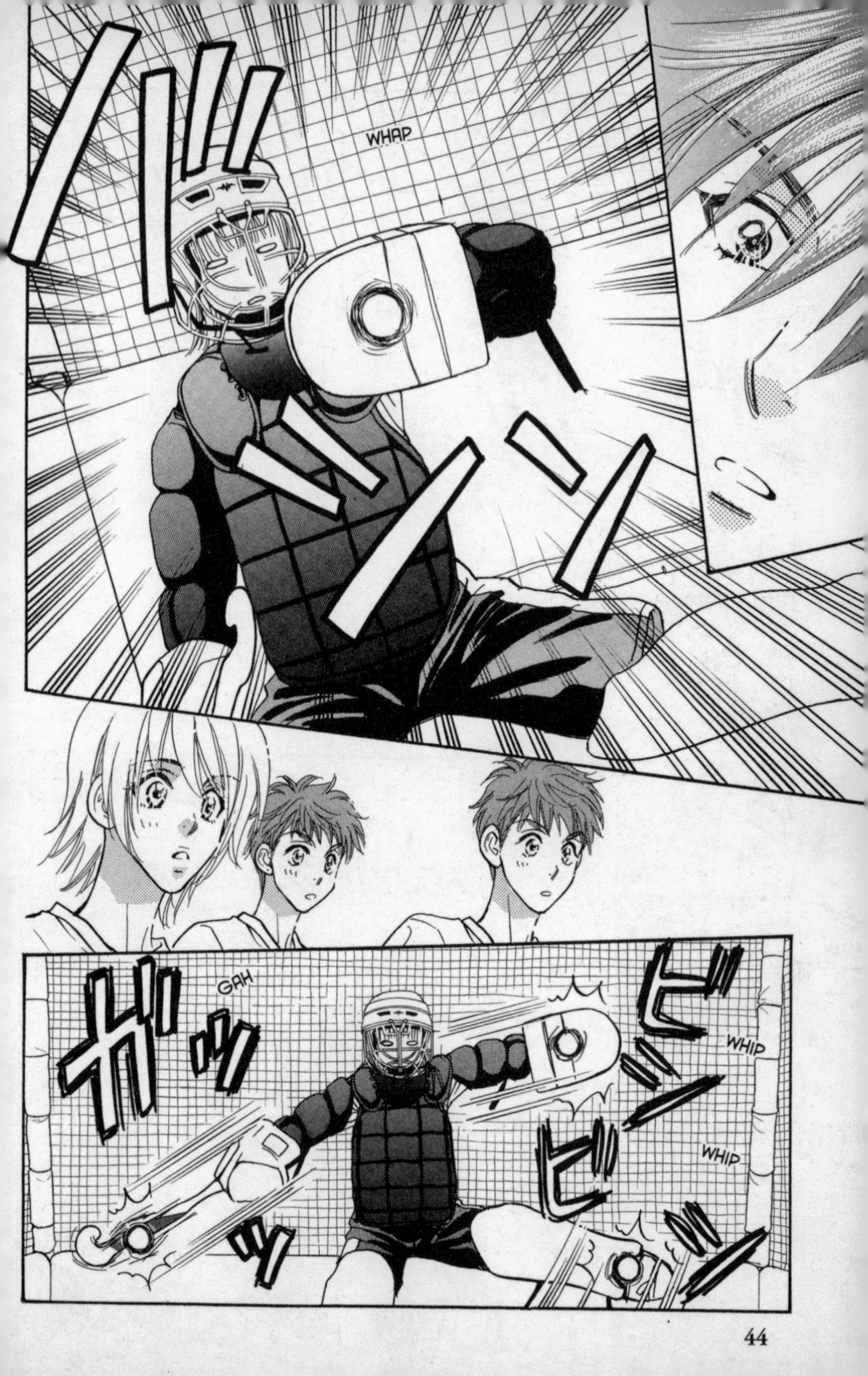
WHAP
WHIP
WHIP
GAH

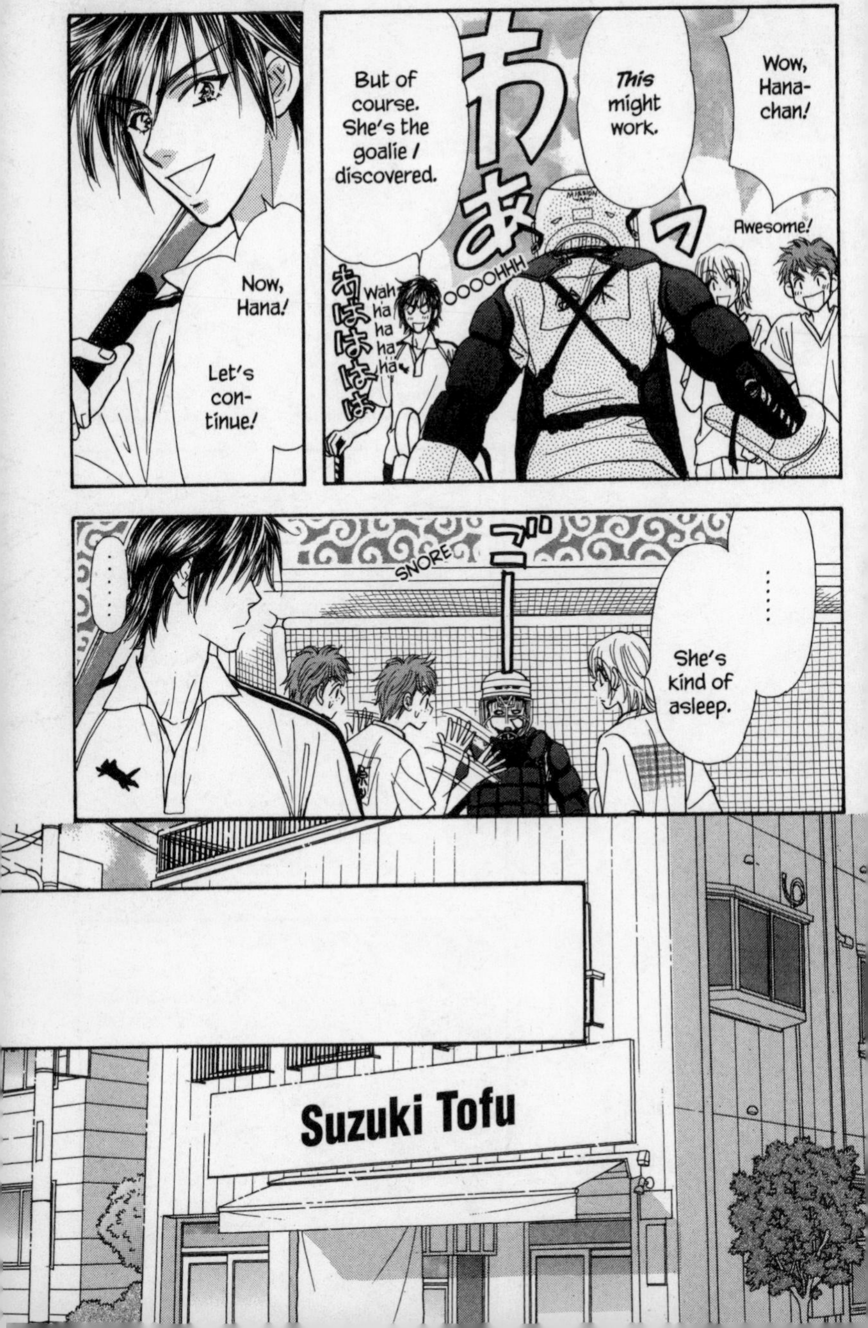
Wow, Hana-chan!
This might work.
わぁっ
OOOOHHH
Awesome!
But of course. She's the goalie I discovered.
あははは
Wah ha ha ha ha
Now, Hana!
Let's continue!
......
She's kind of asleep.
ゴー
SNORE
......
Suzuki Tofu

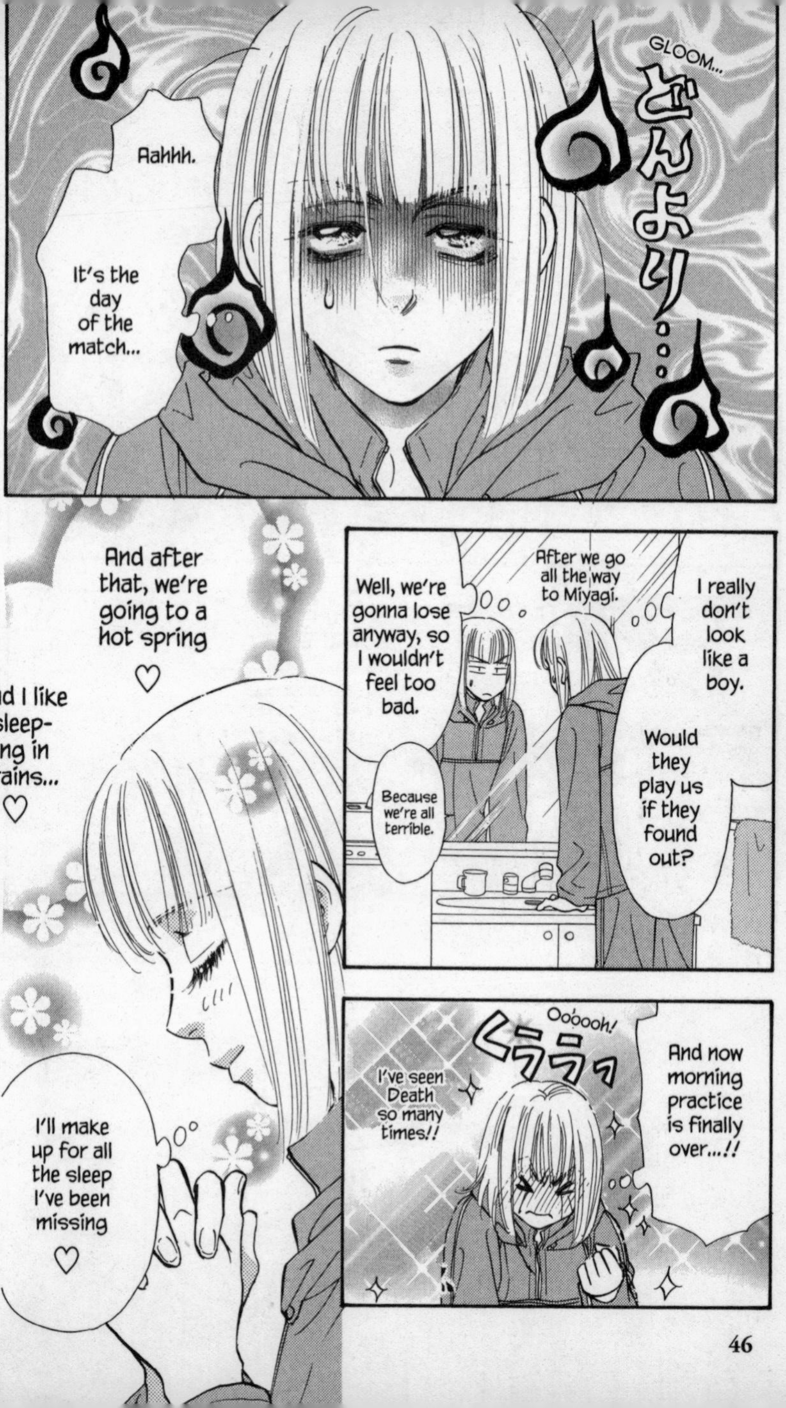
GLOOM...
どんより...
Aahhh.
It's the day of the match...
I really don't look like a boy.
Would they play us if they found out?
After we go all the way to Miyagi.
Well, we're gonna lose anyway, so I wouldn't feel too bad.
Because we're all terrible.
And now morning practice is finally over...!!
Oo'oooh!
くららぁ
I've seen Death so many times!!
And after that, we're going to a hot spring ♡
nd I like sleeping in rains... ♡
I'll make up for all the sleep I've been missing ♡

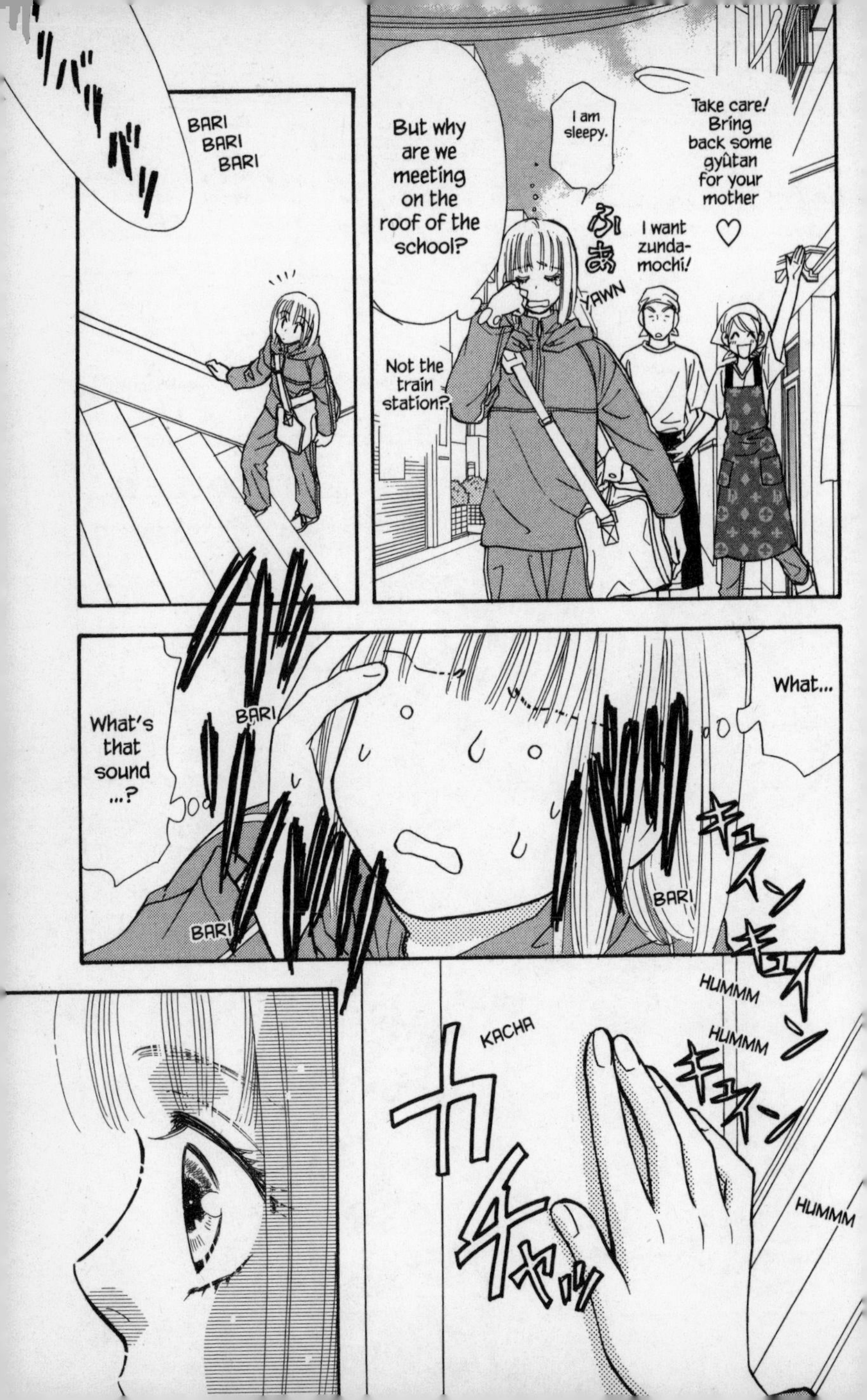
Take care! Bring back some gyûtan for your mother ♡
I want zunda-mochi!
I am sleepy.
ふあ
YAWN
But why are we meeting on the roof of the school?
Not the train station?
BARI BARI BARI
What...
What's that sound ...?
BARI
BARI
BARI
キュイーン
キュイーン
HUMMM
HUMMM
HUMMM
KACHA
カチャッ

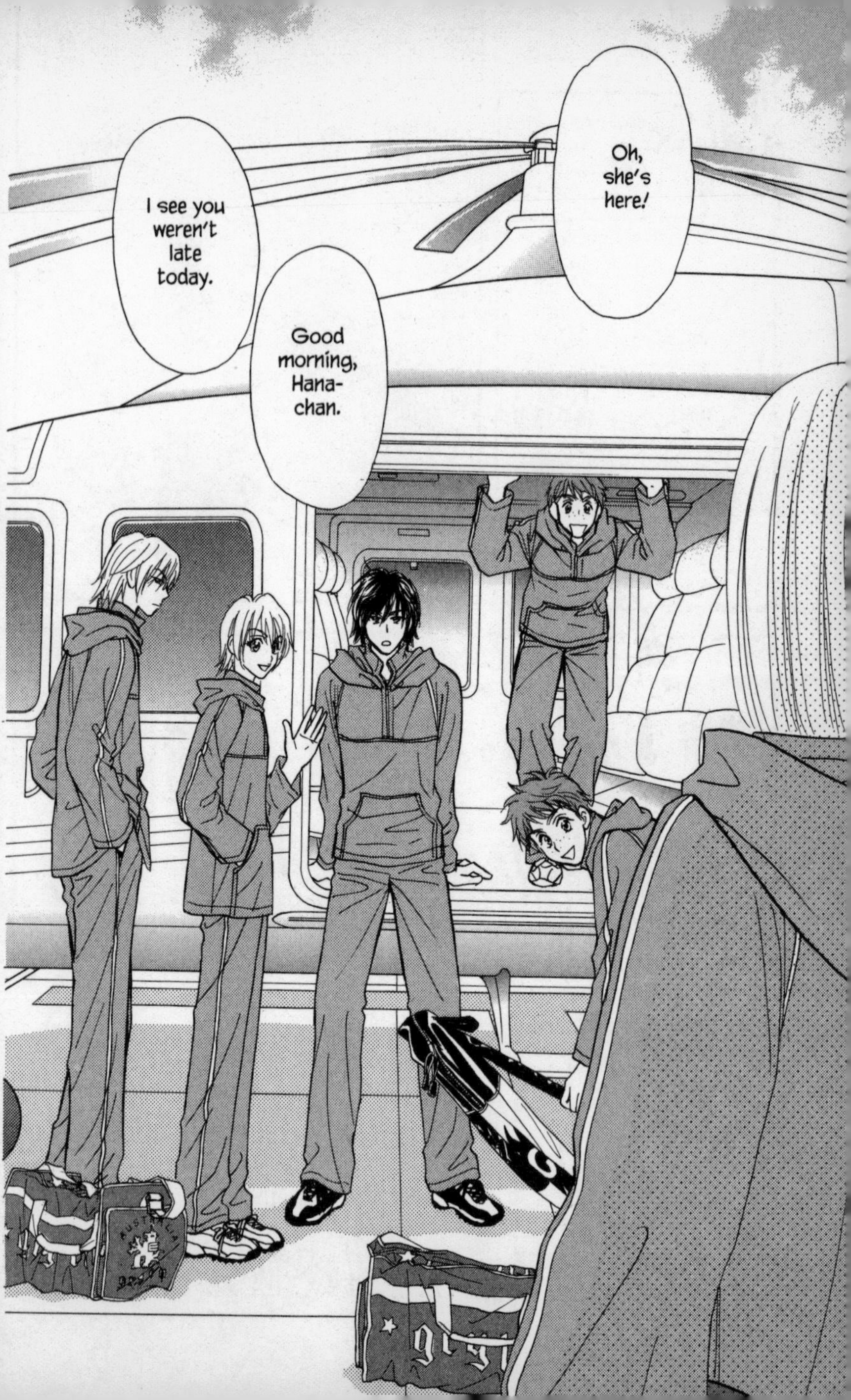
Oh, she's here!
Good morning, Hana-chan.
I see you weren't late today.

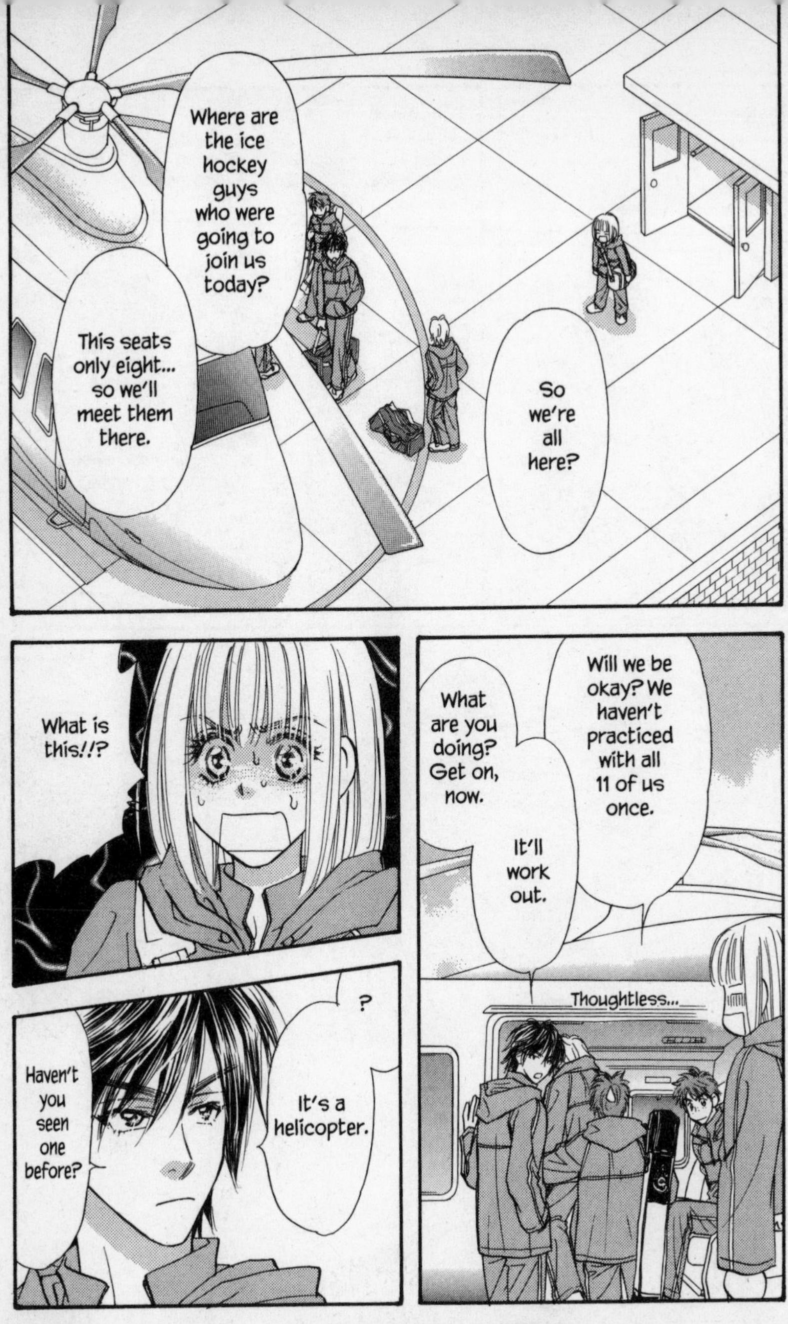
So we're all here?
Where are the ice hockey guys who were going to join us today?
This seats only eight... so we'll meet them there.
Will we be okay? We haven't practiced with all 11 of us once.
What are you doing? Get on, now.
It'll work out.
Thoughtless...
What is this!!?
?
It's a helicopter.
Haven't you seen one before?

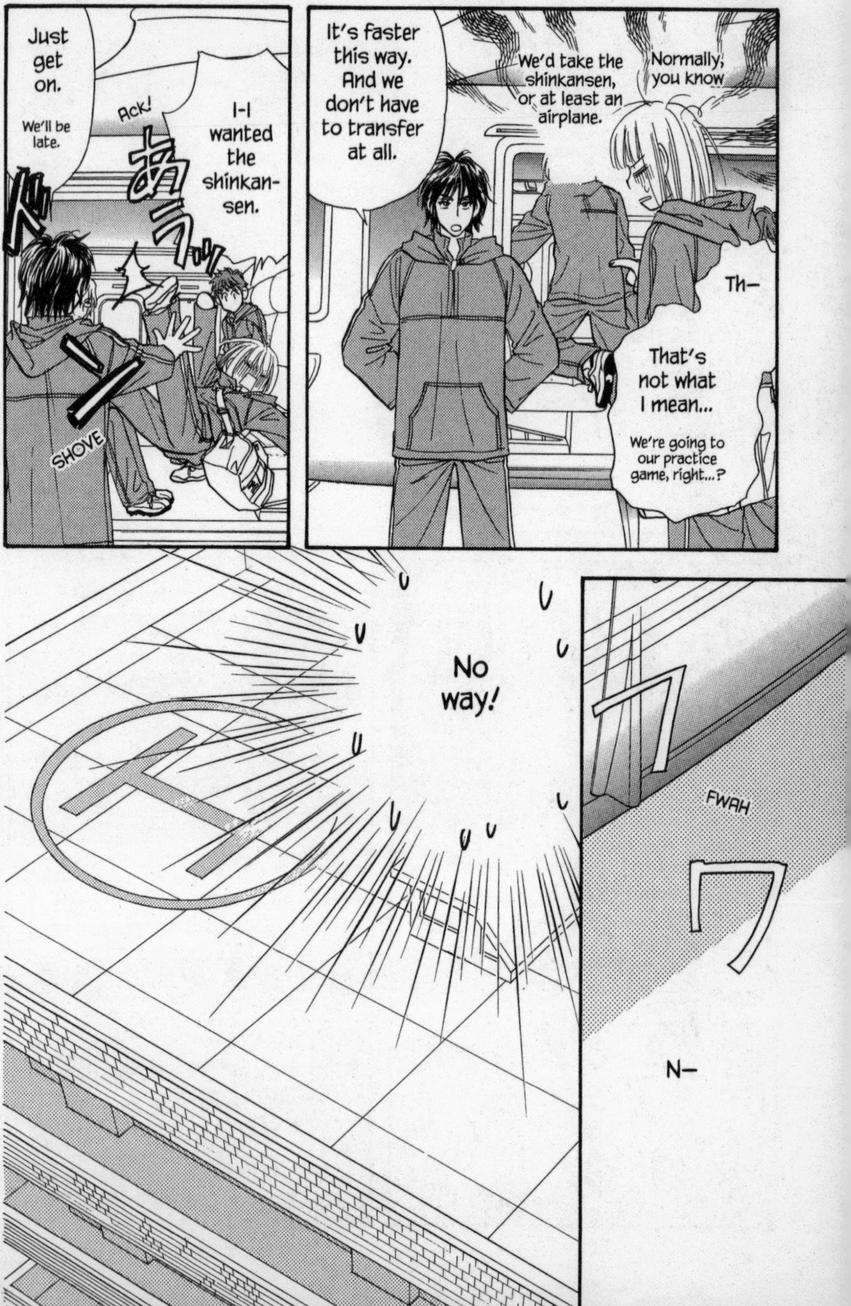
Normally, you know
We'd take the shinkansen, or at least an airplane.
It's faster this way. And we don't have to transfer at all.
Th—
That's not what I mean...
We're going to our practice game, right...?
I-I wanted the shinkansen.
Ack!
Just get on.
We'll be late.
SHOVE
FWAH
N—
No way!

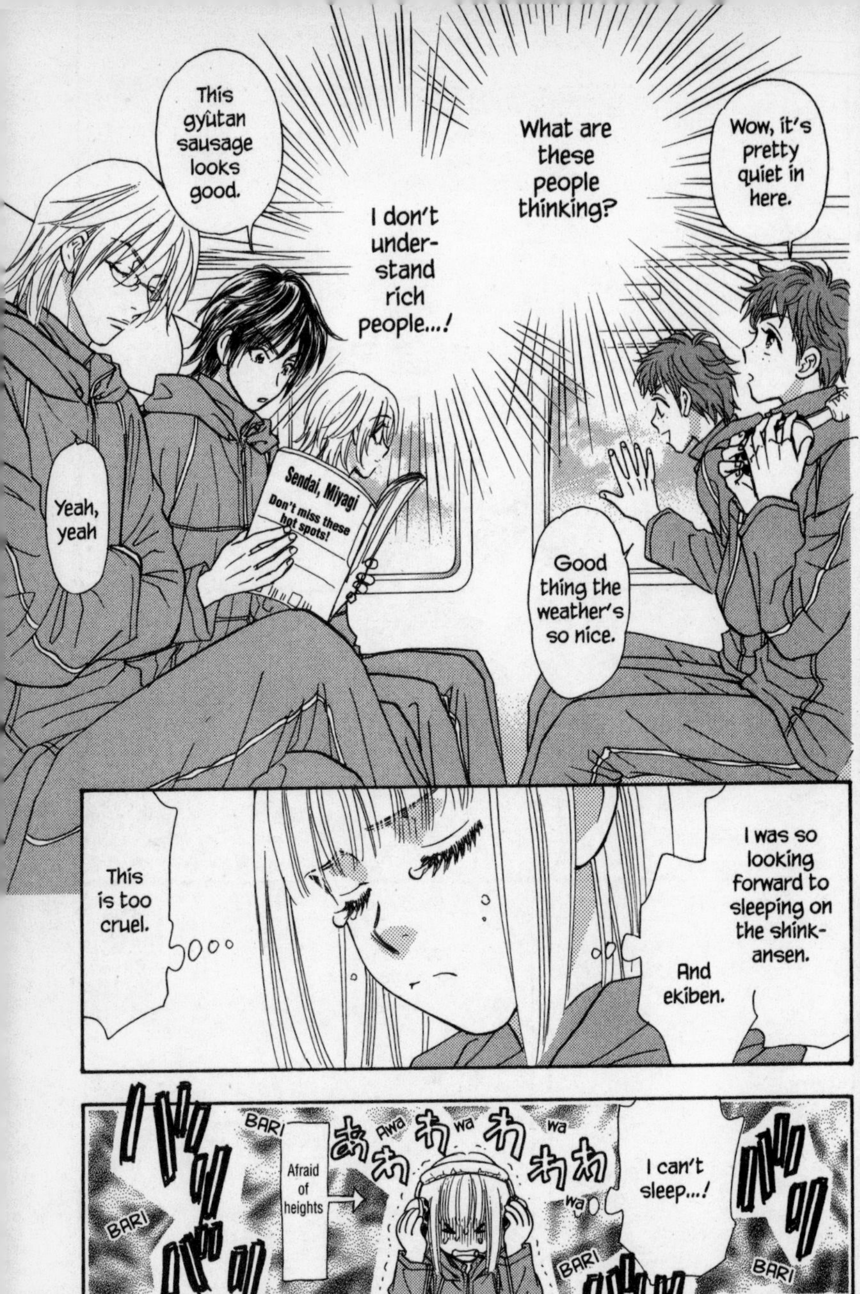

Wow, it's pretty quiet in here.
What are these people thinking?
This gyûtan sausage looks good.
I don't under-stand rich people...!
Good thing the weather's so nice.
Sendai, Miyagi
Don't miss these hot spots!
Yeah, yeah
I was so looking forward to sleeping on the shink-ansen.
And ekiben.
This is too cruel.
BARI
BARI
I can't sleep...!
wa
wa
awa
BARI
Afraid of heights
BARI
BARI

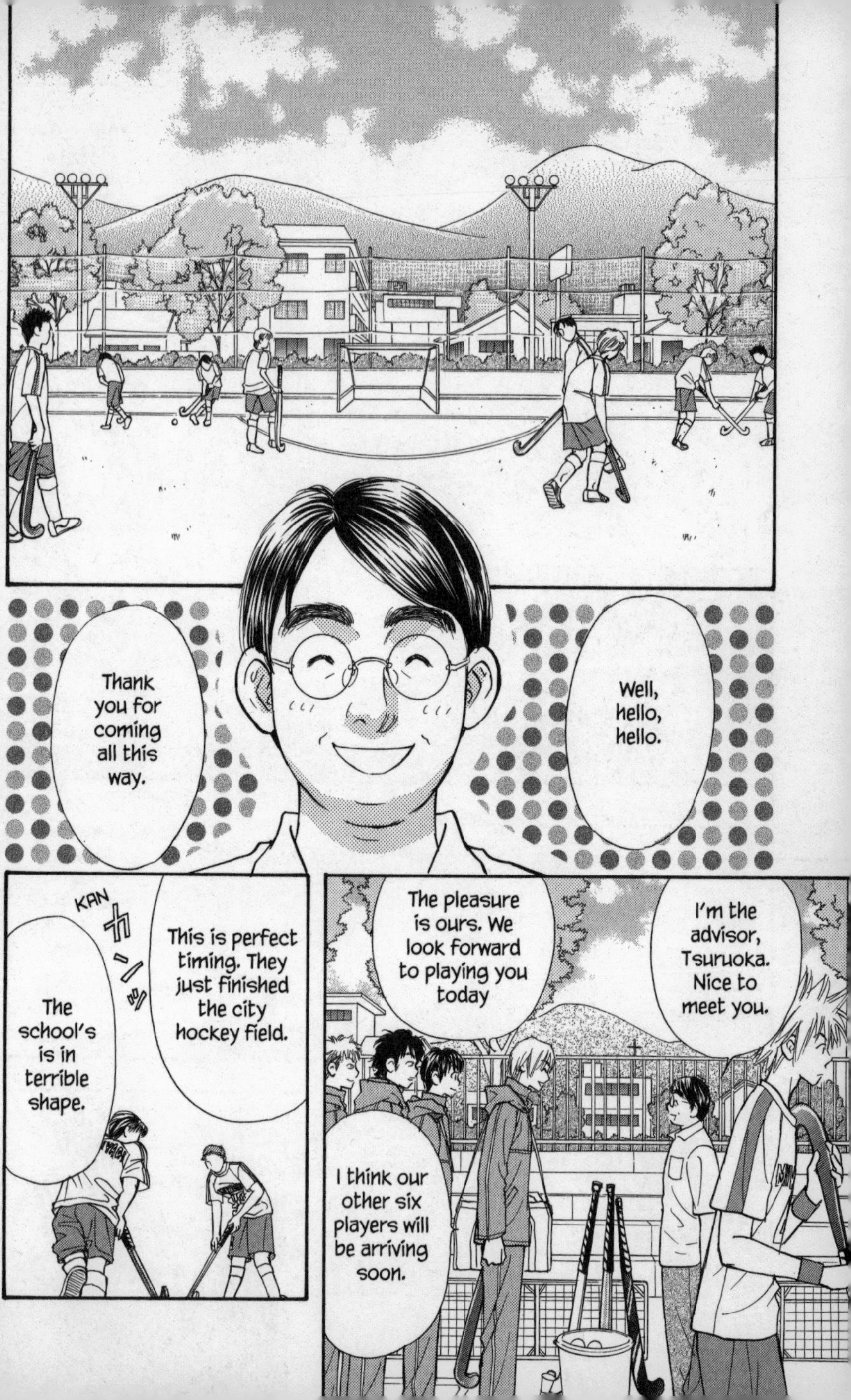
Well, hello, hello.
Thank you for coming all this way.
I'm the advisor, Tsuruoka. Nice to meet you.
The pleasure is ours. We look forward to playing you today
I think our other six players will be arriving soon.
This is perfect timing. They just finished the city hockey field.
KAN
The school's is in terrible shape.

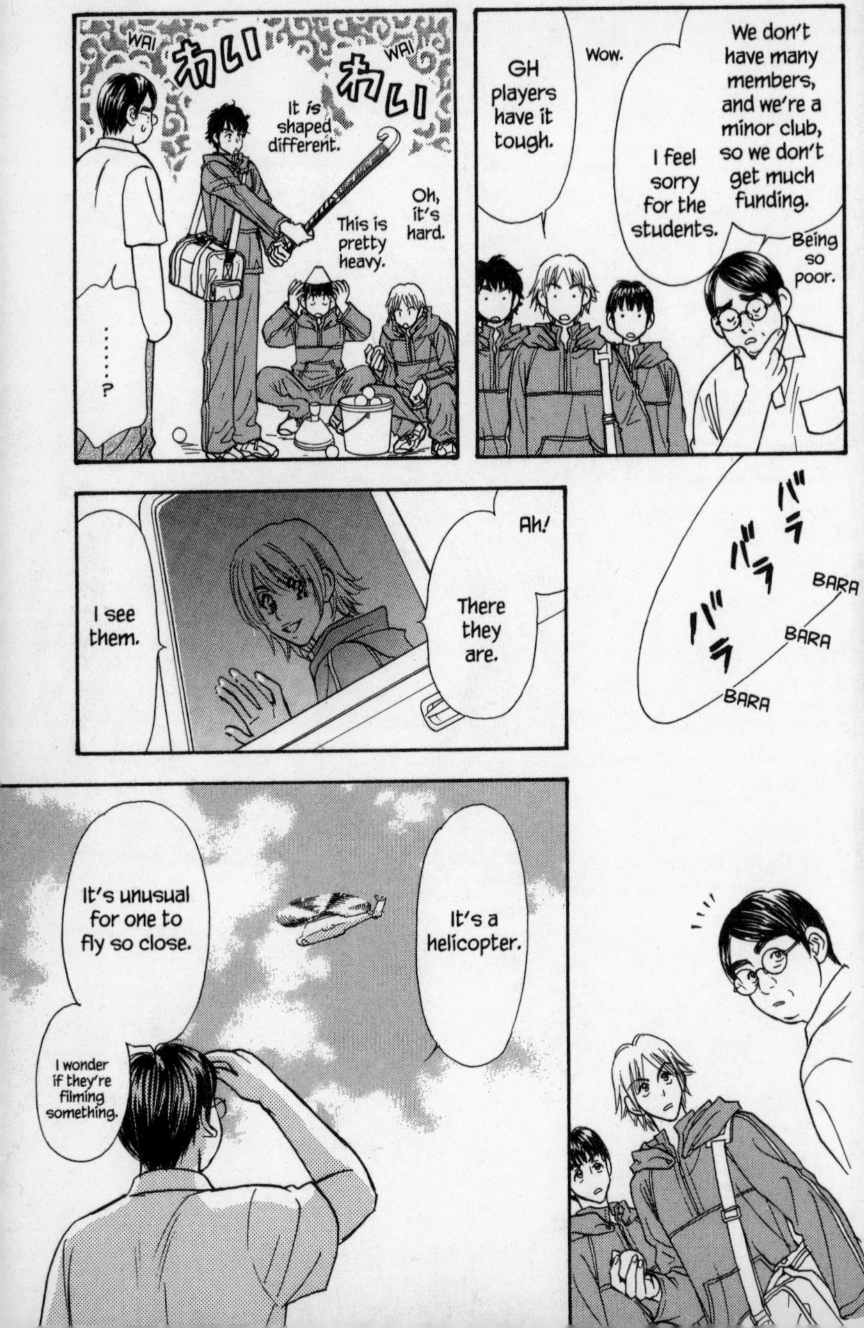
We don't have many members, and we're a minor club, so we don't get much funding.
Being so poor.
I feel sorry for the students.
Wow.
GH players have it tough.
WAI
わい
WAI
わい
It is shaped different.
Oh, it's hard.
This is pretty heavy.
......?
バラ
BARA
バラ
BARA
バラ
BARA
Ah!
There they are.
I see them.
It's a helicopter.
It's unusual for one to fly so close.
I wonder if they're filming something.

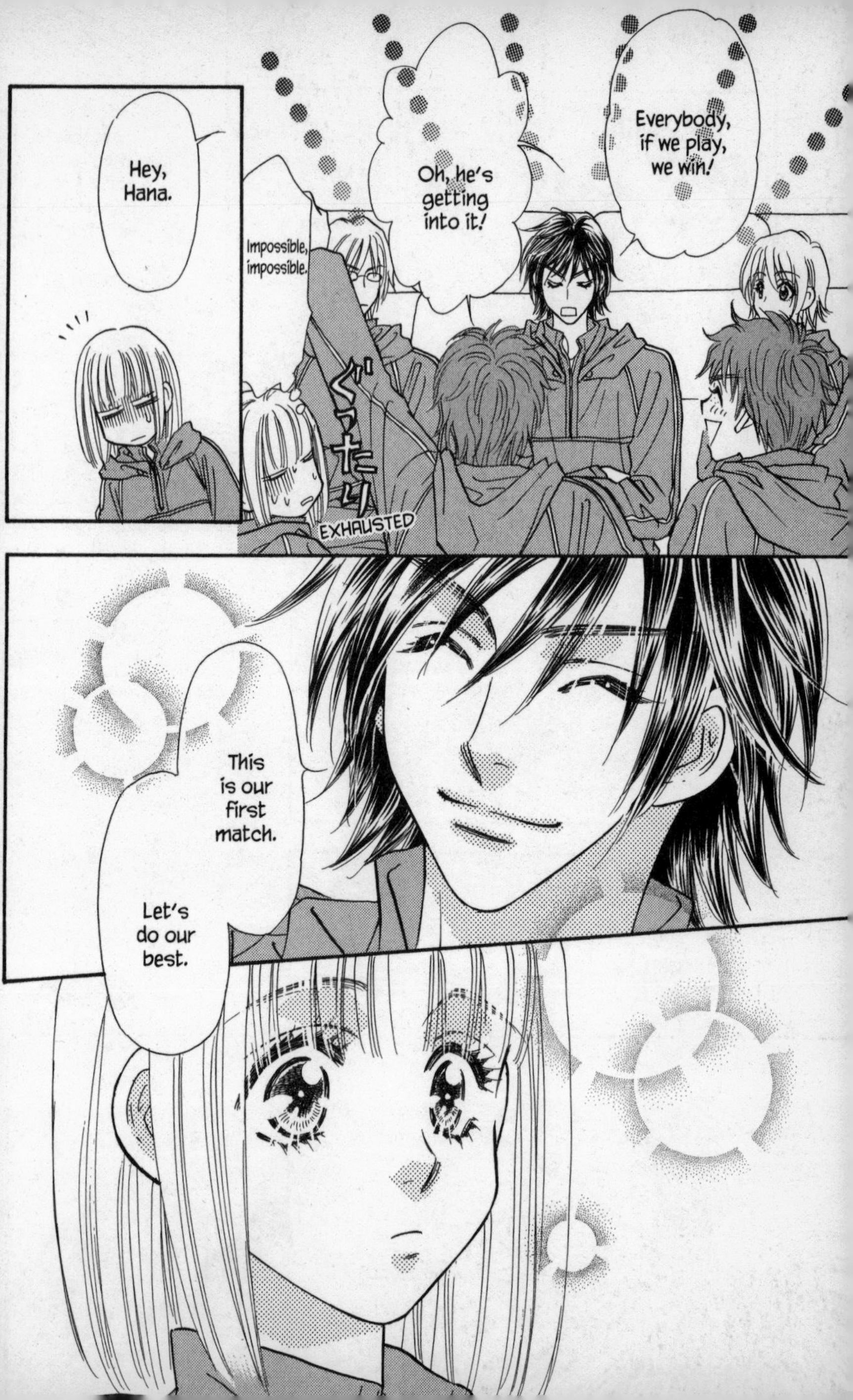
Everybody, if we play, we win!
Oh, he's getting into it!
Impossible, impossible.
ぐったり
EXHAUSTED
Hey, Hana.
This is our first match.
Let's do our best.

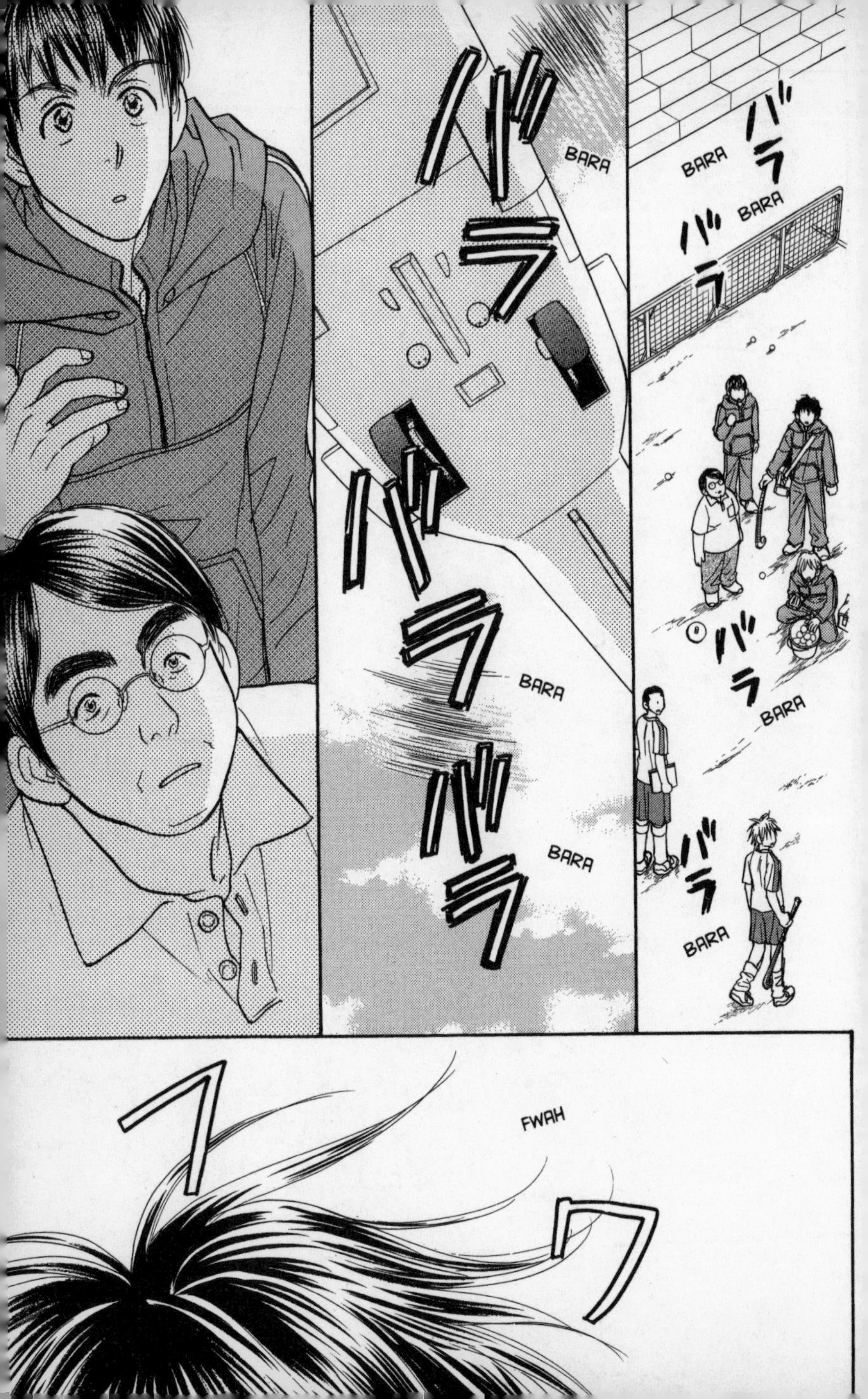
バラ
BARA
バラ
BARA
バラ
BARA
バラ
BARA
バラ
BARA
バラ
BARA
バラ
BARA
FWAH
フワ

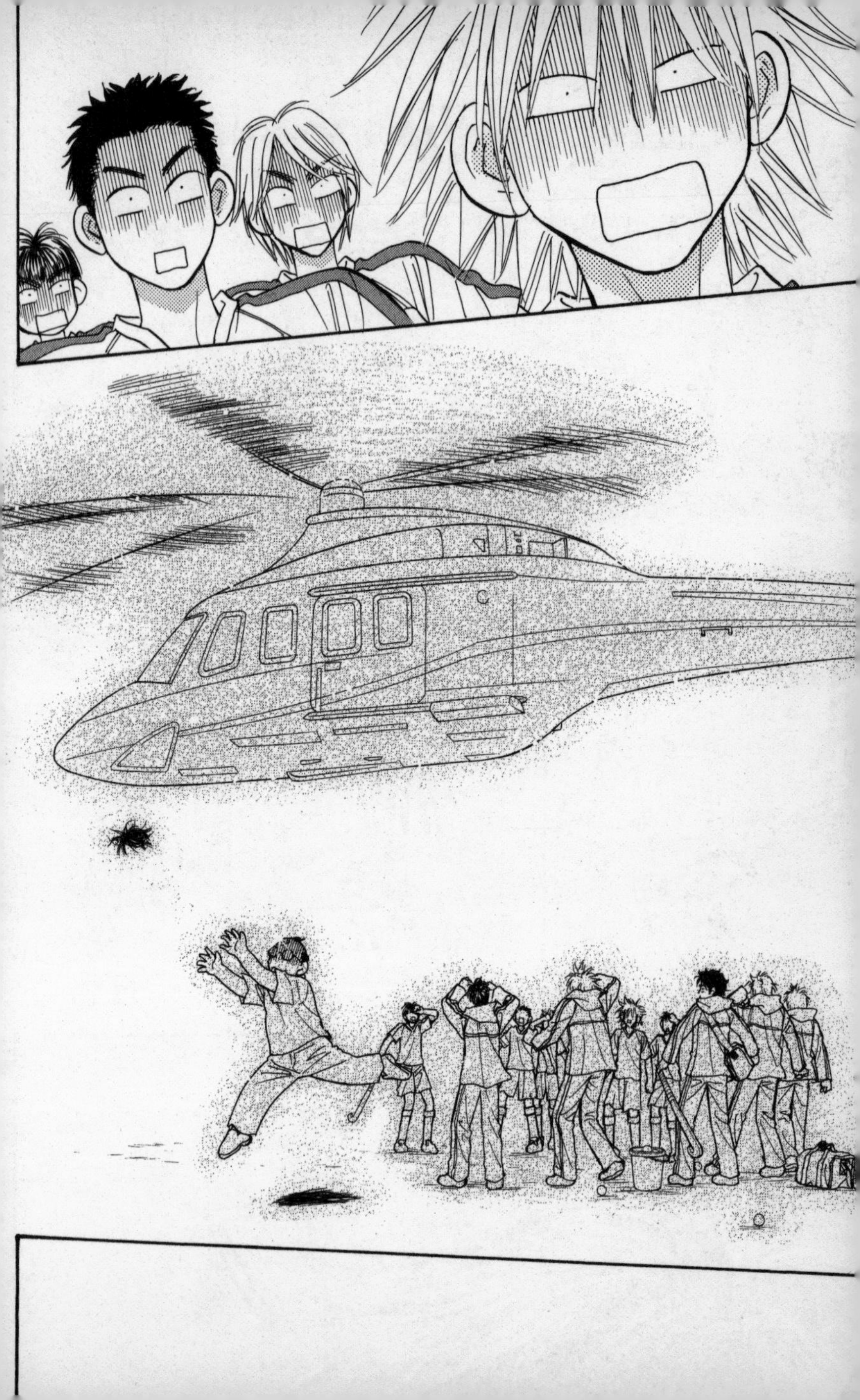

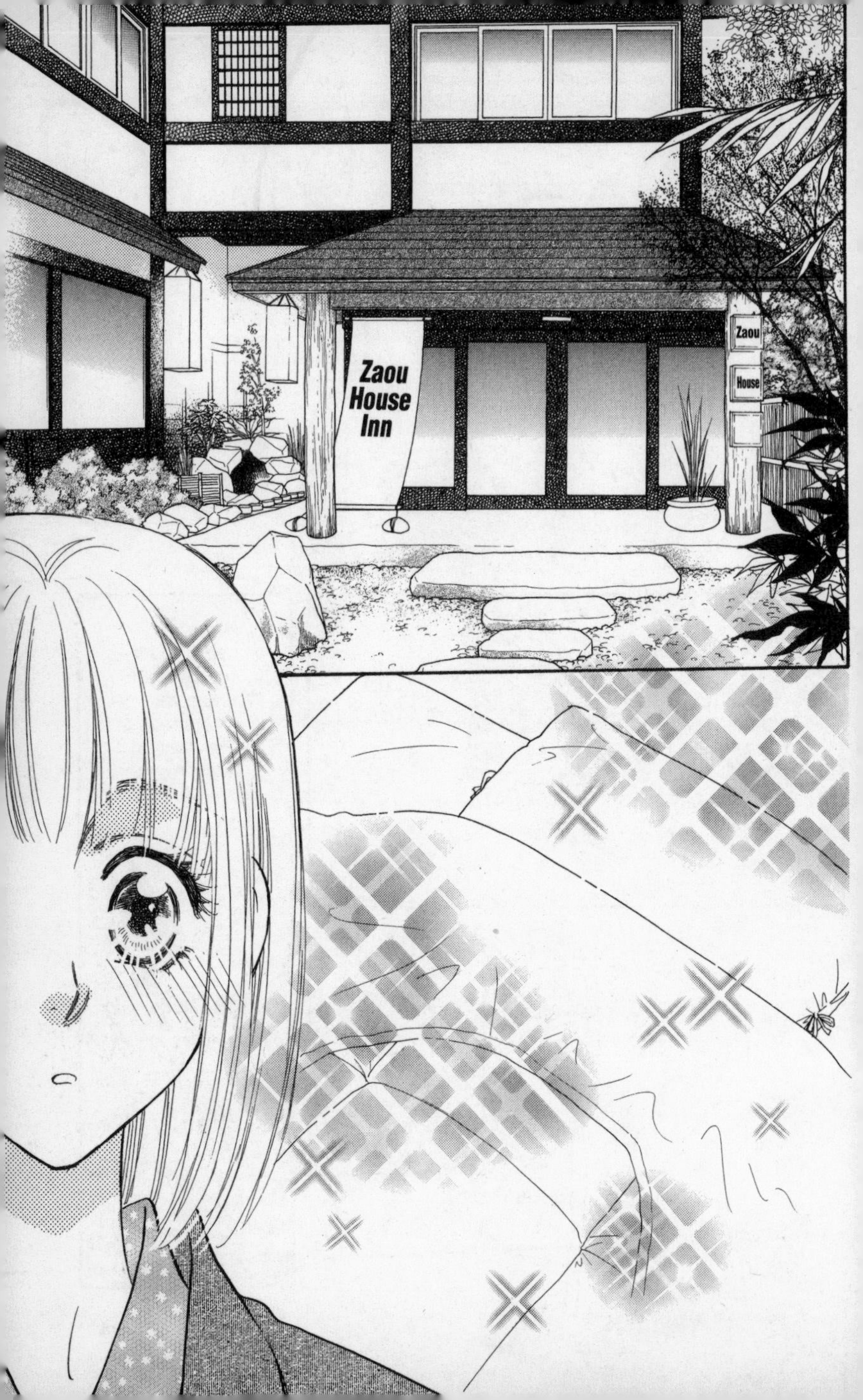
Zaou House Inn
Zaou
House

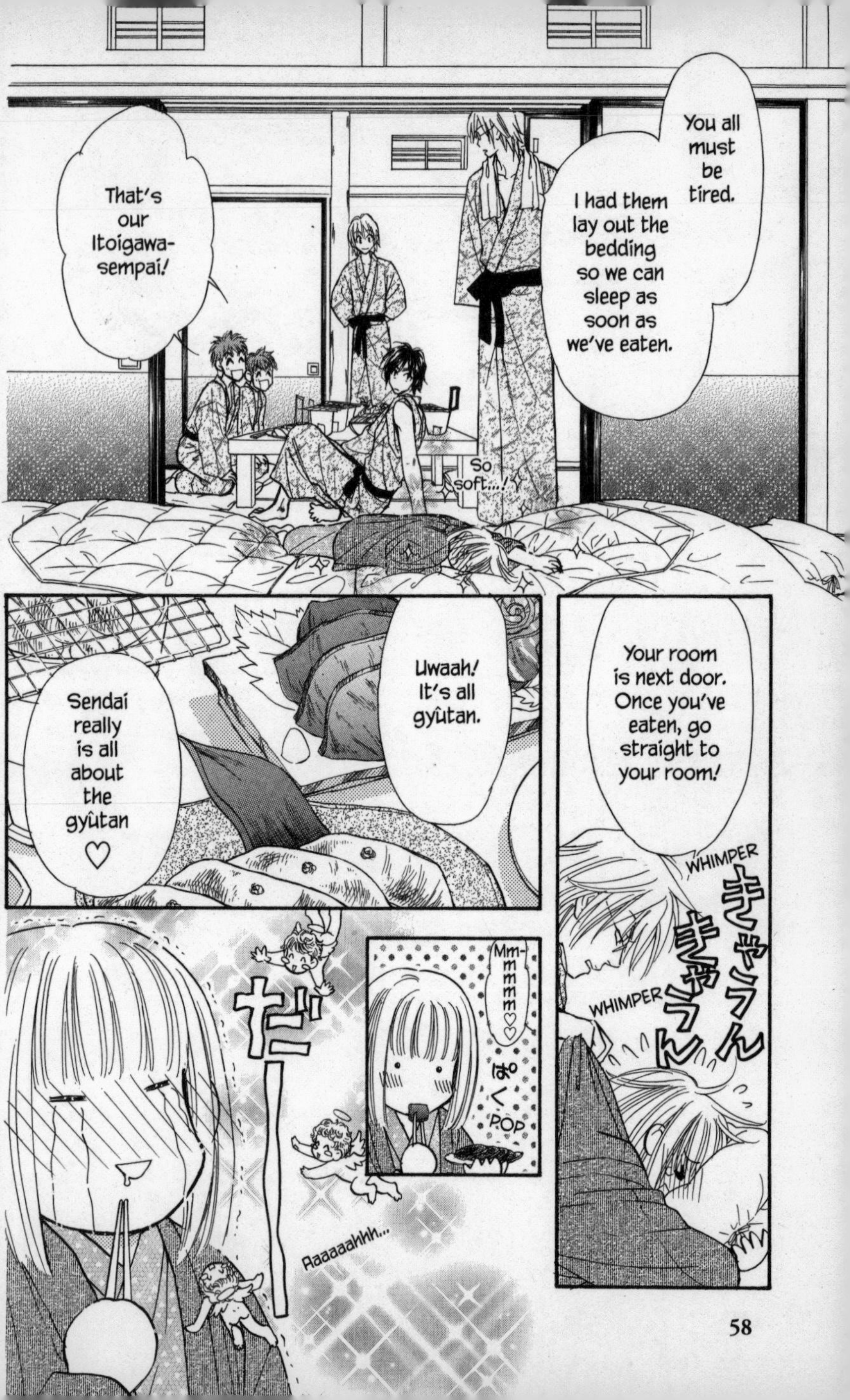
You all must be tired.
I had them lay out the bedding so we can sleep as soon as we've eaten.
That's our Itoigawa-sempai!
So soft...!
Your room is next door. Once you've eaten, go straight to your room!
WHIMPER
きゃうん
WHIMPER
きゃうん
Uwaah! It's all gyûtan.
Sendai really is all about the gyûtan ♡
Mm-mmmmm♡
ぱく
POP
だー
Aaaaaahhh...

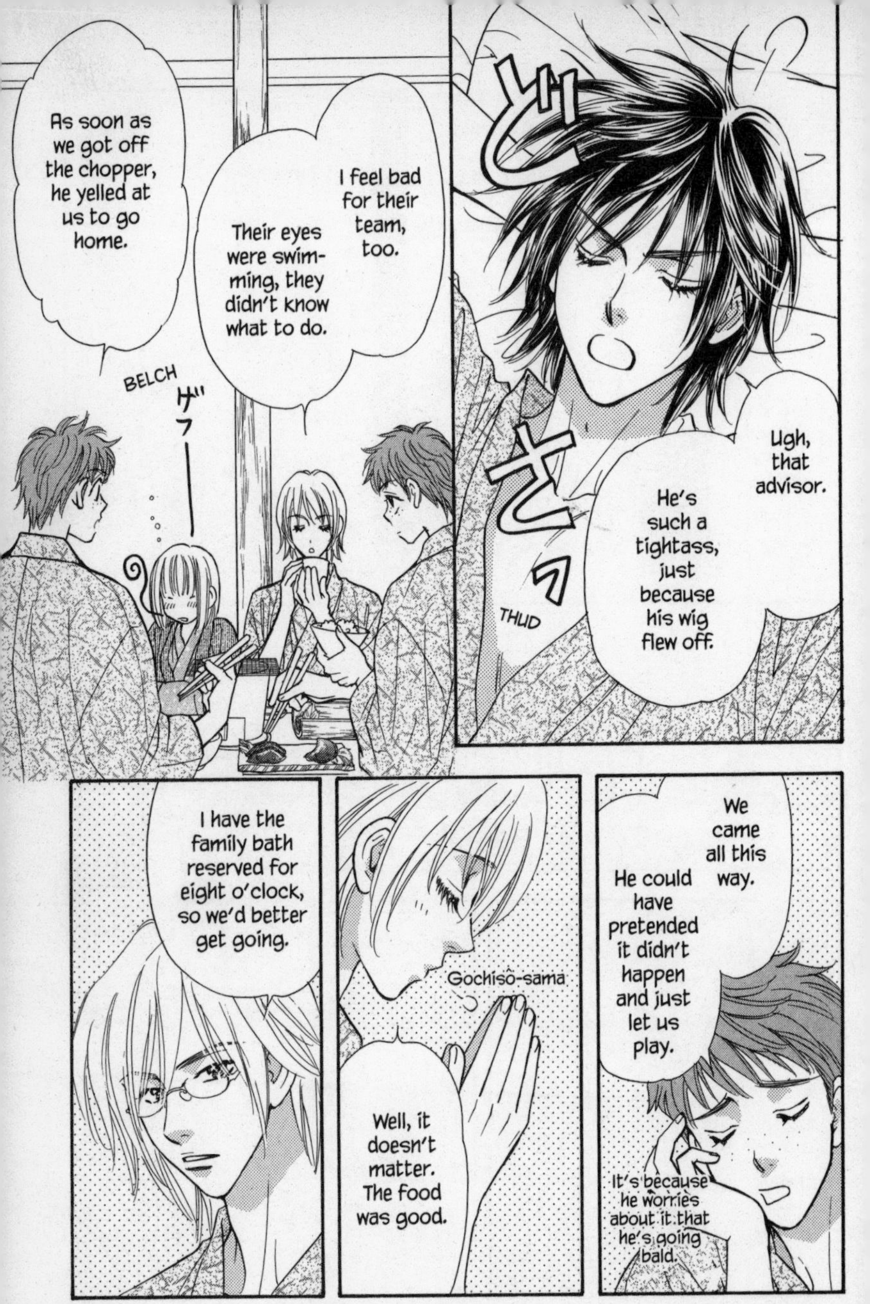
どさっ
THUD
Ugh, that advisor.
He's such a tightass, just because his wig flew off.
I feel bad for their team, too.
Their eyes were swimming, they didn't know what to do.
As soon as we got off the chopper, he yelled at us to go home.
BELCH
ゲフー
We came all this way.
He could have pretended it didn't happen and just let us play.
It's because he worries about it that he's going bald.
Gochisō-sama
Well, it doesn't matter. The food was good.
I have the family bath reserved for eight o'clock, so we'd better get going.

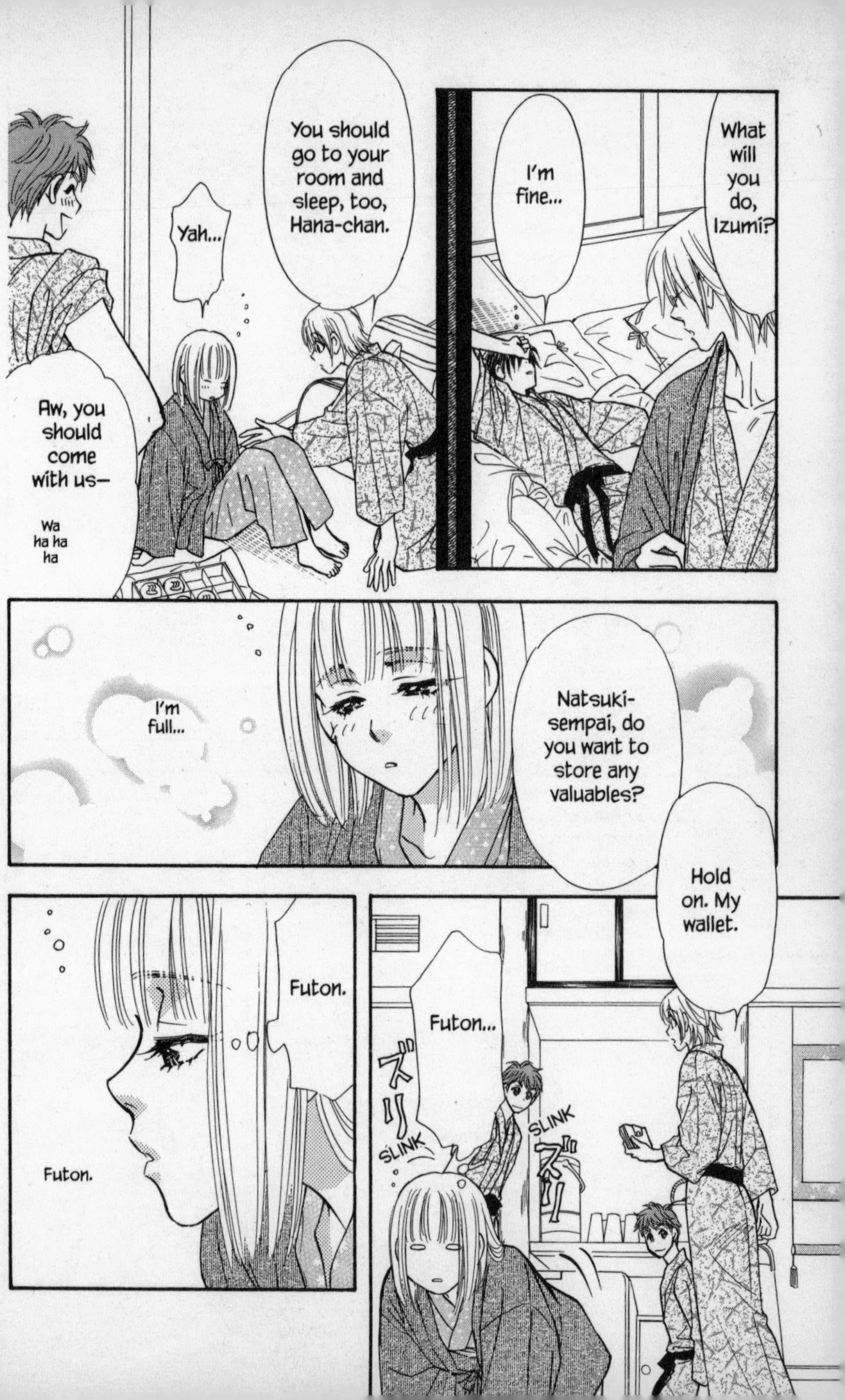
What will you do, Izumi?
I'm fine...
You should go to your room and sleep, too, Hana-chan.
Yah...
Aw, you should come with us—
Wa ha ha ha
Natsuki-sempai, do you want to store any valuables?
I'm full...
Hold on. My wallet.
SLINK
ズリ
Futon...
ズリ
SLINK
Futon.
Futon.

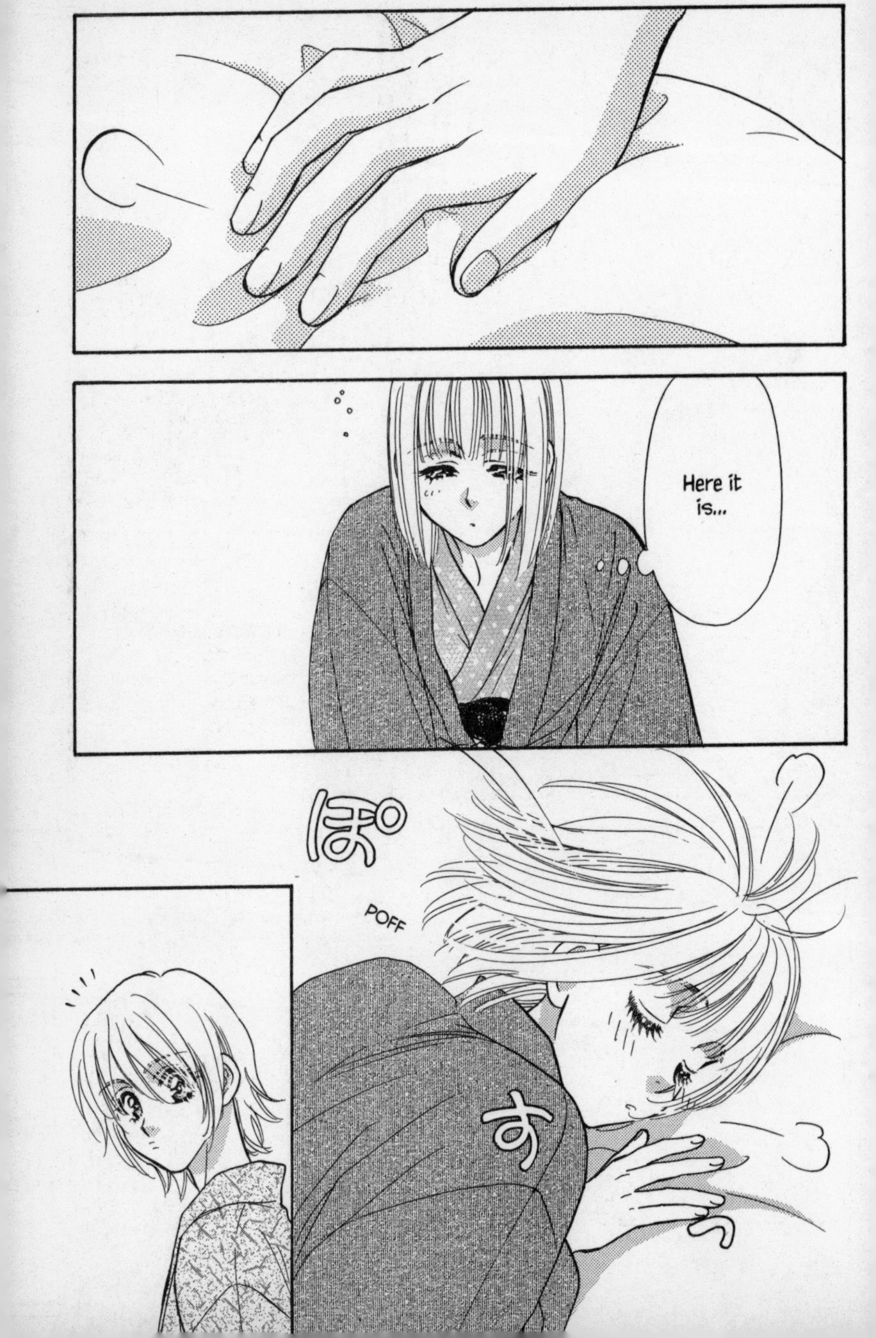
Here it is...
ぽ
POFF
す

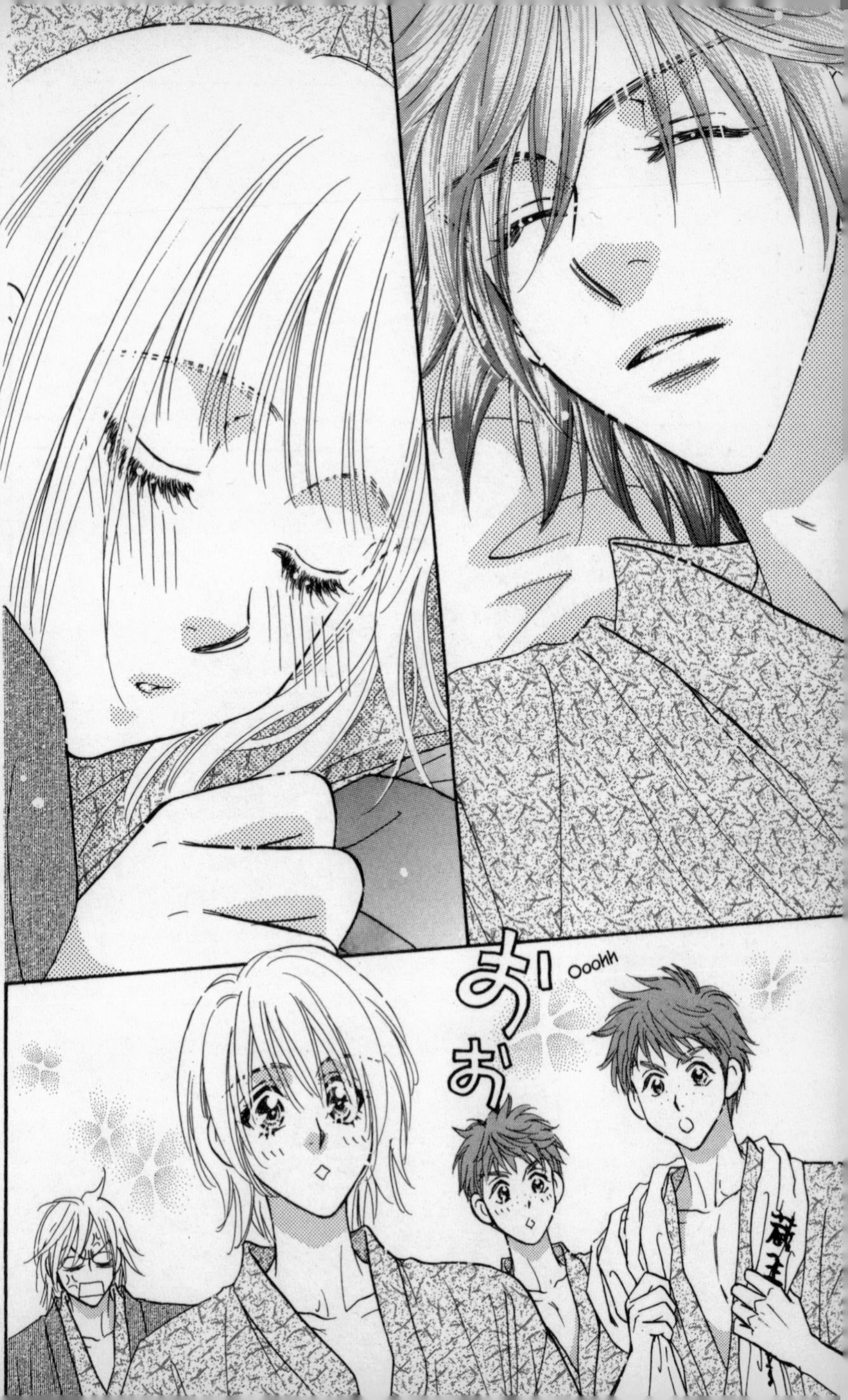
おお
Ooohh

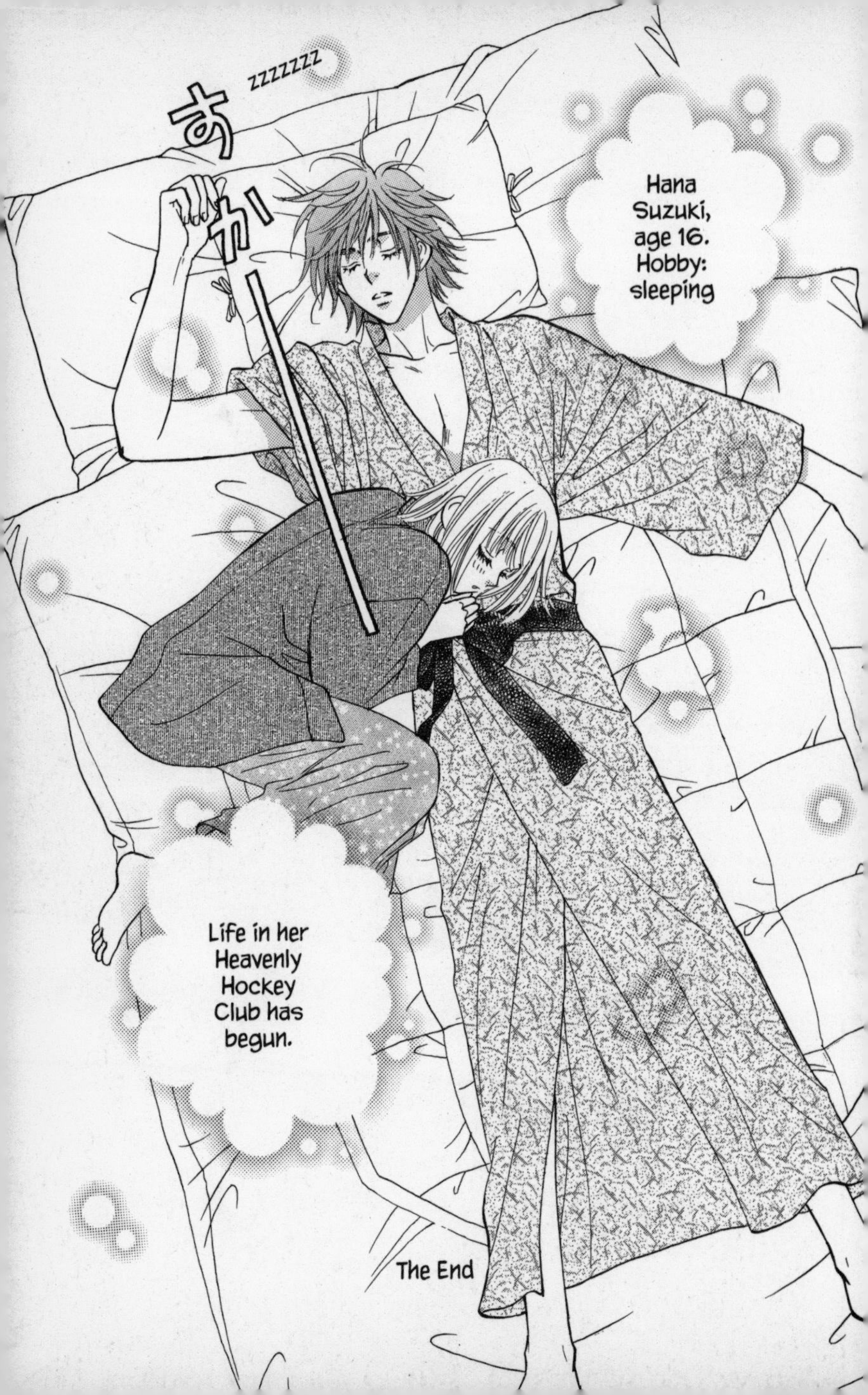
Hana Suzuki, age 16. Hobby: sleeping
すかー
zzzzzzz
Life in her Heavenly Hockey Club has begun.
The End

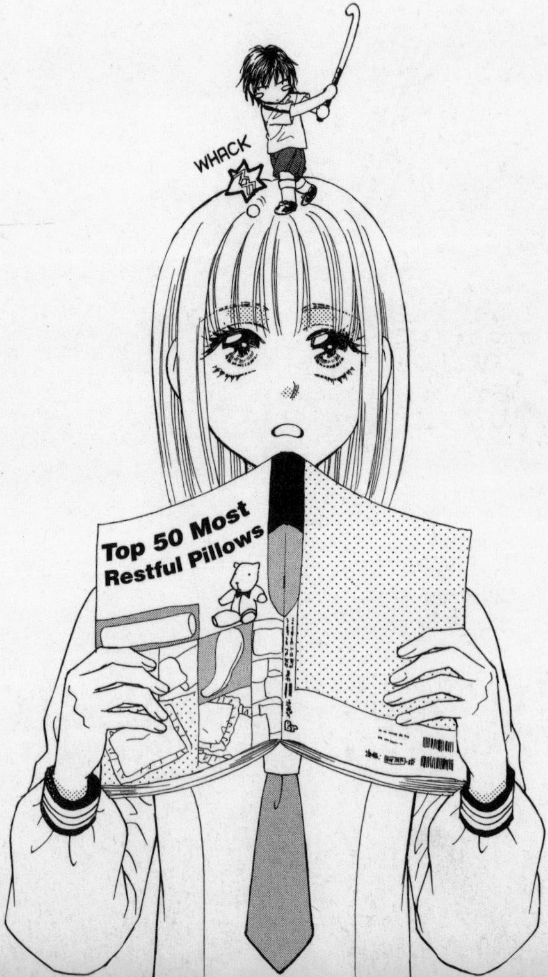
WHACK
Top 50 Most Restful Pillows

Chapter 2: Bravo, Ekiben

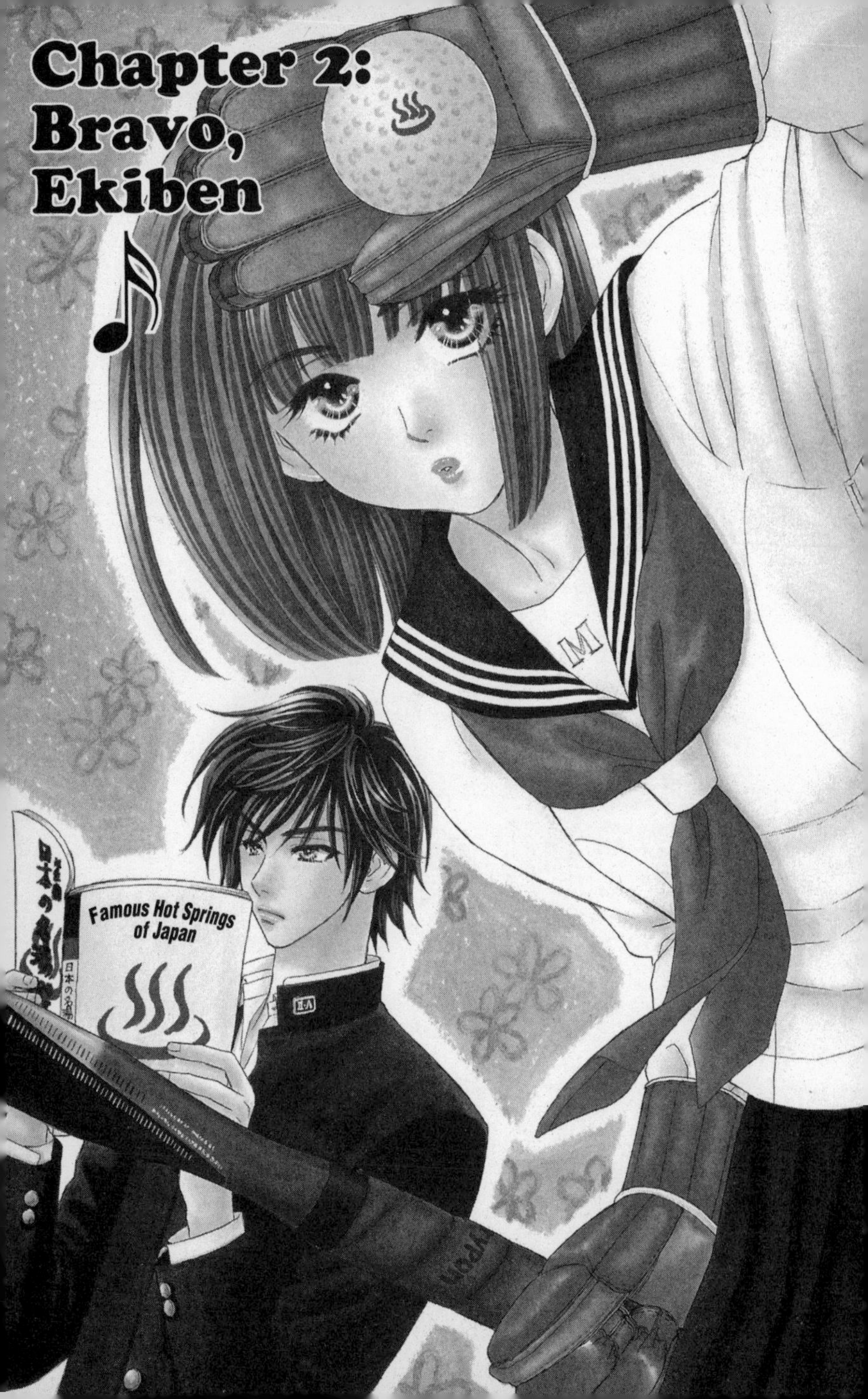
Famous Hot Springs of Japan

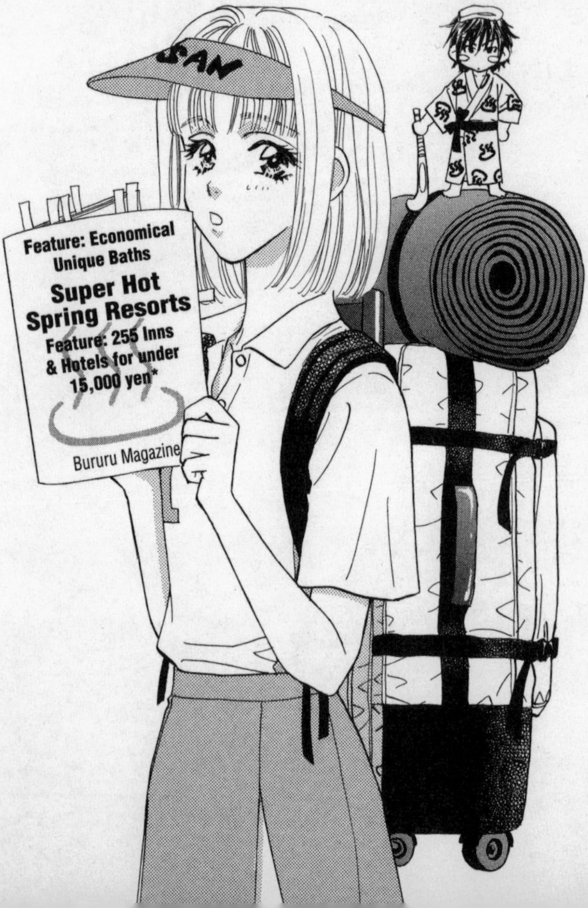
SAN
Feature: Economical Unique Baths
Super Hot Spring Resorts
Feature: 255 Inns & Hotels for under 15,000 yen*
Bururu Magazine

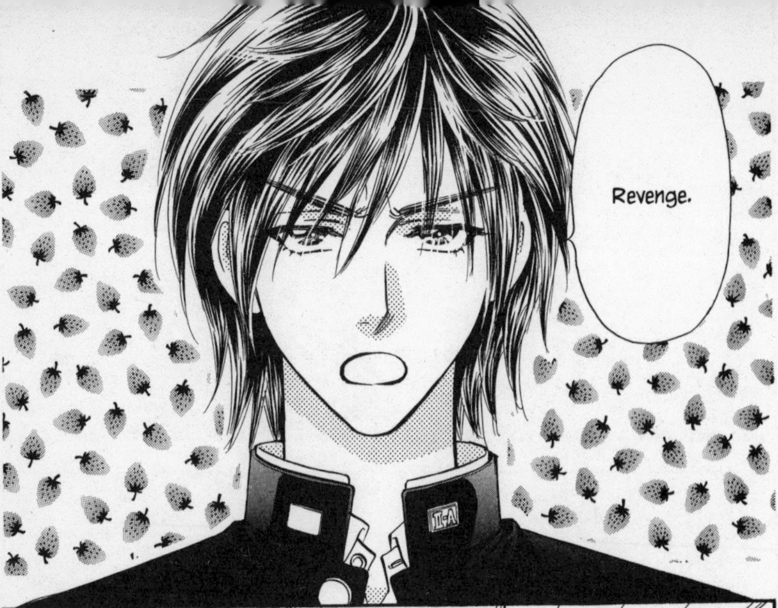
Revenge.
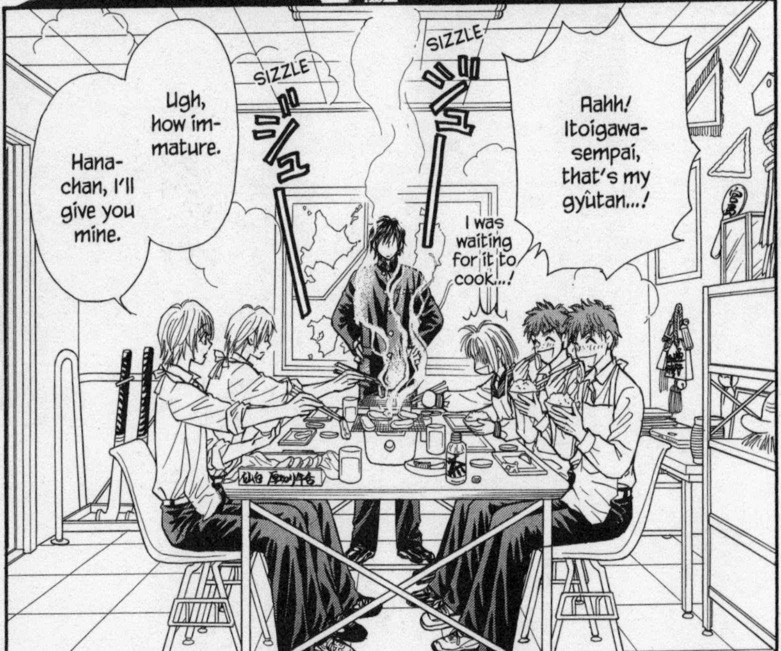
Aahh! Itoigawa-sempai, that's my gyûtan...!
I was waiting for it to cook...!
SIZZLE
SIZZLE
Ugh, how im-mature.
Hana-chan, I'll give you mine.

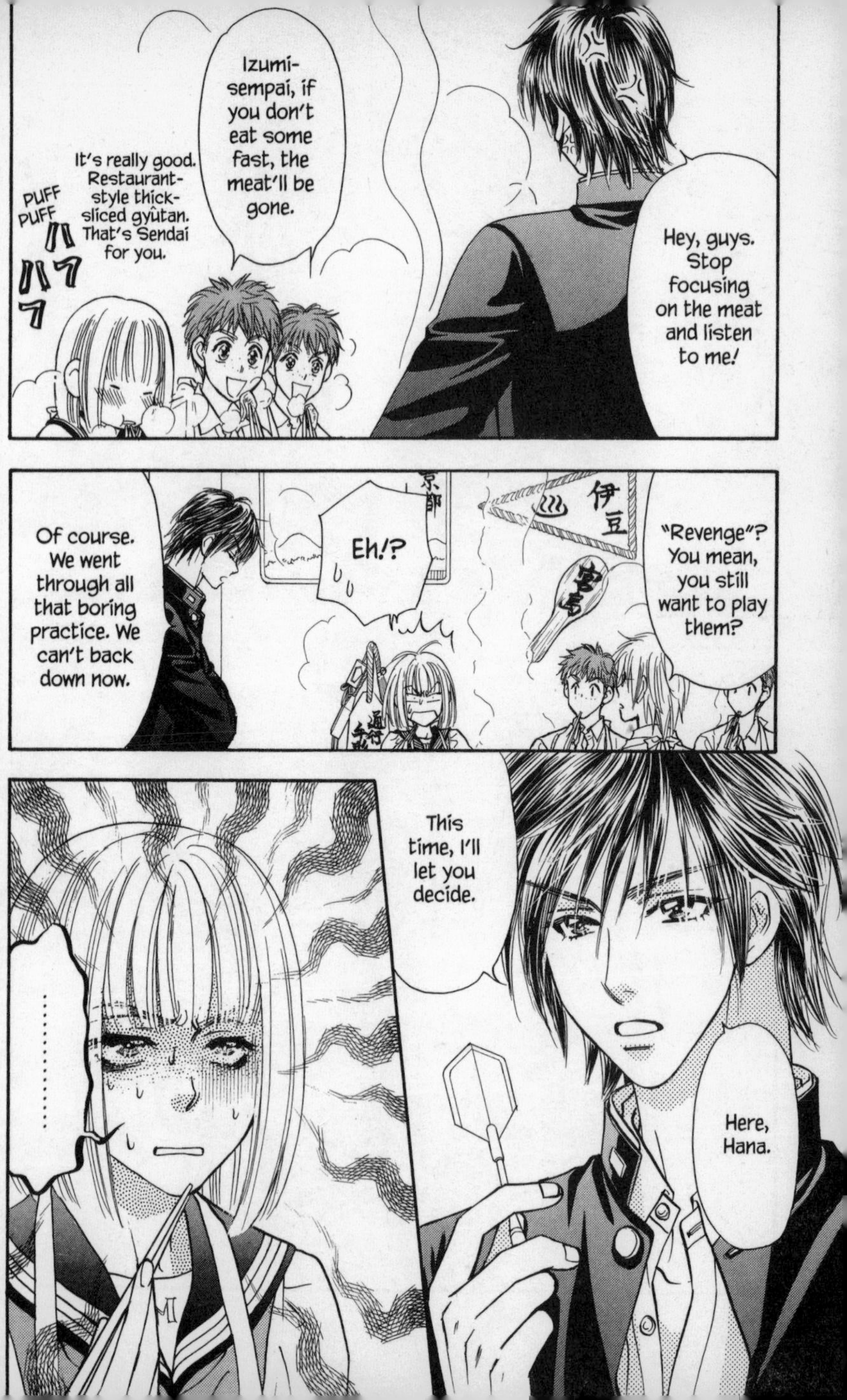
Hey, guys. Stop focusing on the meat and listen to me!
Izumi-sempai, if you don't eat some fast, the meat'll be gone.
It's really good. Restaurant-style thick-sliced gyûtan. That's Sendai for you.
PUFF PUFF
パフパフ
"Revenge"? You mean, you still want to play them?
伊豆
Eh!?
Of course. We went through all that boring practice. We can't back down now.
This time, I'll let you decide.
Here, Hana.
......

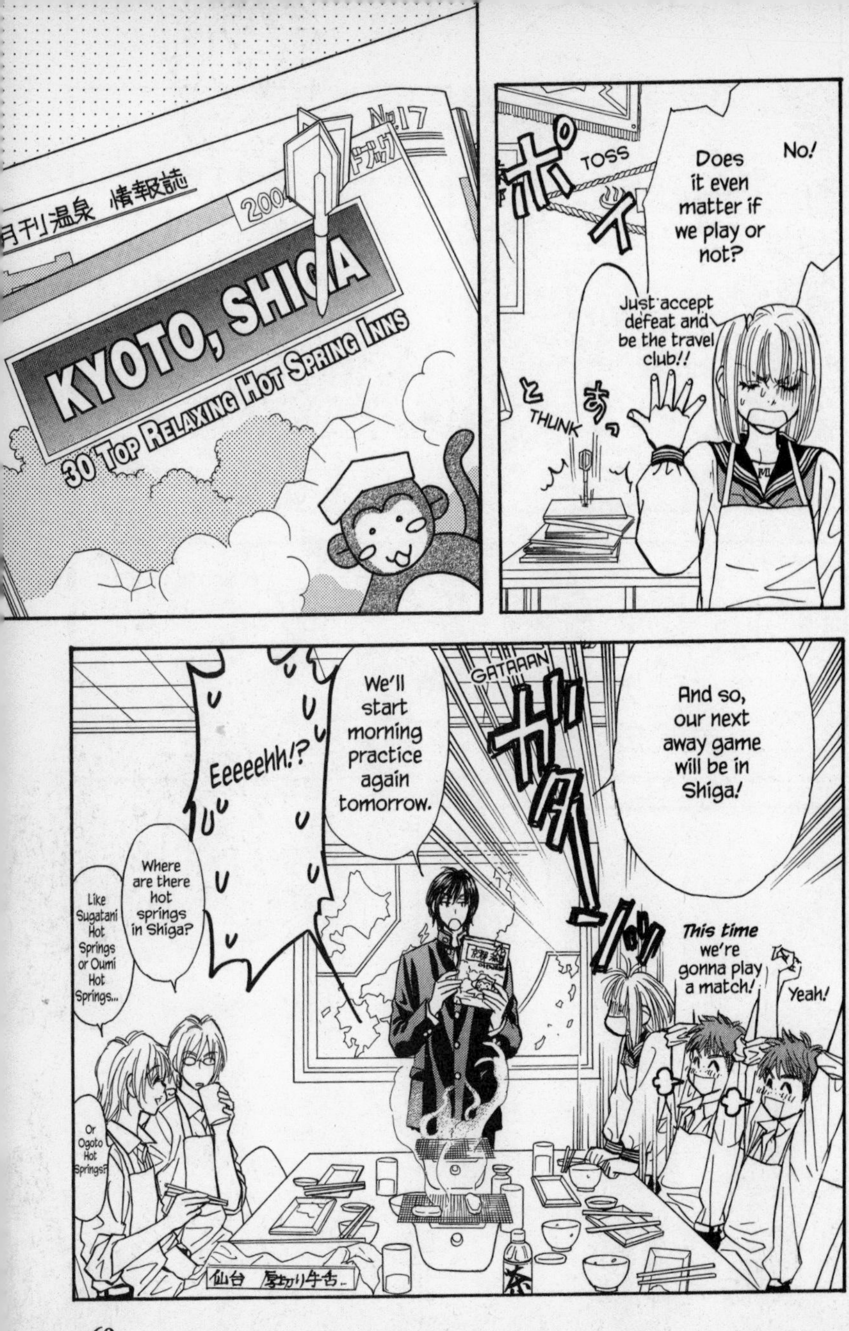

No!
TOSS
Does it even matter if we play or not?
Just accept defeat and be the travel club!!
THUNK
No.17
月刊温泉 情報誌
KYOTO, SHIGA
30 Top Relaxing Hot Spring Inns
And so, our next away game will be in Shiga!
GATAAAN
This time we're gonna play a match!
Yeah!
We'll start morning practice again tomorrow.
Eeeeehh!?
Where are there hot springs in Shiga?
Like Sugatani Hot Springs or Oumi Hot Springs...
Or Ogoto Hot Springs?
仙台 厚切り牛舌

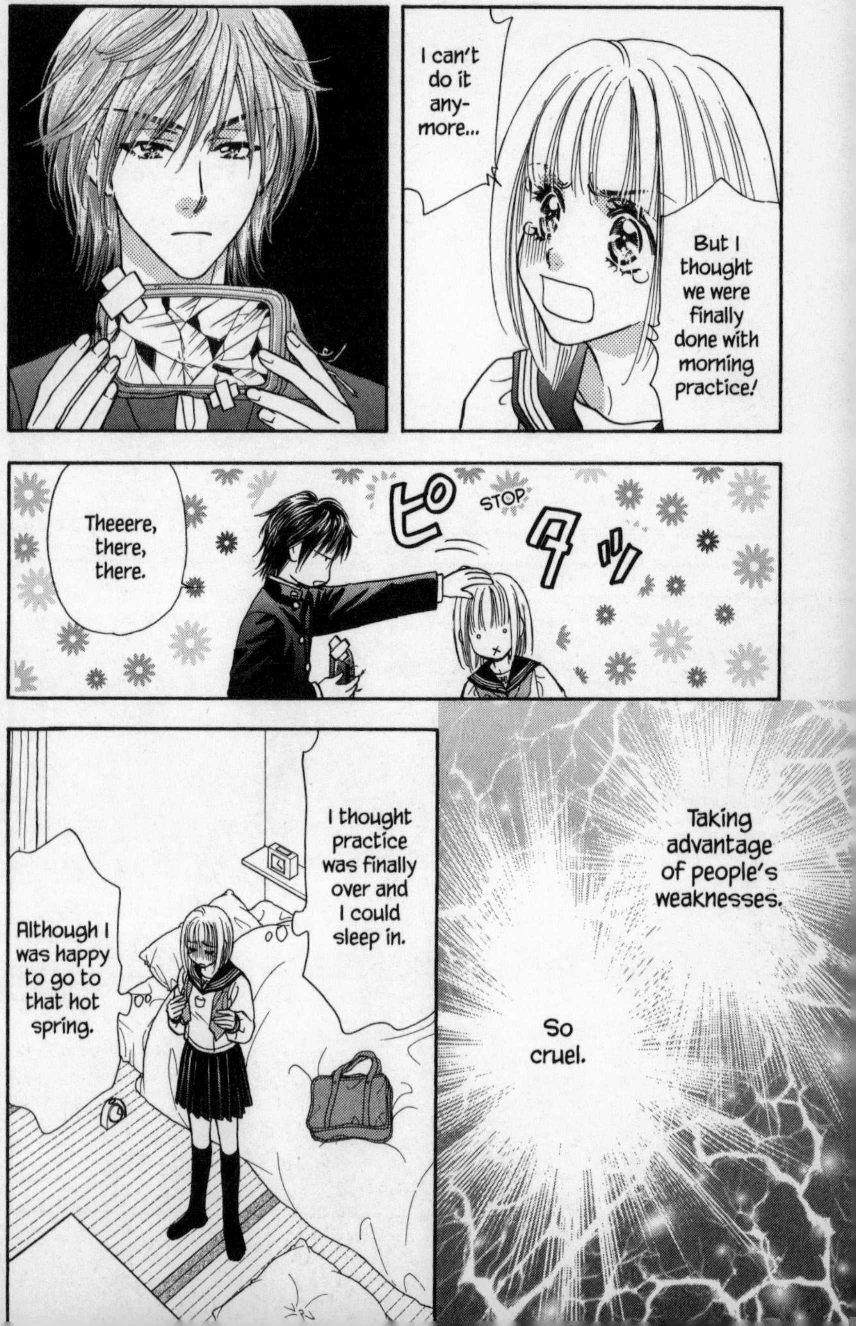
I can't do it anymore...
But I thought we were finally done with morning practice!
ピタッ
STOP
Theeere, there, there.
Taking advantage of people's weaknesses.
So cruel.
I thought practice was finally over and I could sleep in.
Although I was happy to go to that hot spring.

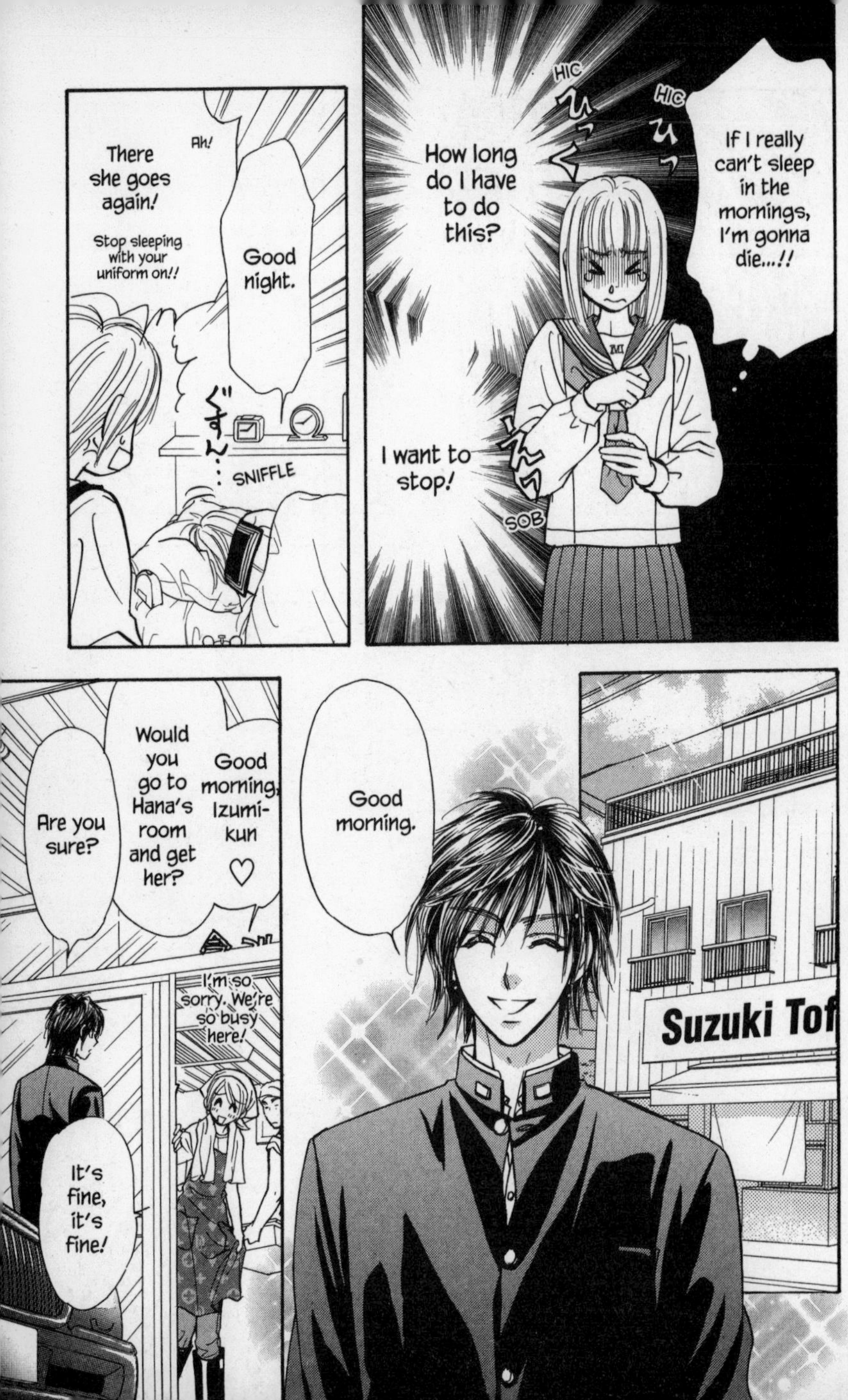

HIC
If I really can't sleep in the mornings, I'm gonna die...!!
HIC
How long do I have to do this?
I want to stop!
SOB
Good night.
Ah!
There she goes again!
Stop sleeping with your uniform on!!
SNIFFLE
Suzuki Tof
Good morning.
Good morning, Izumi-kun ♡
Would you go to Hana's room and get her?
Are you sure?
I'm so sorry. We're so busy here!
It's fine, it's fine!

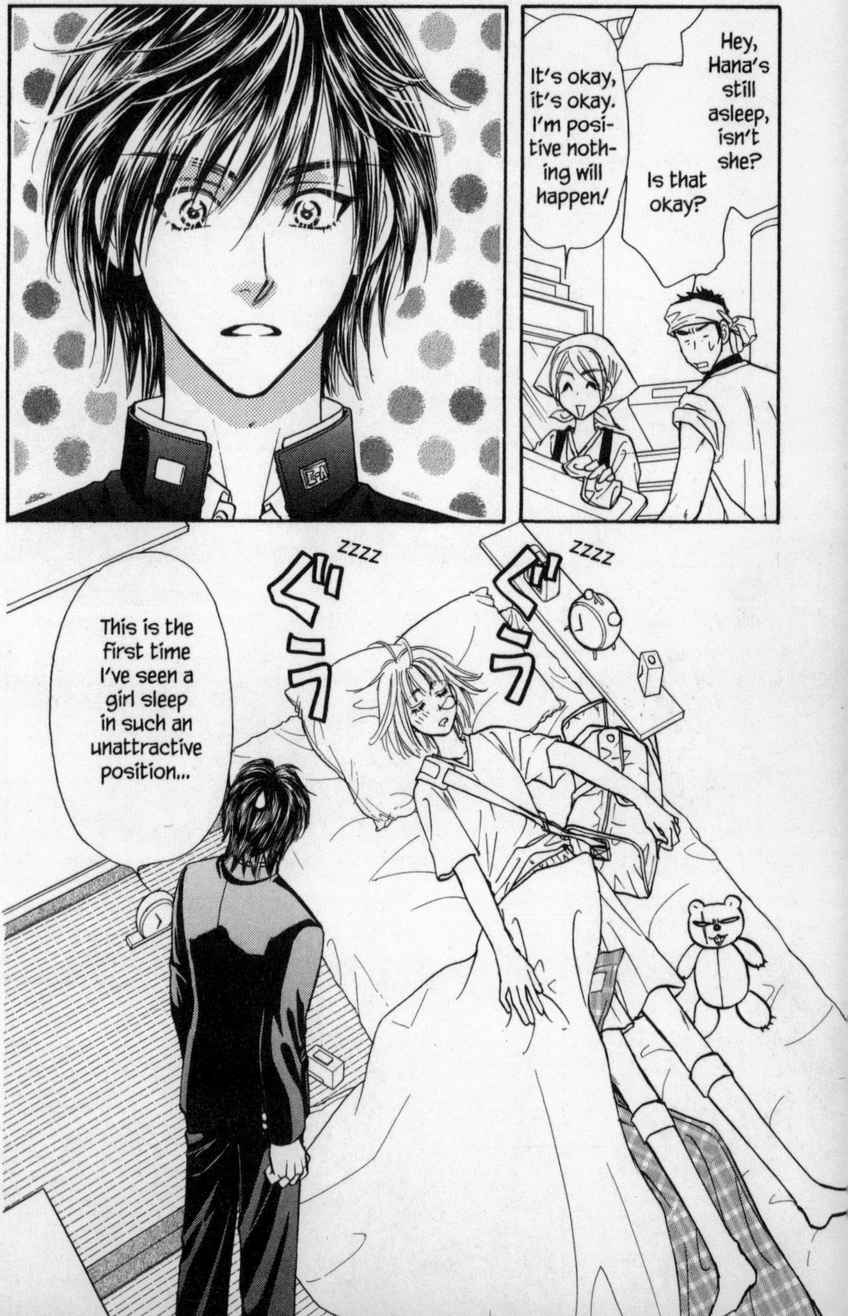
Hey, Hana's still asleep, isn't she?
Is that okay?
It's okay, it's okay. I'm positive nothing will happen!
ZZZZ
ぐう
ZZZZ
ぐう
This is the first time I've seen a girl sleep in such an unattractive position...

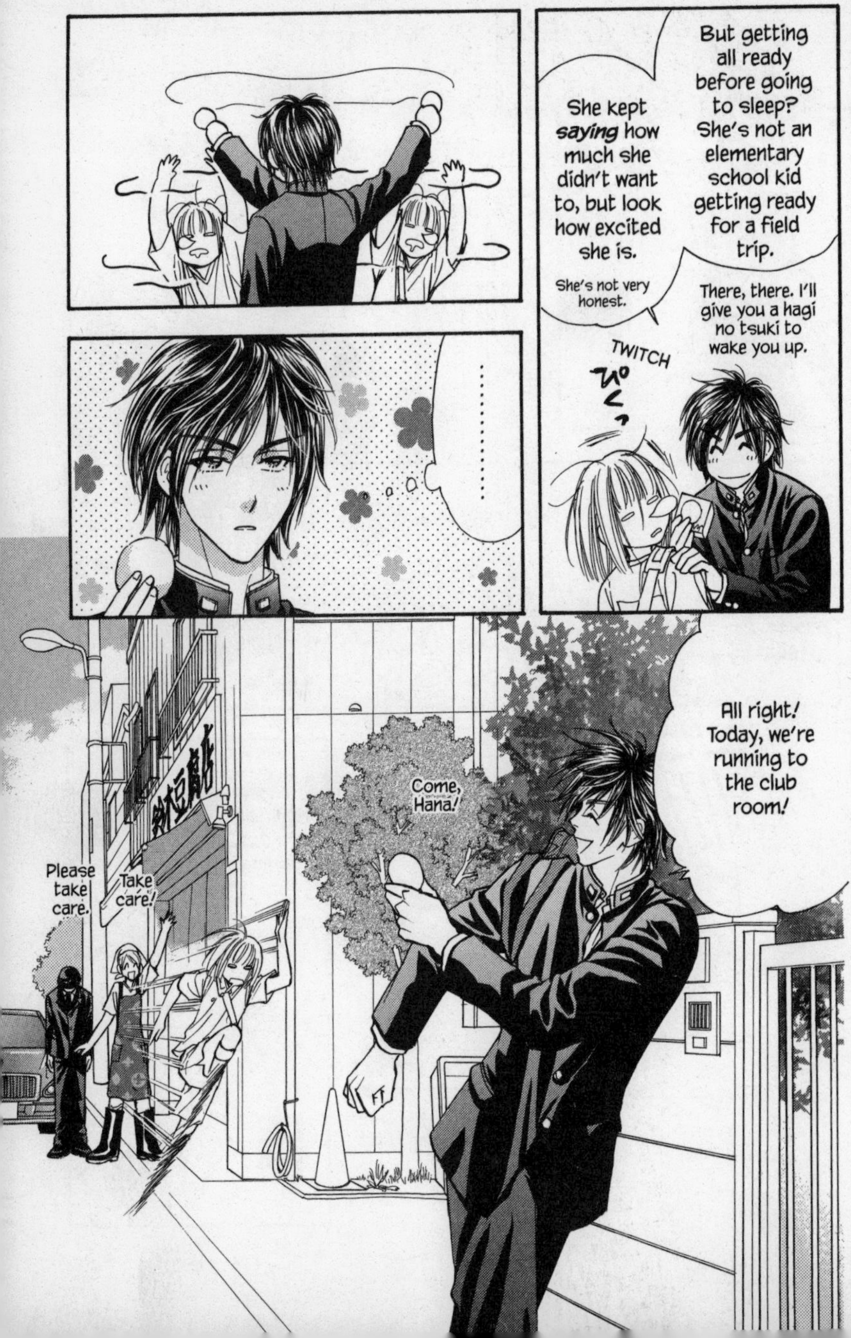
But getting all ready before going to sleep? She's not an elementary school kid getting ready for a field trip.
She kept *saying* how much she didn't want to, but look how excited she is.
She's not very honest.
There, there. I'll give you a hagi no tsuki to wake you up.
TWITCH
ぴく
......
All right! Today, we're running to the club room!
鈴木豆腐店
Come, Hana!
Take care!
Please take care.

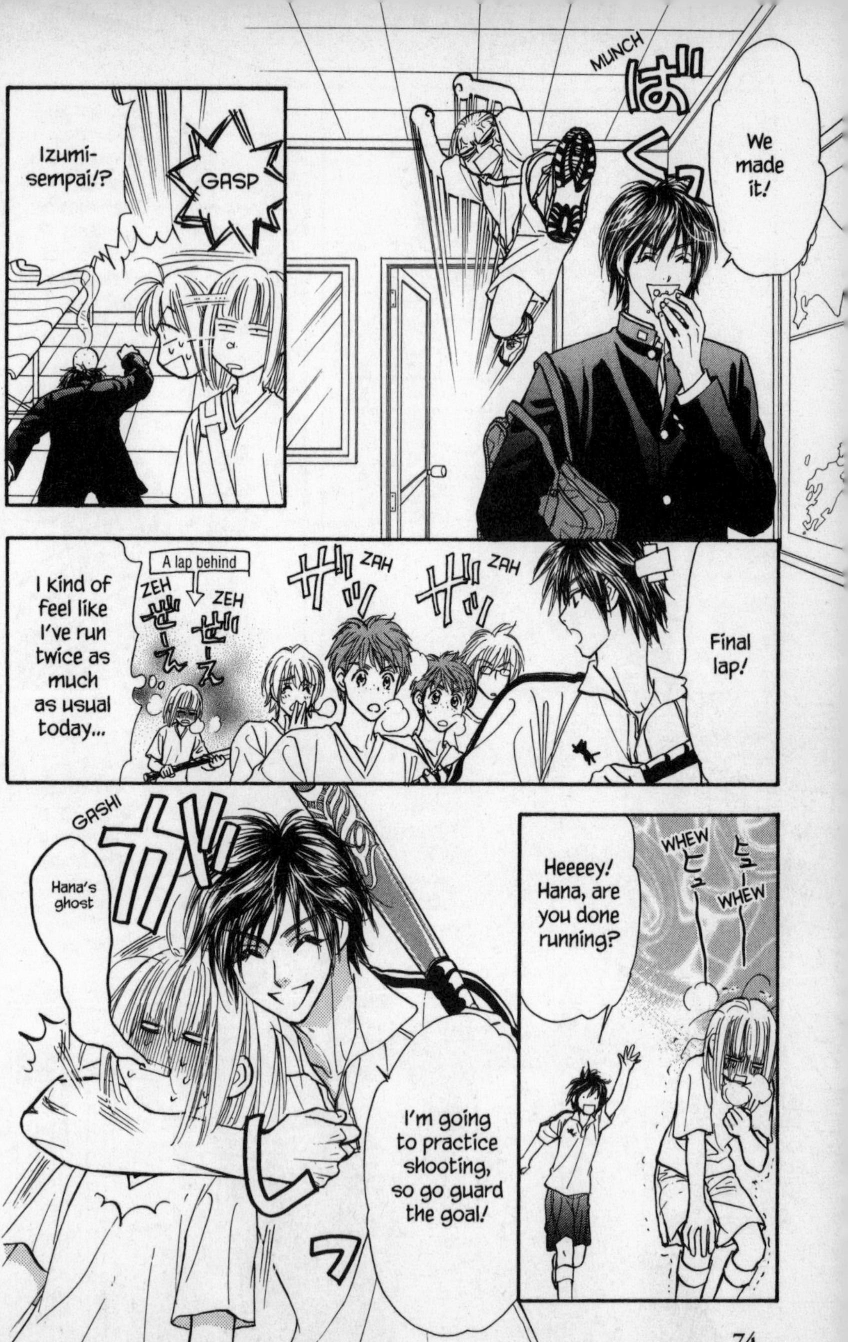

MUNCH
We made it!
Izumi-sempai!?
GASP
Final lap!
ZAH
ZAH
ZEH
ZEH
A lap behind
I kind of feel like I've run twice as much as usual today...
WHEW
WHEW
Heeeey! Hana, are you done running?
GASHI
Hana's ghost
I'm going to practice shooting, so go guard the goal!

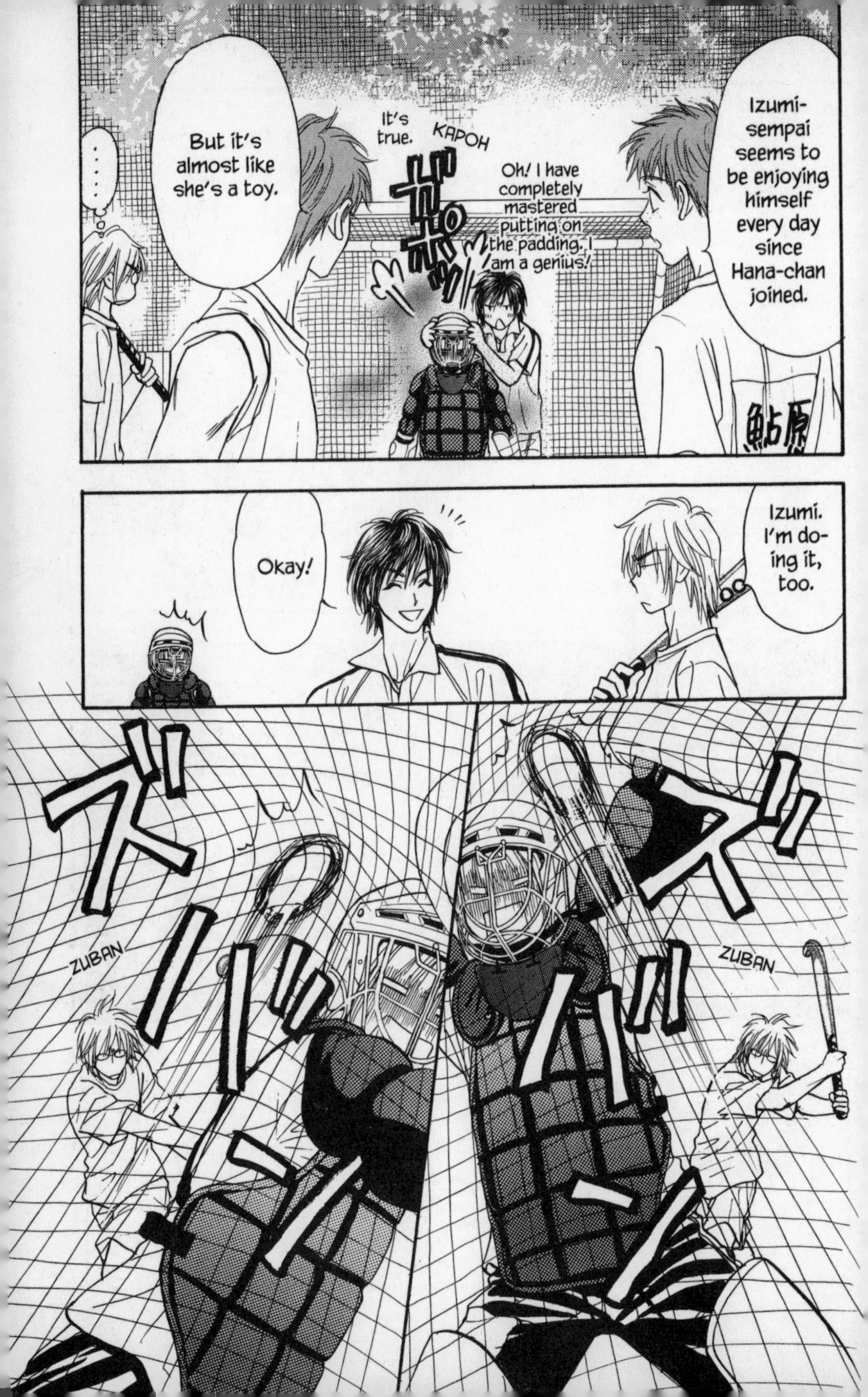
Izumi-sempai seems to be enjoying himself every day since Hana-chan joined.
Oh! I have completely mastered putting on the padding. I am a genius!
KAPOH
It's true.
But it's almost like she's a toy.
......
Izumi. I'm doing it, too.
Okay!
ZUBAN
ZUBAN

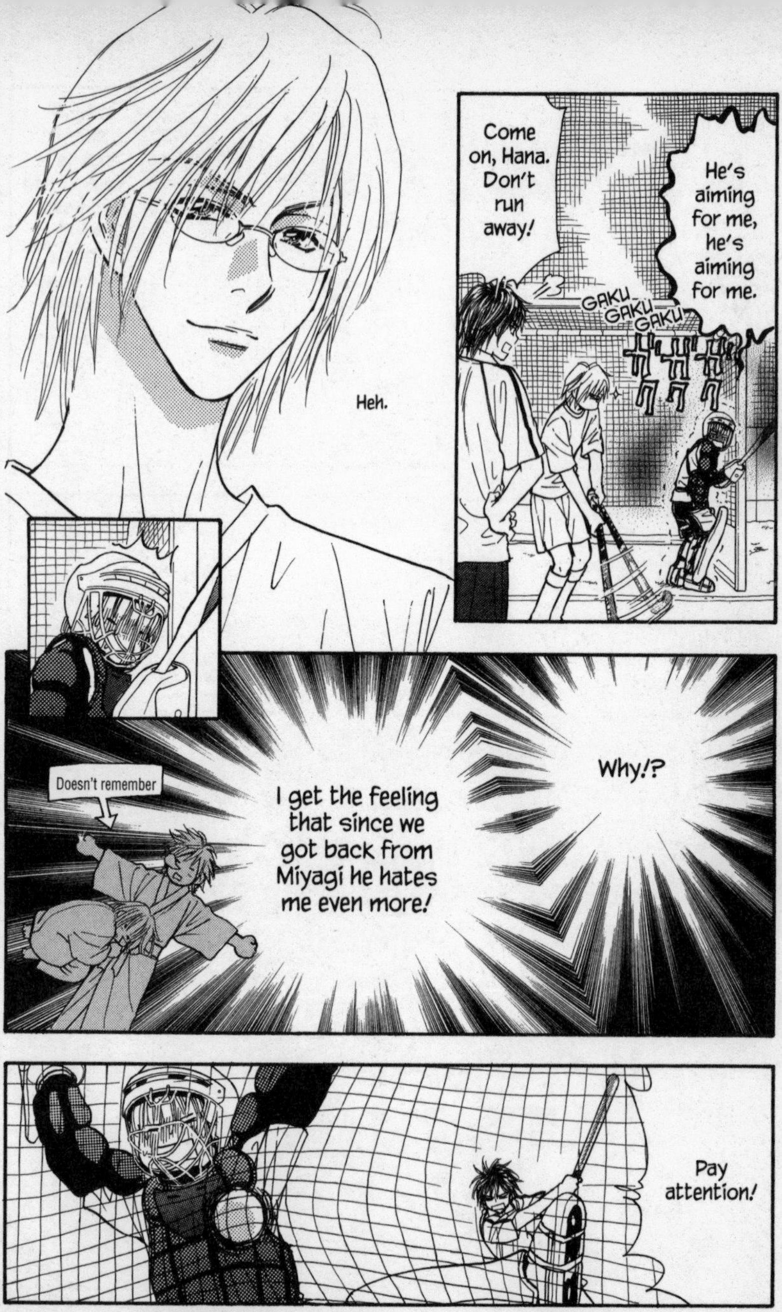
He's aiming for me, he's aiming for me.
Come on, Hana. Don't run away!
GAKU GAKU GAKU
Heh.
Why!?
I get the feeling that since we got back from Miyagi he hates me even more!
Doesn't remember
Pay attention!

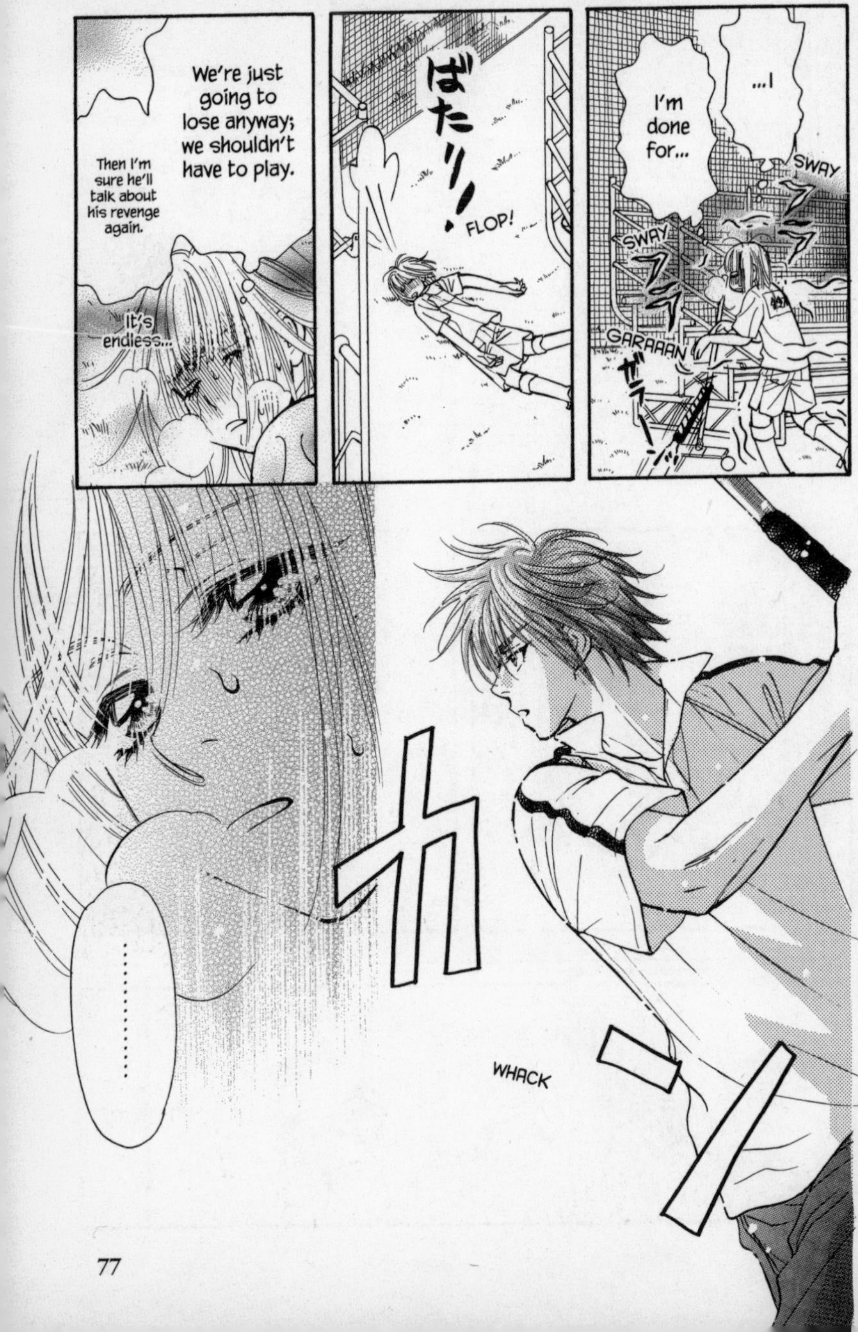
...I
I'm done for...
SWAY
SWAY
GARAAAN
ガラー
ばたリ!
FLOP!
We're just going to lose anyway; we shouldn't have to play.
Then I'm sure he'll talk about his revenge again.
It's endless...
カーン
WHACK
......

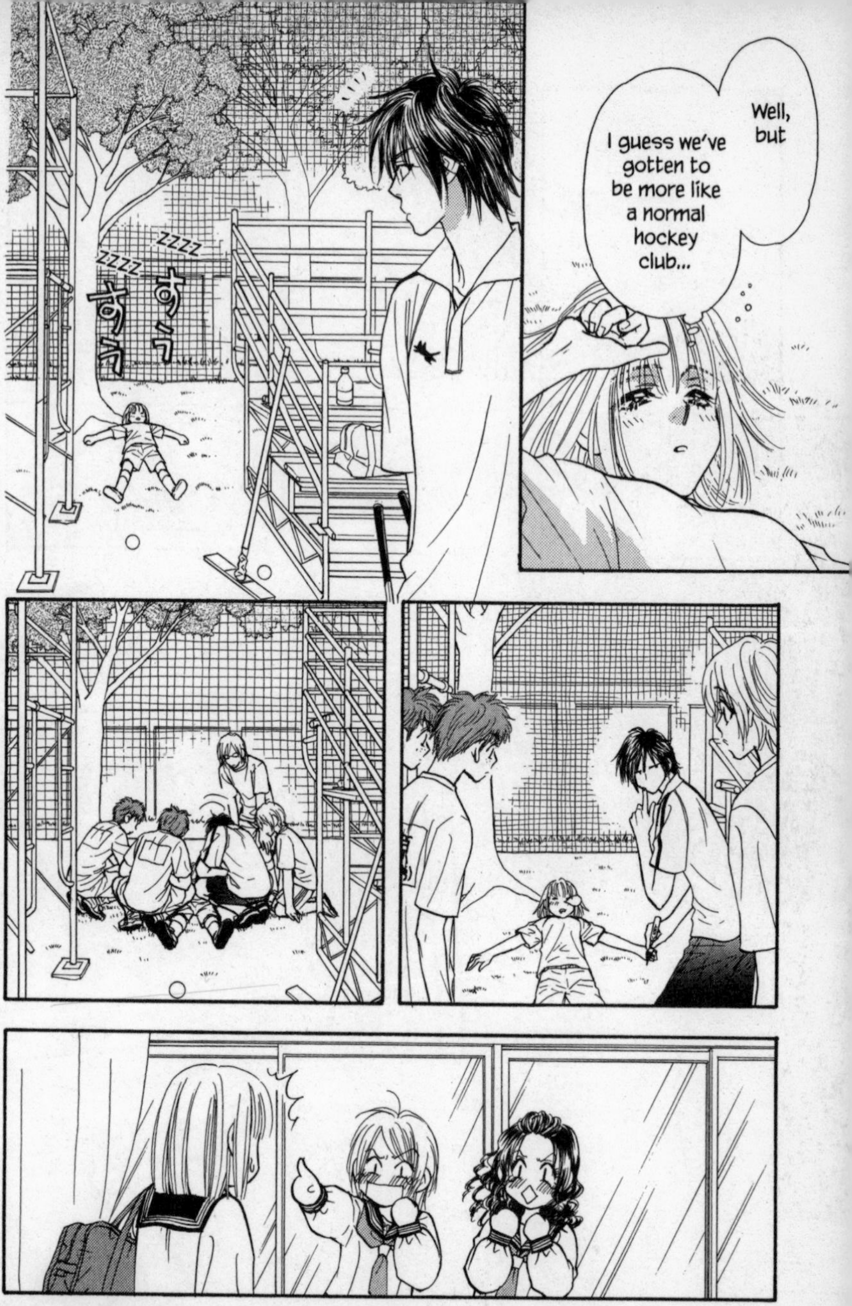
Well, but
I guess we've gotten to be more like a normal hockey club...
ZZZZ
ZZZZ
すぅ
すぅ

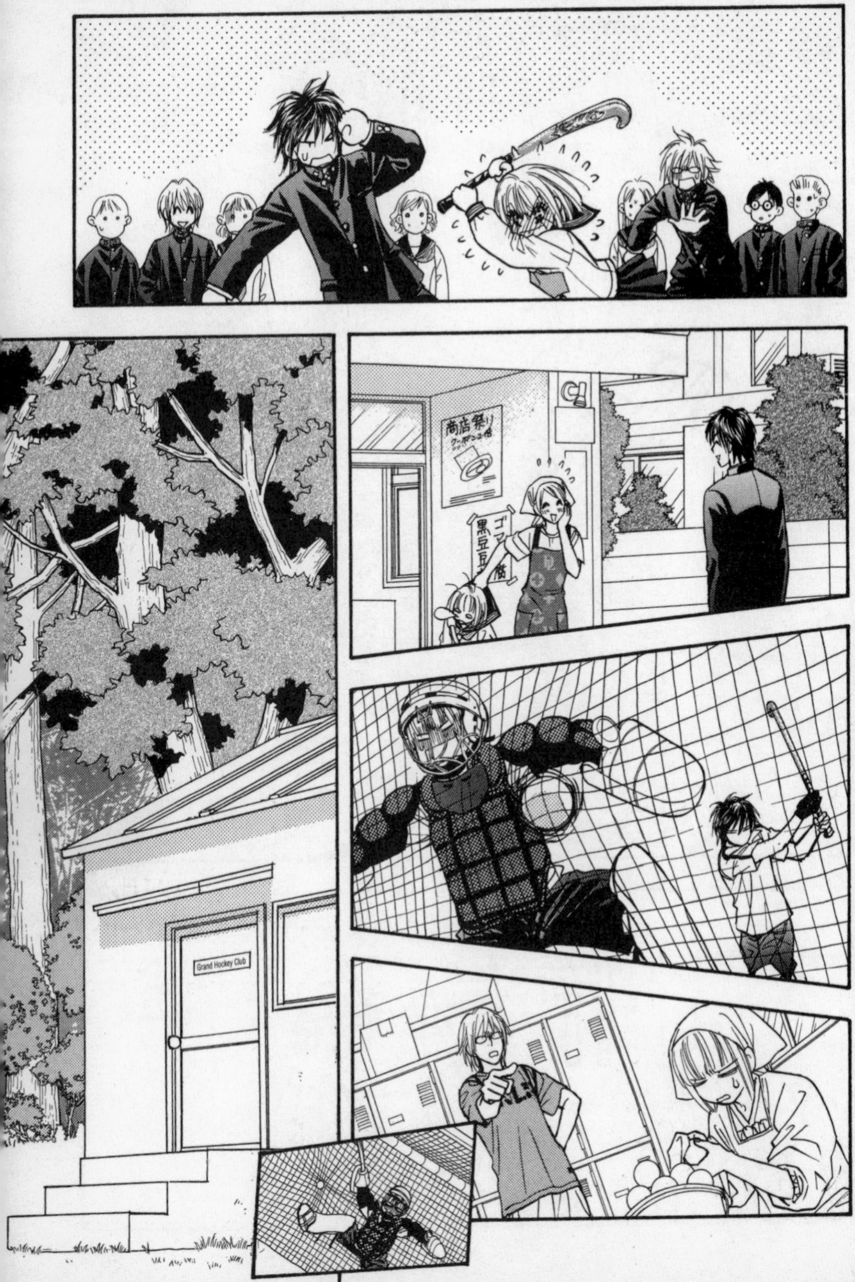

商店祭り
クーポン2倍
Grand Hockey Club

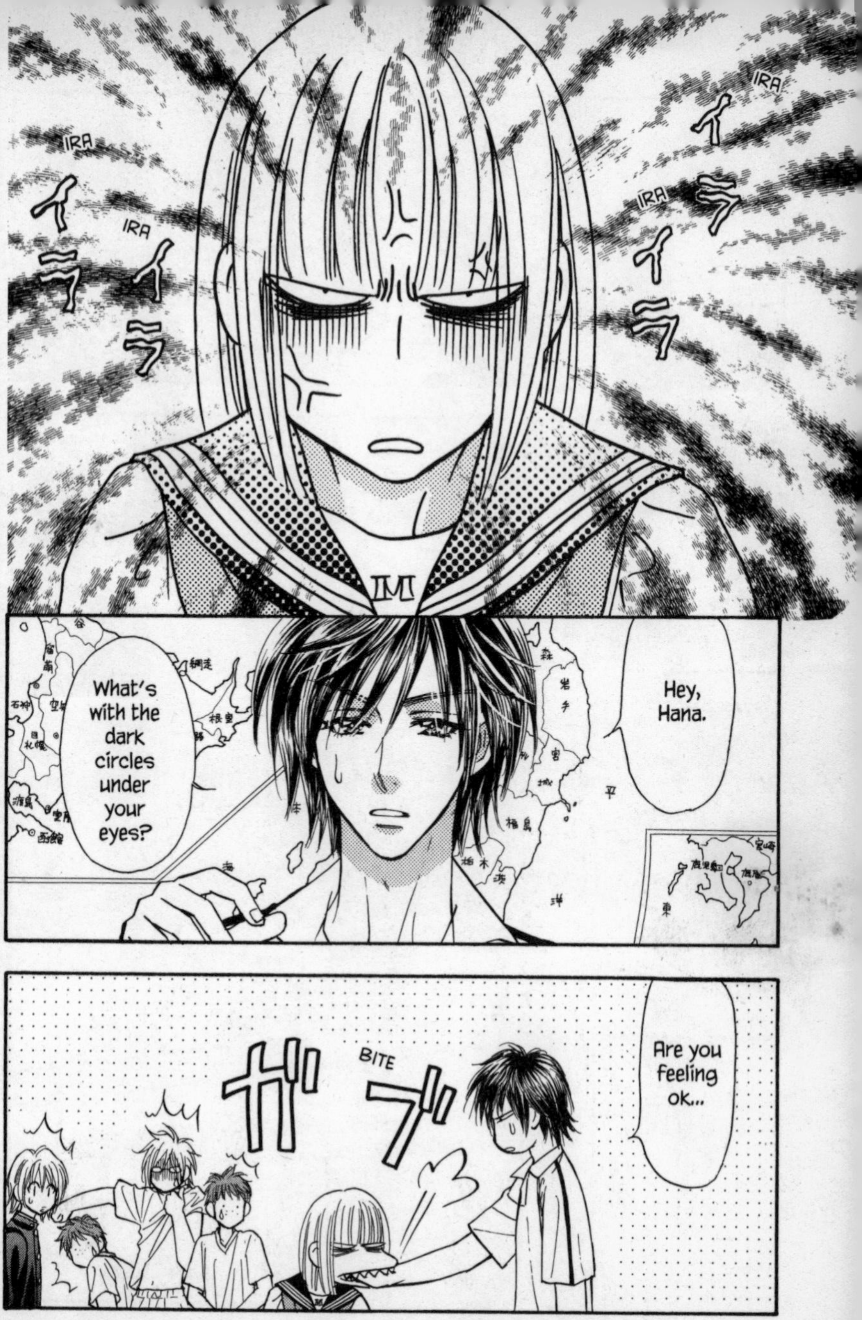
IRA
イラ
IRA
イラ
IRA
イラ
IRA
イラ
Hey, Hana.
What's with the dark circles under your eyes?
Are you feeling ok...
BITE
ガブ

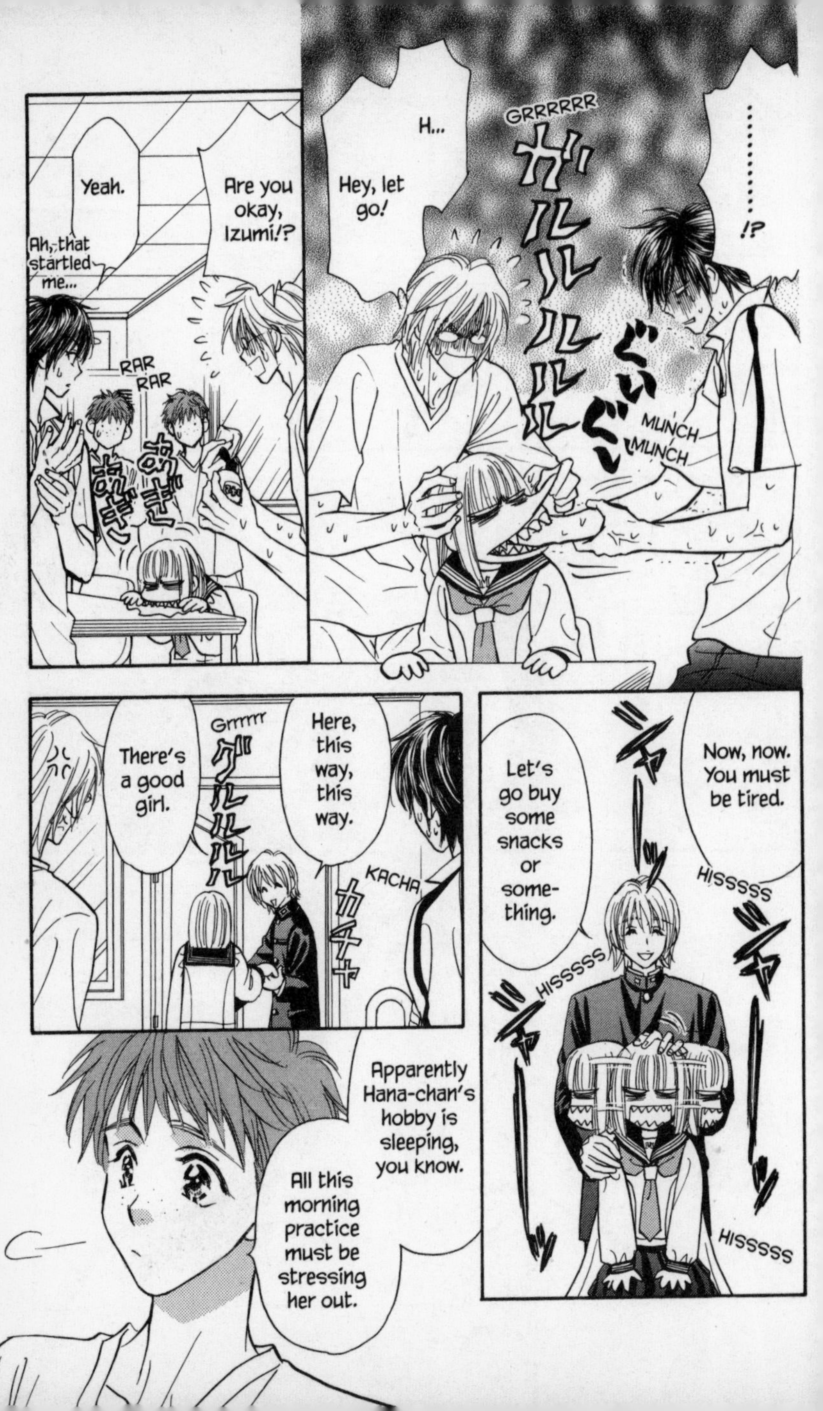
......!?
GRRRRRR
ガルルルル
H...
Hey, let go!
ぐいぐい
MUNCH MUNCH
Are you okay, Izumi!?
Yeah.
Ah, that startled me...
RAR RAR
あぎあぎ
Now, now. You must be tired.
Let's go buy some snacks or something.
HISSSSS
HISSSSS
HISSSSS
Here, this way, this way.
KACHA
カチャ
Grrrrr
グルルル
There's a good girl.
Apparently Hana-chan's hobby is sleeping, you know.
All this morning practice must be stressing her out.

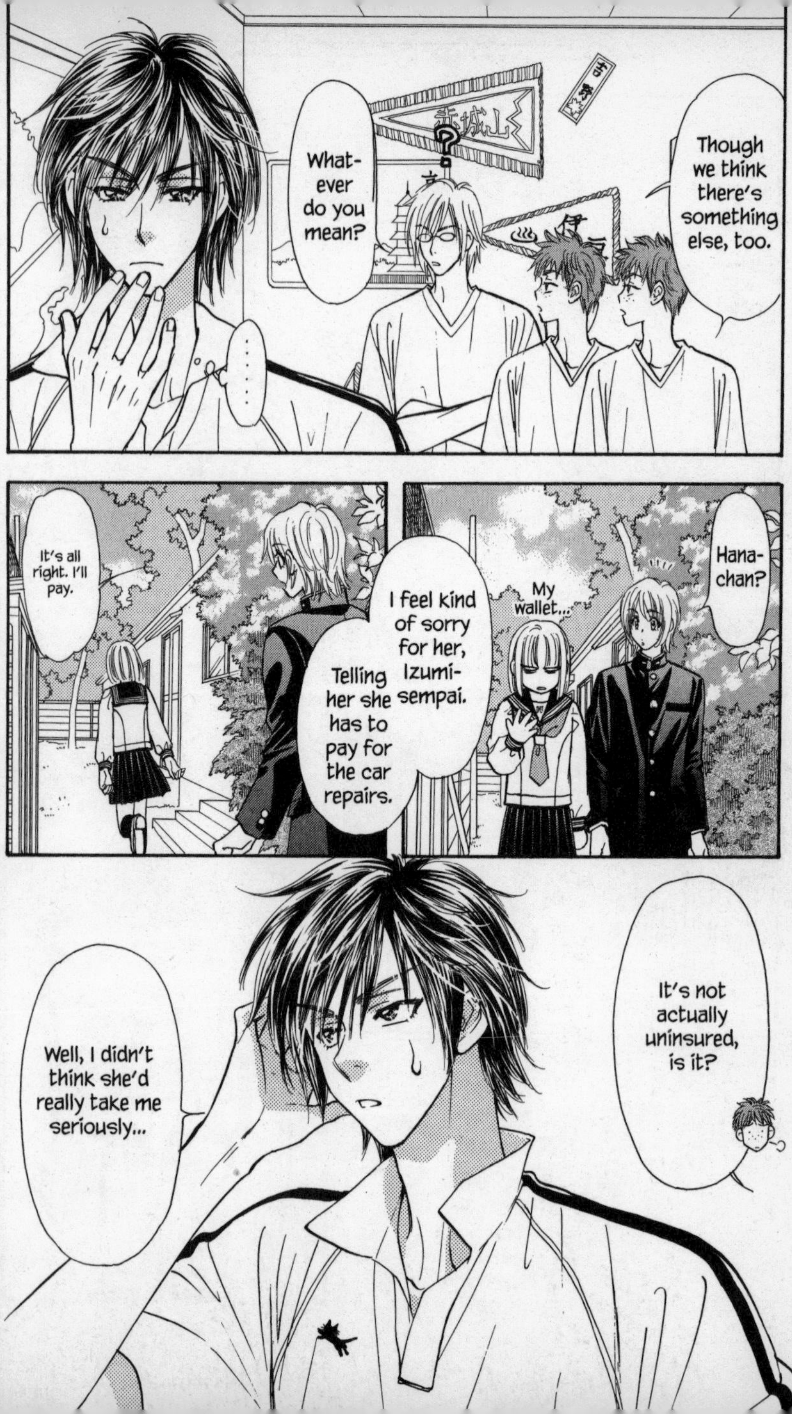
Though we think there's something else, too.
What-ever do you mean?
......
Hana-chan?
My wallet...
I feel kind of sorry for her, Izumi-sempai.
Telling her she has to pay for the car repairs.
It's all right. I'll pay.
It's not actually uninsured, is it?
Well, I didn't think she'd really take me seriously...

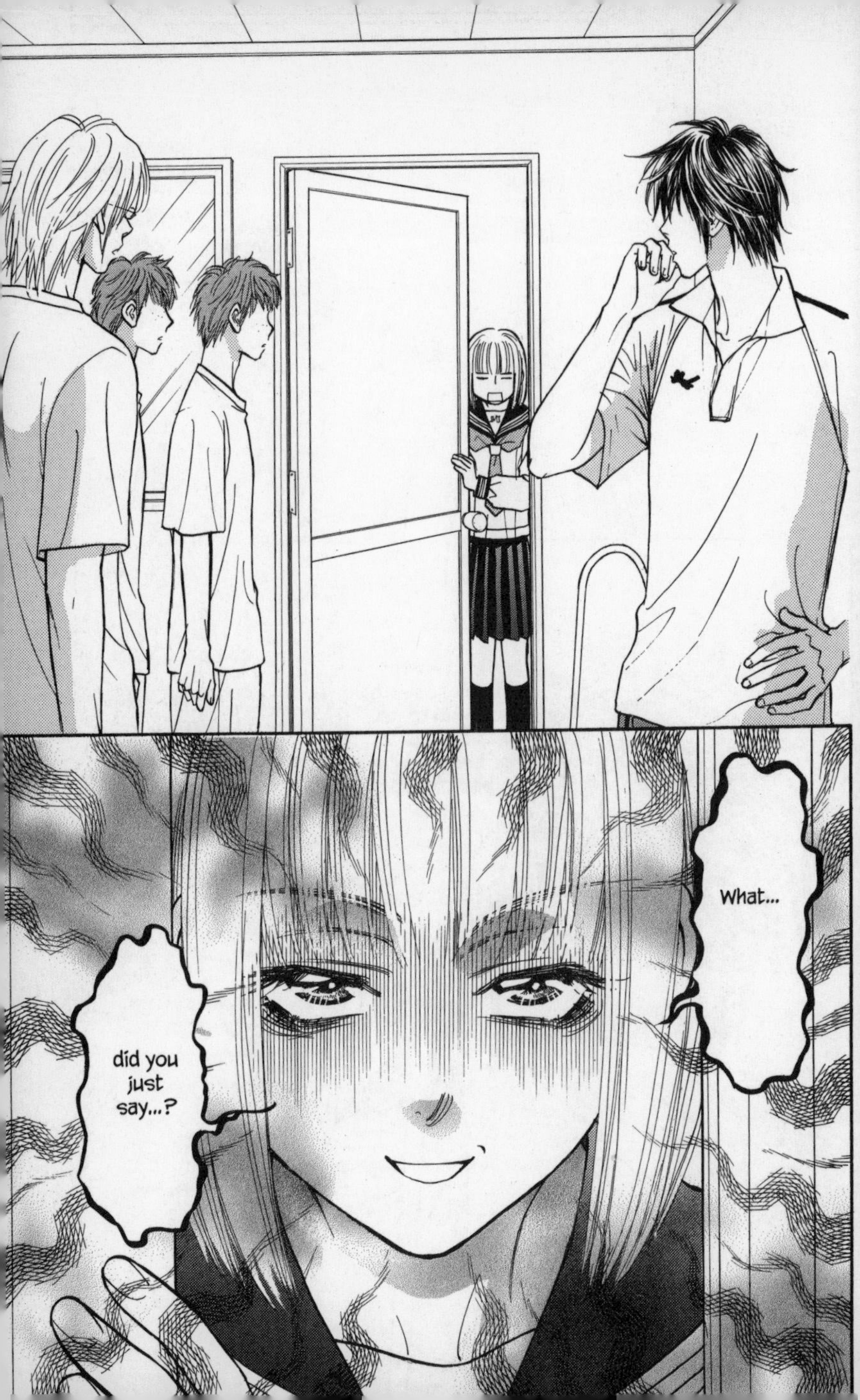
What...
did you just say...?

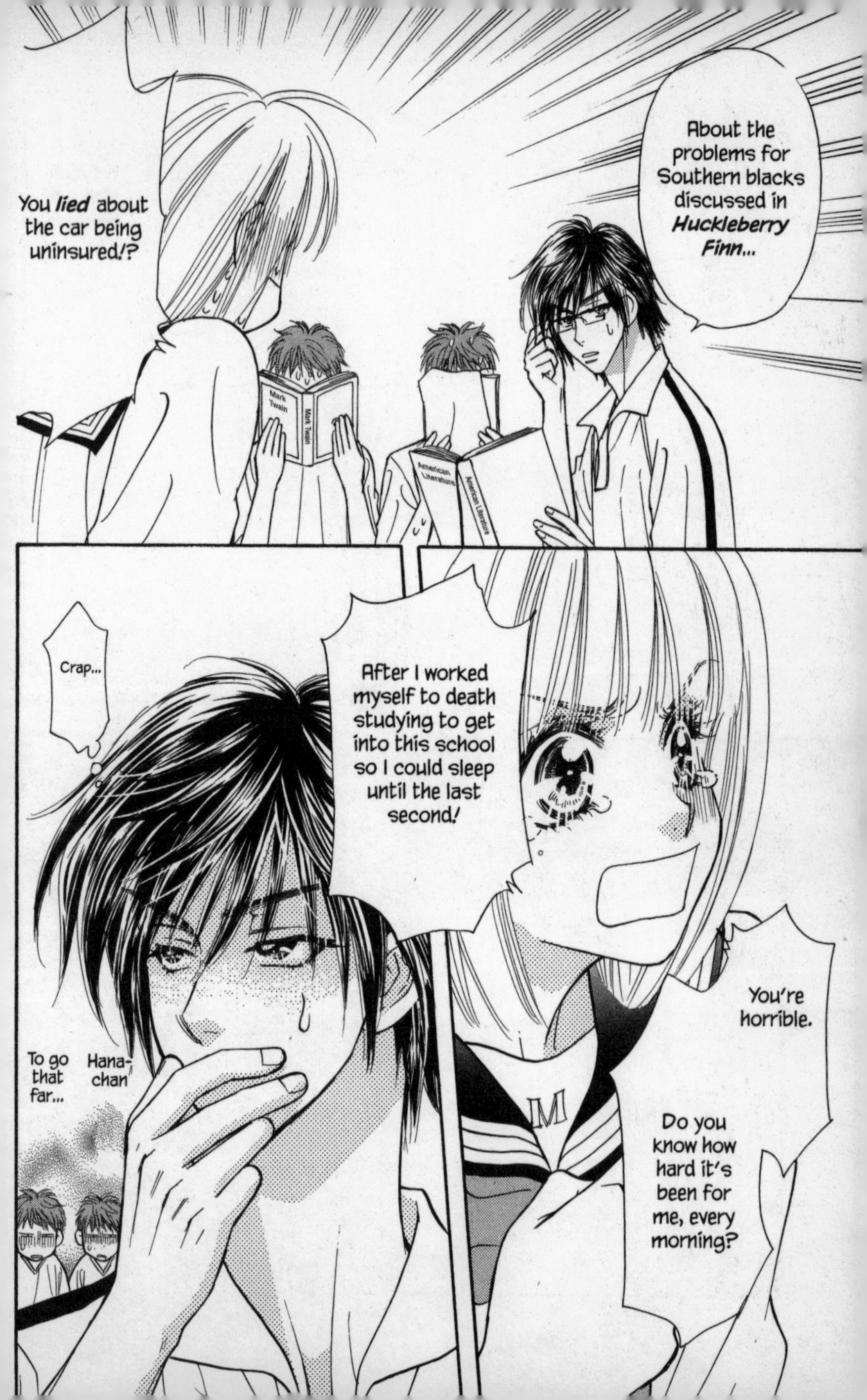
About the problems for Southern blacks discussed in ***Huckleberry Finn***...
American Literature
American Literature
Mark Twain
Mark Twain
You *lied* about the car being uninsured!?
After I worked myself to death studying to get into this school so I could sleep until the last second!
You're horrible.
Do you know how hard it's been for me, every morning?
Crap...
Hana-chan
To go that far...

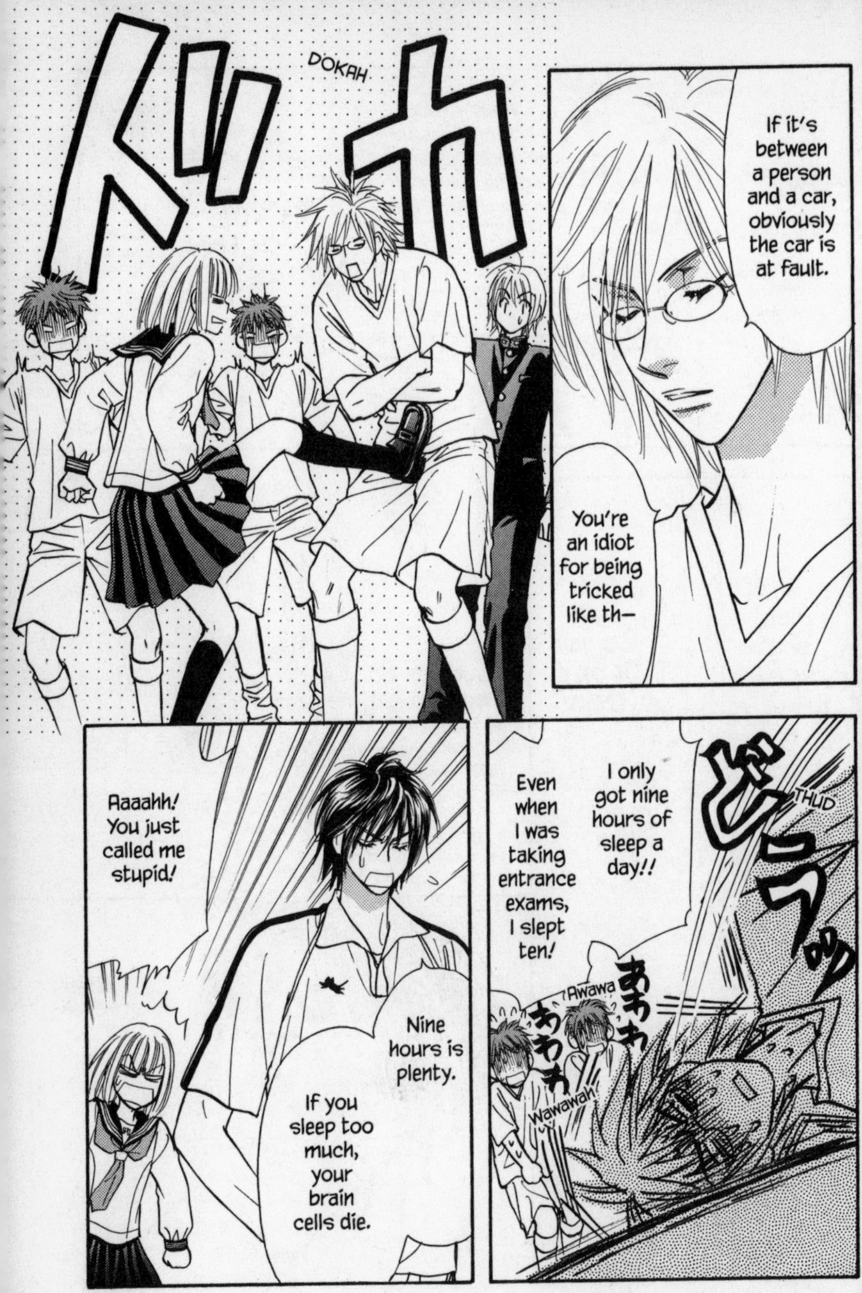
If it's between a person and a car, obviously the car is at fault.
You're an idiot for being tricked like th—
DOKAH
THUD
I only got nine hours of sleep a day!!
Even when I was taking entrance exams, I slept ten!
Awawa
Wawawah!
Aaaahh! You just called me stupid!
Nine hours is plenty.
If you sleep too much, your brain cells die.

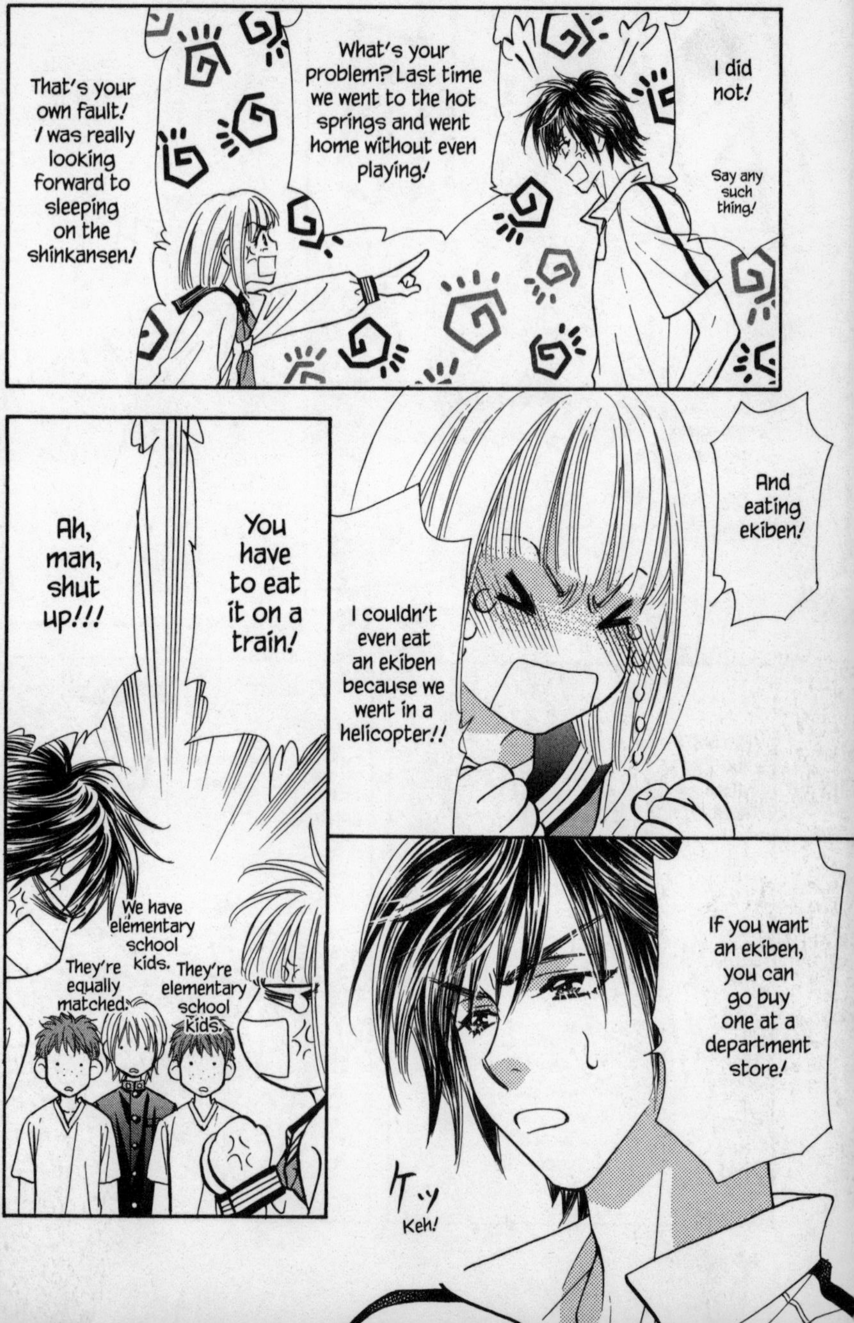
I did not!
Say any such thing!
What's your problem? Last time we went to the hot springs and went home without even playing!
That's your own fault! I was really looking forward to sleeping on the shinkansen!
And eating ekiben!
I couldn't even eat an ekiben because we went in a helicopter!!
If you want an ekiben, you can go buy one at a department store!
Keh!
You have to eat it on a train!
Ah, man, shut up!!!
We have elementary school kids.
They're elementary school kids.
They're equally matched.

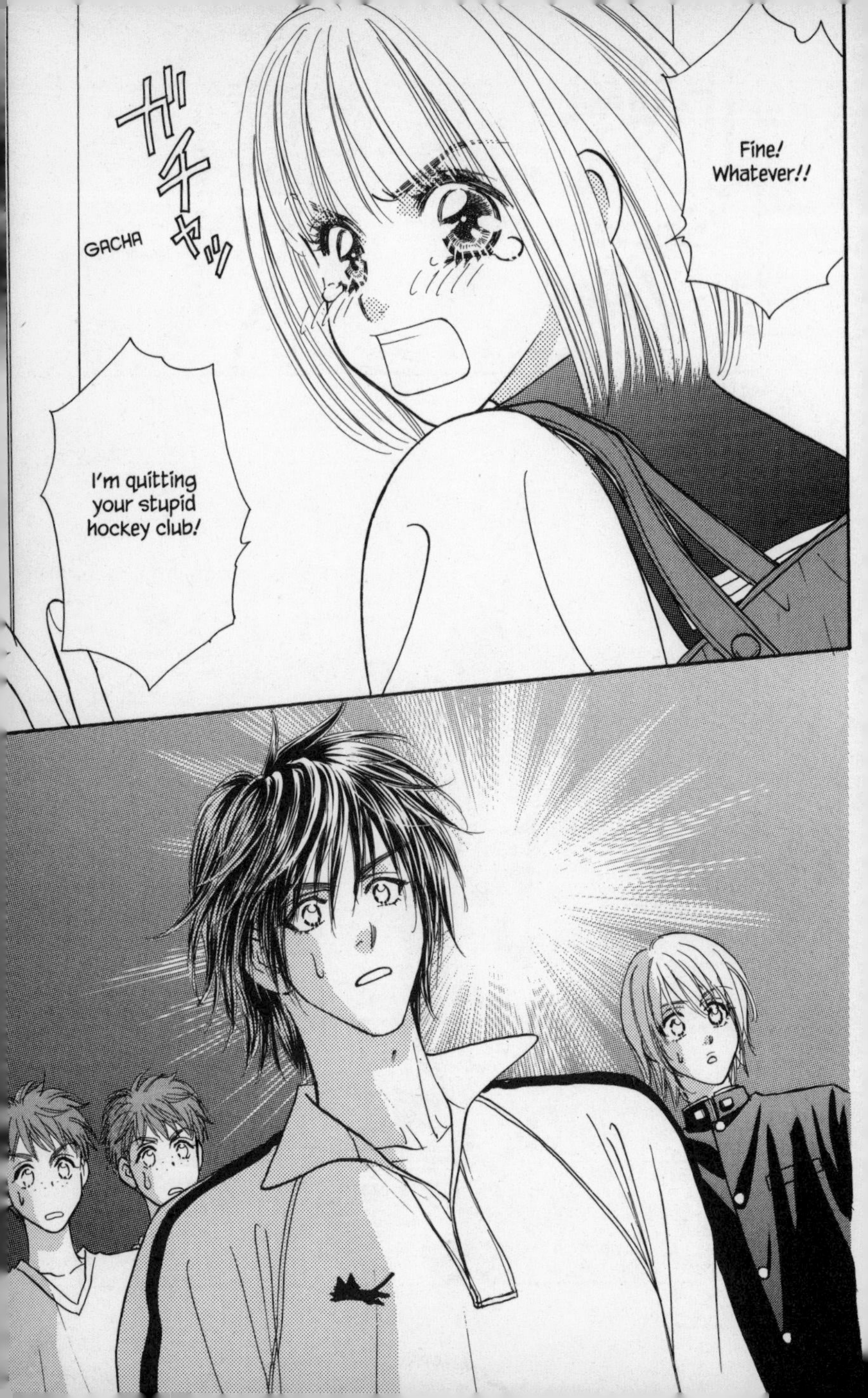
Fine! Whatever!!
ガチャッ
GACHA
I'm quitting your stupid hockey club!

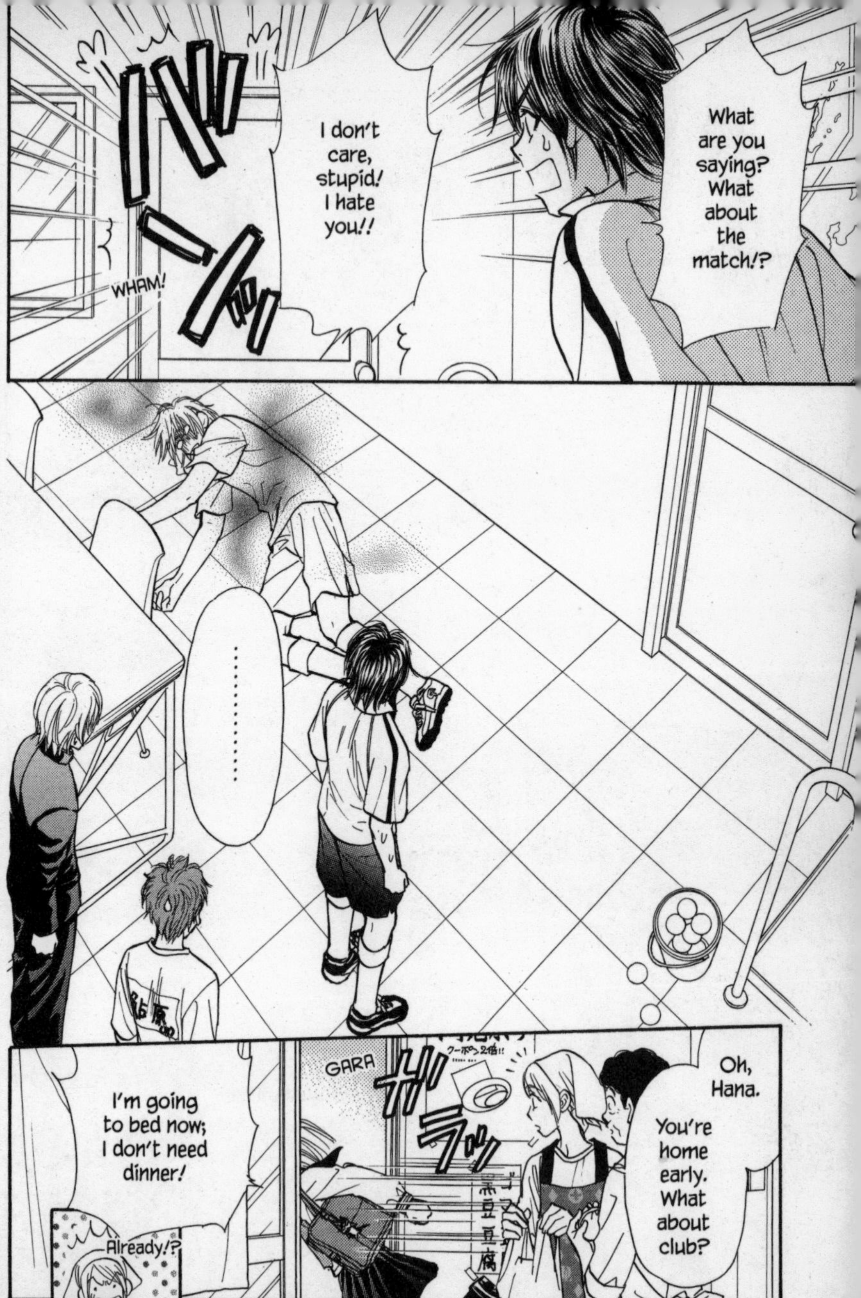
What are you saying? What about the match!?
I don't care, stupid! I hate you!!
WHAM!
......
Oh, Hana.
You're home early. What about club?
GARA
I'm going to bed now; I don't need dinner!
Already!?

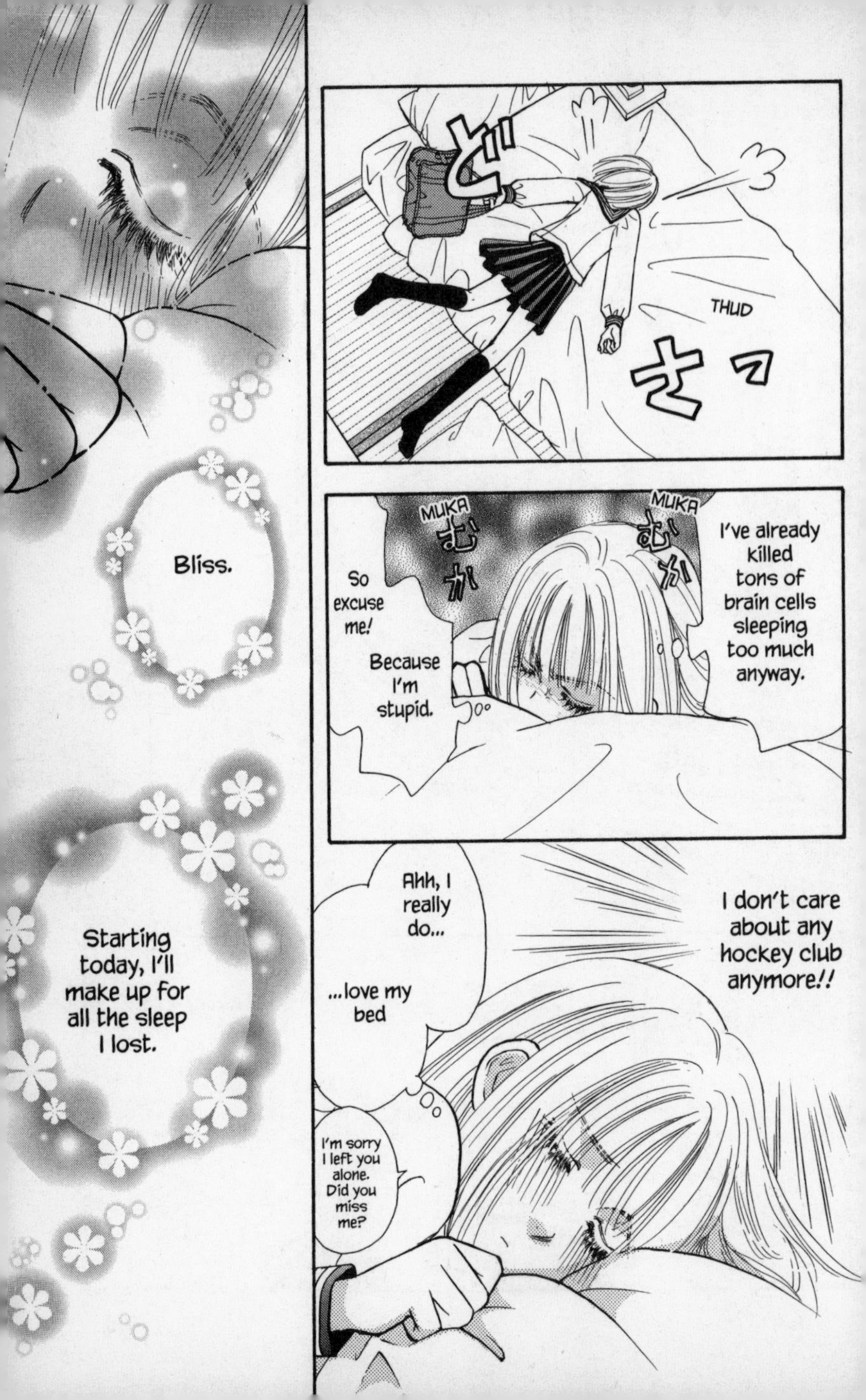
ど
THUD
さっ
MUKA
むか
MUKA
むか
I've already killed tons of brain cells sleeping too much anyway.
So excuse me!
Because I'm stupid.
I don't care about any hockey club anymore!!
Ahh, I really do...
...love my bed
I'm sorry I left you alone. Did you miss me?
Bliss.
Starting today, I'll make up for all the sleep I lost.

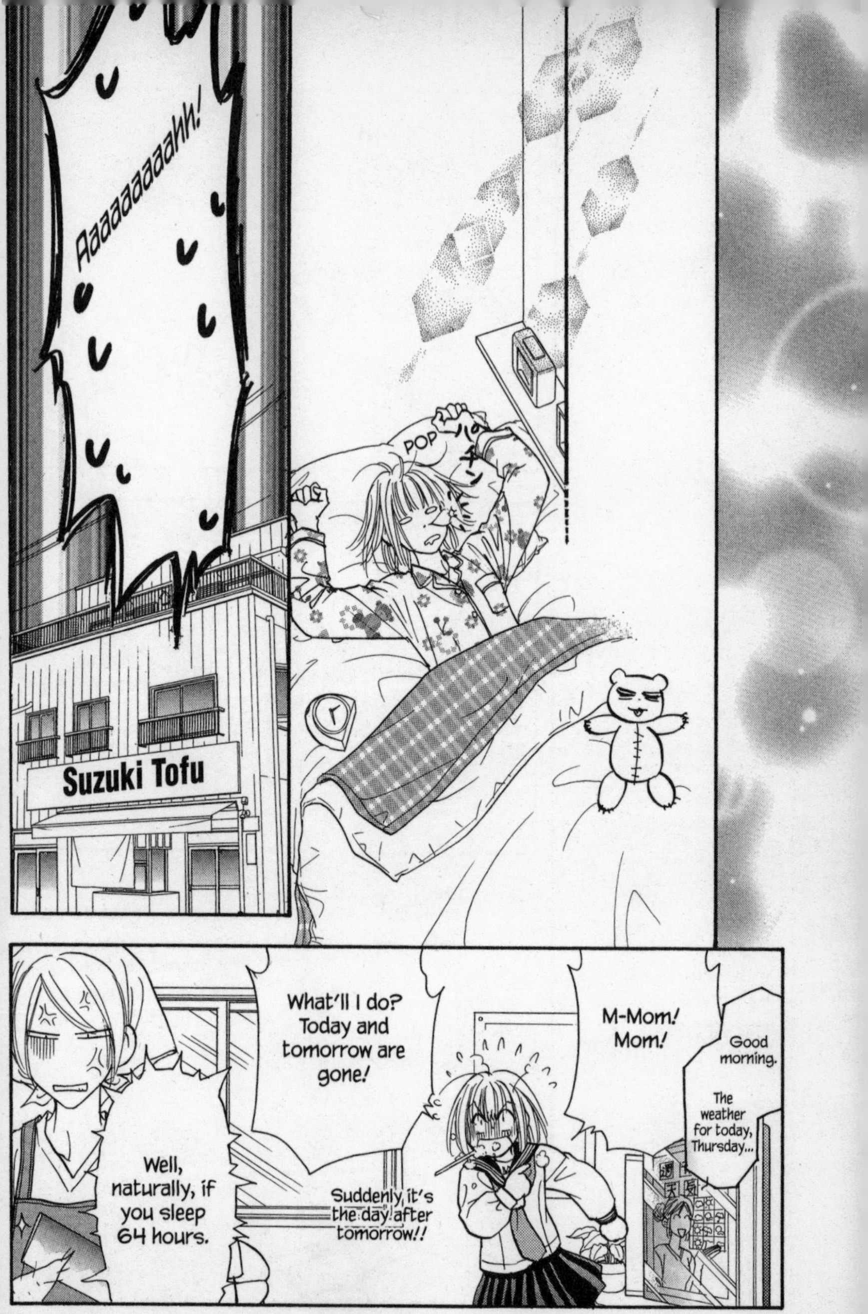
POP
Aaaaaaaaahh!
Suzuki Tofu
Good morning.
The weather for today, Thursday...
M-Mom! Mom!
What'll I do? Today and tomorrow are gone!
Suddenly it's the day after tomorrow!!
Well, naturally, if you sleep 64 hours.

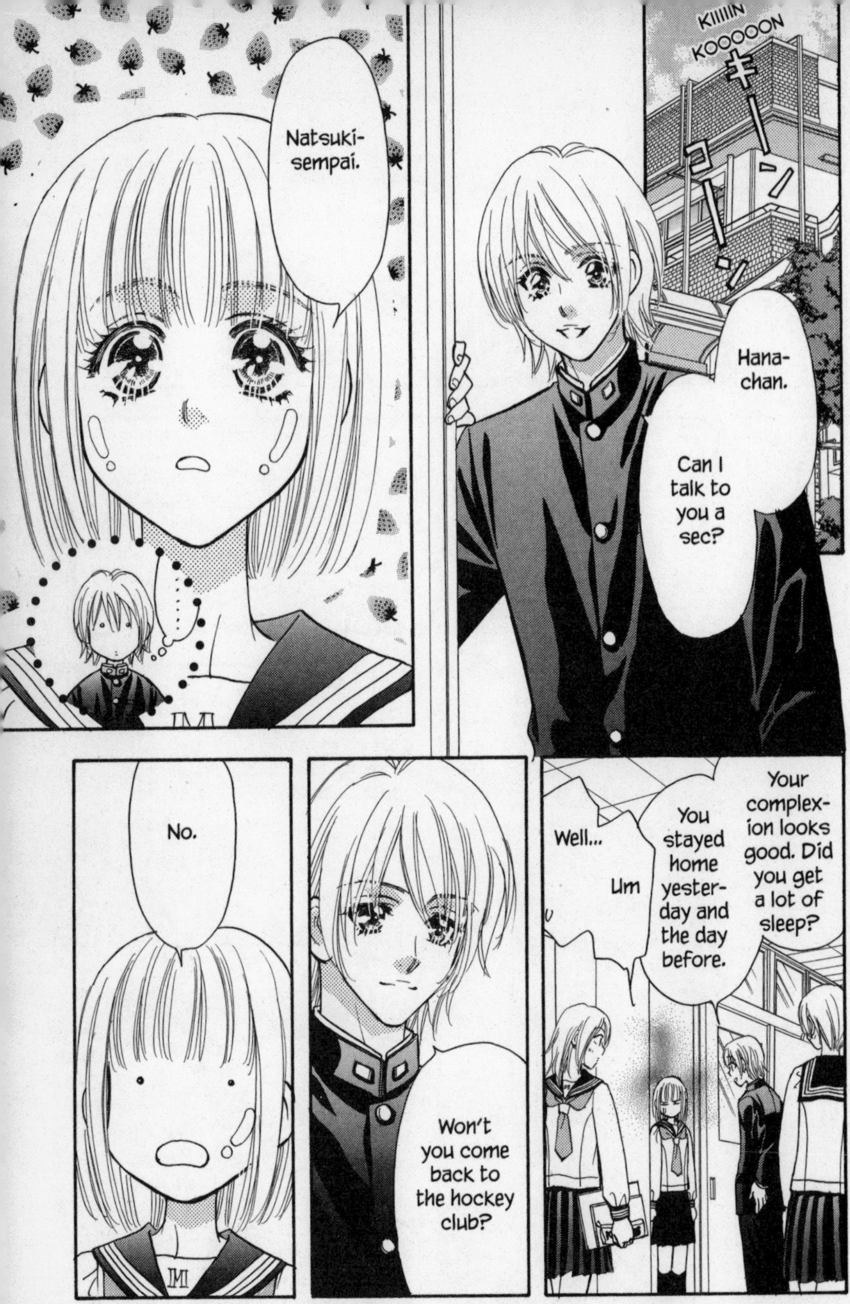
KIIIIIN KOOOOON
キーンコーン
Hana-chan.
Can I talk to you a sec?
Natsuki-sempai.
Your complexion looks good. Did you get a lot of sleep?
You stayed home yesterday and the day before.
Well...
Um
Won't you come back to the hockey club?
No.

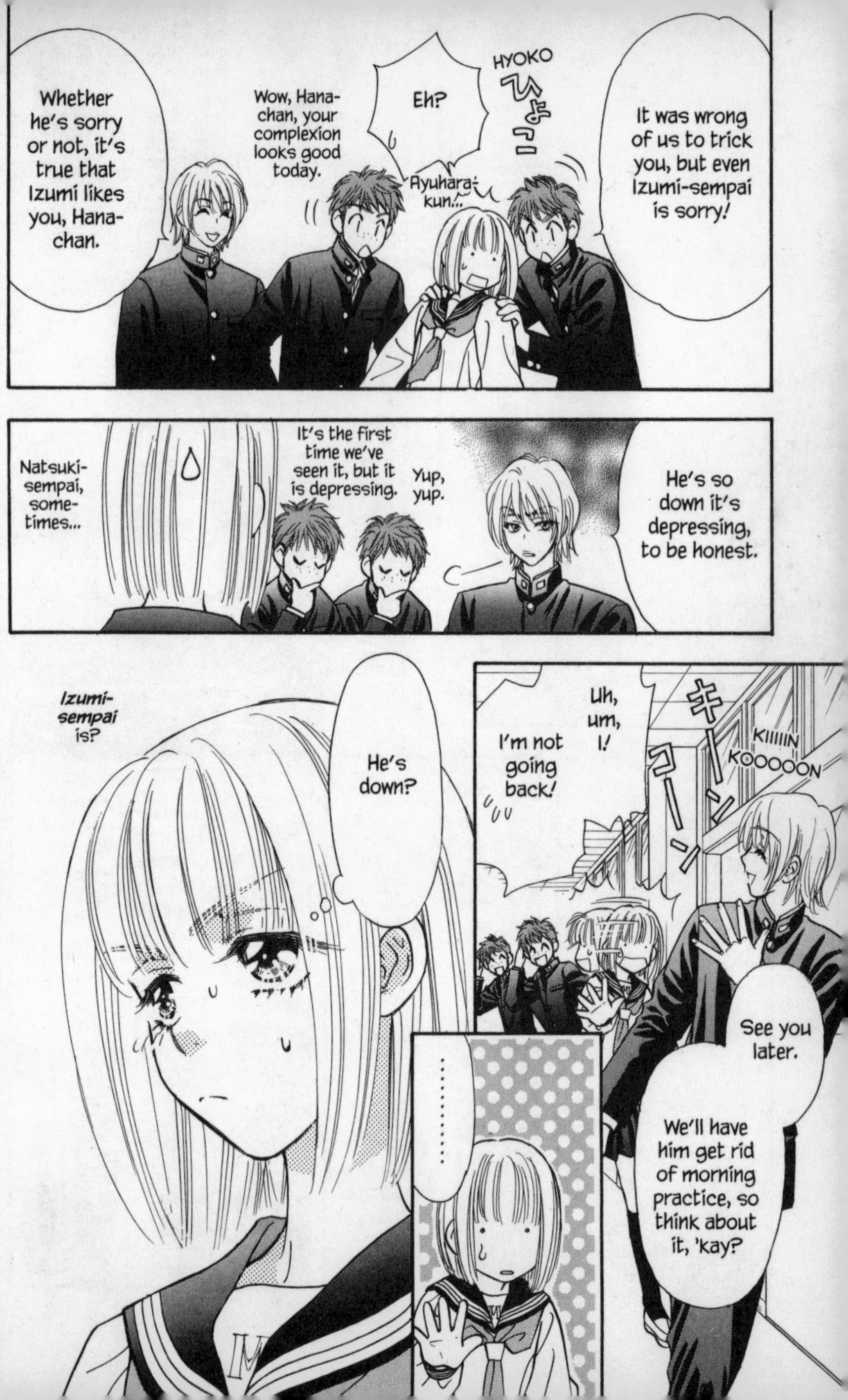
It was wrong of us to trick you, but even Izumi-sempai is sorry!
HYOKO
Eh?
Ayuhara-kun...
Wow, Hana-chan, your complexion looks good today.
Whether he's sorry or not, it's true that Izumi likes you, Hana-chan.
He's so down it's depressing, to be honest.
Yup, yup.
It's the first time we've seen it, but it is depressing.
Natsuki-sempai, sometimes...
KIIIIN KOOOOON
Uh, um, I!
I'm not going back!
See you later.
We'll have him get rid of morning practice, so think about it, 'kay?
......
He's down?
Izumi-sempai is?

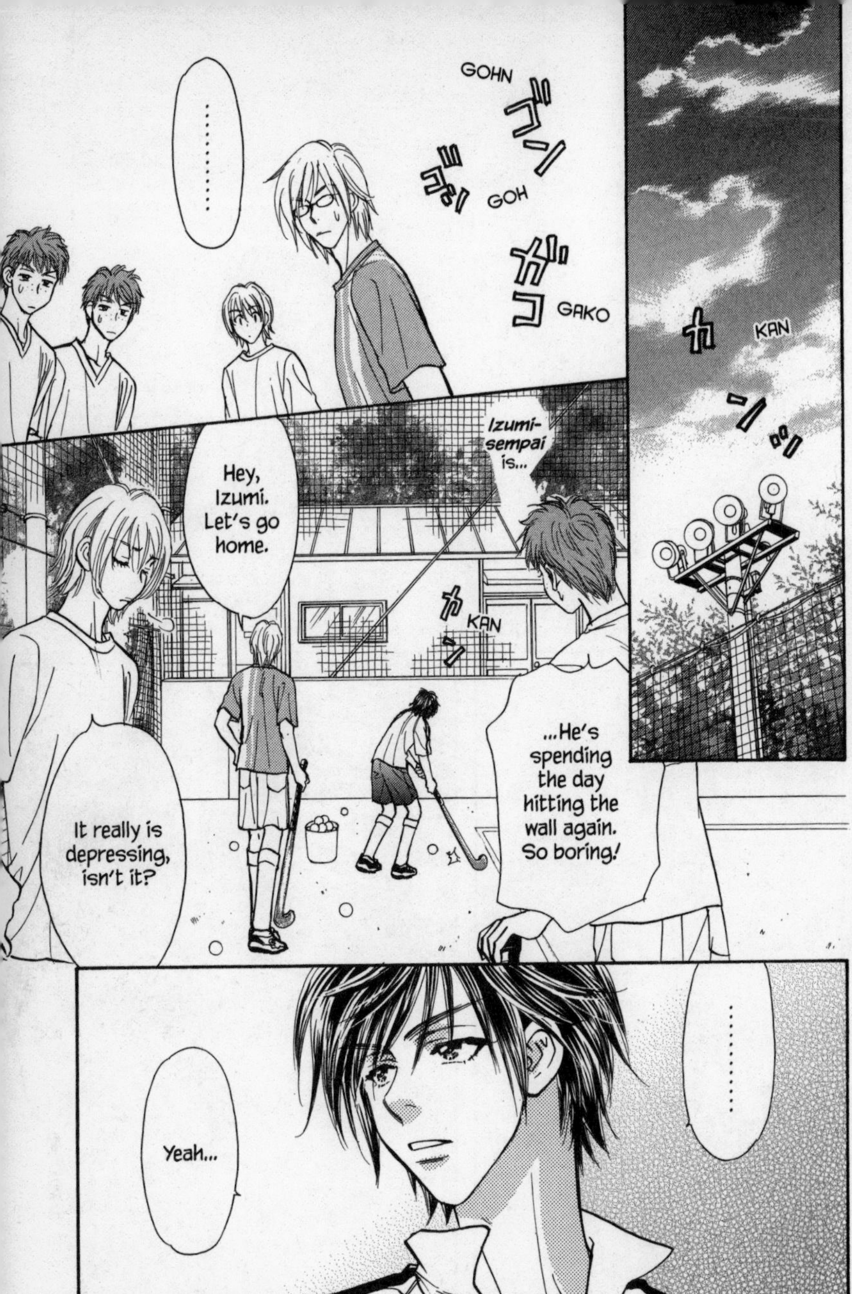
KAN
GOHN
GOH
GAKO
……
Izumi-sempai is...
...He's spending the day hitting the wall again. So boring!
Hey, Izumi. Let's go home.
KAN
It really is depressing, isn't it?
……
Yeah...

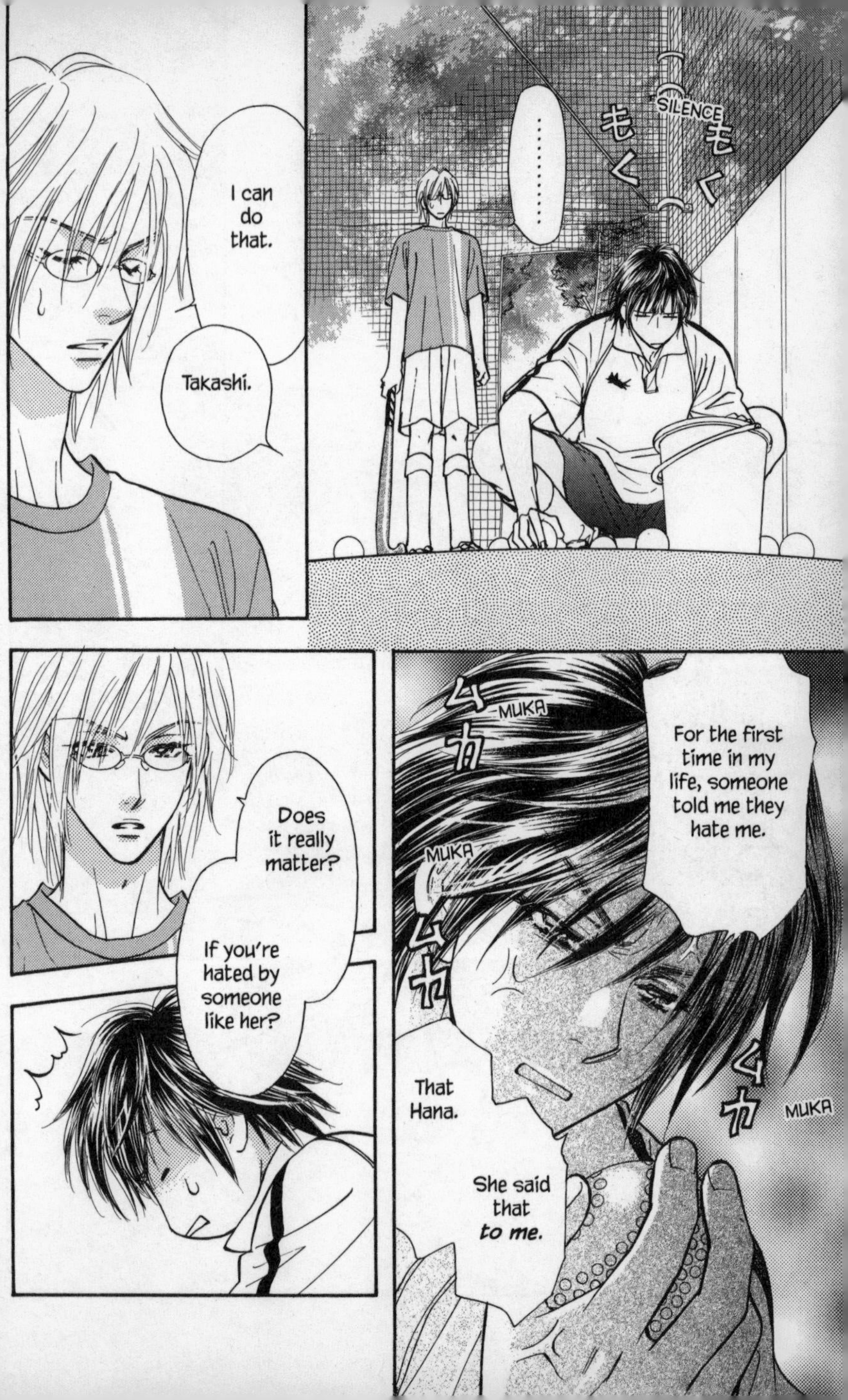

......
SILENCE
もくもく
I can do that.
Takashi.
ムカ
MUKA
ムカ
MUKA
For the first time in my life, someone told me they hate me.
ムカ
MUKA
That Hana.
She said that *to me.*
Does it really matter?
If you're hated by someone like her?

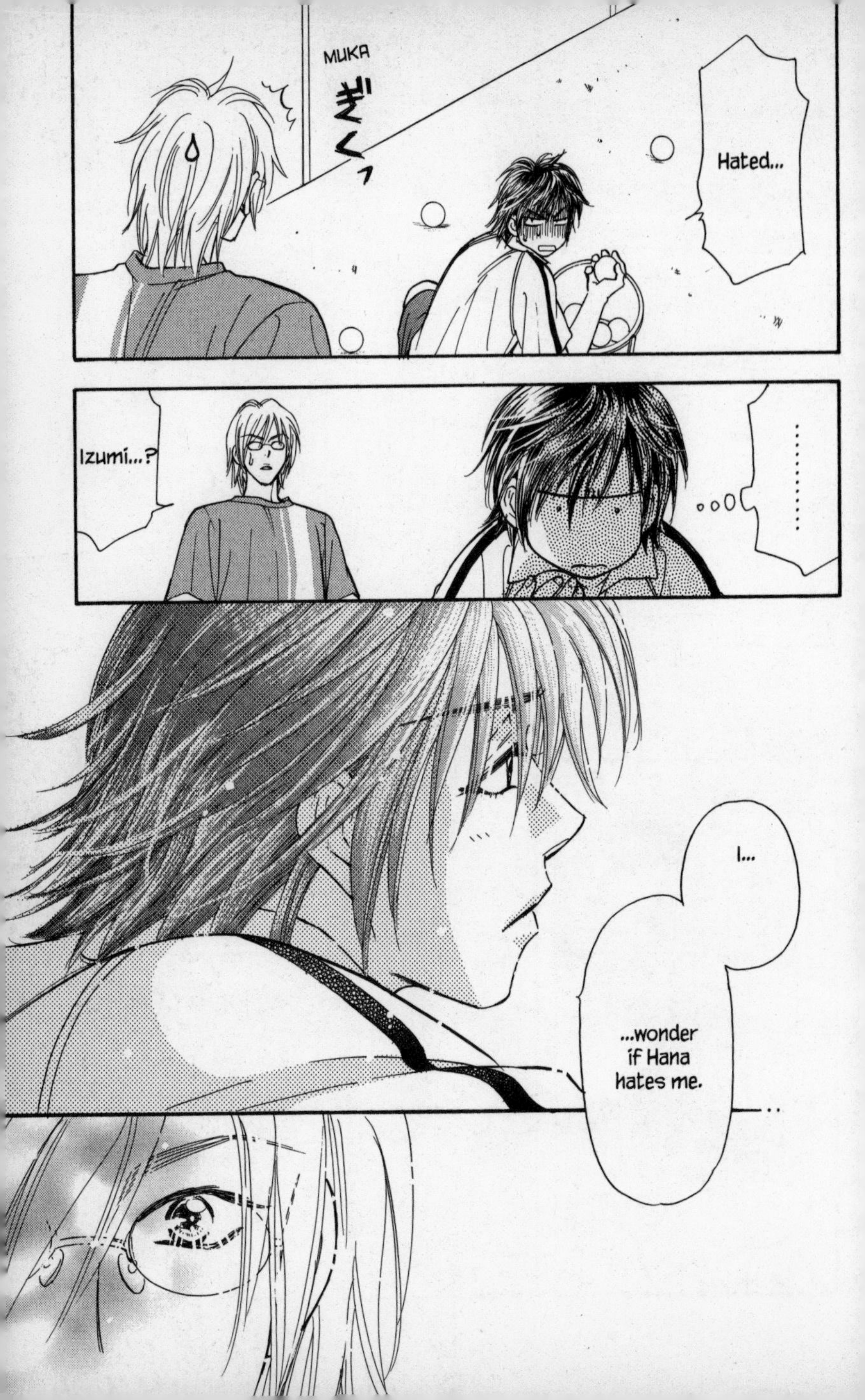

Hated...
MUKA
......
Izumi...?
I...
...wonder if Hana hates me.

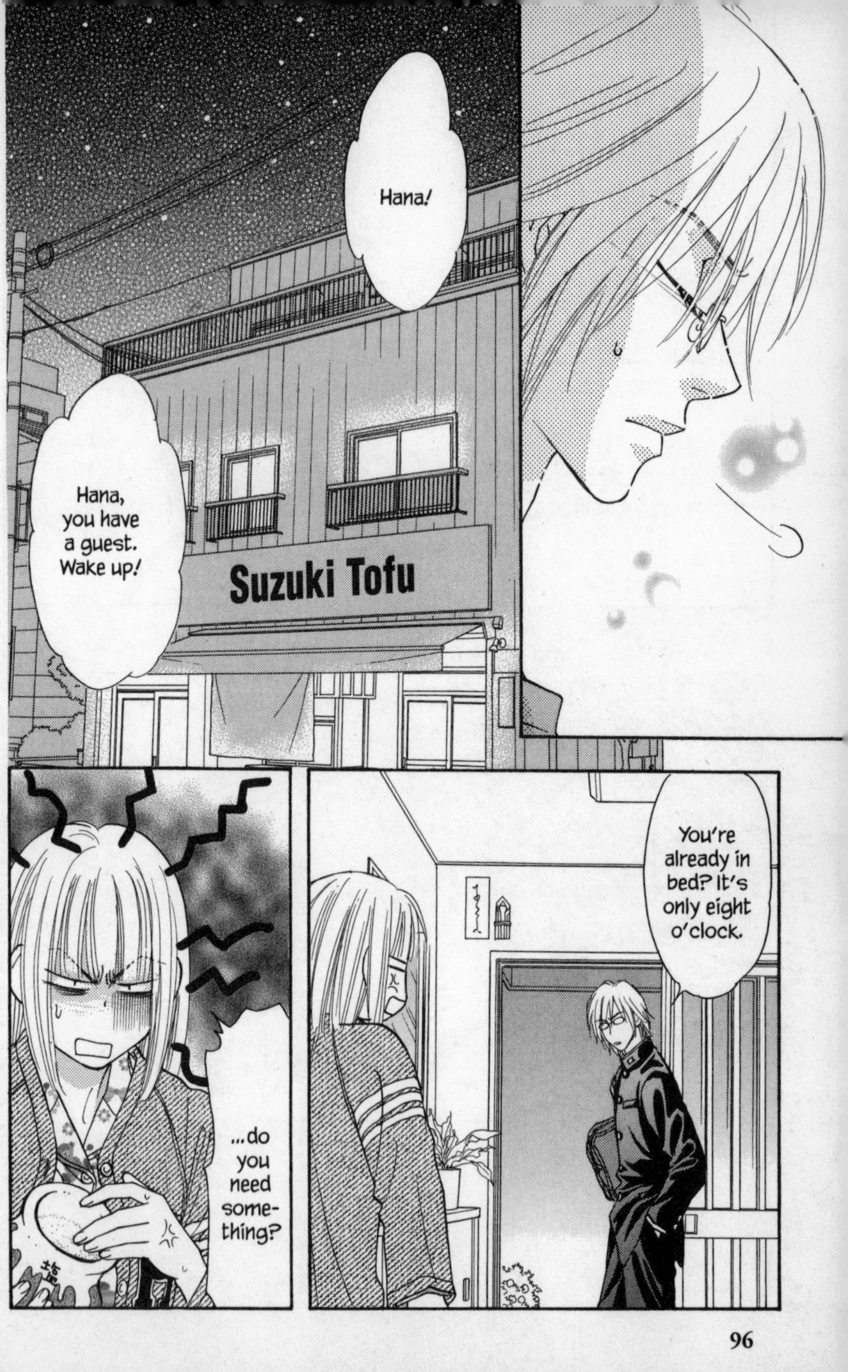
Hana!
Hana, you have a guest. Wake up!
Suzuki Tofu
You're already in bed? It's only eight o'clock.
...do you need something?

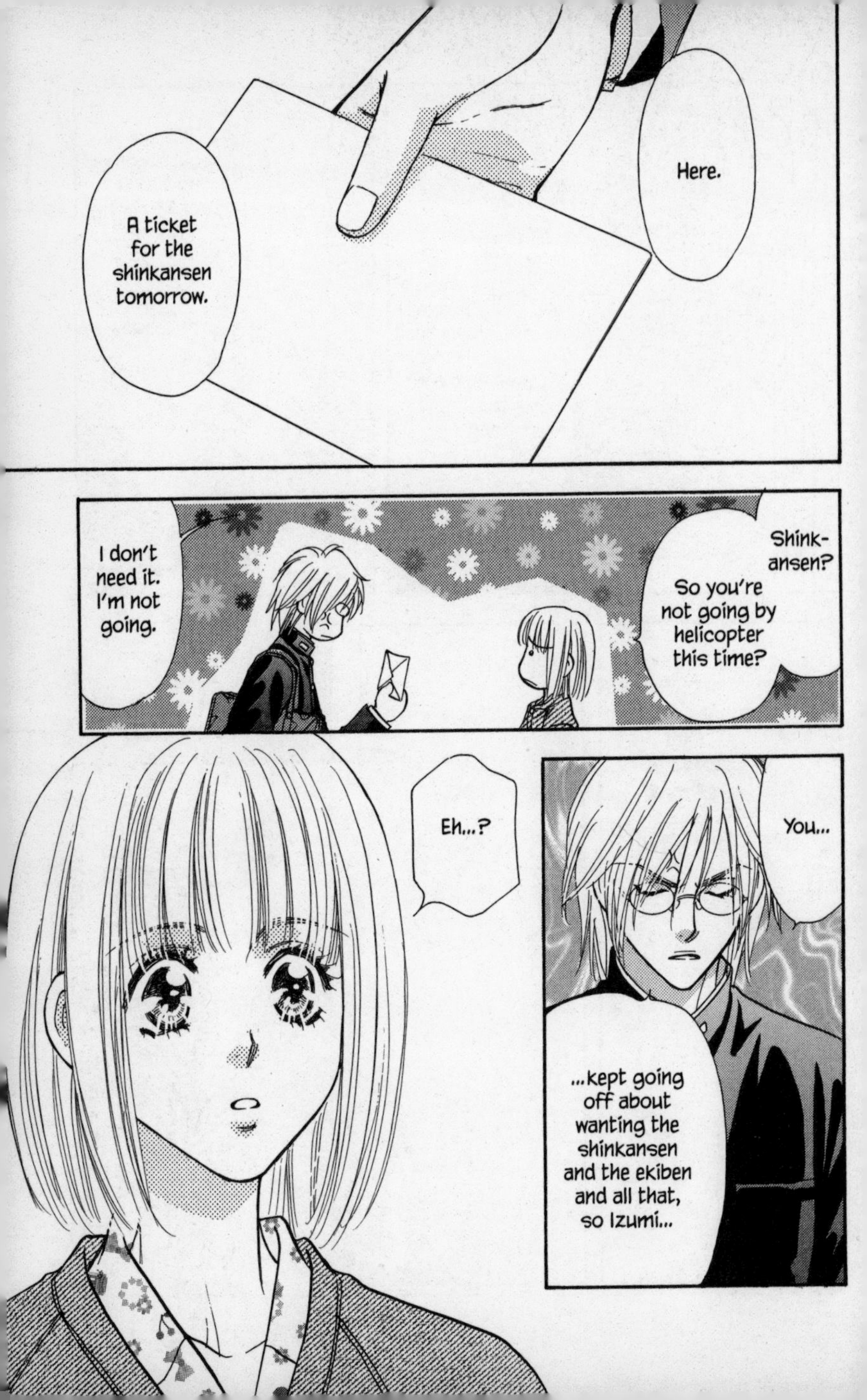
Here.
A ticket for the shinkansen tomorrow.
Shink-ansen?
So you're not going by helicopter this time?
I don't need it. I'm not going.
You...
...kept going off about wanting the shinkansen and the ekiben and all that, so Izumi...
Eh...?

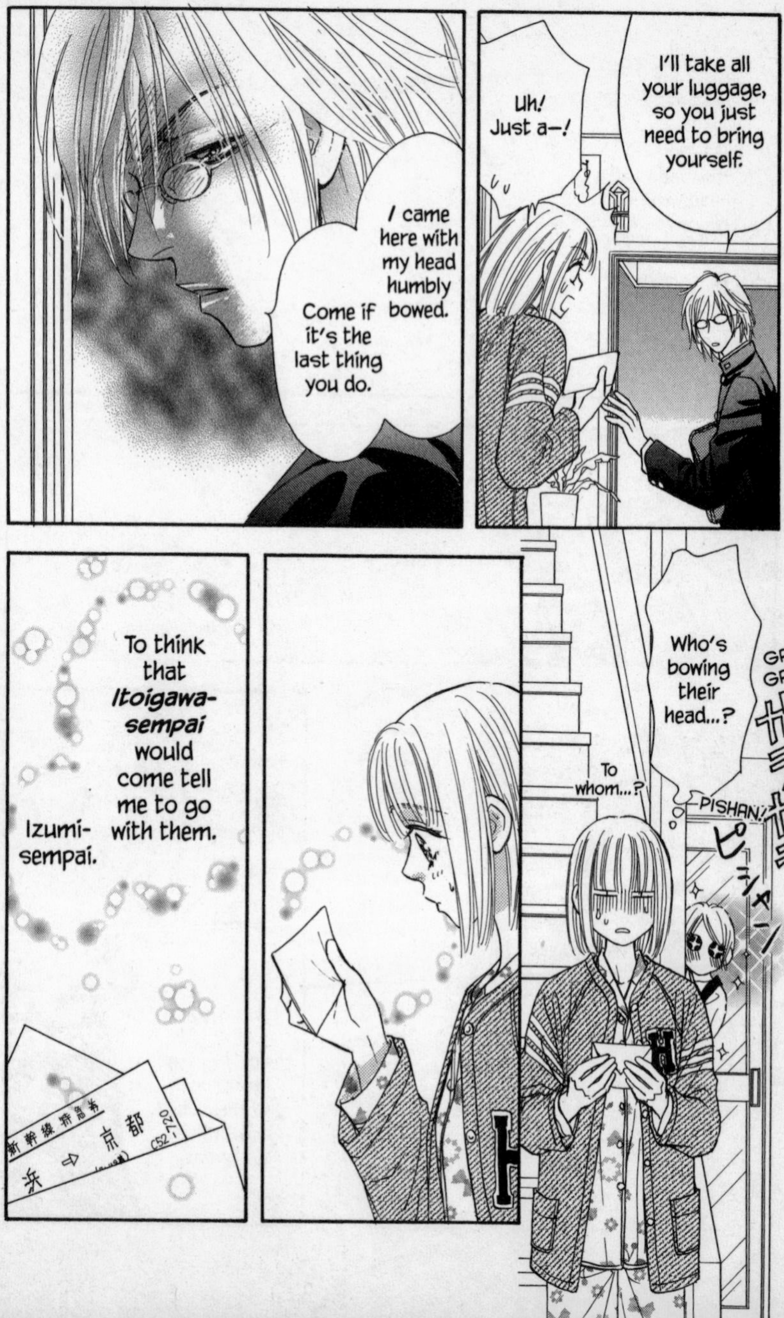
I'll take all your luggage, so you just need to bring yourself.
Uh! Just a—!
I came here with my head humbly bowed.
Come if it's the last thing you do.
Who's bowing their head...?
GARA GARA
ガラガラ
To whom...?
PISHAN!
ピシャーン!
To think that *Itoigawa-sempai* would come tell me to go with them.
Izumi-sempai.
新幹線特急券
浜 ⇨ 京都
C52-720

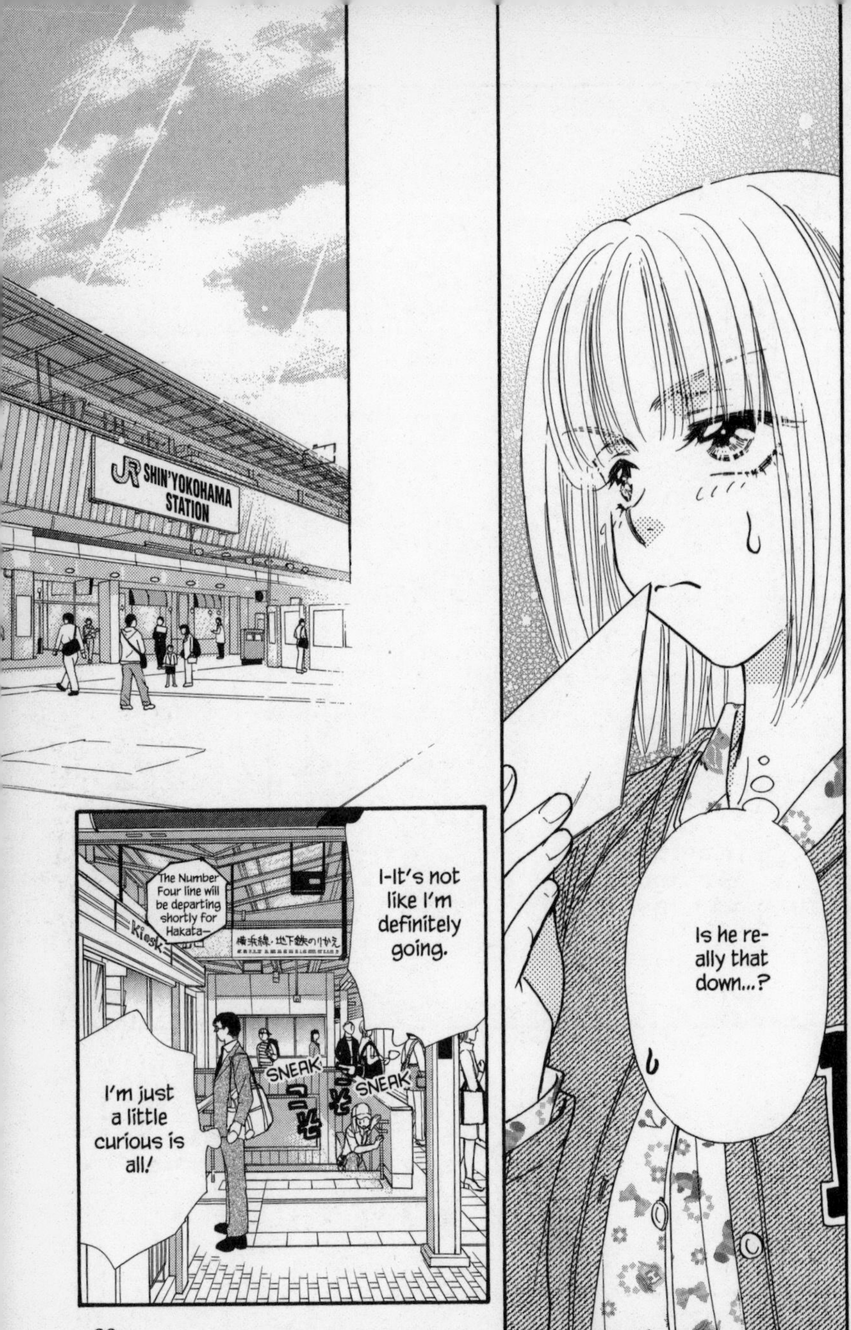
Is he re-ally that down...?
JR SHIN'YOKOHAMA STATION
I-It's not like I'm definitely going.
The Number Four line will be departing shortly for Hakata—
横浜線・地下鉄のりかえ
Kiosk
SNEAK
SNEAK
I'm just a little curious is all!

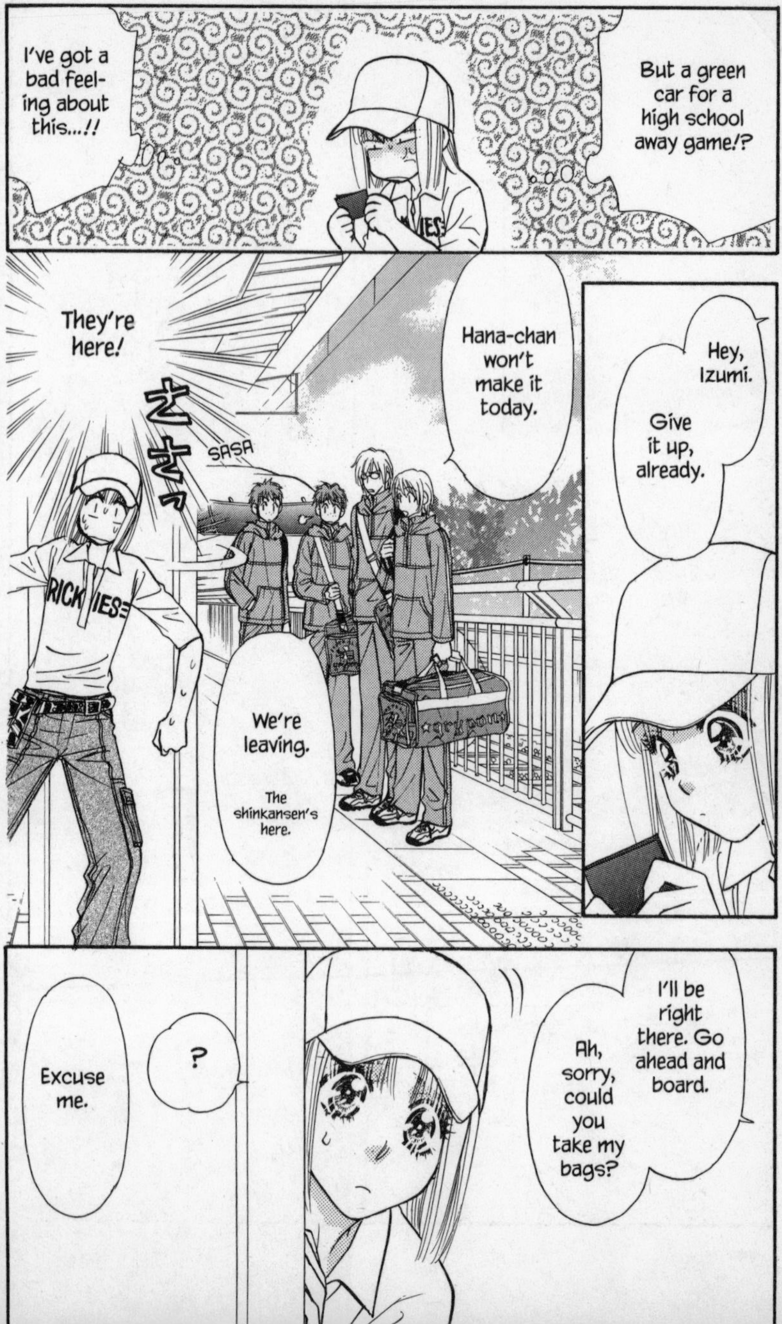
But a green car for a high school away game!?
I've got a bad feeling about this...!!
Hey, Izumi.
Give it up, already.
Hana-chan won't make it today.
They're here!
SASA
We're leaving.
The shinkansen's here.
I'll be right there. Go ahead and board.
Ah, sorry, could you take my bags?
?
Excuse me.

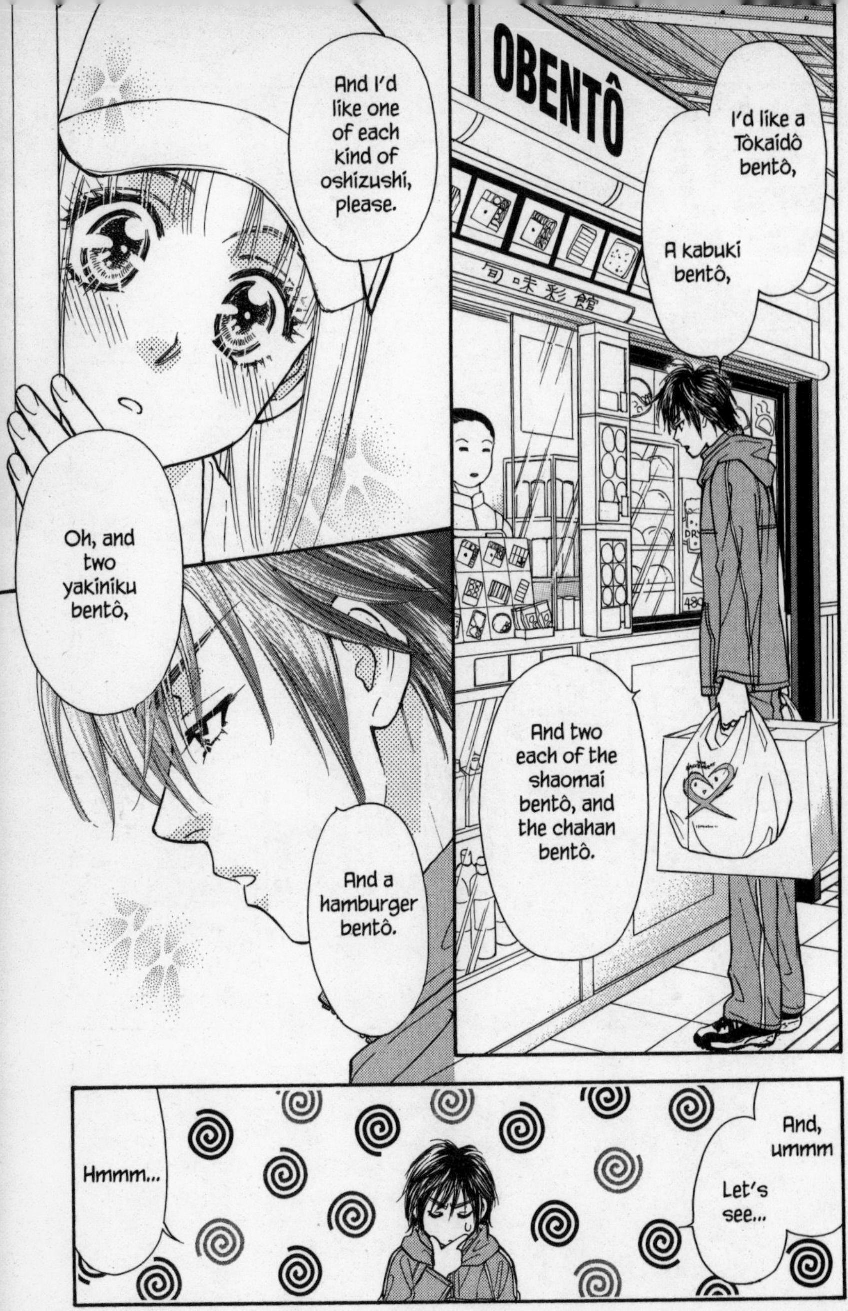
OBENTÔ
旬味彩館
I'd like a Tôkaidô bentô,
A kabuki bentô,
And two each of the shaomai bentô, and the chahan bentô.
And I'd like one of each kind of oshizushi, please.
Oh, and two yakiniku bentô,
And a hamburger bentô.
And, ummm
Let's see...
Hmmm...

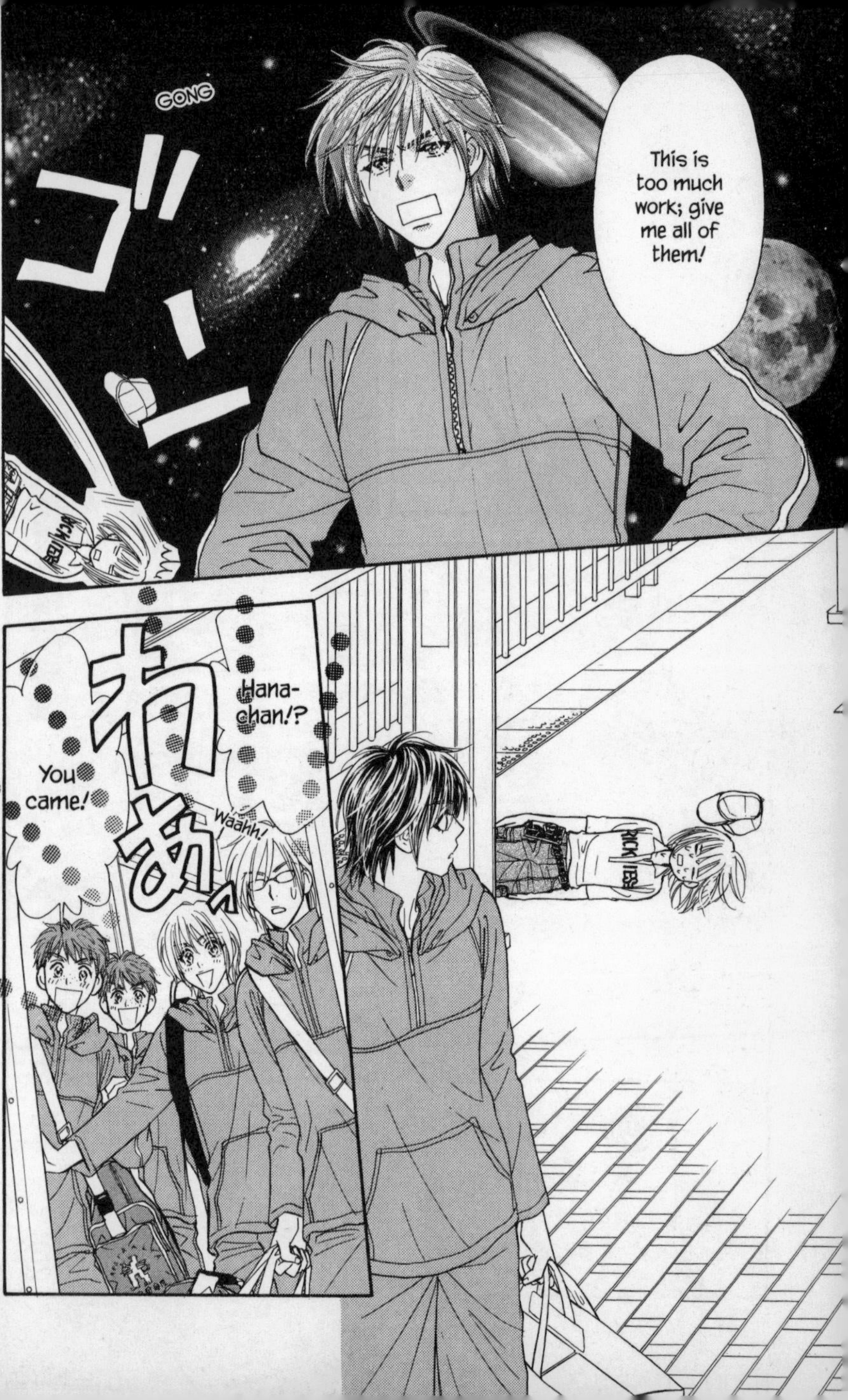
This is too much work; give me all of them!
GONG
Hana-chan!?
Waahh!
You came!

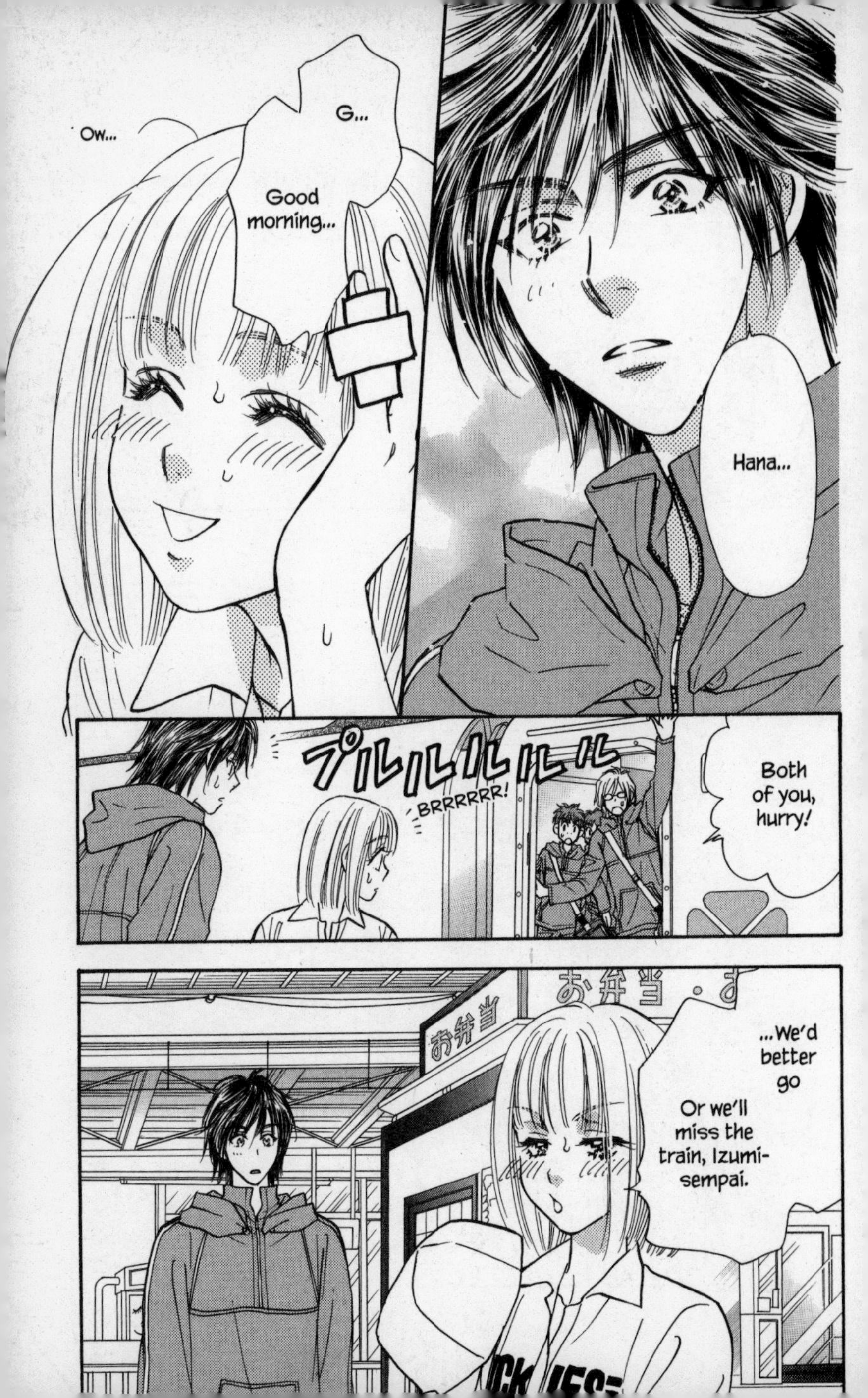
Hana...
G...
Good morning...
Ow...
Both of you, hurry!
プルルルルル
BRRRRRR!
...We'd better go
Or we'll miss the train, Izumi-sempai.
お弁当
お弁当

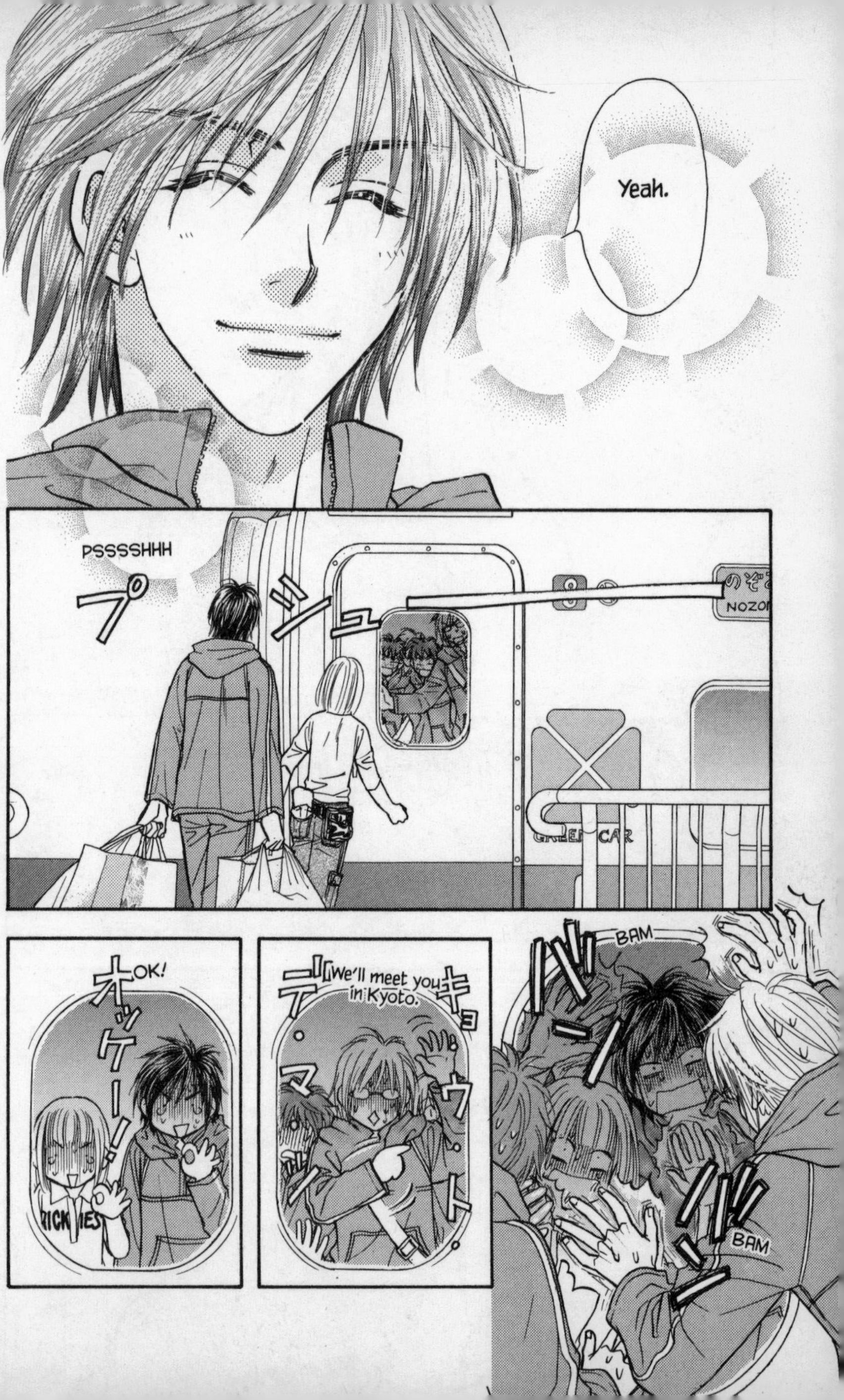

Yeah.
PSSSSHHH
プシュ
BAM
BAM
We'll meet you in Kyoto.
OK!
オッケー!

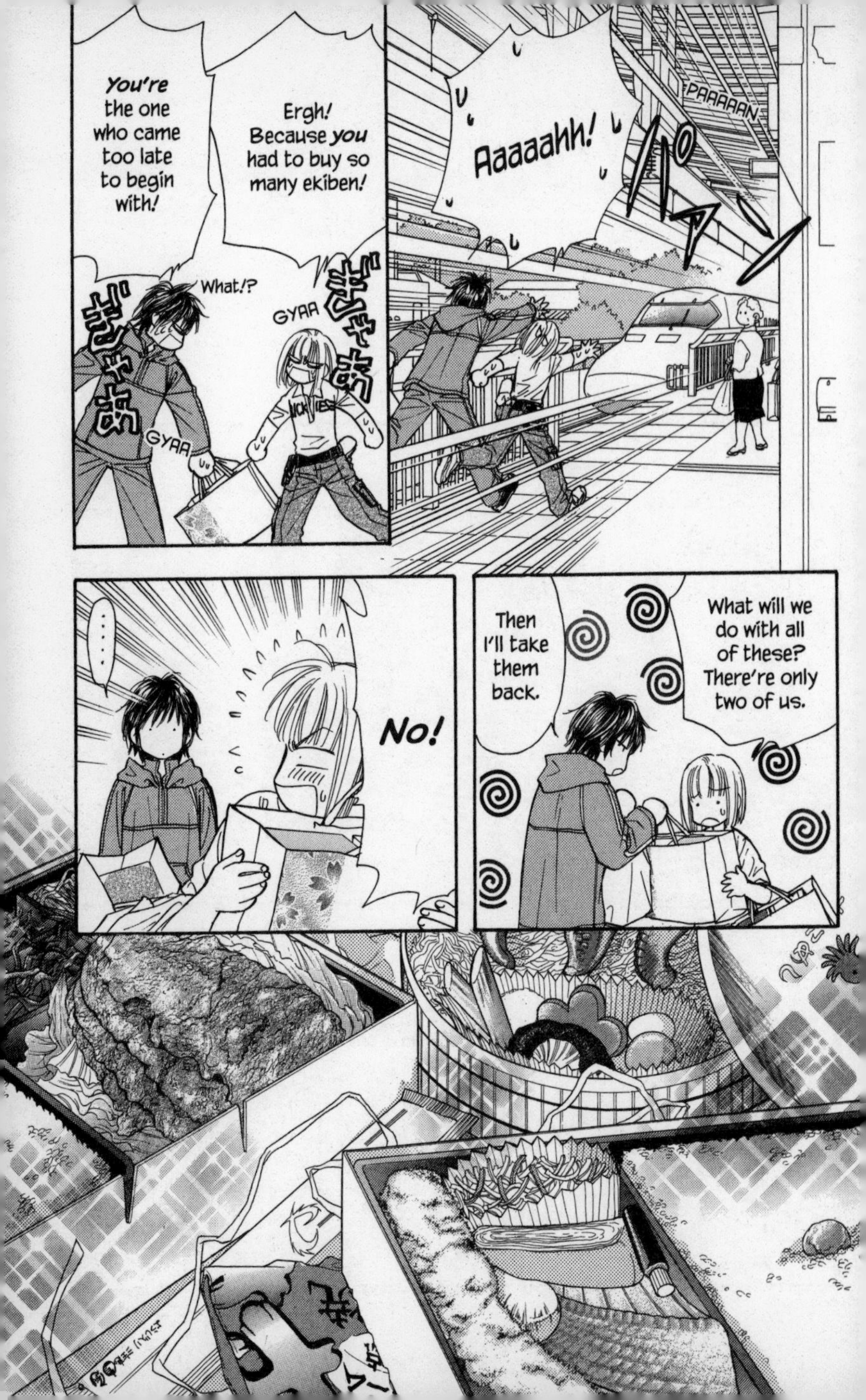
PAAAAAAN
Aaaaahh!
Ergh! Because *you* had to buy so many ekiben!
You're the one who came too late to begin with!
GYAA
What!?
GYAA
What will we do with all of these? There're only two of us.
Then I'll take them back.
No!
......

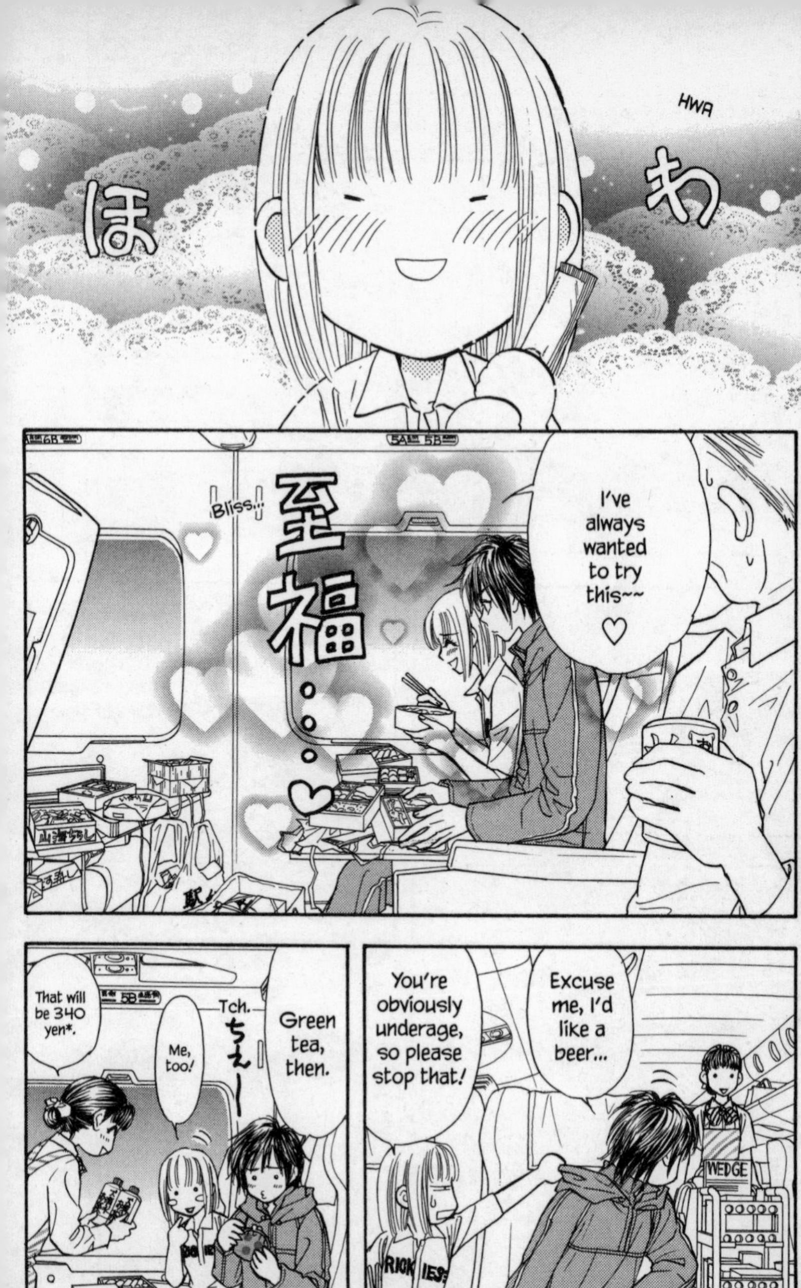
HWA
ほ
わ
I've always wanted to try this~~ ♥
至福…
Bliss...
Excuse me, I'd like a beer...
You're obviously underage, so please stop that!
WEDGE
Green tea, then.
Tch.
ちぇ～
Me, too!
That will be 340 yen*.

*$3.40

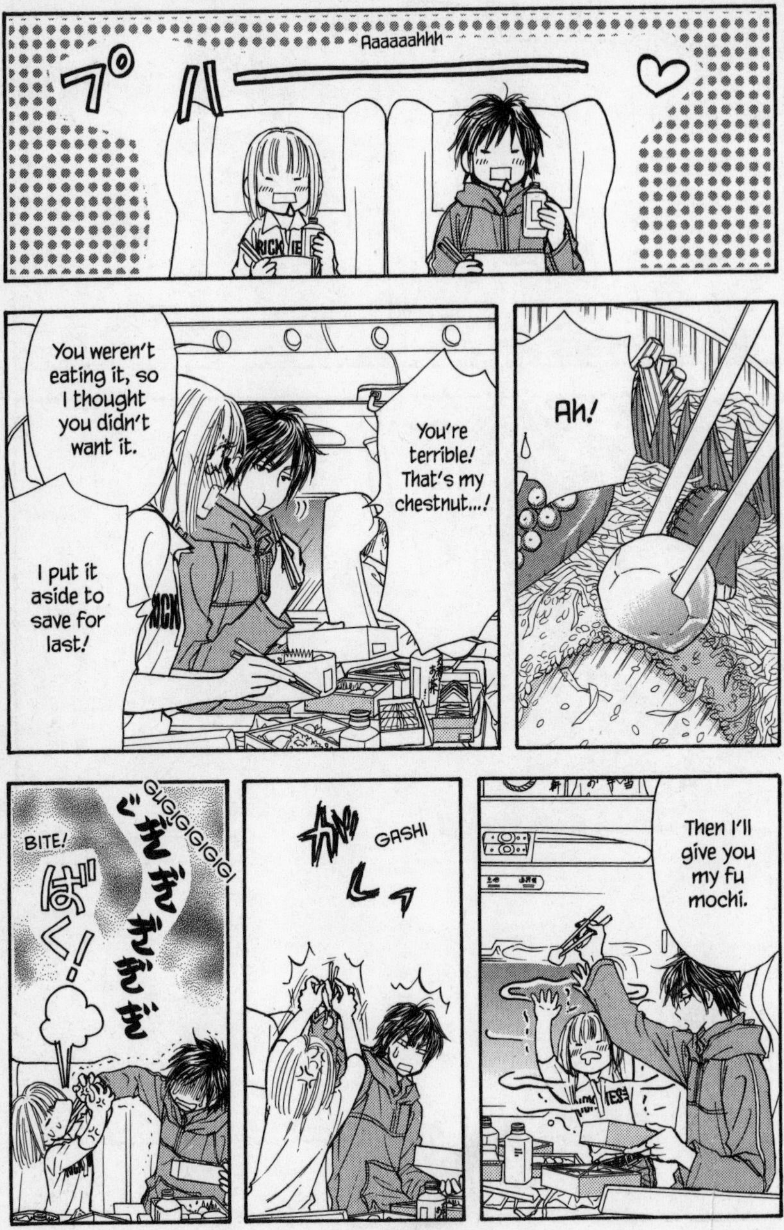
プハー
Aaaaaahhh
Ah!
You're terrible! That's my chestnut...!
You weren't eating it, so I thought you didn't want it.
I put it aside to save for last!
Then I'll give you my fu mochi.
GASHI
GIGIGIGIGI
ぱく!
BITE!

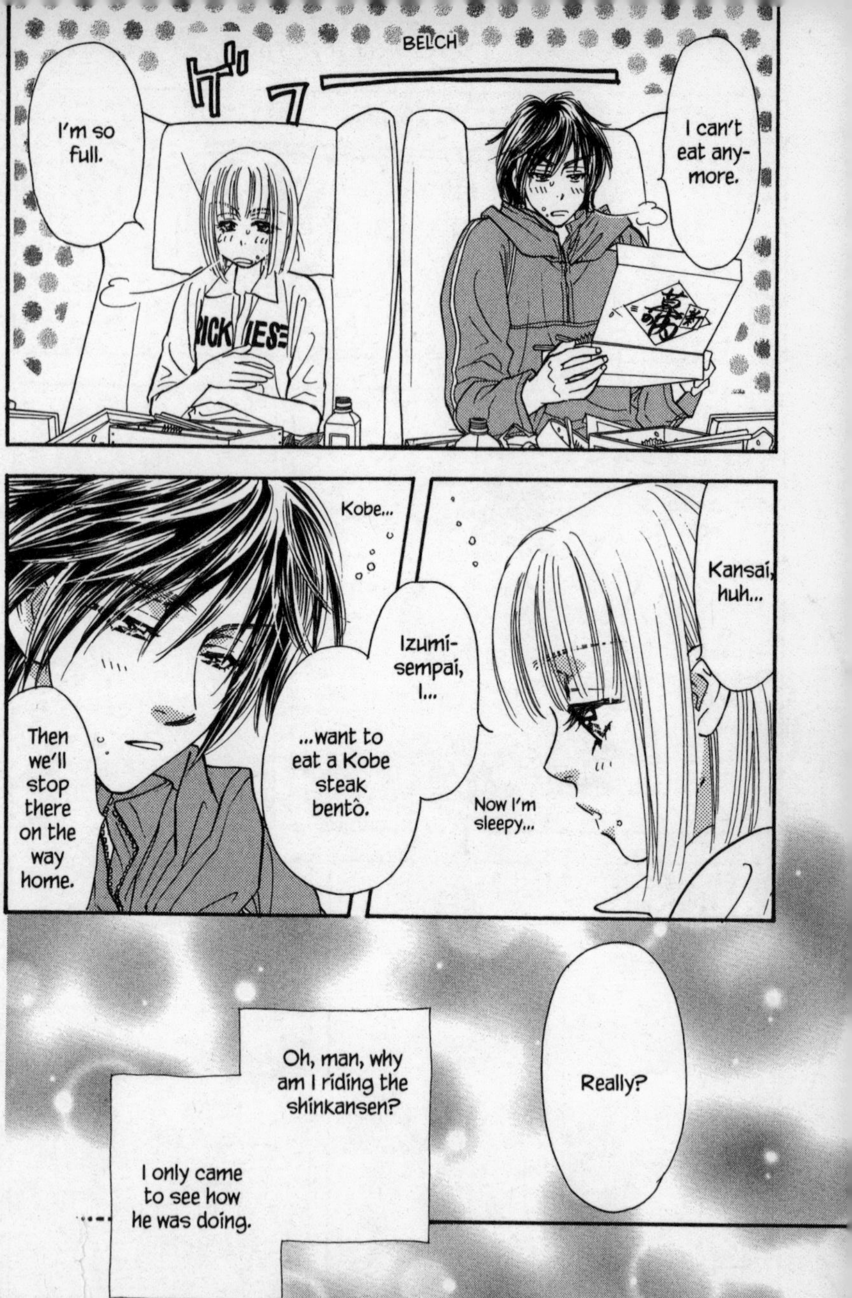
BELCH
I can't eat anymore.
I'm so full.
Kansai, huh...
Now I'm sleepy...
Kobe...
Izumi-sempai, I...
...want to eat a Kobe steak bentô.
Then we'll stop there on the way home.
Really?
Oh, man, why am I riding the shinkansen?
I only came to see how he was doing.

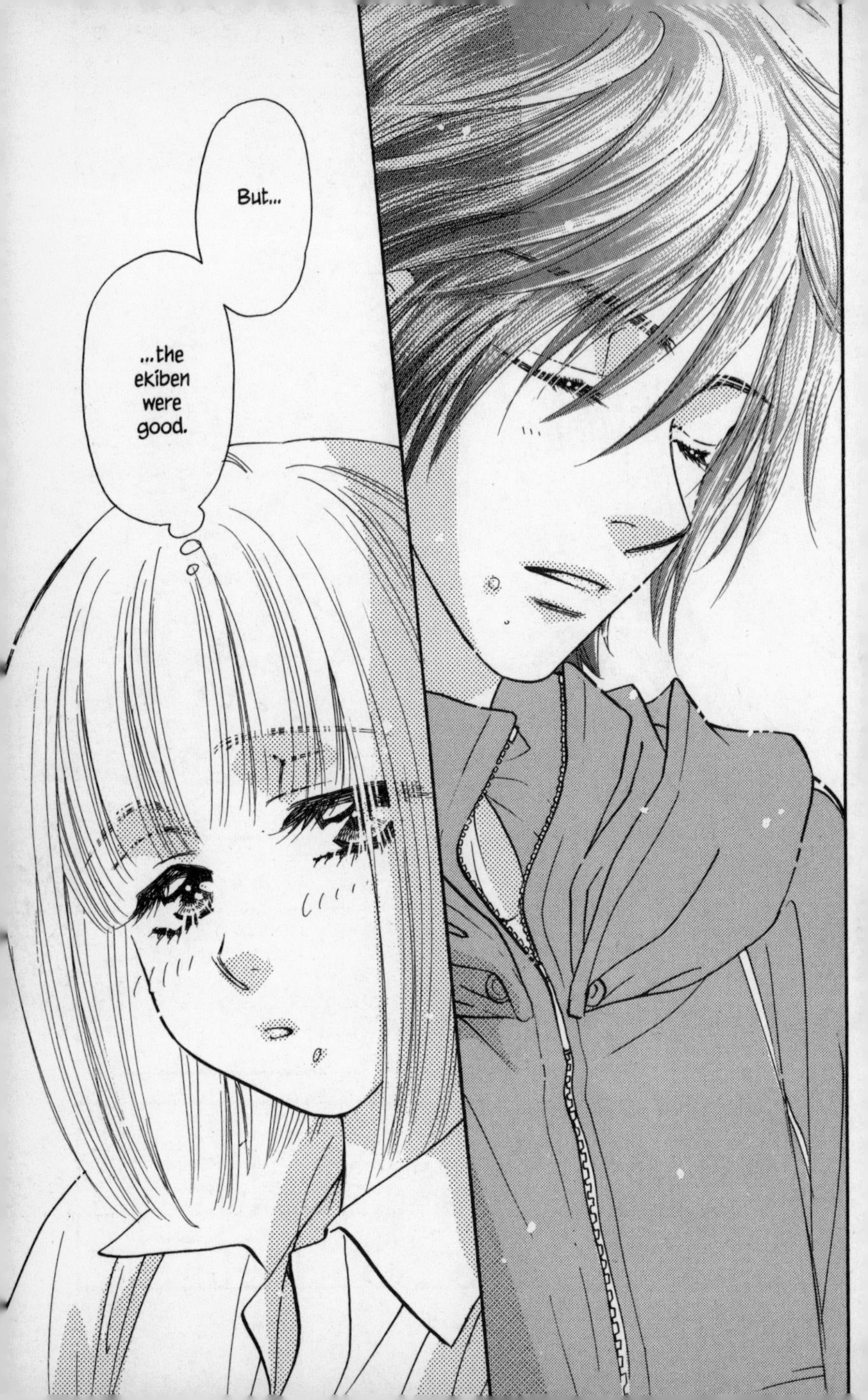
But...
...the ekiben were good.

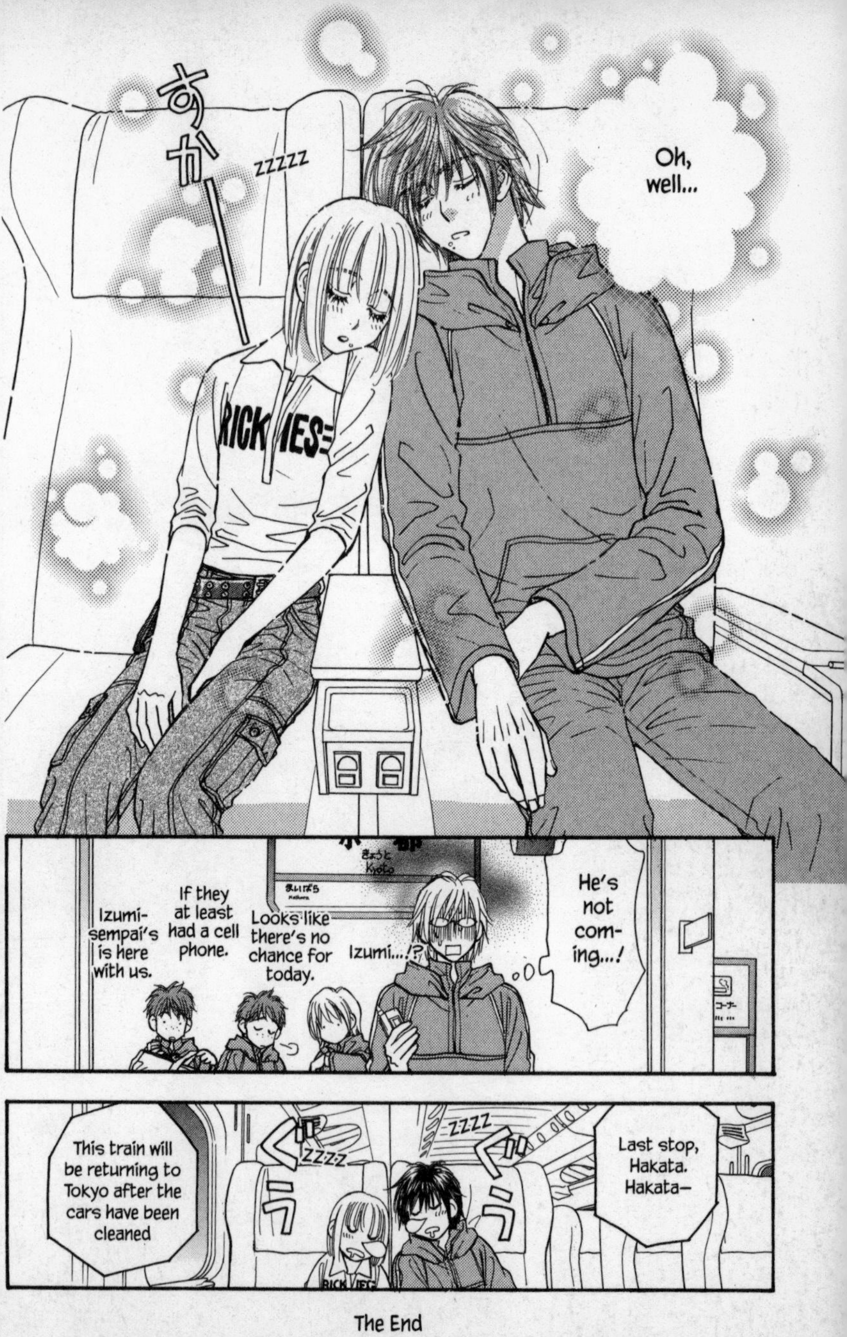
Oh, well...
zzzzz
すかー
He's not com-ing...!
Izumi...!?
Looks like there's no chance for today.
If they at least had a cell phone.
Izumi-sempai's is here with us.
Last stop, Hakata. Hakata—
ぐぅ
zzzz
ぐぅ
zzzz
This train will be returning to Tokyo after the cars have been cleaned

The End

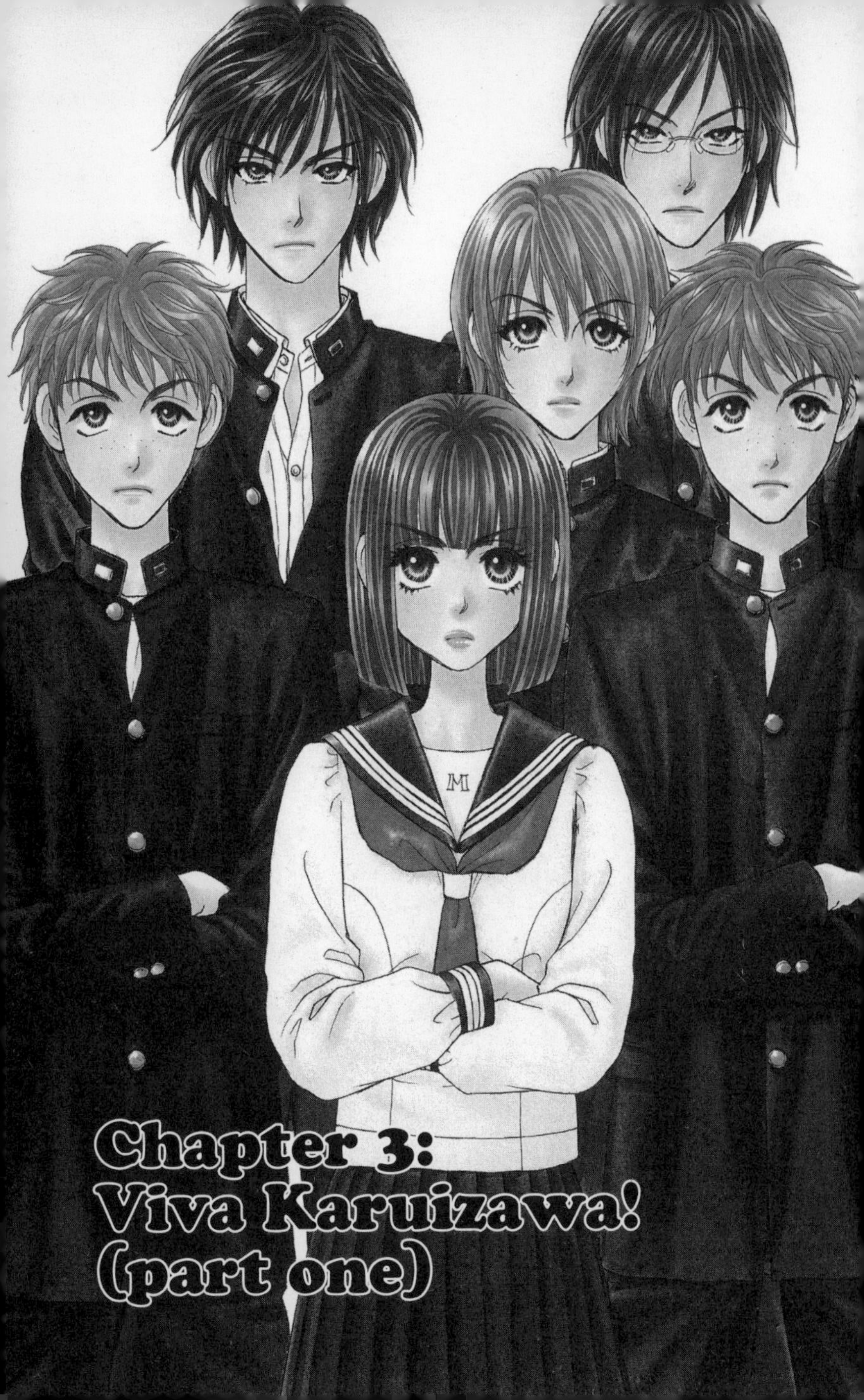

Chapter 3: Viva Karuizawa! (part one)

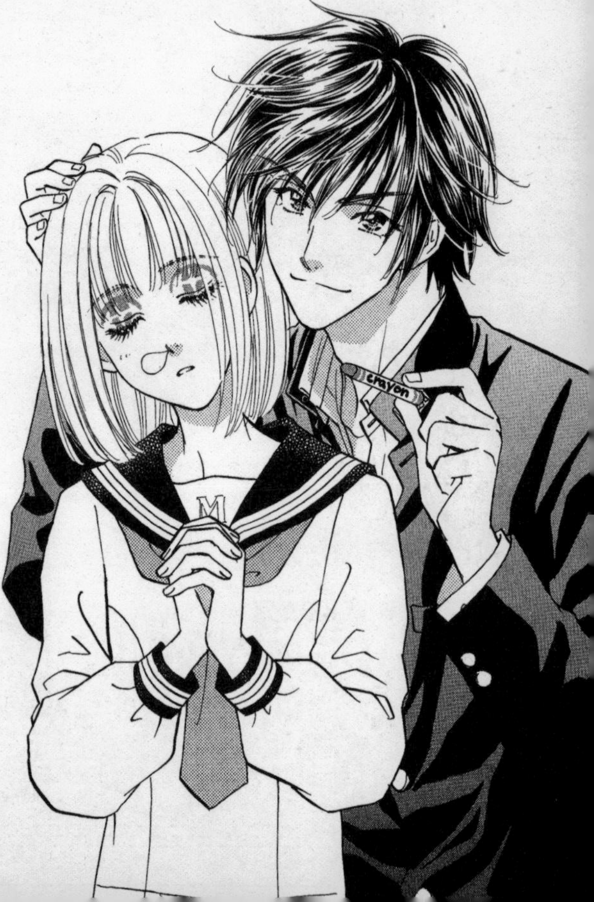
crayon

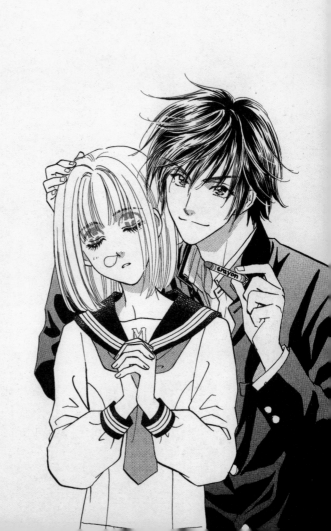

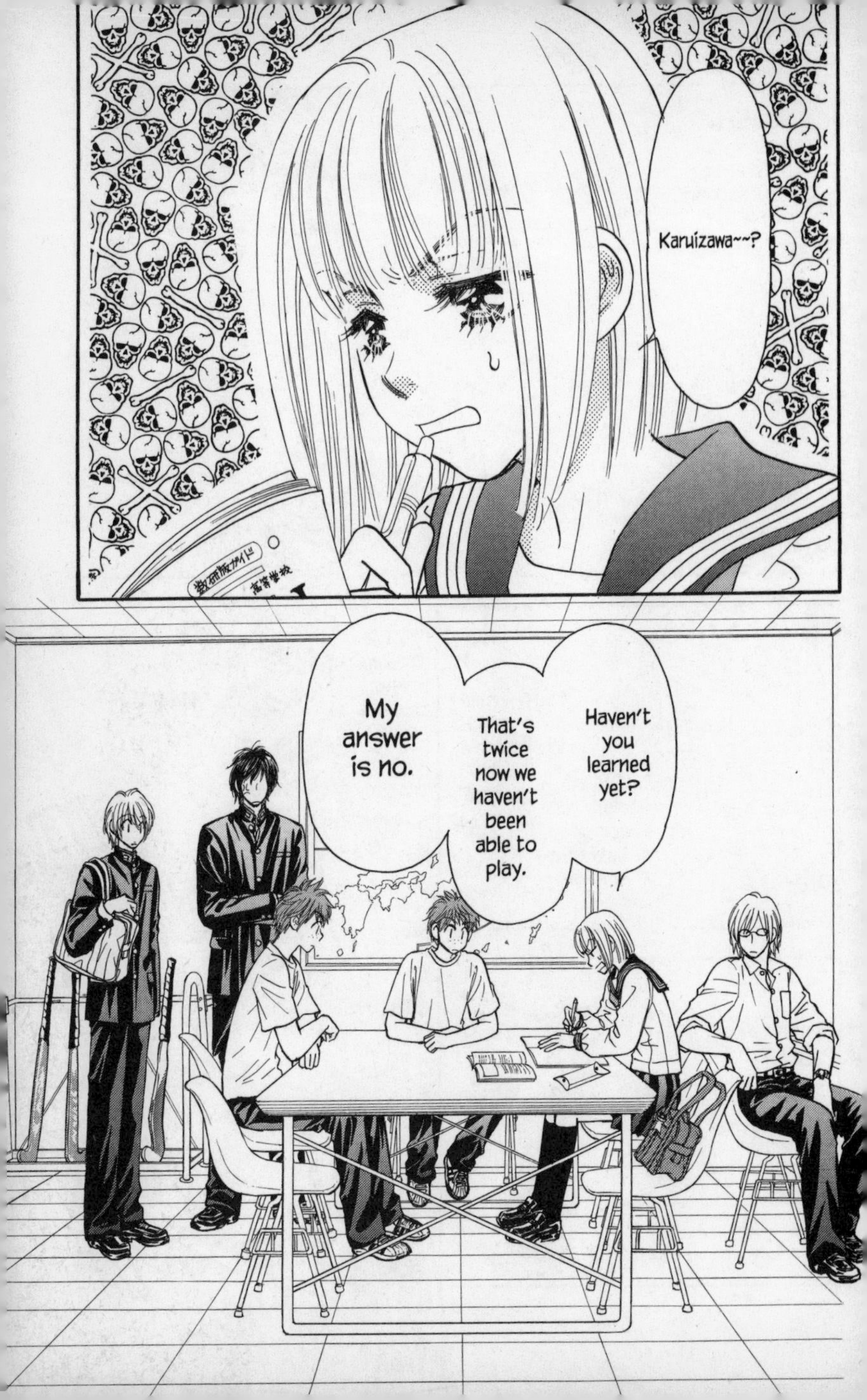
Karuizawa~~?
数研版ガイド
高等学校
Haven't you learned yet?
That's twice now we haven't been able to play.
My answer is no.

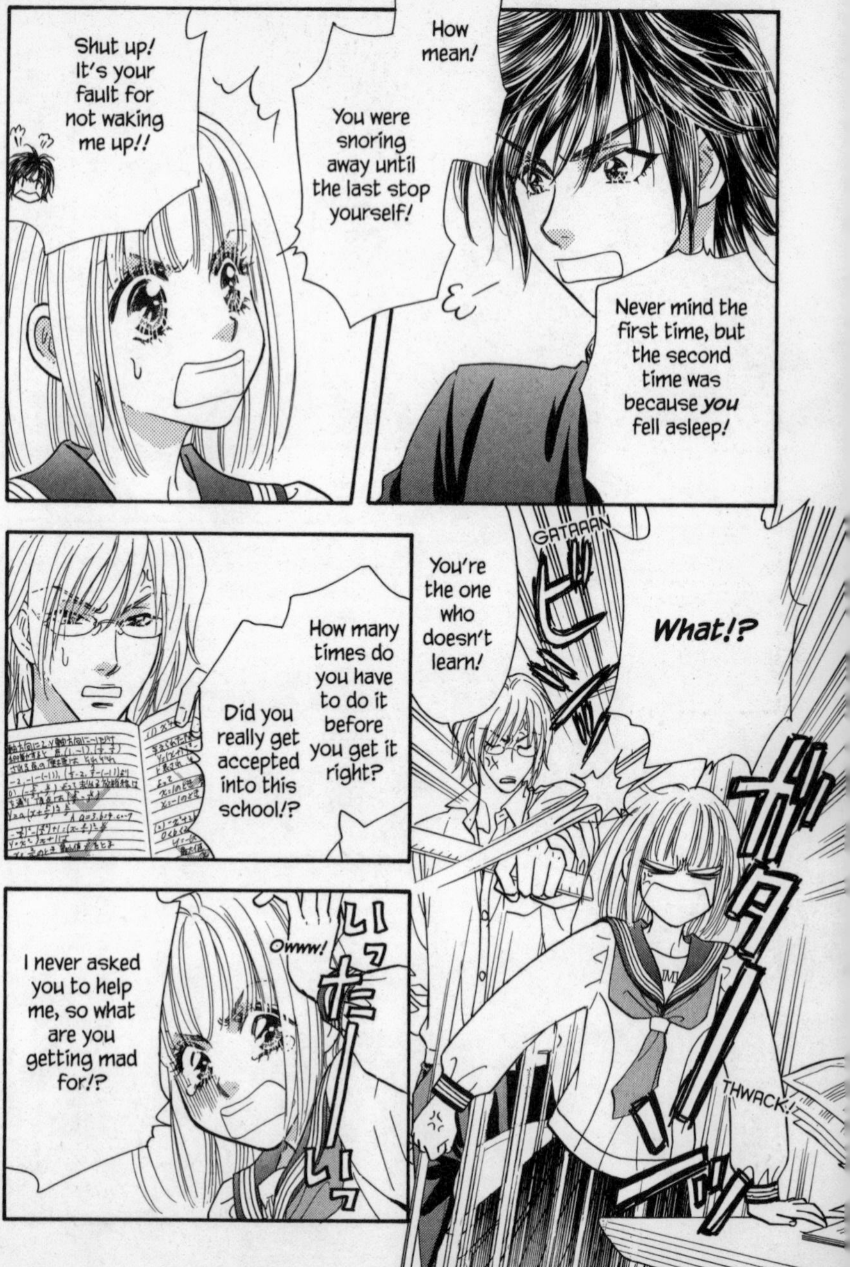
How mean!
You were snoring away until the last stop yourself!
Never mind the first time, but the second time was because *you* fell asleep!
Shut up! It's your fault for not waking me up!!
GATAAAN
What!?
You're the one who doesn't learn!
THWACK!
How many times do you have to do it before you get it right?
Did you really get accepted into this school!?
Owww!
I never asked you to help me, so what are you getting mad for!?

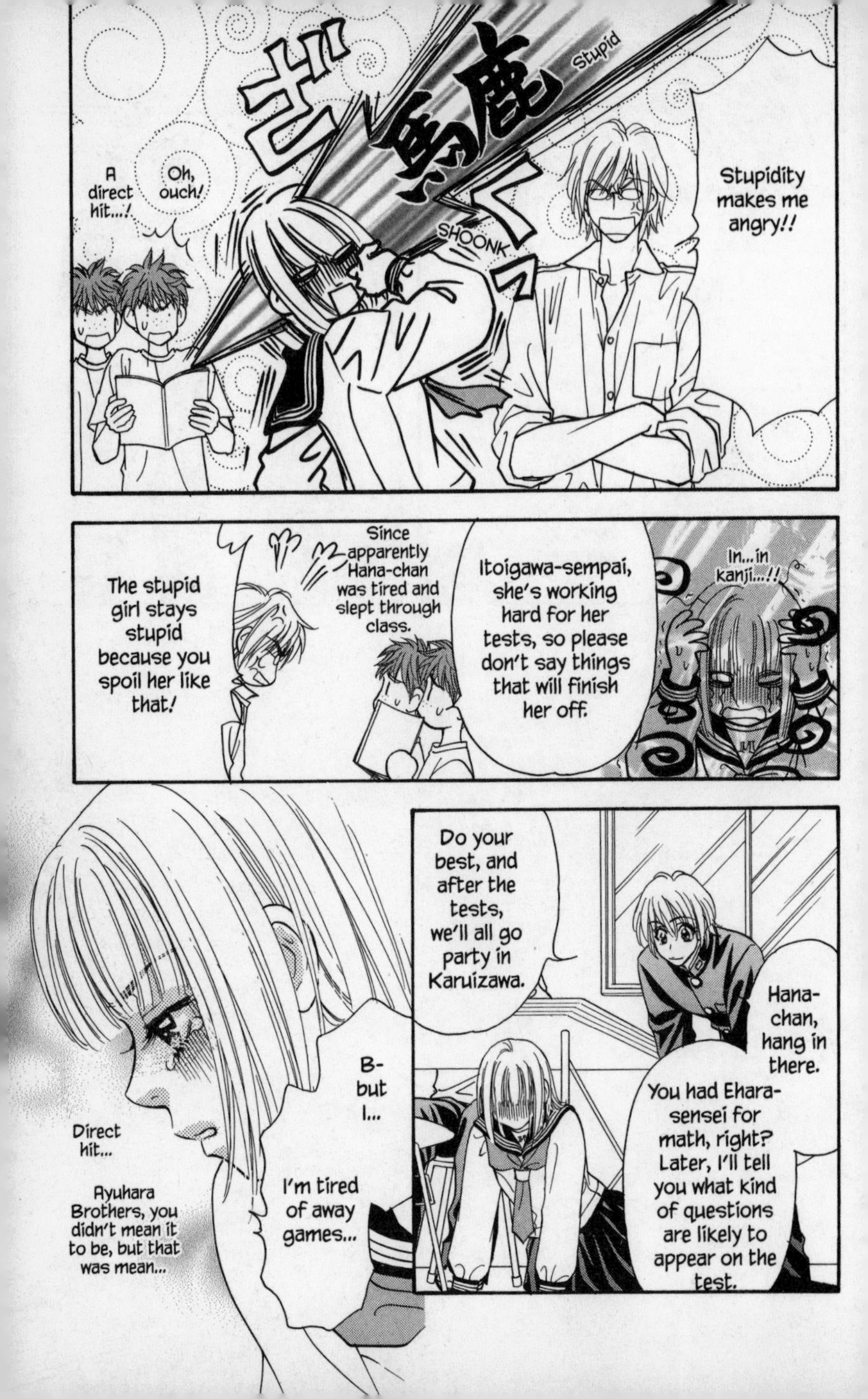

Stupidity makes me angry!!
Stupid
SHOONK
Oh, ouch!
A direct hit...!
In...in kanji...!!
Itoigawa-sempai, she's working hard for her tests, so please don't say things that will finish her off.
Since apparently Hana-chan was tired and slept through class.
The stupid girl stays stupid because you spoil her like that!
Hana-chan, hang in there.
You had Ehara-sensei for math, right? Later, I'll tell you what kind of questions are likely to appear on the test.
Do your best, and after the tests, we'll all go party in Karuizawa.
B-but I...
I'm tired of away games...
Direct hit...
Ayuhara Brothers, you didn't mean it to be, but that was mean...

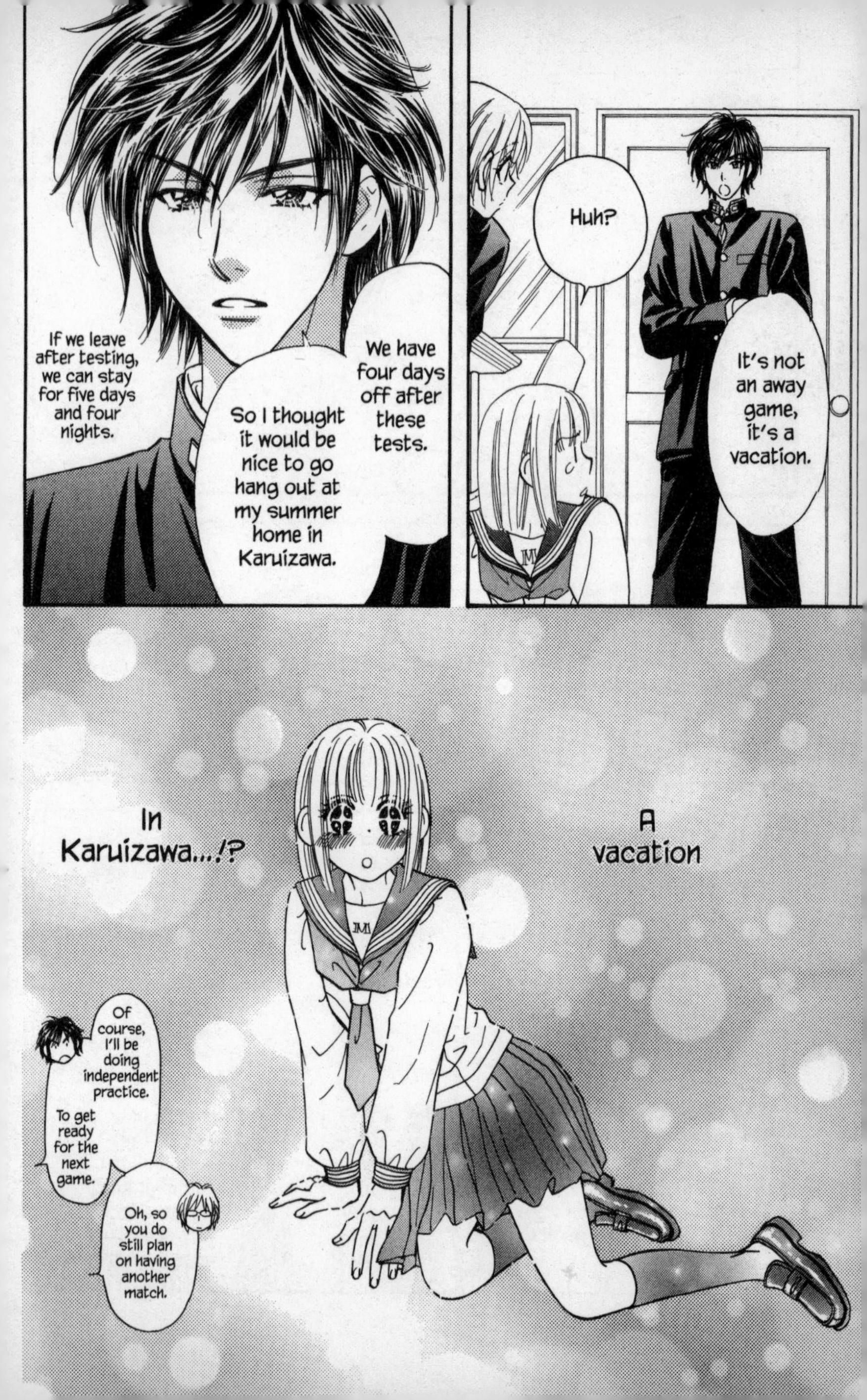
Huh?
It's not an away game, it's a vacation.
We have four days off after these tests.
So I thought it would be nice to go hang out at my summer home in Karuizawa.
If we leave after testing, we can stay for five days and four nights.
A vacation
In Karuizawa...!?
Of course, I'll be doing independent practice.
To get ready for the next game.
Oh, so you do still plan on having another match.

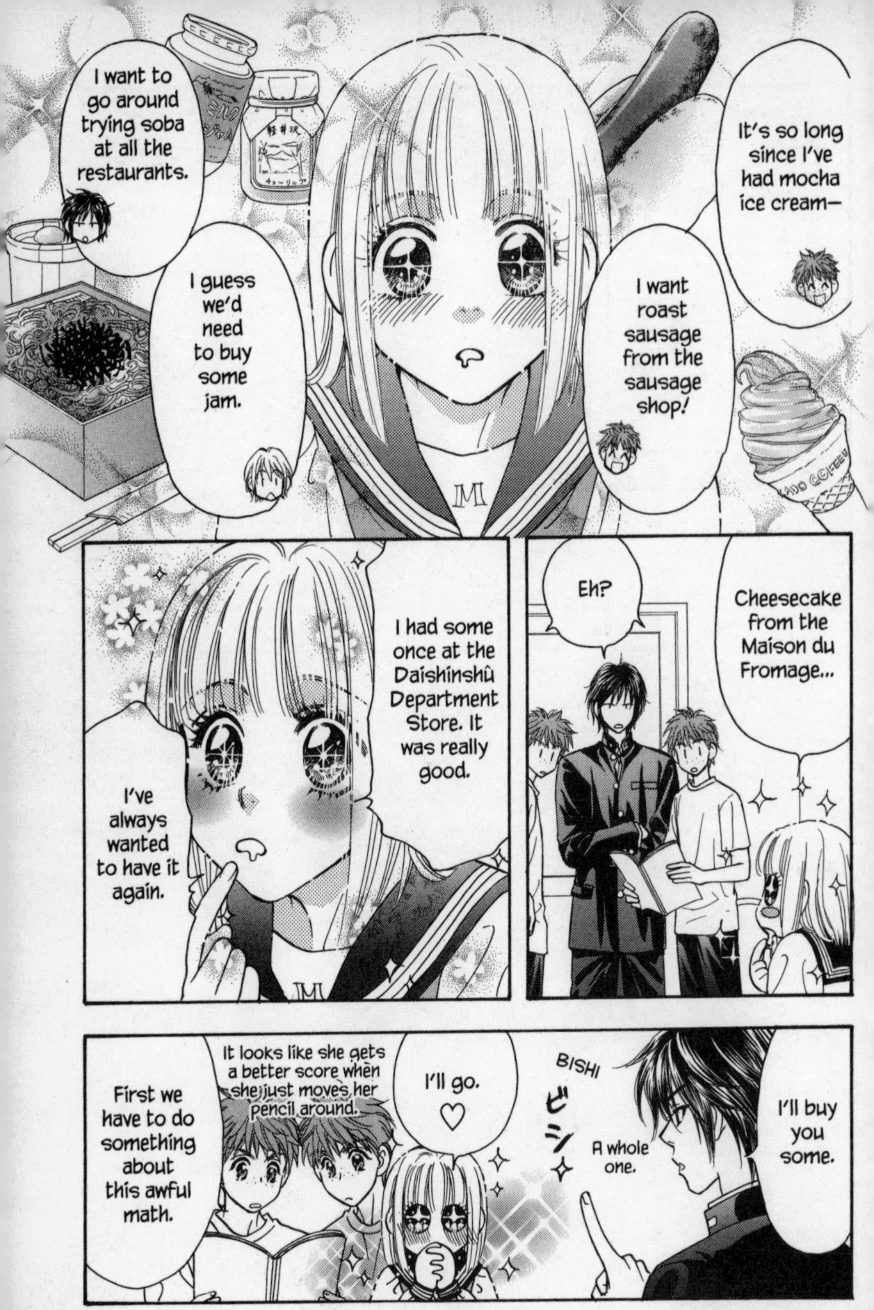
It's so long since I've had mocha ice cream—
I want roast sausage from the sausage shop!
I want to go around trying soba at all the restaurants.
I guess we'd need to buy some jam.
Cheesecake from the Maison du Fromage...
Eh?
I had some once at the Daishinshû Department Store. It was really good.
I've always wanted to have it again.
I'll buy you some.
BISHI
ビシ
A whole one.
I'll go. ♡
It looks like she gets a better score when she just moves her pencil around.
First we have to do something about this awful math.

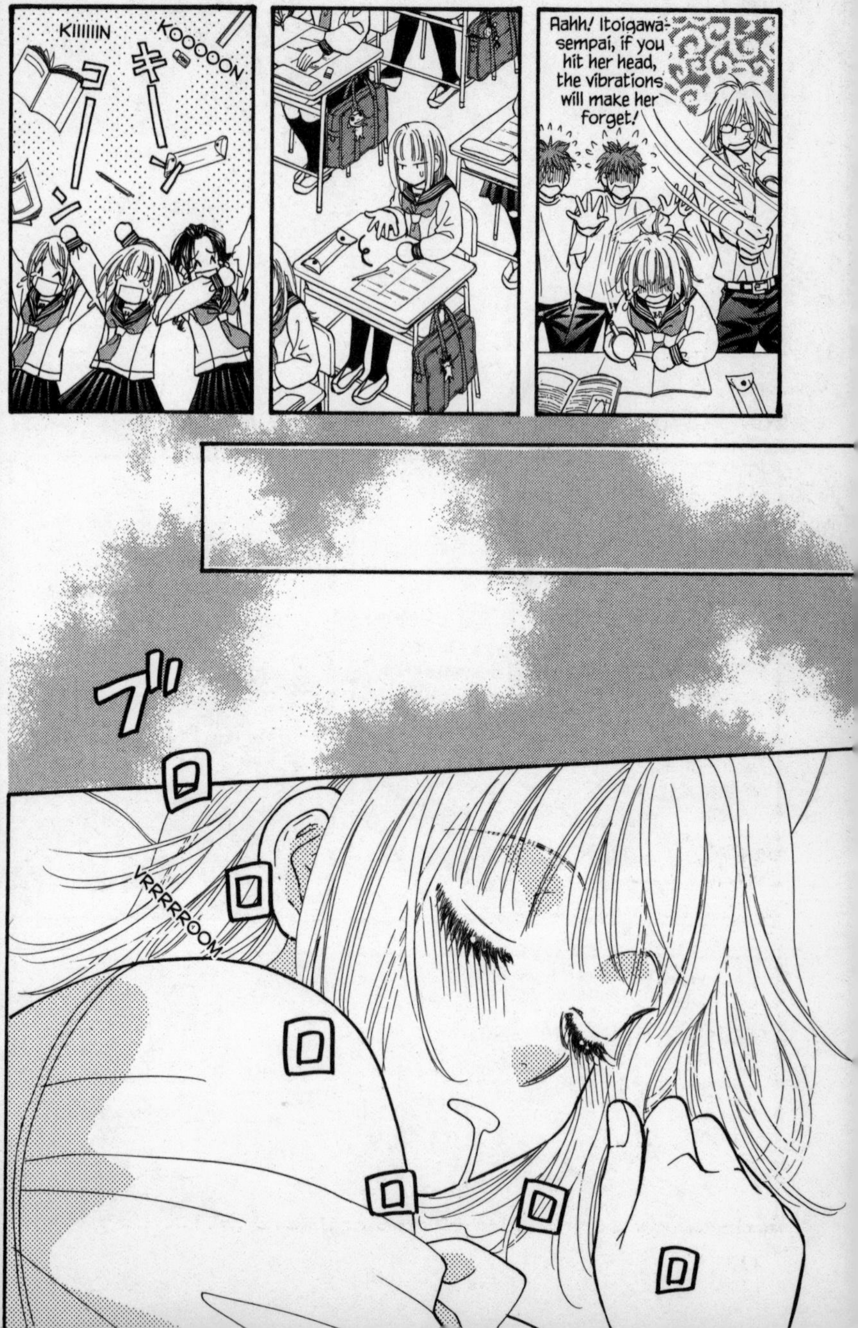
Aahh! Itoigawa-sempai, if you hit her head, the vibrations will make her forget!
KIIIIIN
KOOOOON
ブロロロロロ
VRRRRROOM

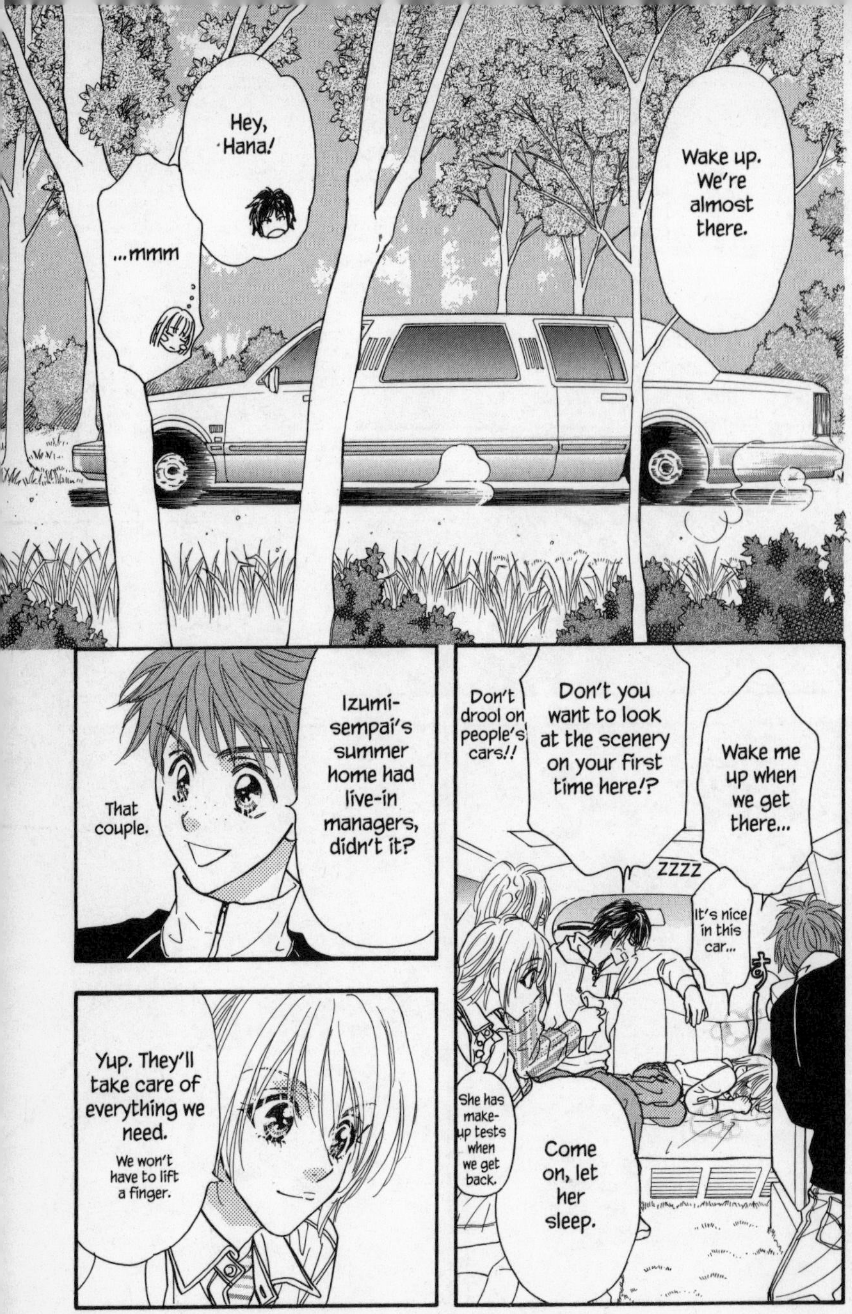
Wake up. We're almost there.
Hey, Hana!
...mmm
Wake me up when we get there...
Don't you want to look at the scenery on your first time here!?
Don't drool on people's cars!!
ZZZZ
It's nice in this car...
She has make-up tests when we get back.
Come on, let her sleep.
Izumi-sempai's summer home had live-in managers, didn't it?
That couple.
Yup. They'll take care of everything we need.
We won't have to lift a finger.

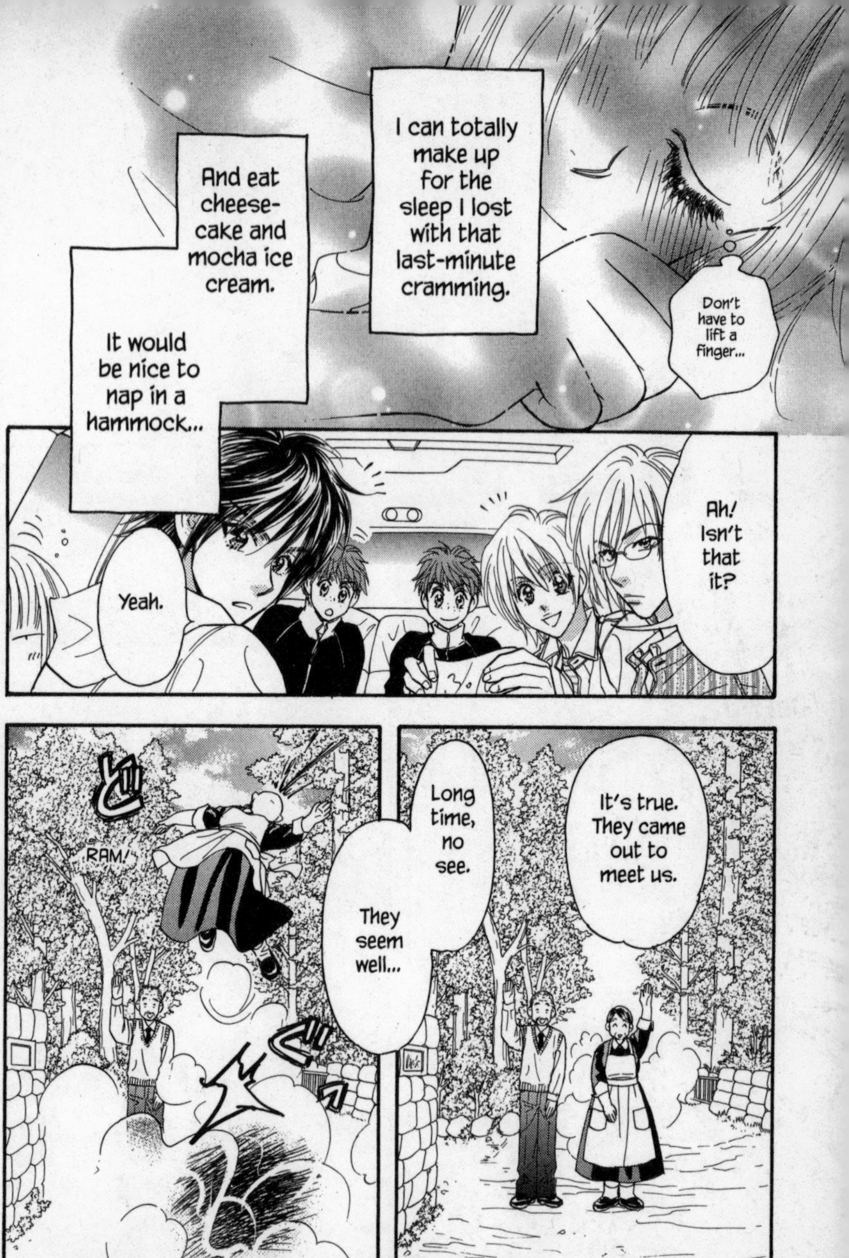
Don't have to lift a finger...
I can totally make up for the sleep I lost with that last-minute cramming.
And eat cheese-cake and mocha ice cream.
It would be nice to nap in a hammock...
Ah! Isn't that it?
Yeah.
It's true. They came out to meet us.
Long time, no see.
They seem well...
RAM!

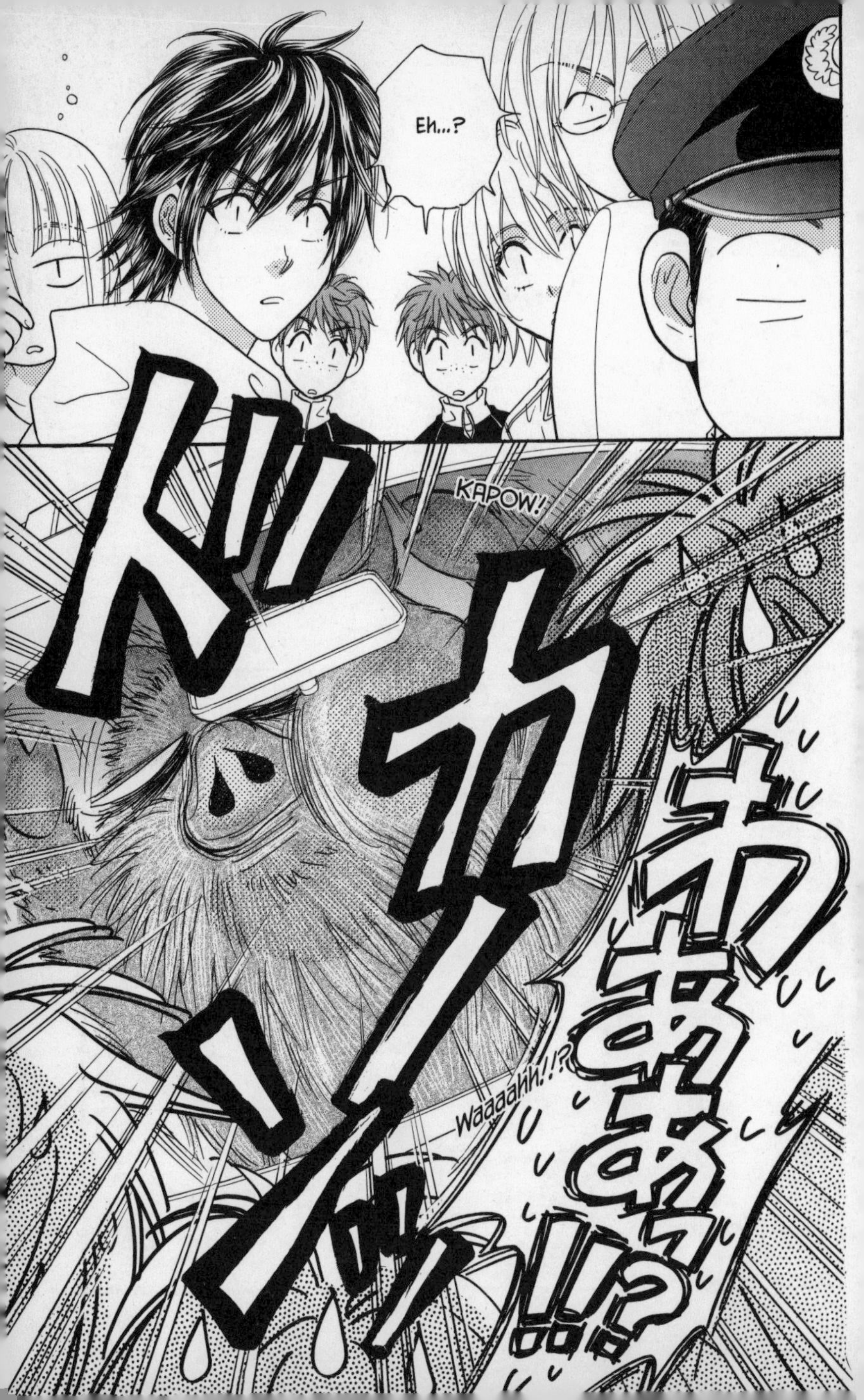
Eh...?
KAPOW!
Waaaahh!!?

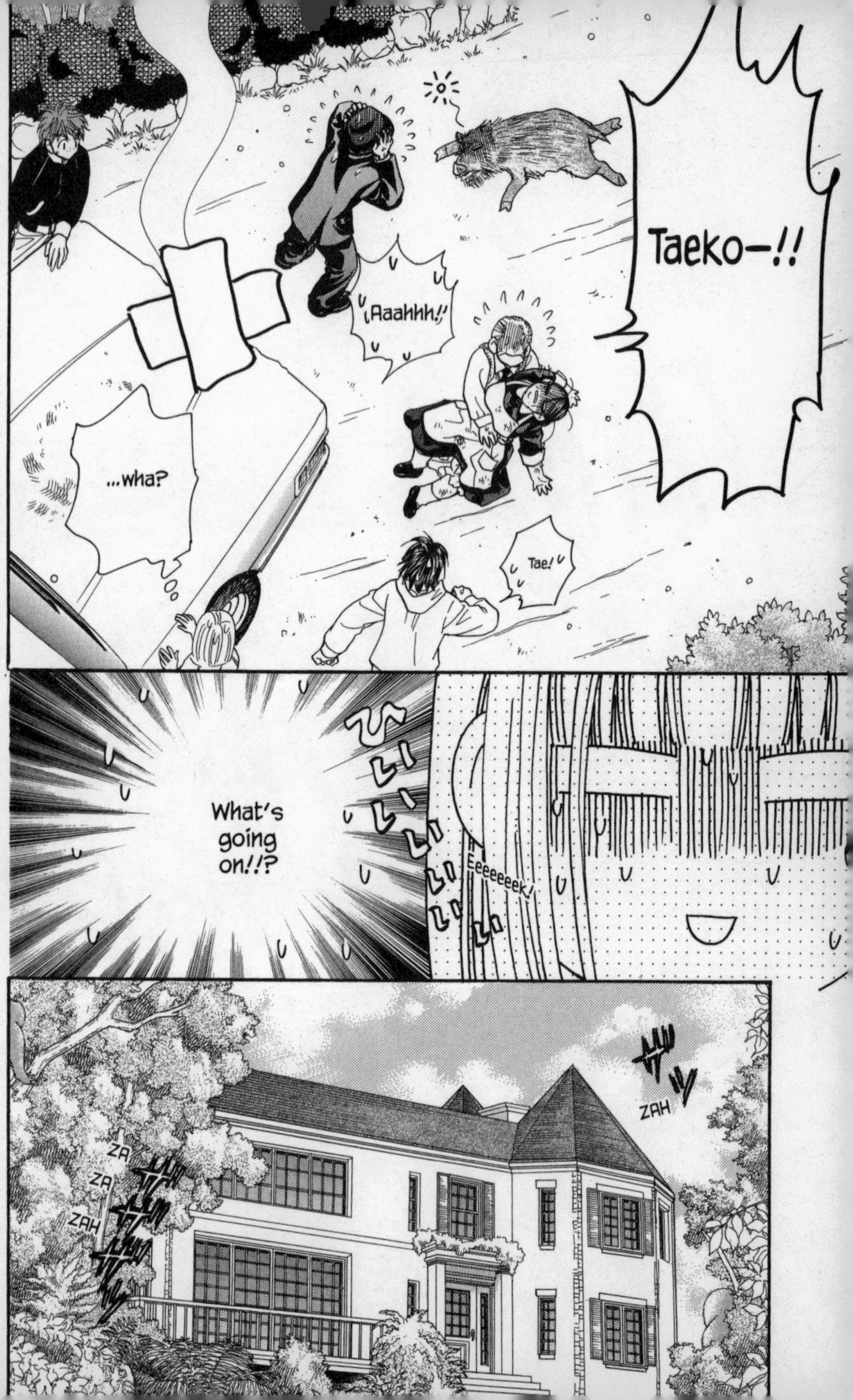
Taeko—!!
¡Aaahhh!!
Tae!
...wha?
Eeeeeeek!
What's going on!!?
ZAH
ZA
ZA
ZAH

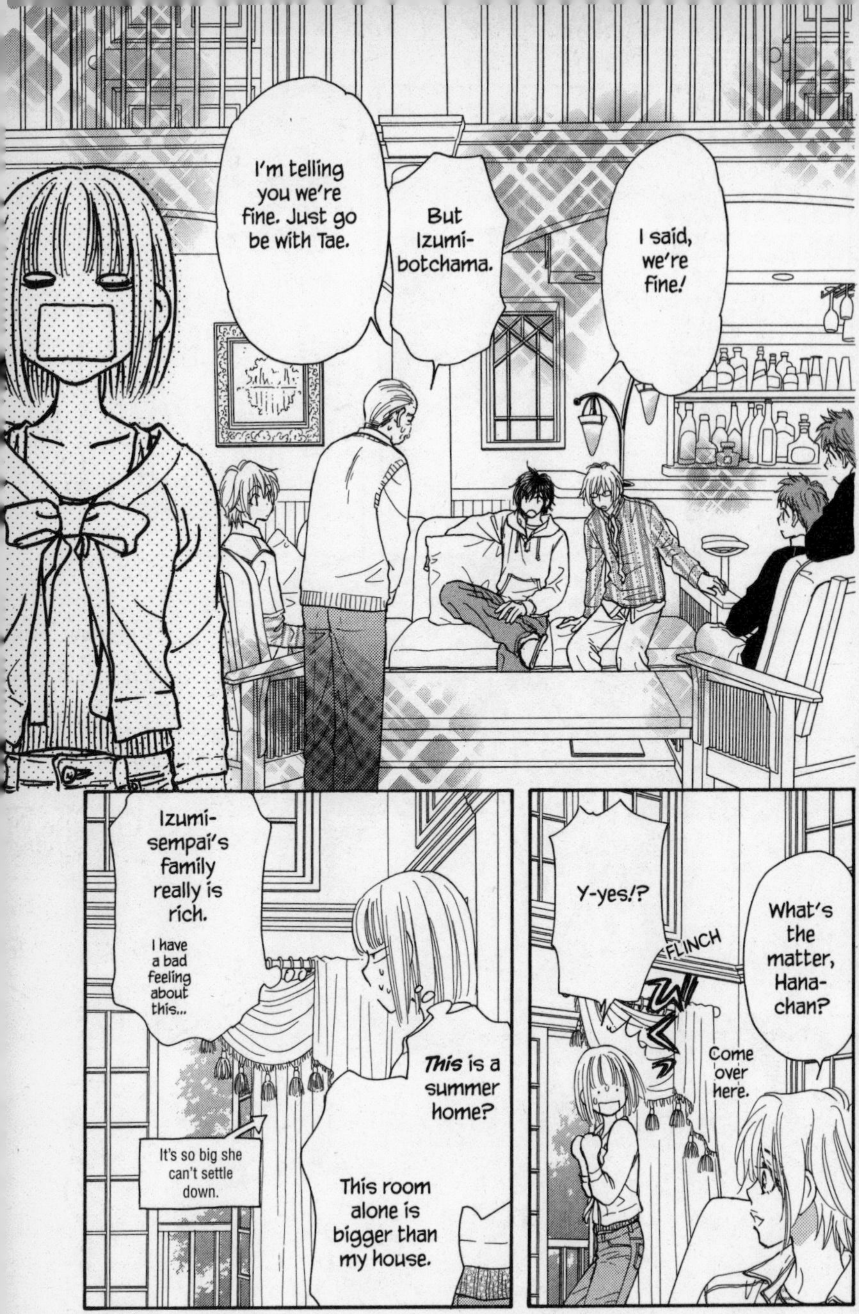
I'm telling you we're fine. Just go be with Tae.
But Izumi-botchama.
I said, we're fine!
What's the matter, Hana-chan?
Come over here.
Y-yes!?
FLINCH
Izumi-sempai's family really is rich.
I have a bad feeling about this...
This is a summer home?
This room alone is bigger than my house.
It's so big she can't settle down.

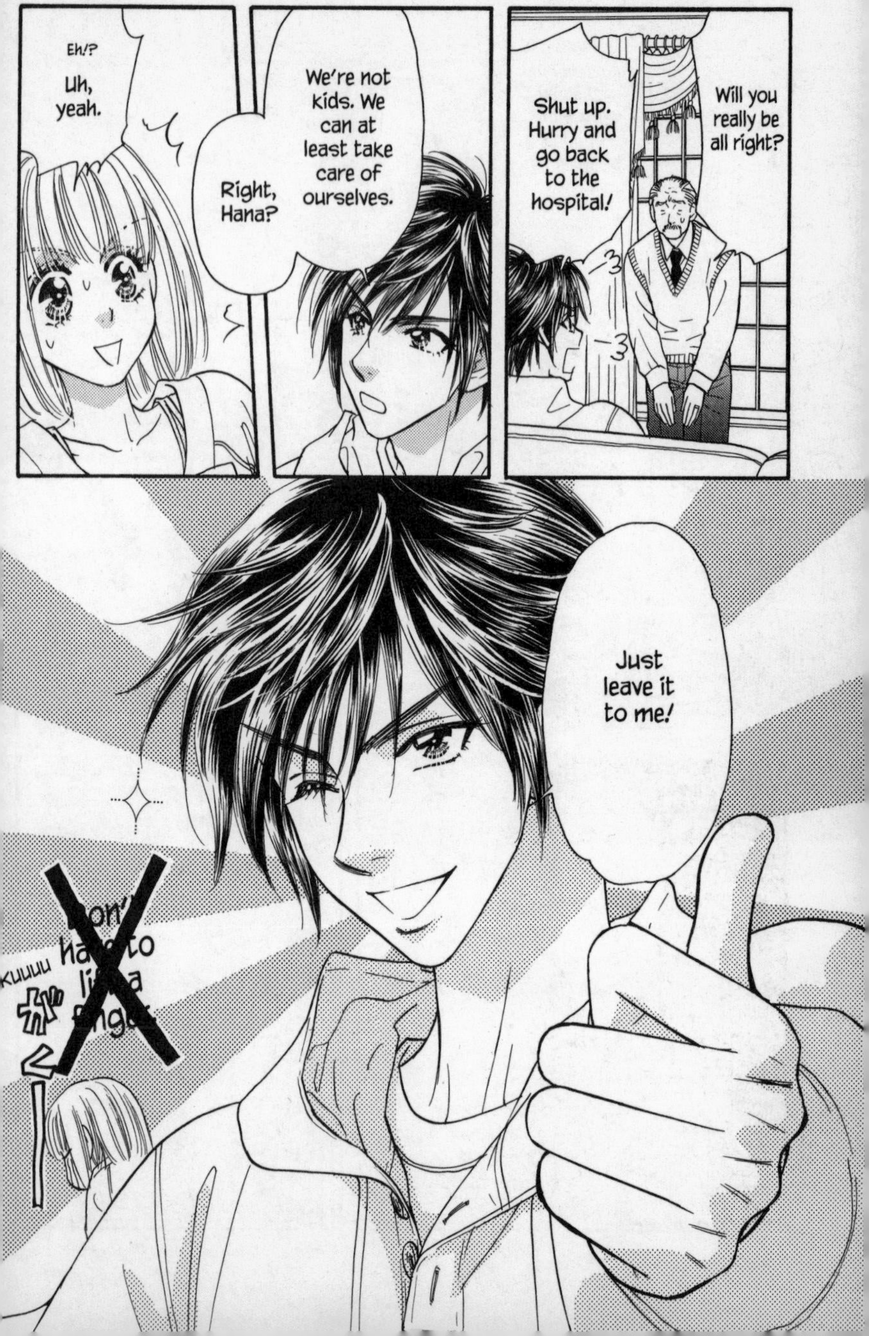

Will you really be all right?
Shut up. Hurry and go back to the hospital!
We're not kids. We can at least take care of ourselves.
Right, Hana?
Eh!?
Uh, yeah.
Just leave it to me!
Kuuuu

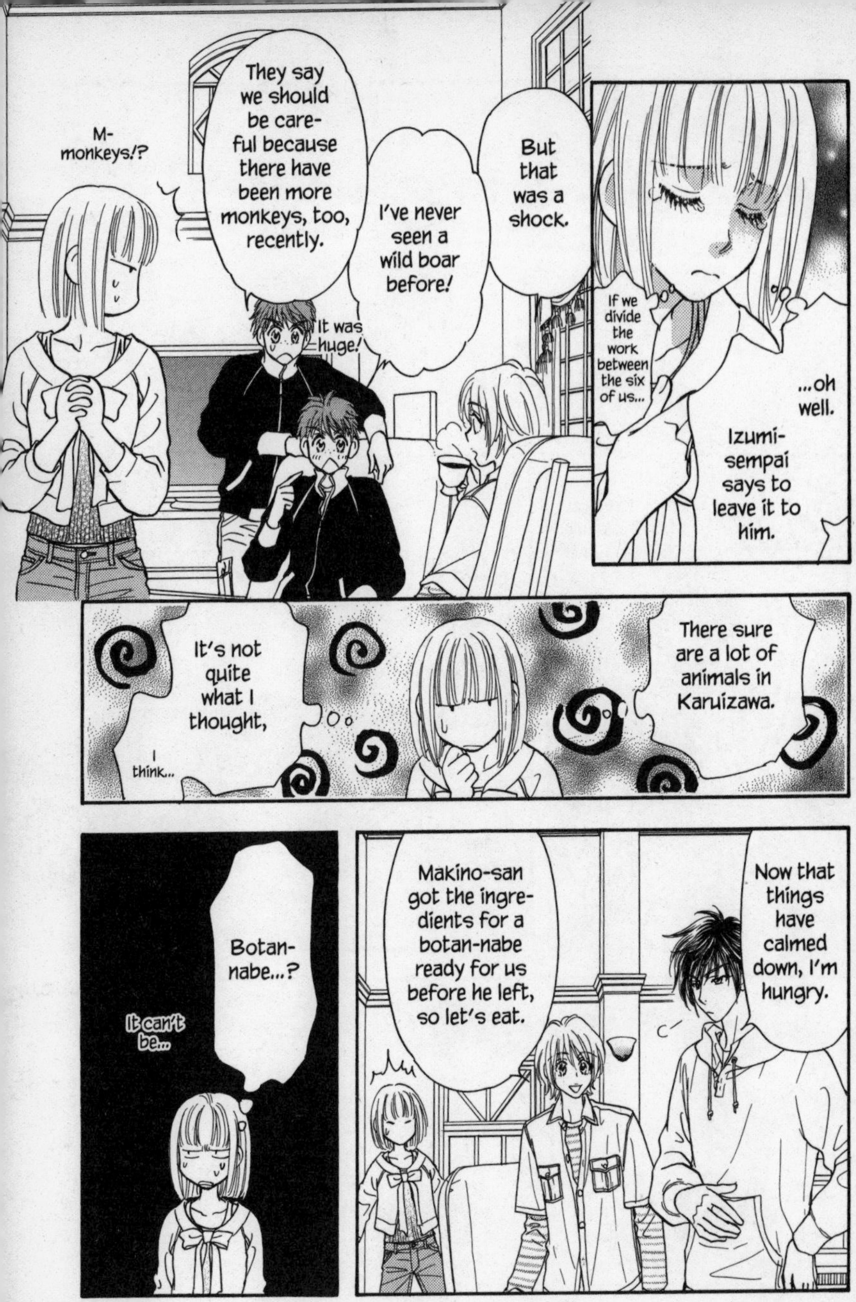
If we divide the work between the six of us...
...oh well.
Izumi-sempai says to leave it to him.
But that was a shock.
I've never seen a wild boar before!
It was huge!
They say we should be care-ful because there have been more monkeys, too, recently.
M-monkeys!?
There sure are a lot of animals in Karuizawa.
It's not quite what I thought,
I think...
Now that things have calmed down, I'm hungry.
Makino-san got the ingre-dients for a botan-nabe ready for us before he left, so let's eat.
Botan-nabe...?
It can't be...

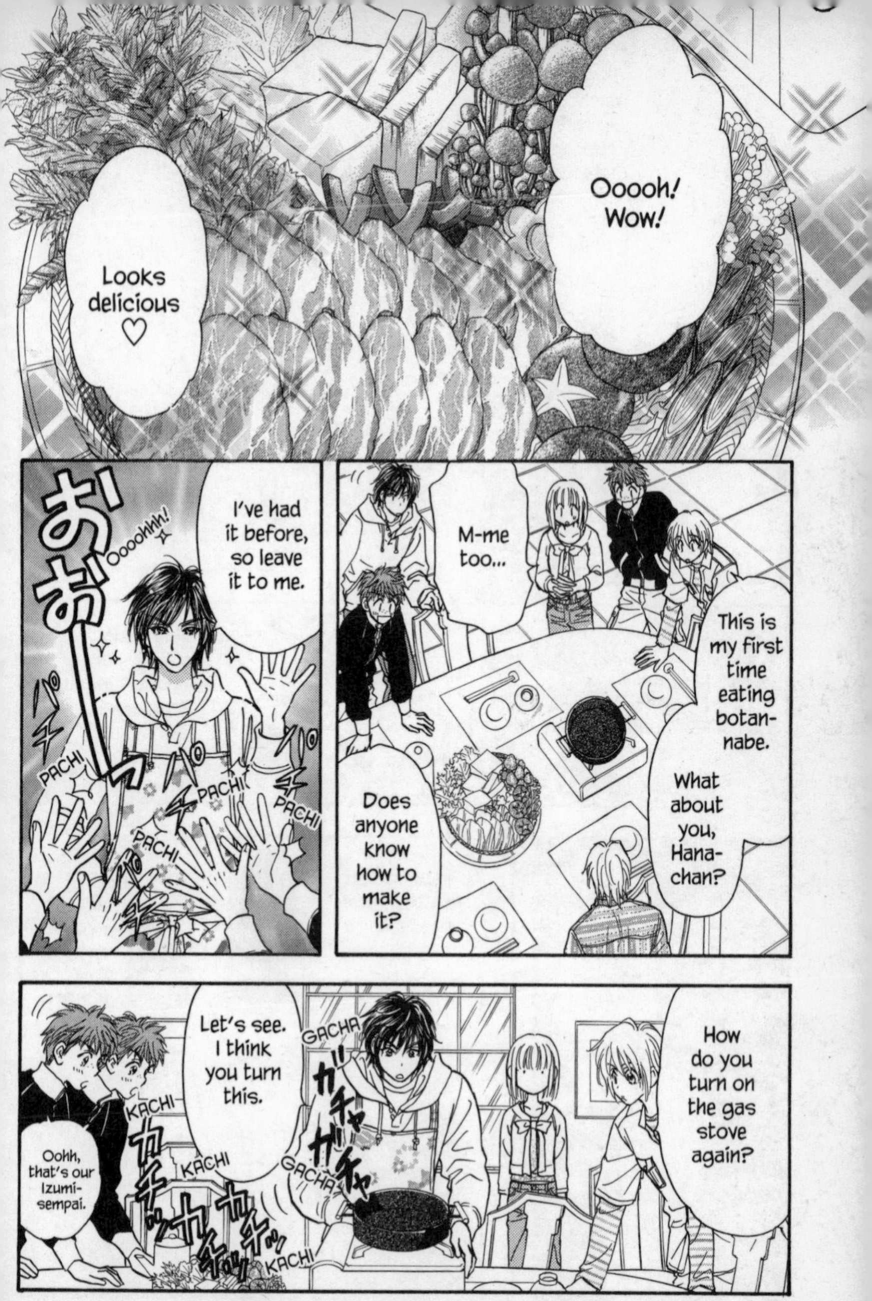
Ooooh! Wow!
Looks delicious ♡
This is my first time eating botan-nabe.
M-me too...
What about you, Hana-chan?
Does anyone know how to make it?
I've had it before, so leave it to me.
おおーっ
Oooohh!
パ パ パ パ
PACHI PACHI PACHI PACHI
How do you turn on the gas stove again?
ガチャ ガチャ
GACHA GACHA
Let's see. I think you turn this.
カチッ カチッ カチッ カチッ
KACHI KACHI KACHI
Oohh, that's our Izumi-sempai.

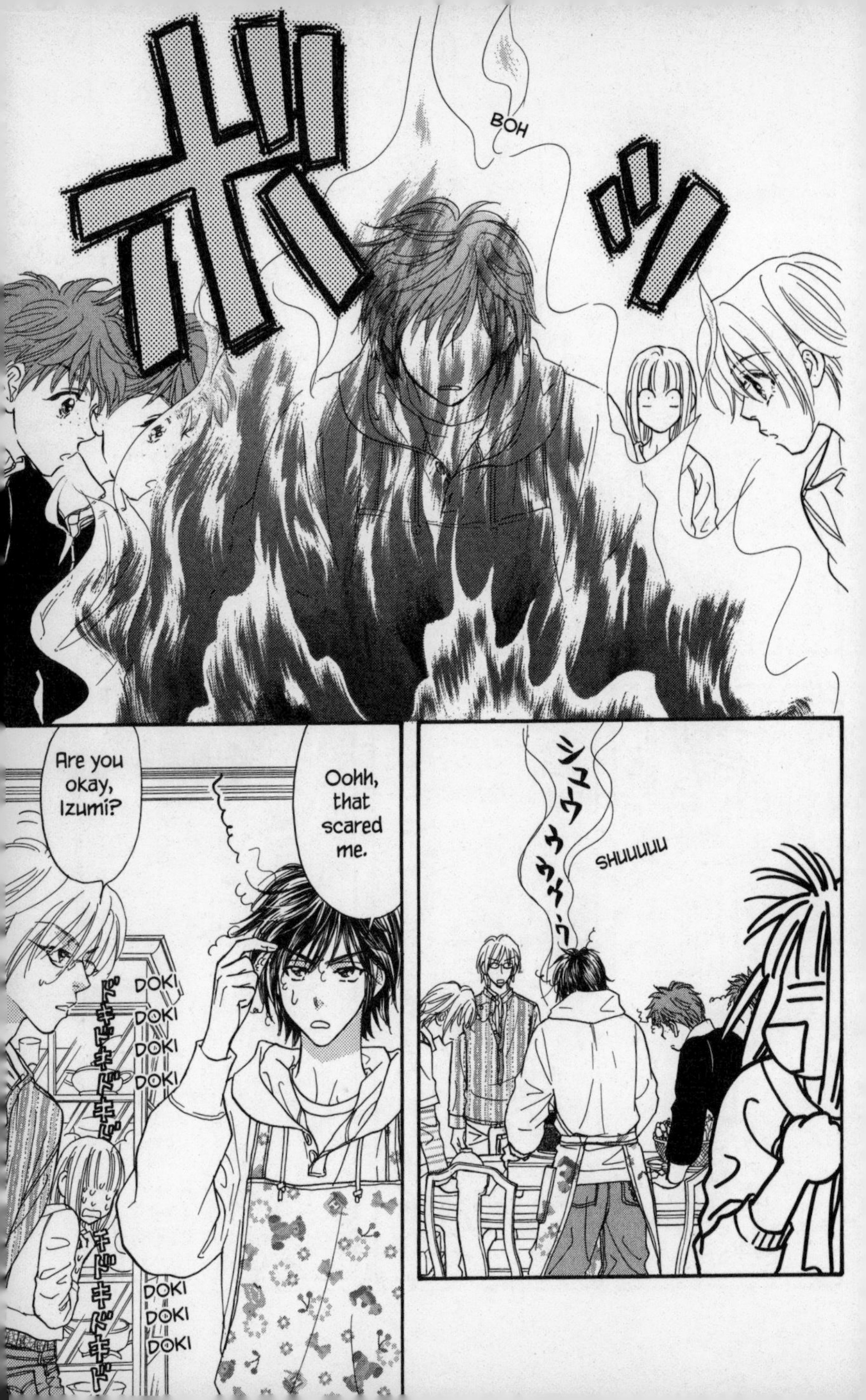
ボッ
BOH
SHUUUUU
Oohh, that scared me.
Are you okay, Izumi?
DOKI DOKI DOKI DOKI
DOKI DOKI DOKI

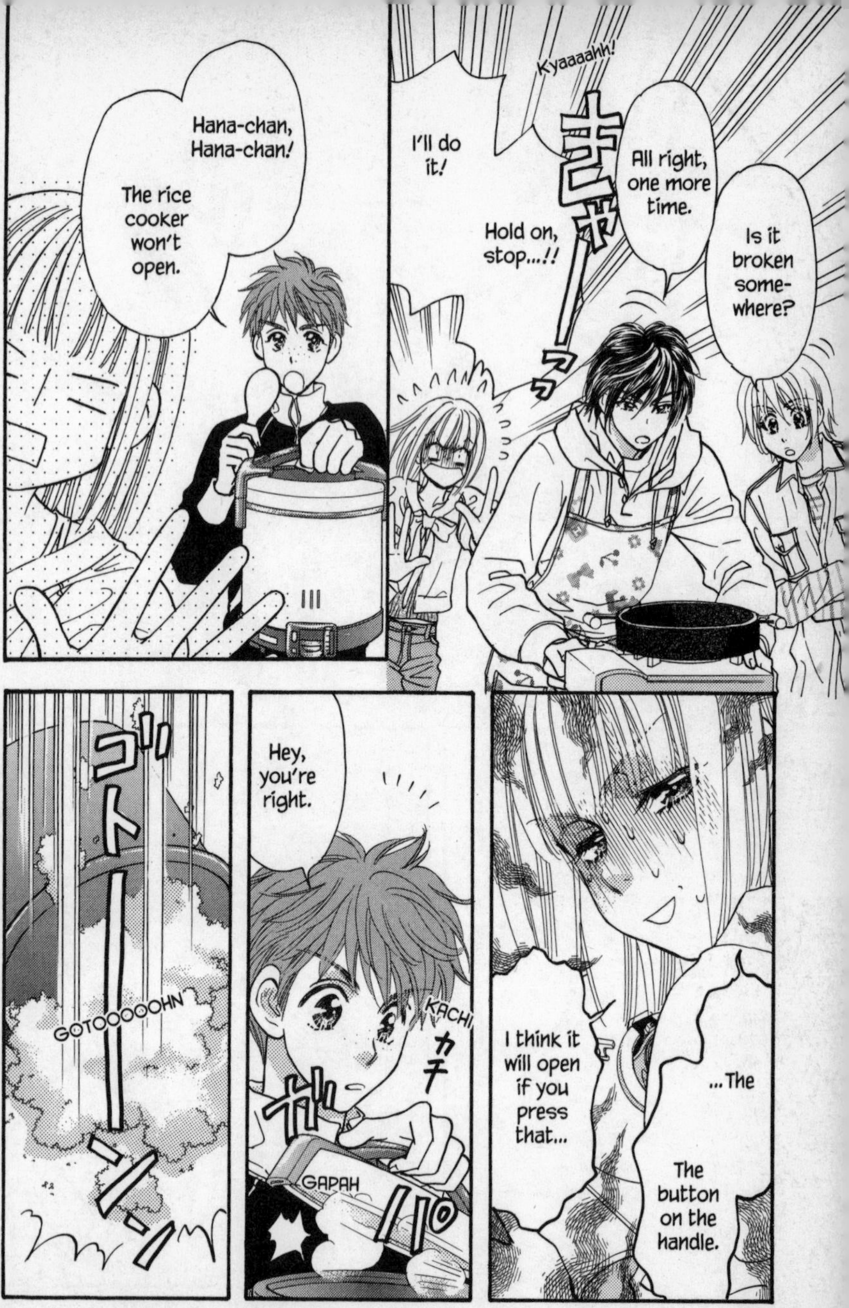
Is it broken somewhere?
All right, one more time.
Kyaaaahh!
Hold on, stop...!!
I'll do it!
Hana-chan, Hana-chan!
The rice cooker won't open.
...The
The button on the handle.
I think it will open if you press that...
Hey, you're right.
KACHI
GAPAH
GOTOOOOOHN

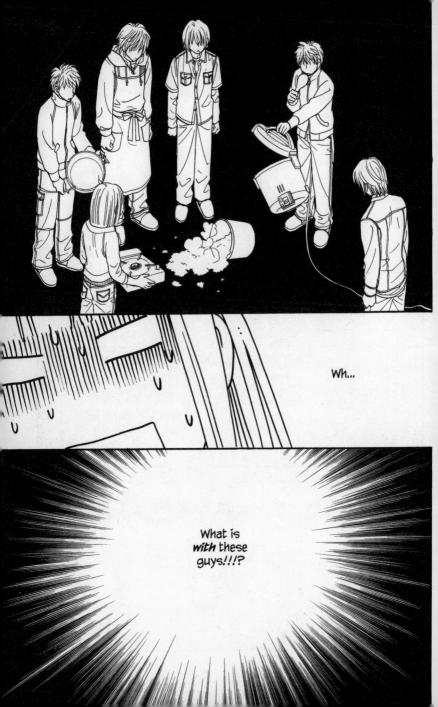

Wh...

What is *with* these guys!!!?

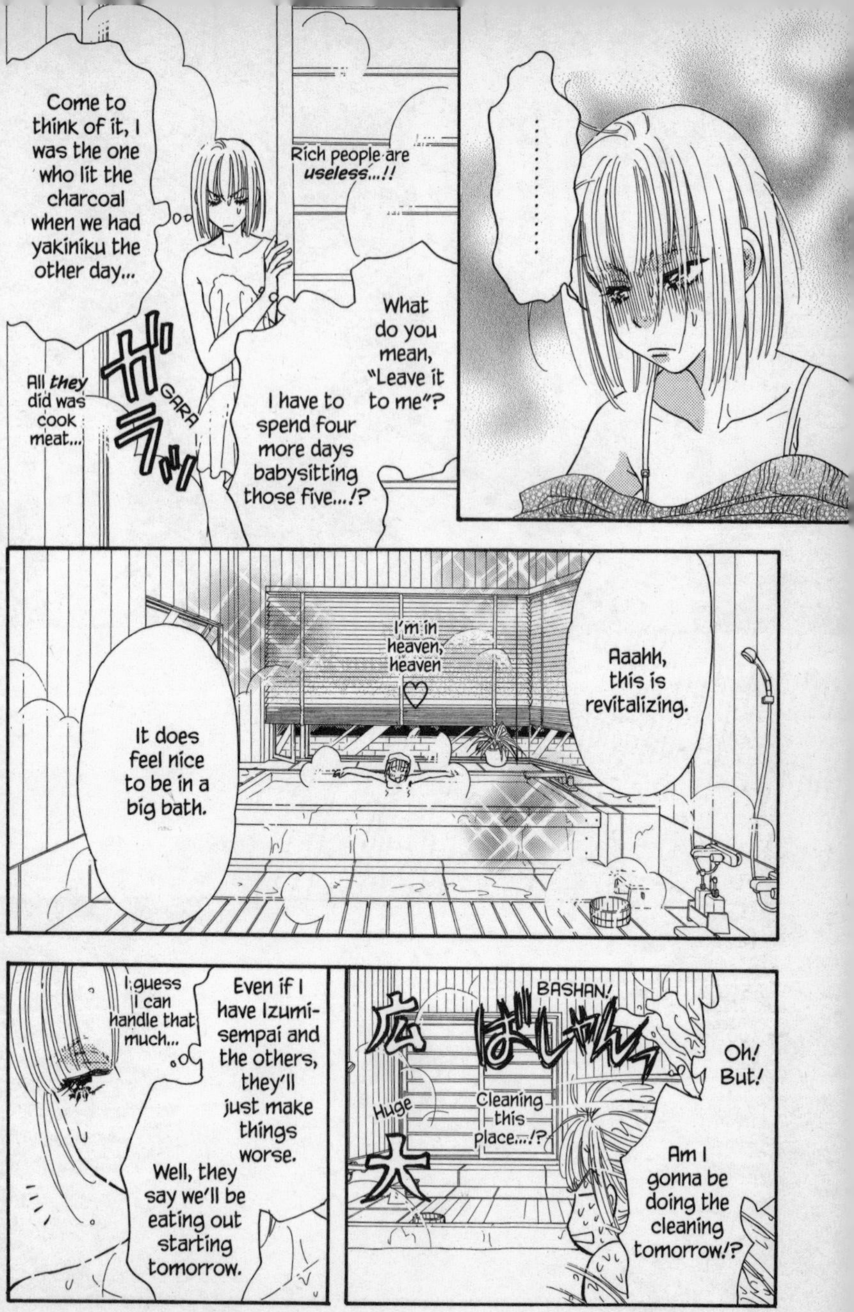

......
Rich people are *useless*...!!
What do you mean, "Leave it to me"?
I have to spend four more days babysitting those five...!?
Come to think of it, I was the one who lit the charcoal when we had yakiniku the other day...
GARA
All *they* did was cook meat...
Aaahh, this is revitalizing.
I'm in heaven, heaven ♡
It does feel nice to be in a big bath.
Oh! But!
BASHAN!
Cleaning this place...!?
Huge
Am I gonna be doing the cleaning tomorrow!?
Even if I have Izumi-sempai and the others, they'll just make things worse.
I guess I can handle that much...
Well, they say we'll be eating out starting tomorrow.

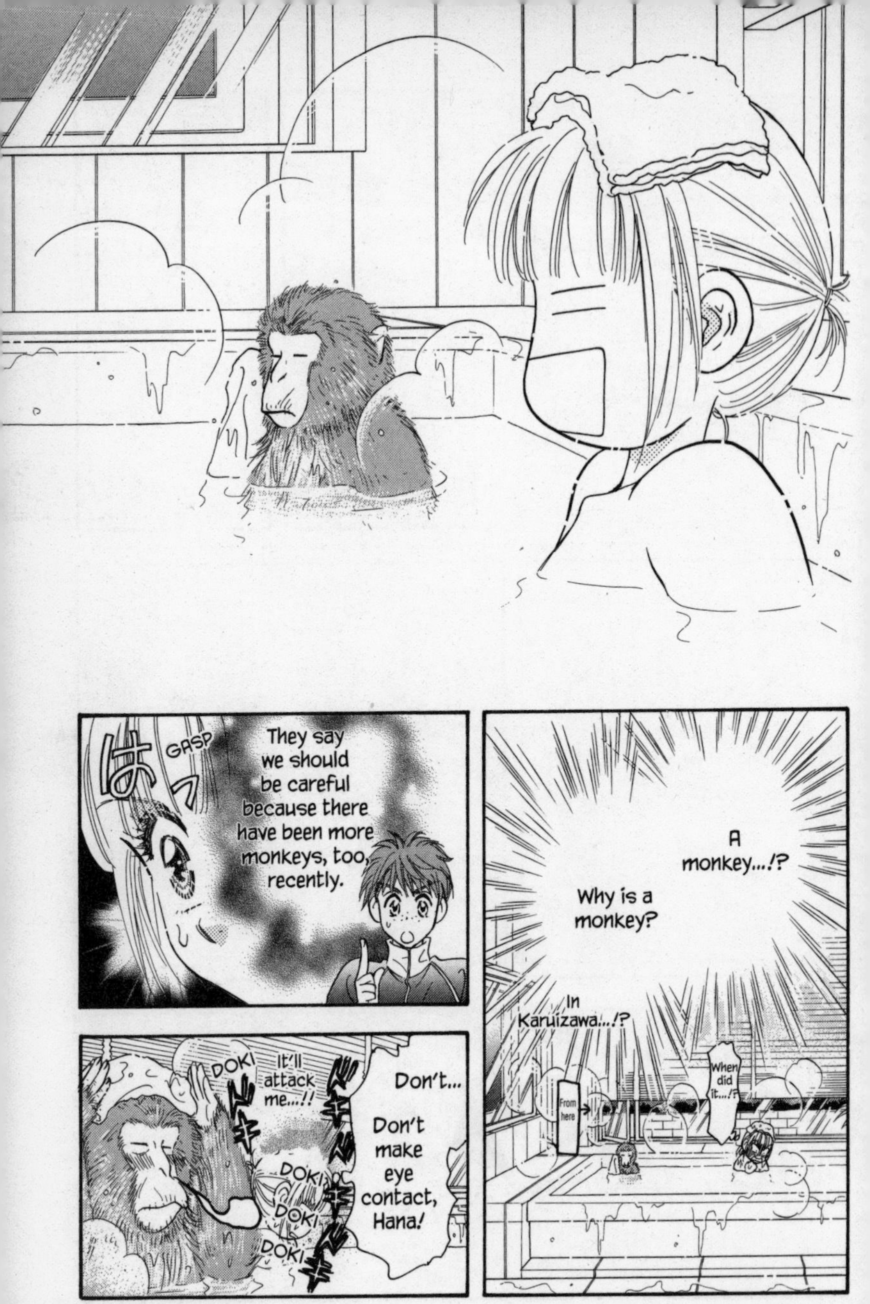
A monkey...!?
Why is a monkey?
In Karuizawa...!?
When did it...!?
From here
はっ
GASP
They say we should be careful because there have been more monkeys, too, recently.
Don't...
Don't make eye contact, Hana!
It'll attack me...!!
DOKI
DOKI
DOKI
DOKI

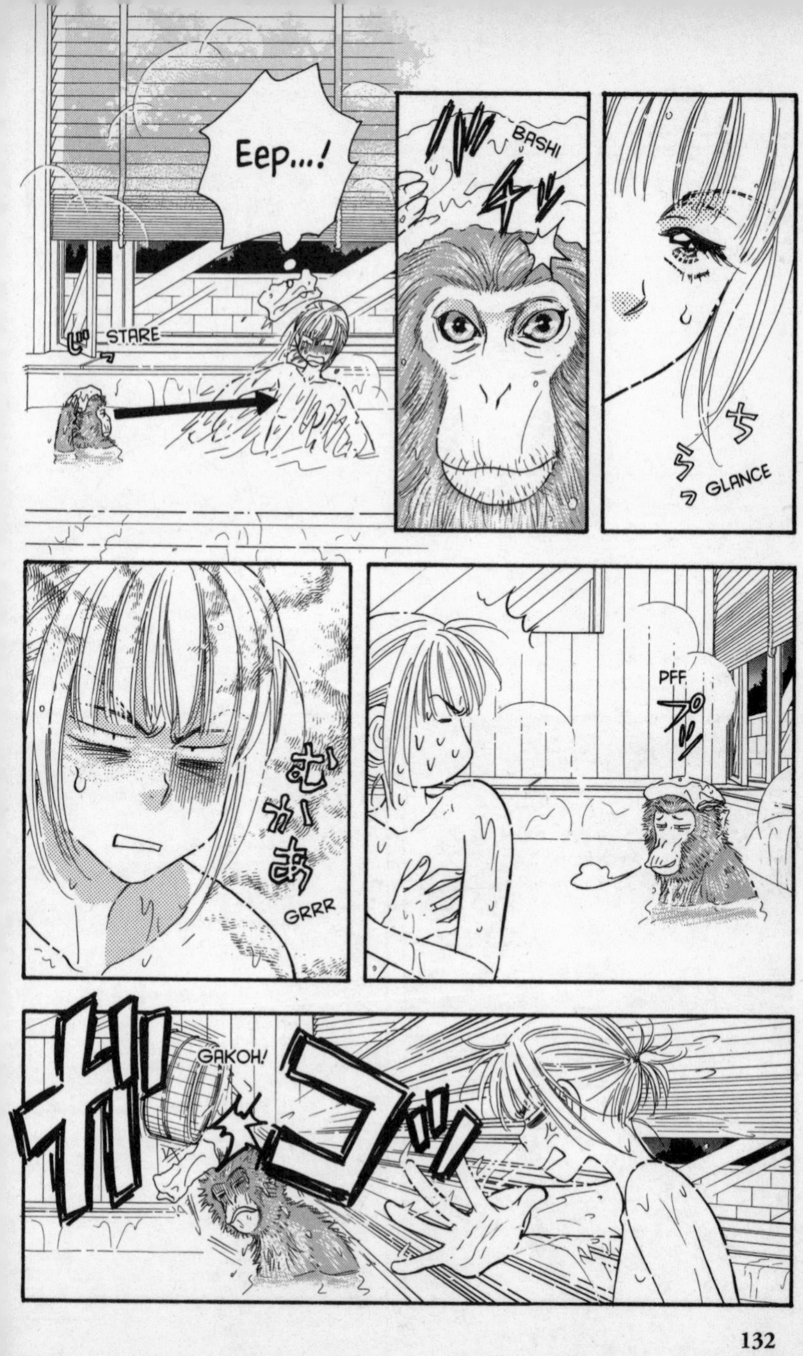
GLANCE
BASHI
Eep...!
STARE
PFF
GRRR
GAKOH!

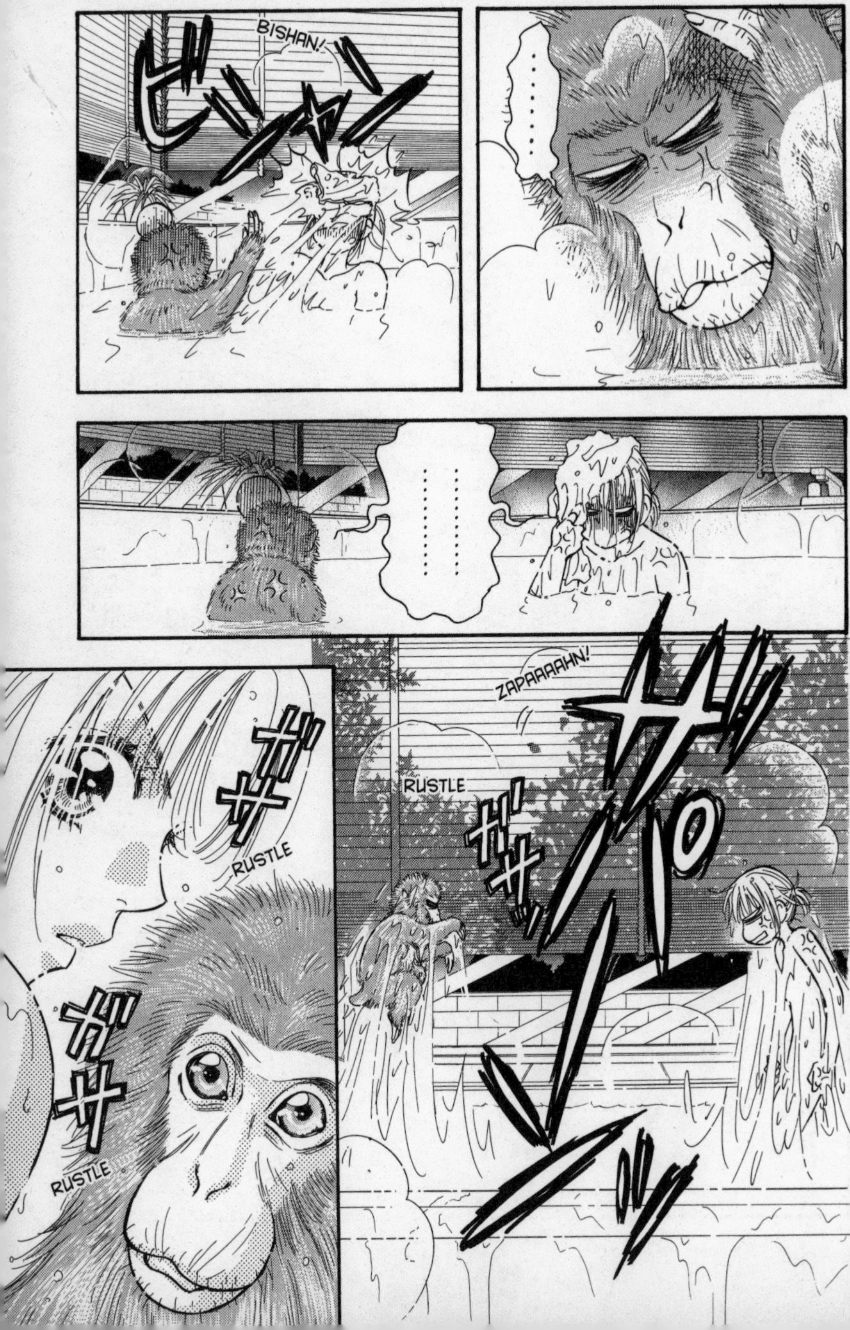
......
BISHAN!
....
ZAPAAAAAHN!
RUSTLE
RUSTLE
RUSTLE

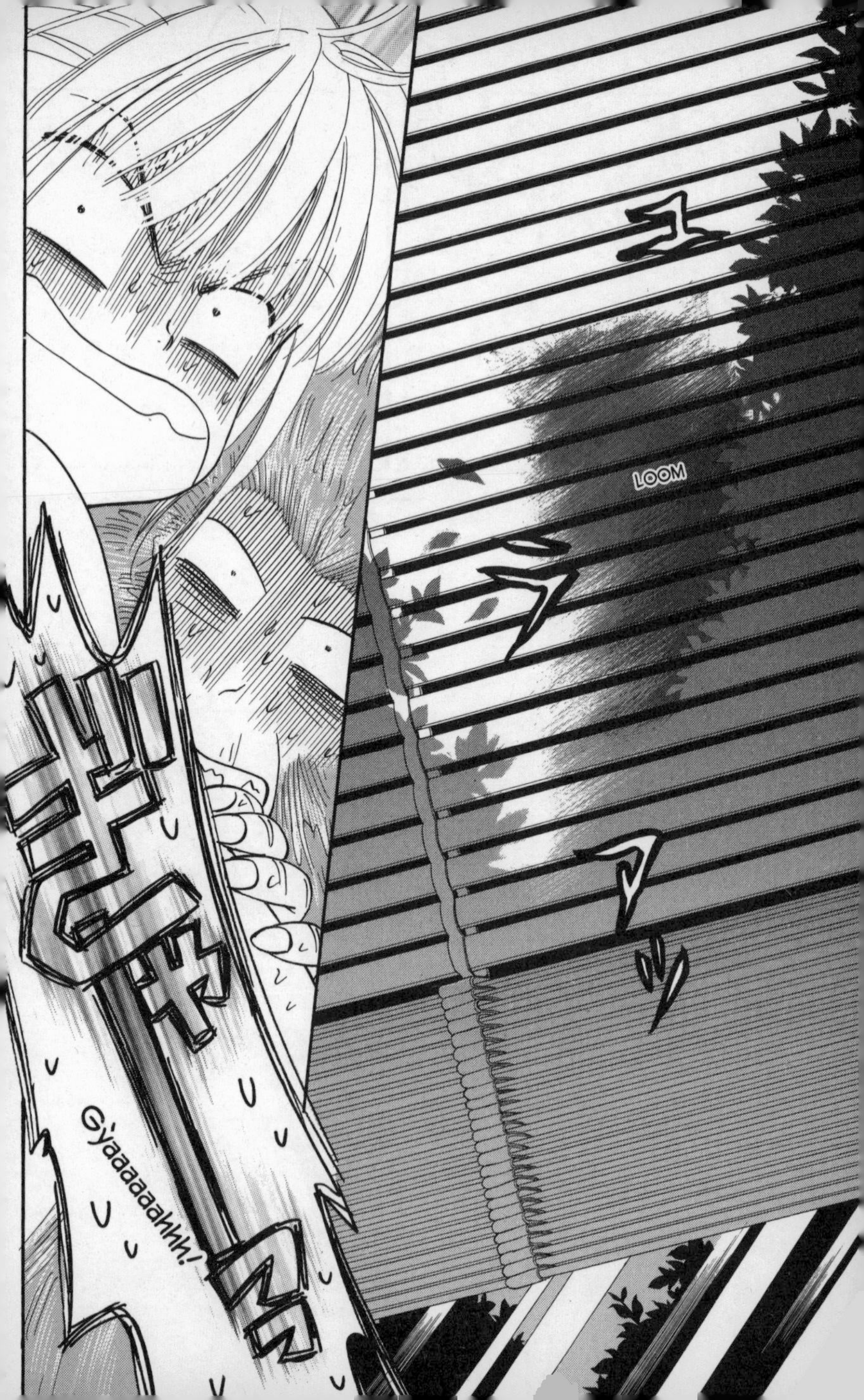
LOOM
Gyaaaaaaahhh!

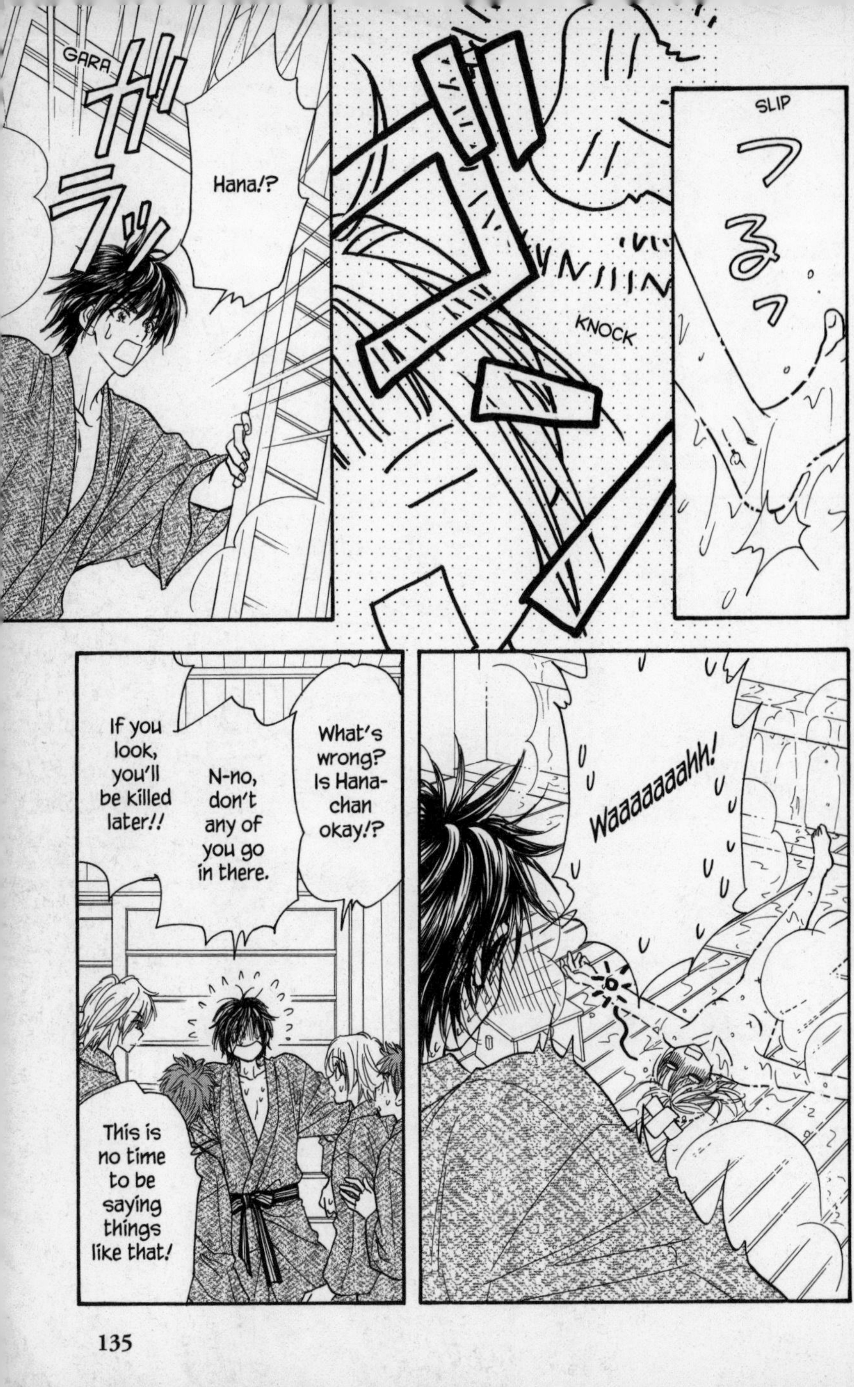
SLIP
つるっ
KNOCK
GARA
ガラッ
Hana!?
Waaaaaaahh!
What's wrong? Is Hana-chan okay!?
N-no, don't any of you go in there.
If you look, you'll be killed later!!
This is no time to be saying things like that!

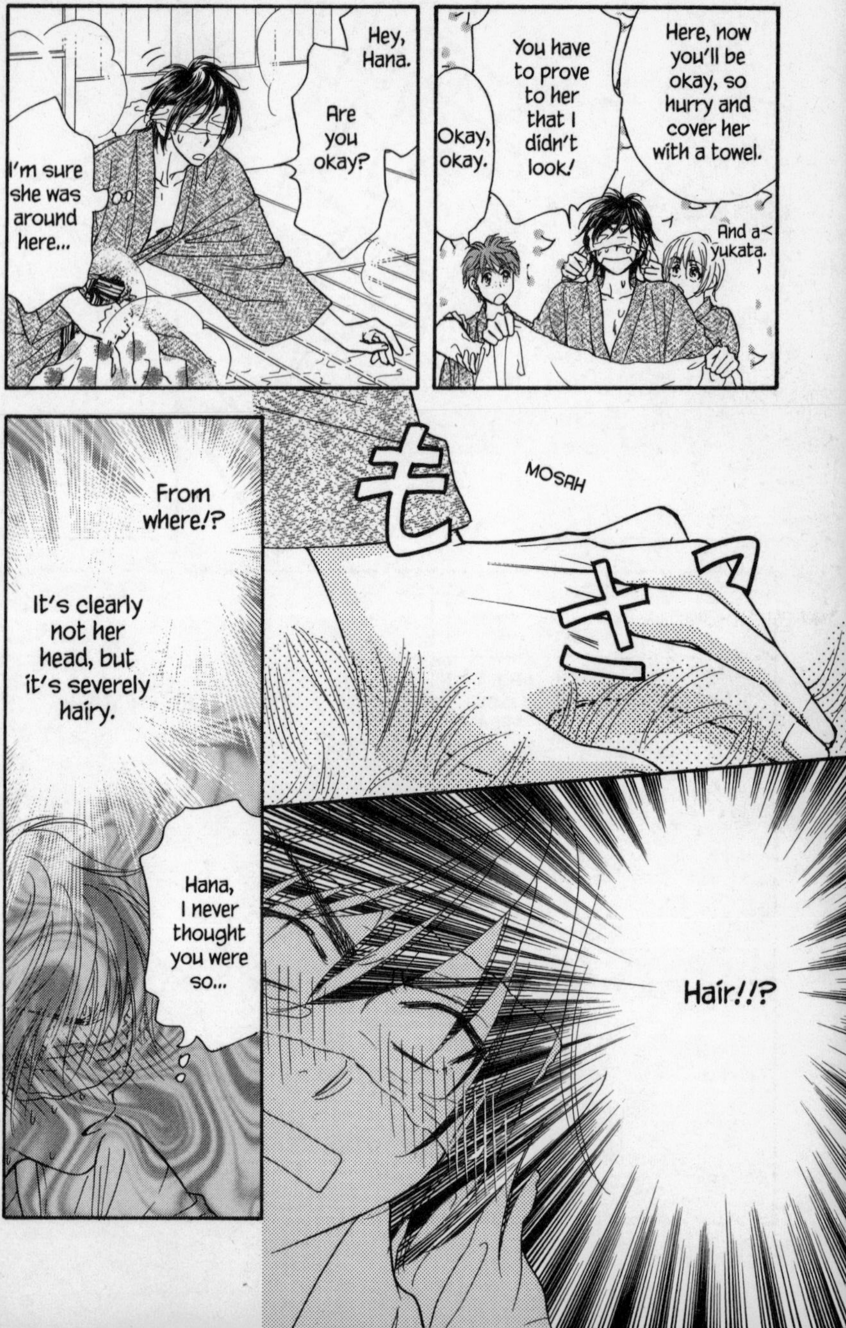
Here, now you'll be okay, so hurry and cover her with a towel.
You have to prove to her that I didn't look!
Okay, okay.
And a yukata.
Hey, Hana.
Are you okay?
I'm sure she was around here...
もさ
MOSAH
Hair!!?
From where!?
It's clearly not her head, but it's severely hairy.
Hana, I never thought you were so...

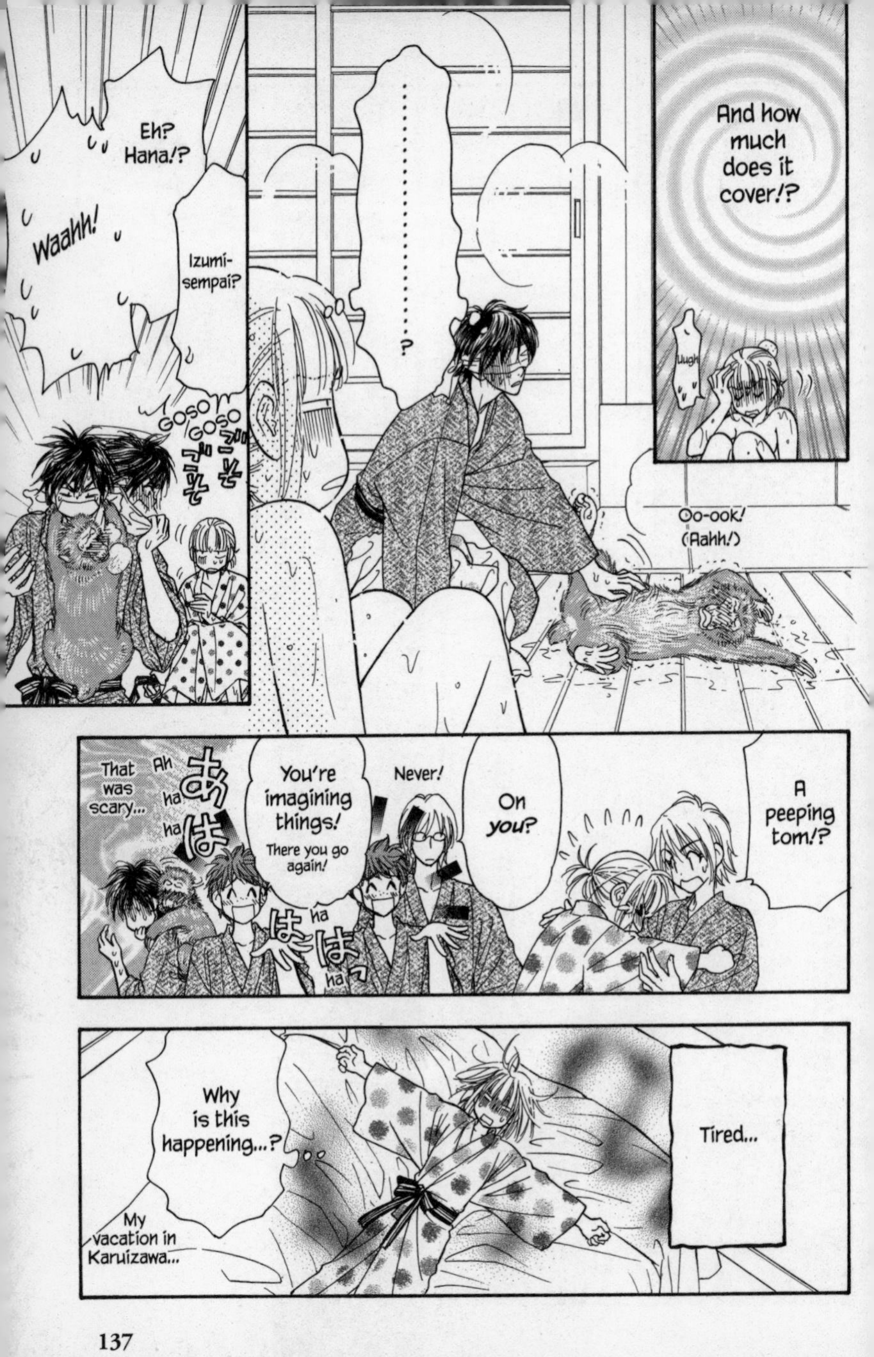

And how much does it cover!?
Uugh
......?
Oo-ook! (Aahh!)
Eh? Hana!?
Waahh!
Izumi-sempai?
GOSO GOSO
ごそごそ
A peeping tom!?
On *you*?
Never!
You're imagining things!
There you go again!
ha ha
はは
Ah ha ha
あは
That was scary...
Tired...
Why is this happening...?
My vacation in Karuizawa...

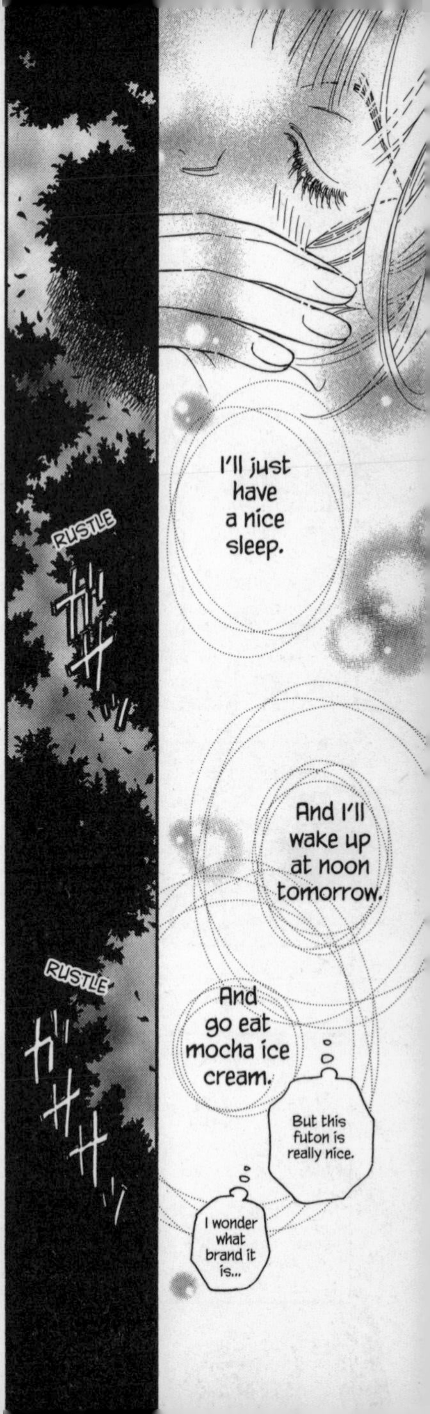
I'll just have a nice sleep.
And I'll wake up at noon tomorrow.
And go eat mocha ice cream.
But this futon is really nice.
I wonder what brand it is...
RUSTLE
RUSTLE

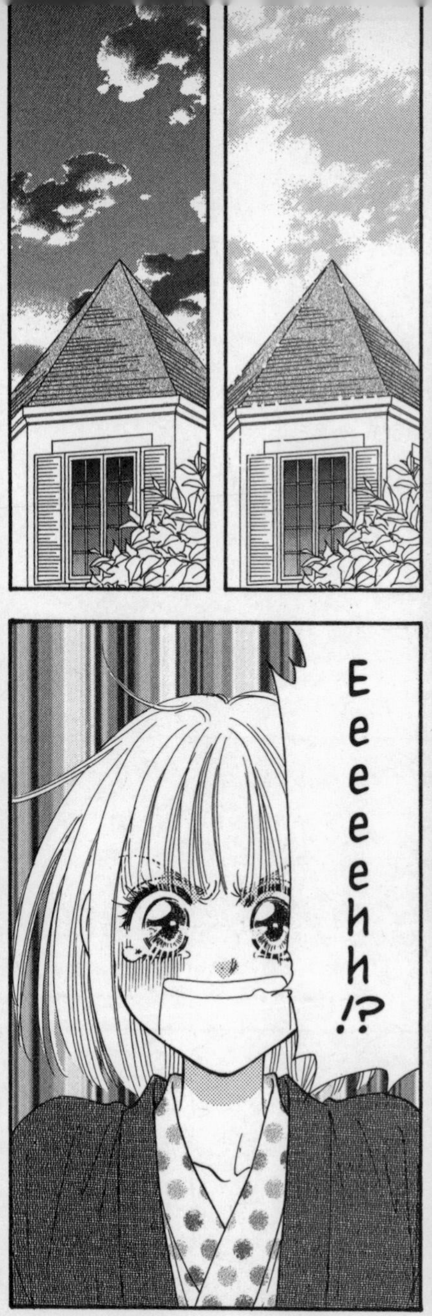
Eeeeehh!?

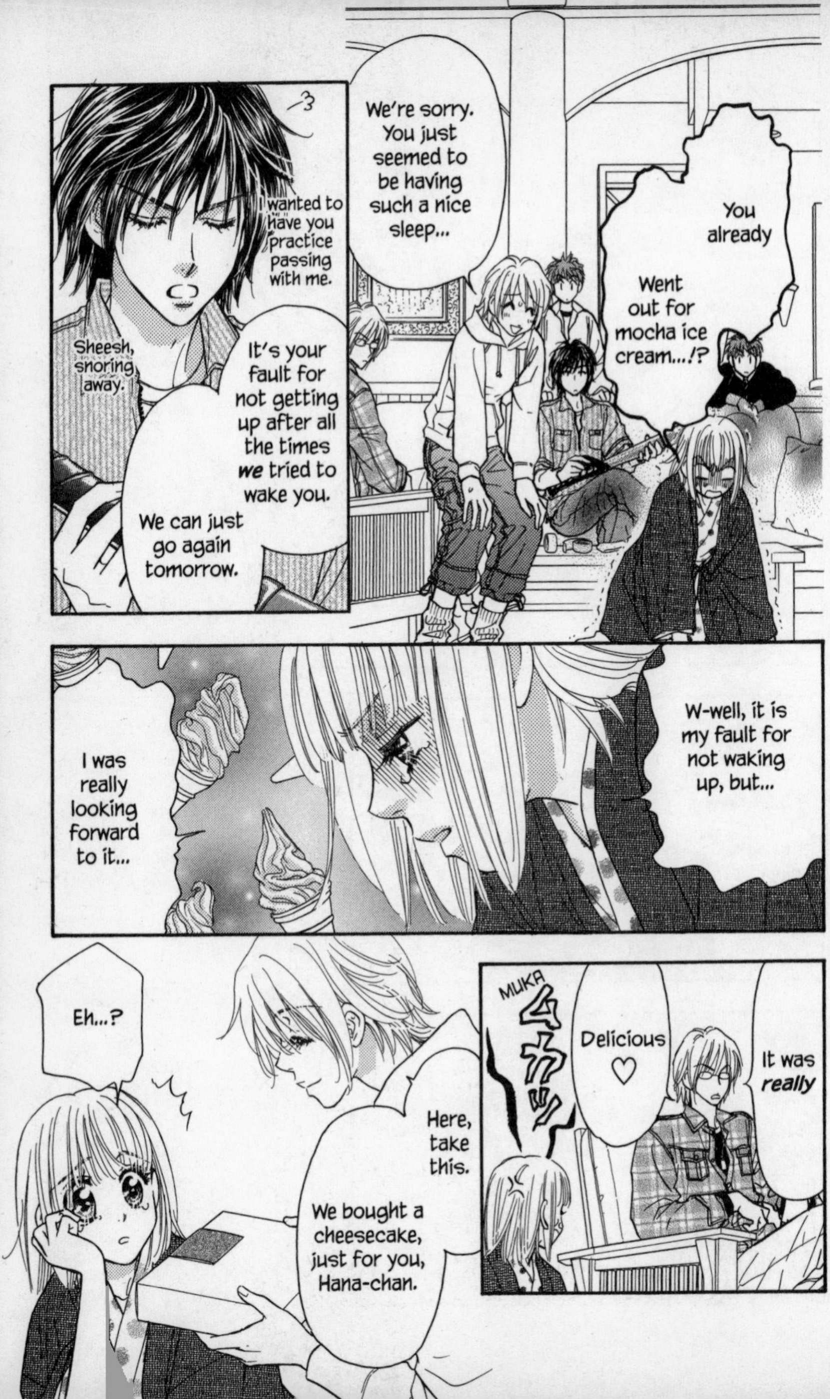
You already
Went out for mocha ice cream...!?
We're sorry. You just seemed to be having such a nice sleep...
I wanted to have you practice passing with me.
Sheesh, snoring away.
It's your fault for not getting up after all the times *we* tried to wake you.
We can just go again tomorrow.
W-well, it is my fault for not waking up, but...
I was really looking forward to it...
It was *really*
Delicious ♥
MUKA
ムカッ
Here, take this.
We bought a cheesecake, just for you, Hana-chan.
Eh...?

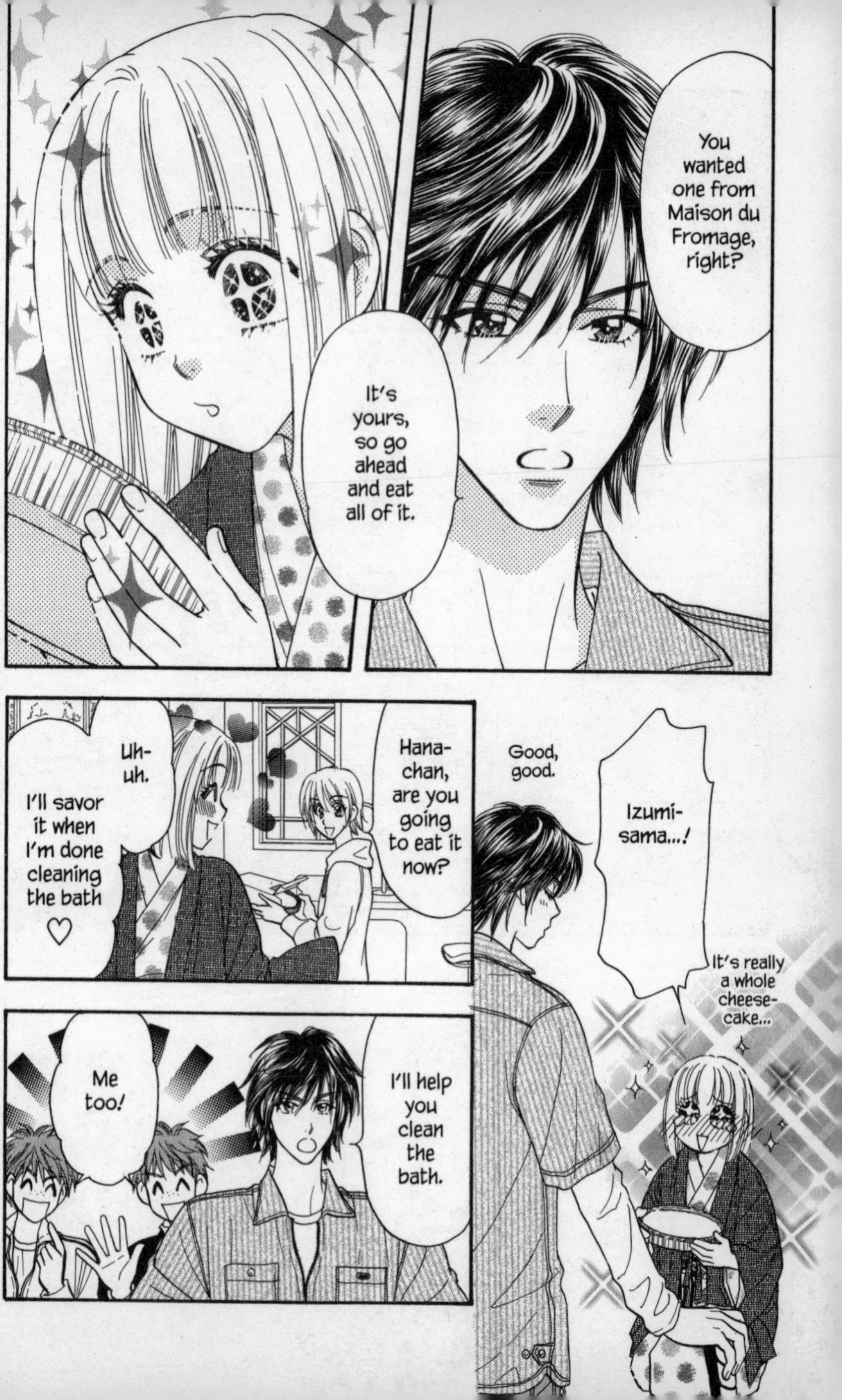
You wanted one from Maison du Fromage, right?
It's yours, so go ahead and eat all of it.
Izumi-sama...!
Good, good.
It's really a whole cheese-cake...
Hana-chan, are you going to eat it now?
Uh-uh.
I'll savor it when I'm done cleaning the bath ♡
I'll help you clean the bath.
Me too!

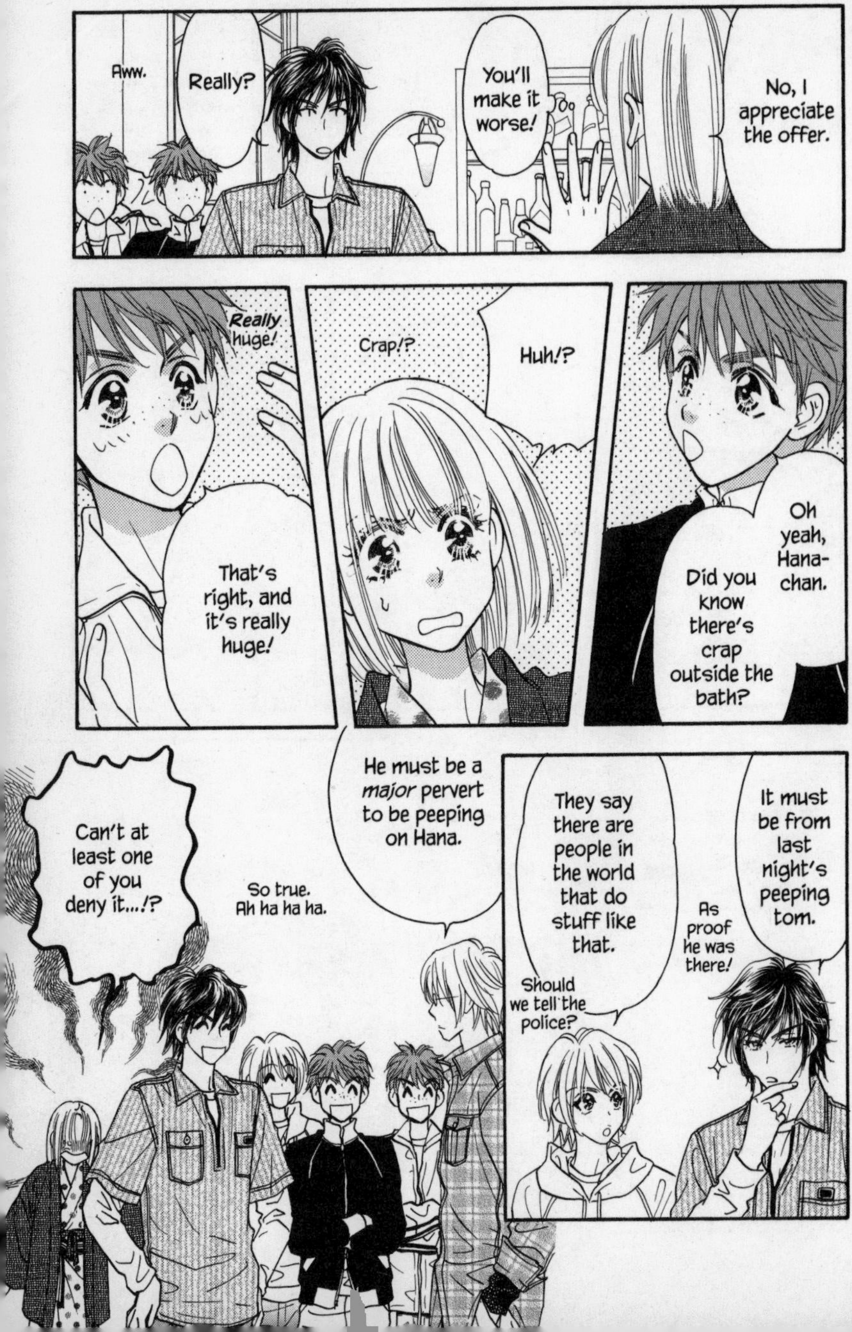
No, I appreciate the offer.
You'll make it worse!
Really?
Aww.
Oh yeah, Hana-chan.
Did you know there's crap outside the bath?
Huh!?
Crap!?
Really huge!
That's right, and it's really huge!
It must be from last night's peeping tom.
They say there are people in the world that do stuff like that.
As proof he was there!
Should we tell the police?
He must be a *major* pervert to be peeping on Hana.
So true. Ah ha ha ha.
Can't at least one of you deny it...!?

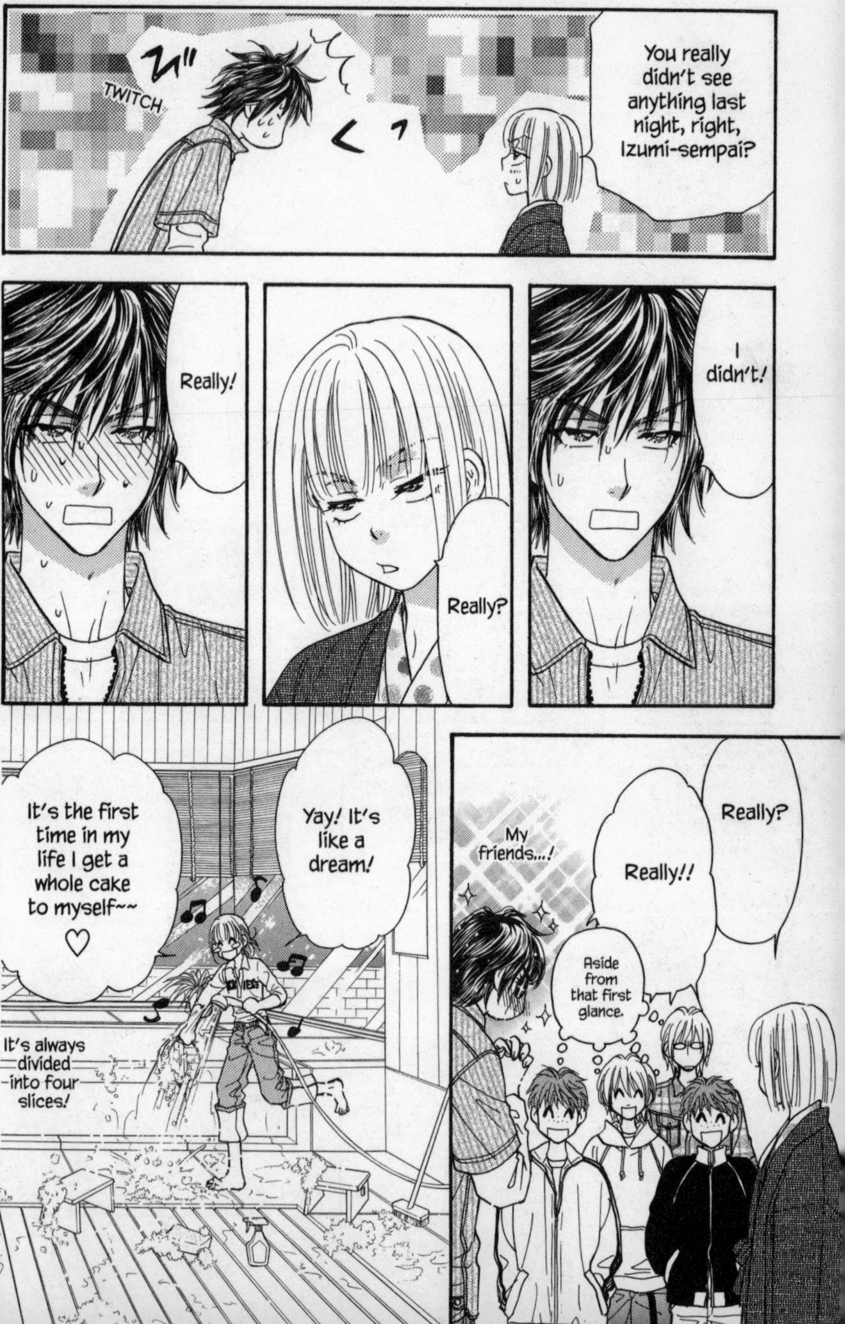
You really didn't see anything last night, right, Izumi-sempai?
TWITCH
I didn't!
Really?
Really!
Really?
Really!!
Aside from that first glance.
My friends...!
Yay! It's like a dream!
It's the first time in my life I get a whole cake to myself~~ ♡
It's always divided into four slices!

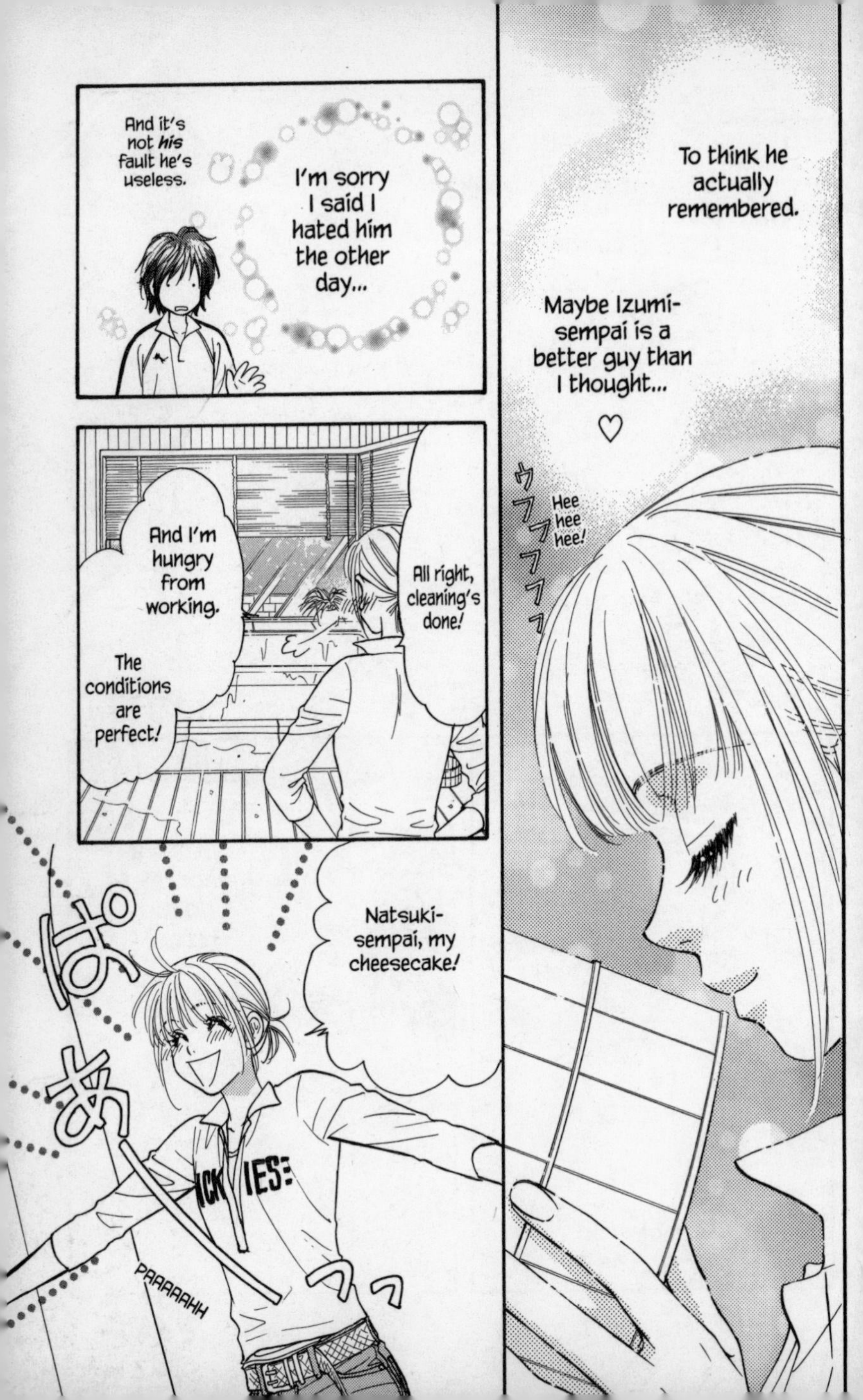
To think he actually remembered.
Maybe Izumi-sempai is a better guy than I thought... ♡
ウフフフフ
Hee hee hee!
I'm sorry I said I hated him the other day...
And it's not *his* fault he's useless.
All right, cleaning's done!
And I'm hungry from working.
The conditions are perfect!
Natsuki-sempai, my cheesecake!
ぱあ〜っ
PAAAAAHH

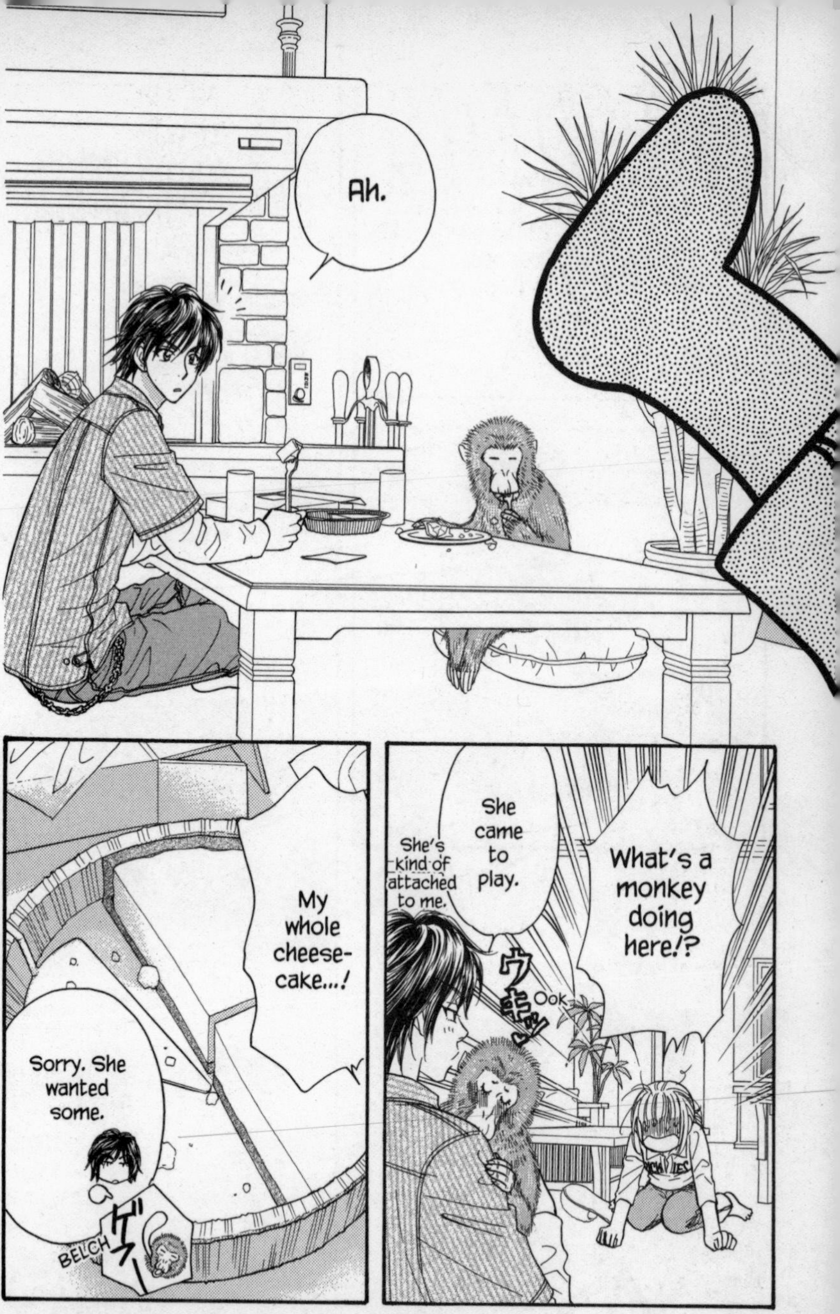
Ah.
What's a monkey doing here!?
She came to play.
She's kind of attached to me.
Ook
My whole cheese-cake...!
Sorry. She wanted some.
BELCH

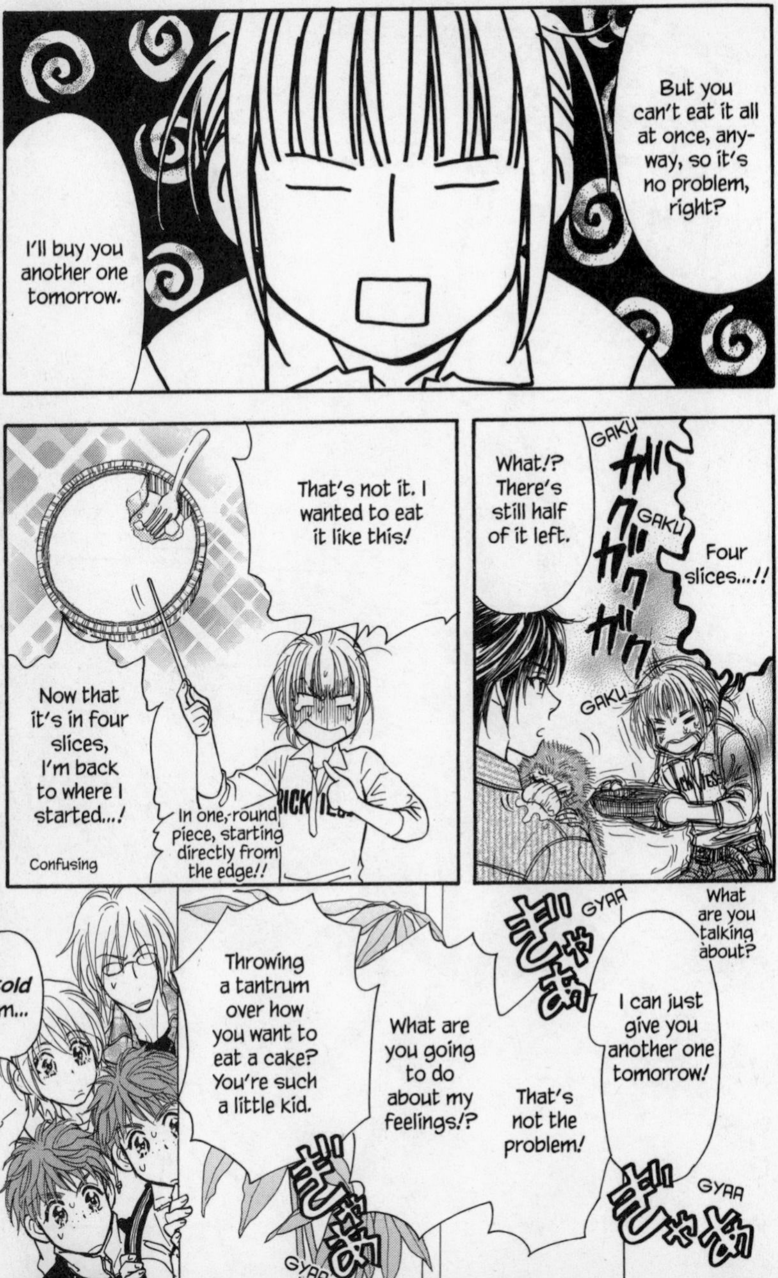
But you can't eat it all at once, any-way, so it's no problem, right?
I'll buy you another one tomorrow.
GAKU
What!? There's still half of it left.
GAKU
Four slices...!!
GAKU
That's not it. I wanted to eat it like this!
In one, round piece, starting directly from the edge!!
Now that it's in four slices, I'm back to where I started...!
Confusing
GYAA
What are you talking about?
I can just give you another one tomorrow!
GYAA
That's not the problem!
What are you going to do about my feelings!?
Throwing a tantrum over how you want to eat a cake? You're such a little kid.
GYAA
I *told* him...

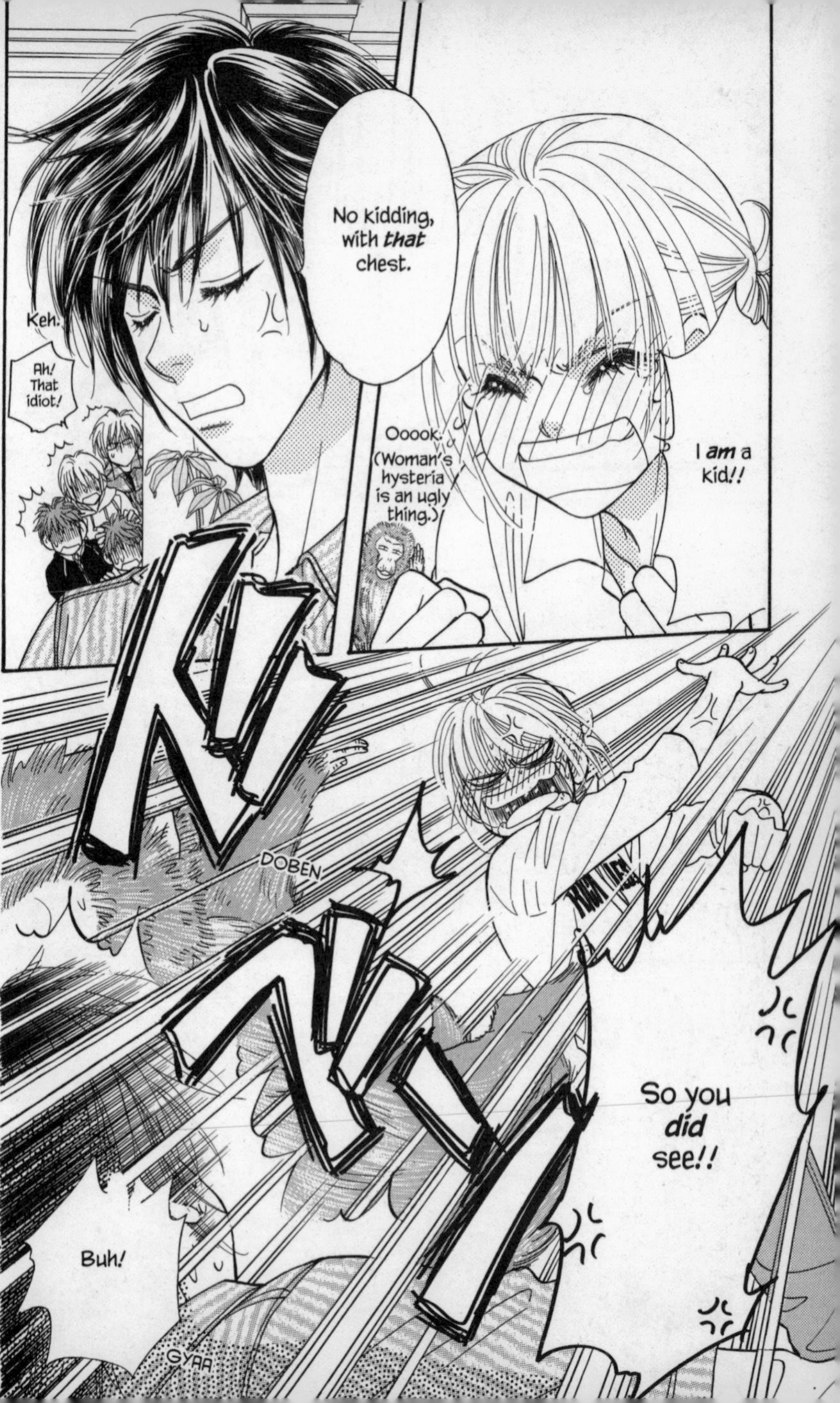
I *am* a kid!!
No kidding, with *that* chest.
Ooook. (Woman's hysteria is an ugly thing.)
Keh.
Ah! That idiot!
So you *did* see!!
DOBEN
Buh!
GYAA

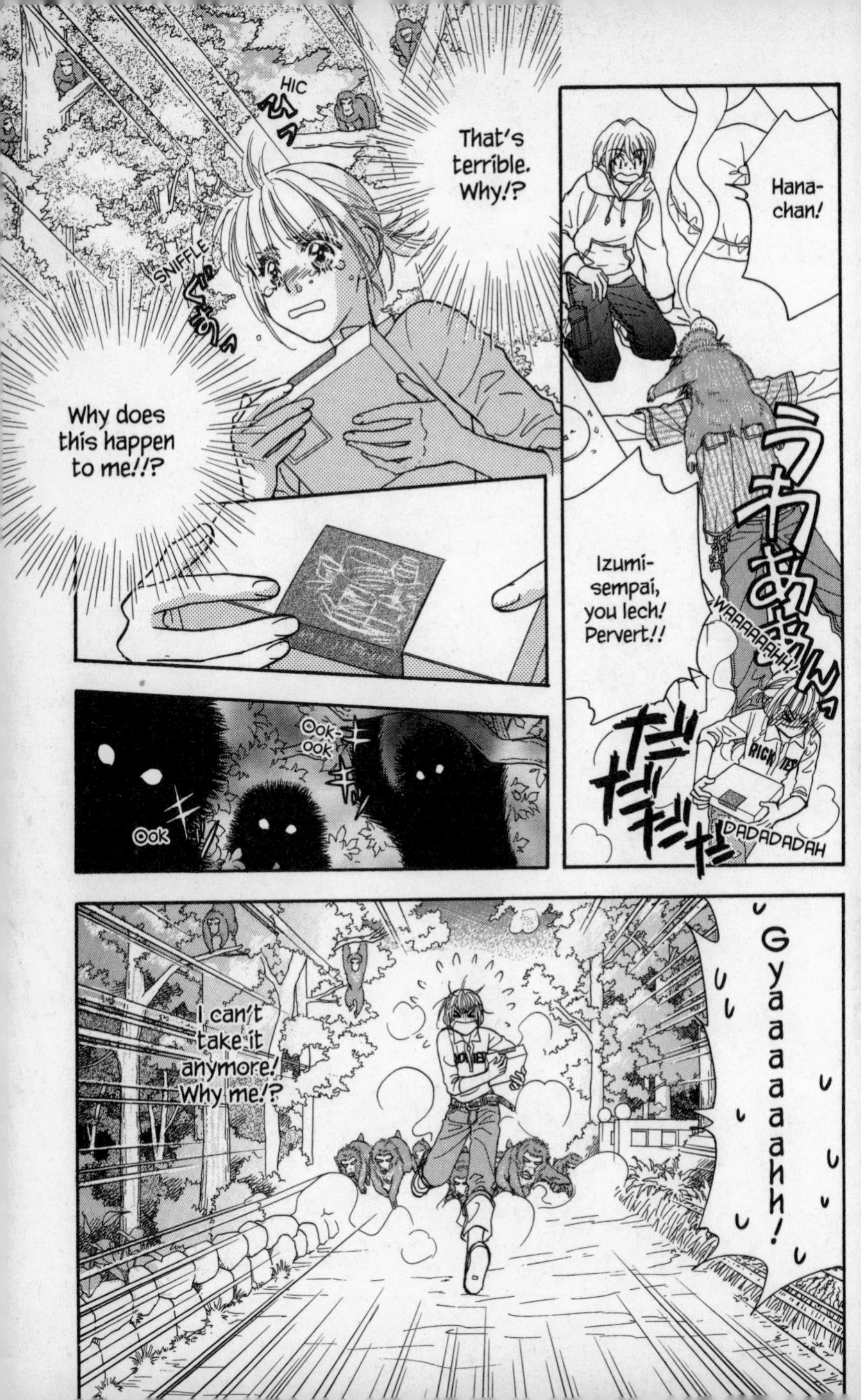
Hana-chan!
Izumi-sempai, you lech! Pervert!!
WAAAAAAHH!
DADADADAH
HIC
That's terrible. Why!?
SNIFFLE
Why does this happen to me!!?
Ook-ook
Ook
Gyaaaaaahh!
I can't take it anymore! Why me!?

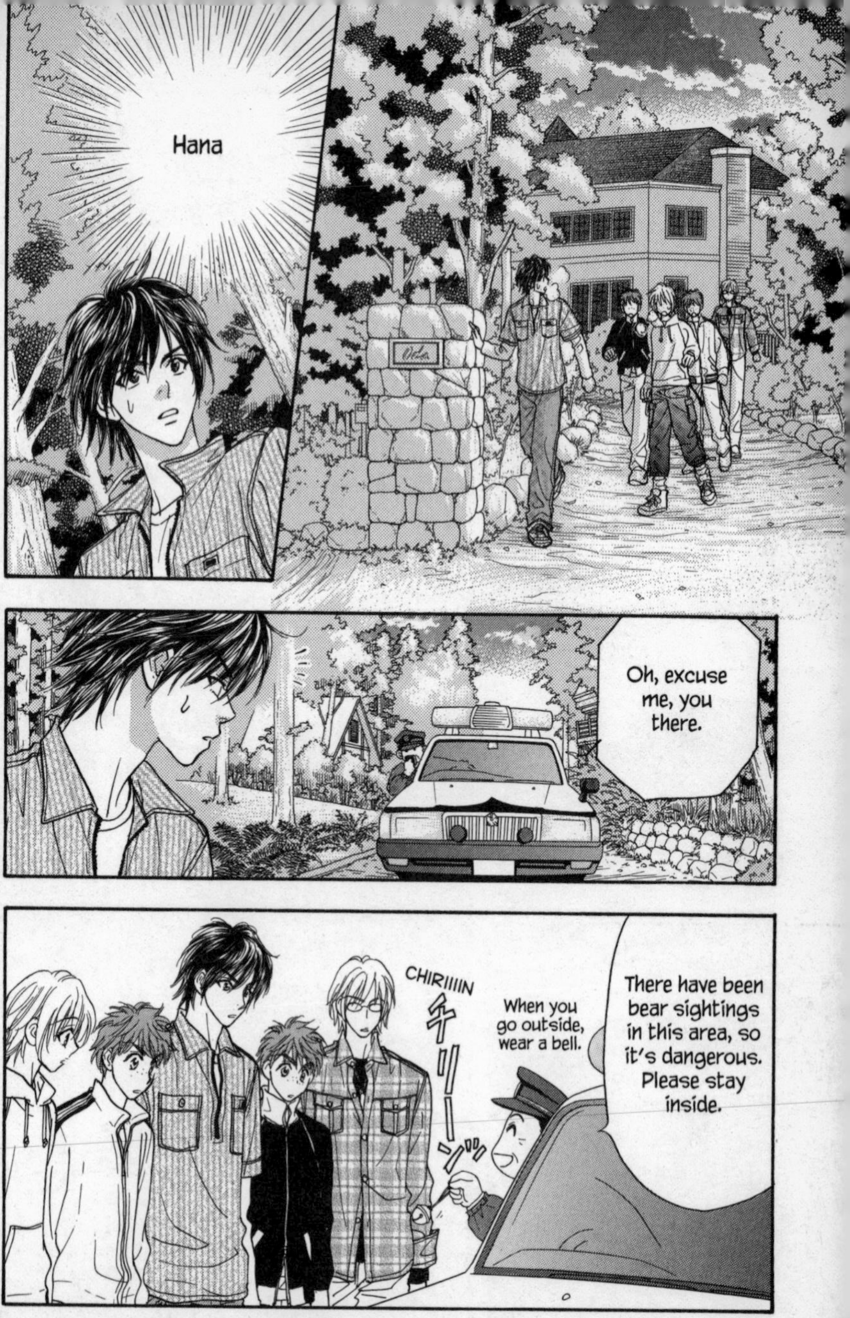
Hana
Oh, excuse me, you there.
There have been bear sightings in this area, so it's dangerous. Please stay inside.
When you go outside, wear a bell.
CHIRIIIN

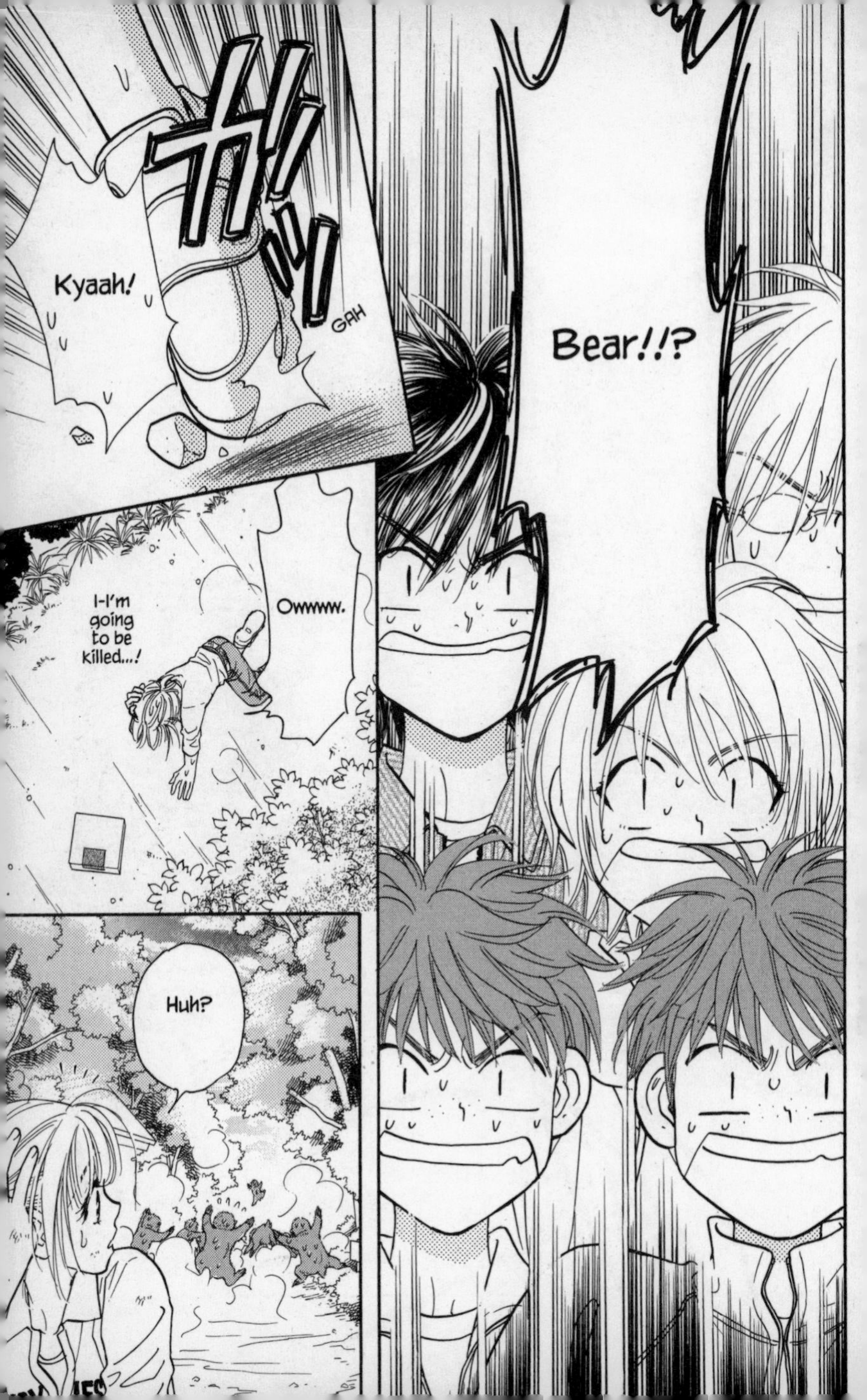
Bear!!?
GAH
Kyaah!
Owwww.
I-I'm going to be killed...!
Huh?

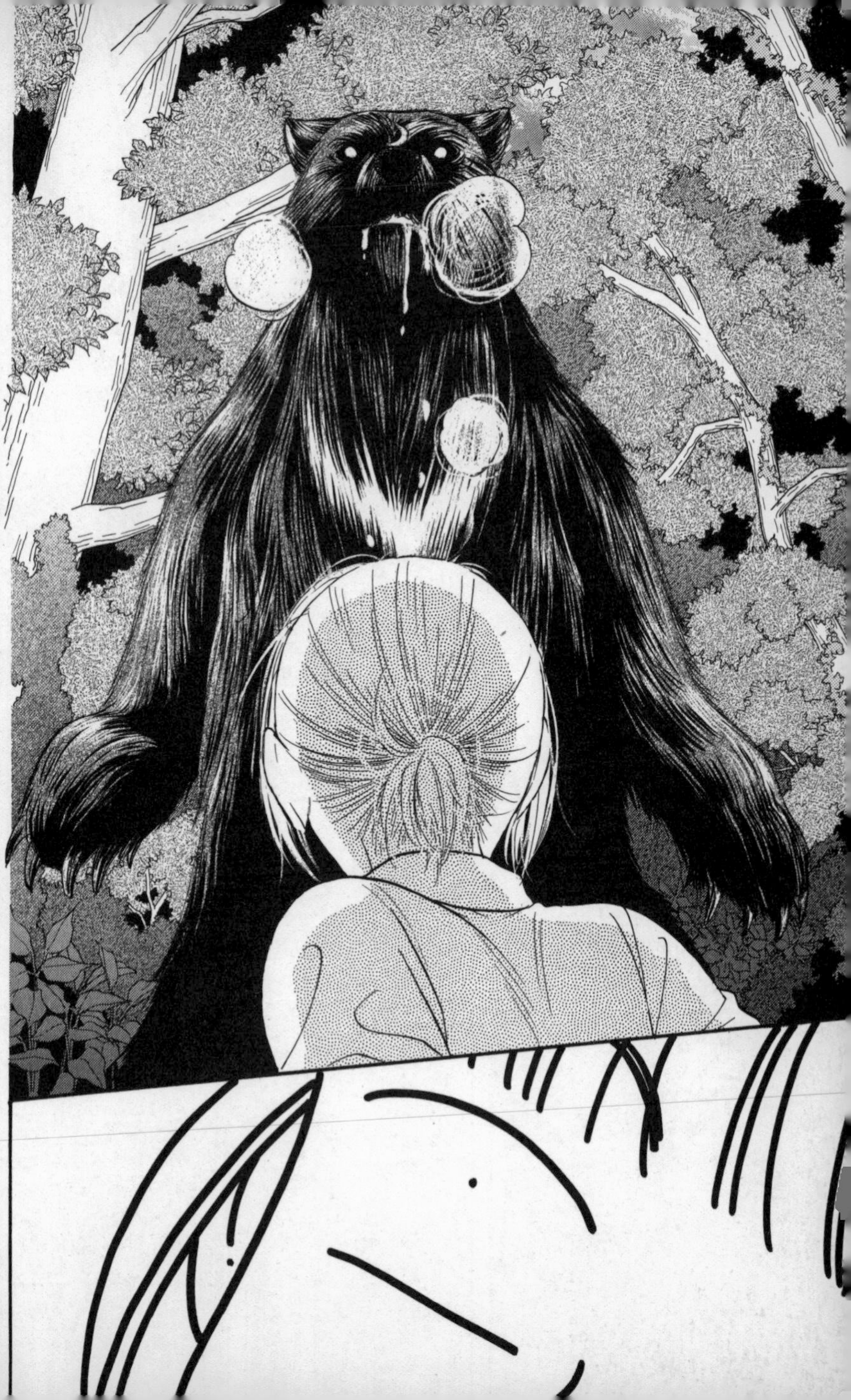

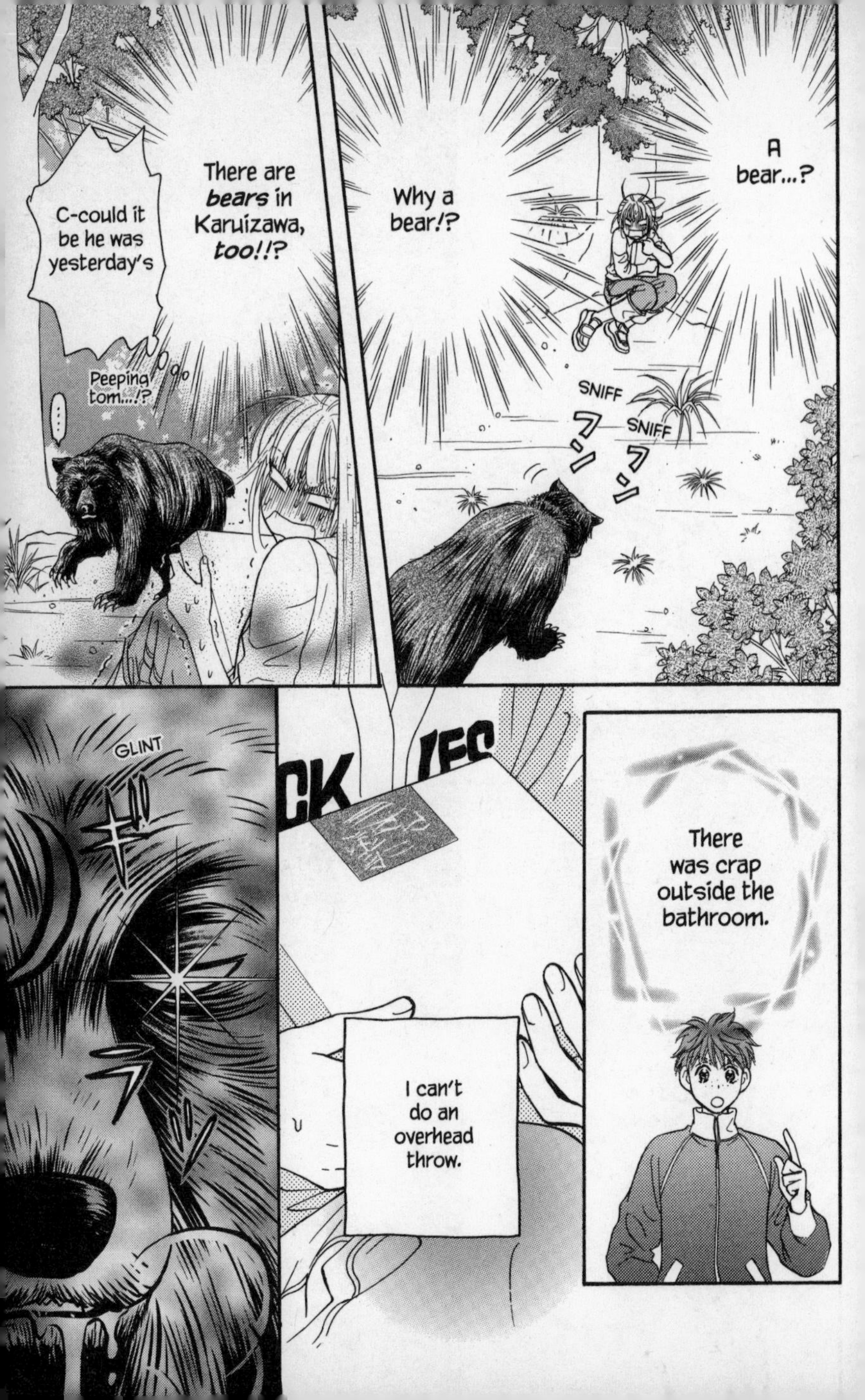
A bear...?
Why a bear!?
SNIFF
SNIFF
There are *bears* in Karuizawa, *too!!?*
C-could it be he was yesterday's
Peeping tom...!?
...
There was crap outside the bathroom.
I can't do an overhead throw.
GLINT

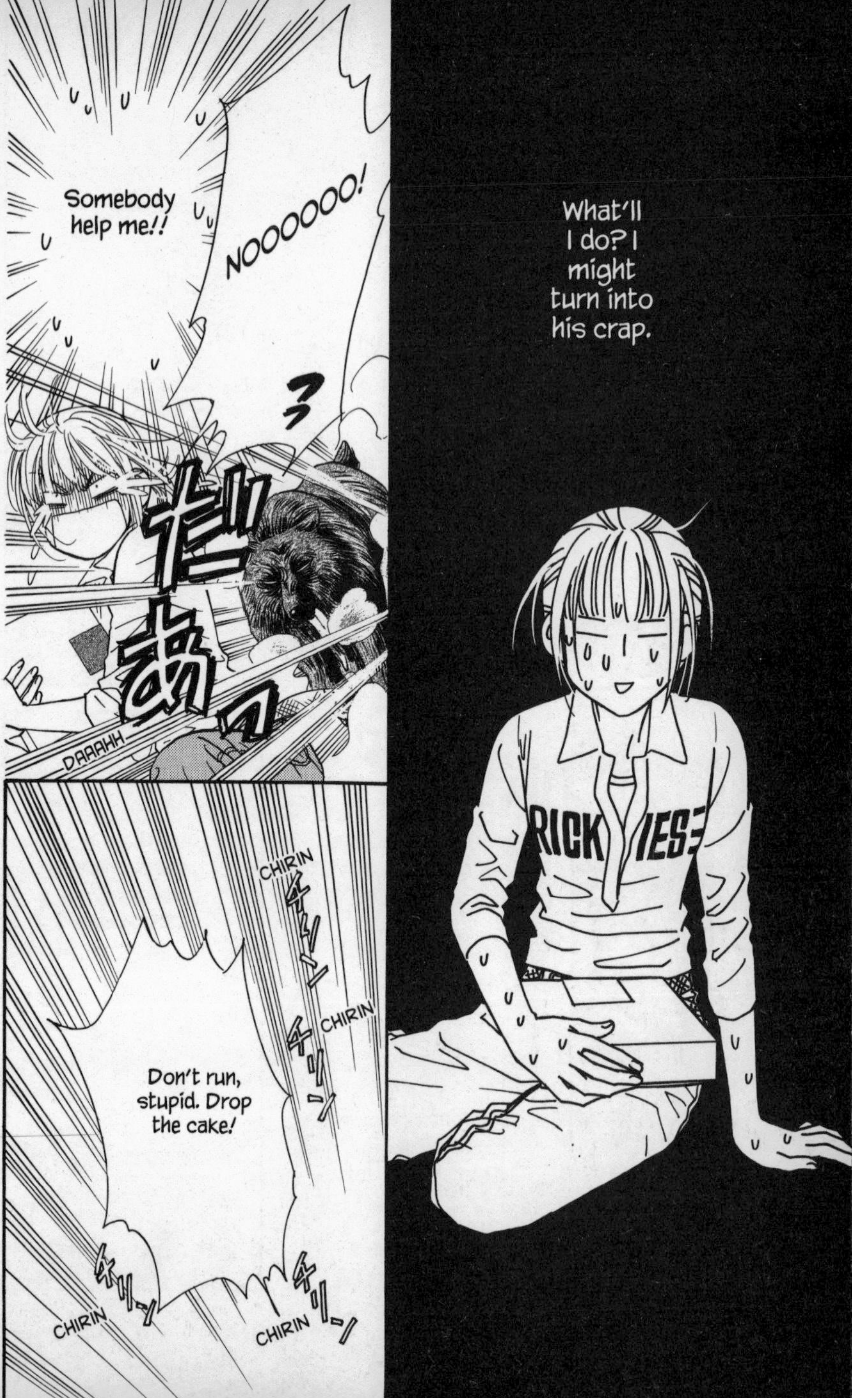
What'll I do? I might turn into his crap.
Somebody help me!!
NOOOOOO!
DAAAHH
Don't run, stupid. Drop the cake!
CHIRIN
CHIRIN
CHIRIN
CHIRIN

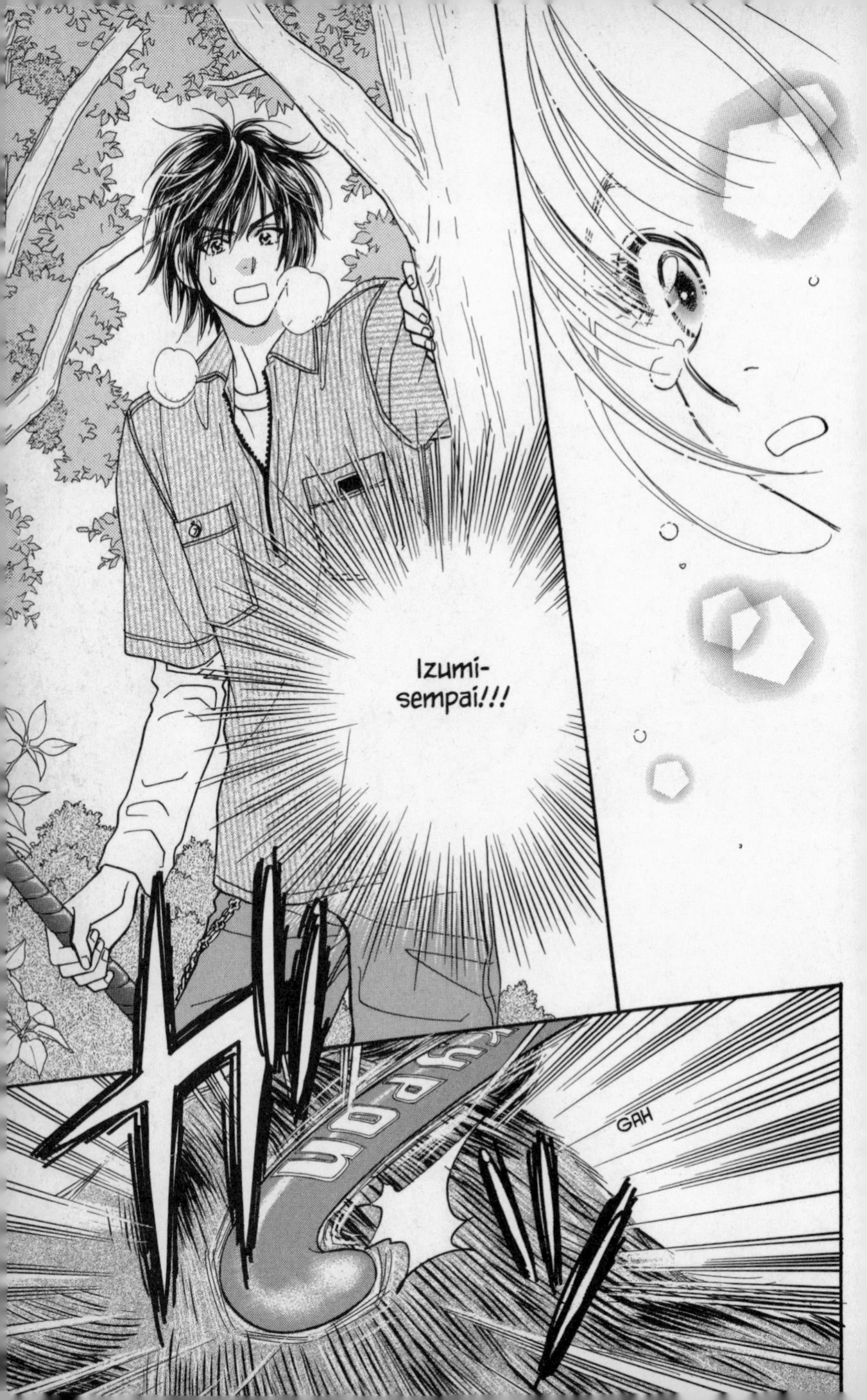
Izumi-
sempai!!!
GAH

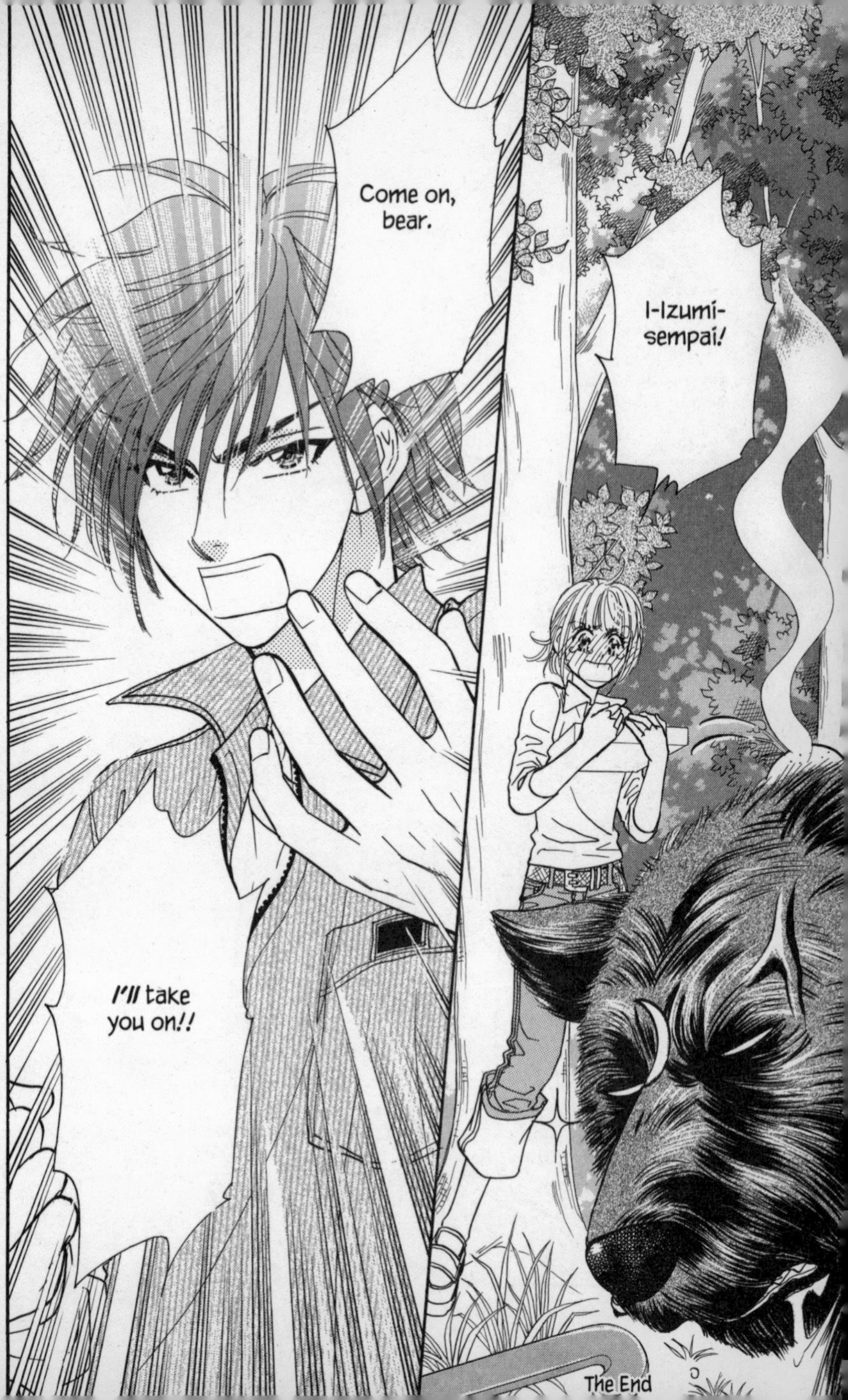
I-Izumi-sempai!
The End
Come on, bear.
I'll take you on!!

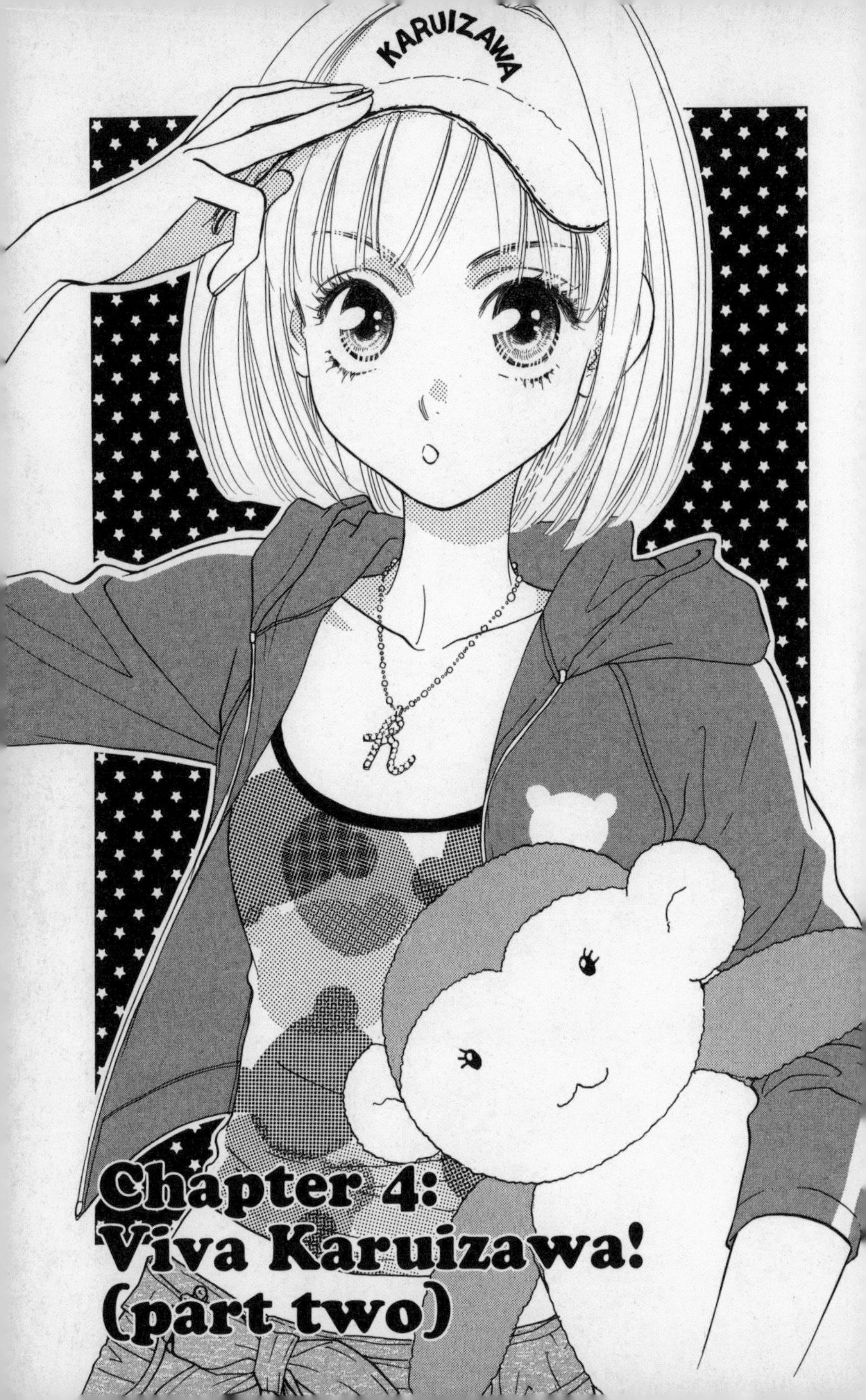
KARUIZAWA
Chapter 4:
Viva Karuizawa!
(part two)

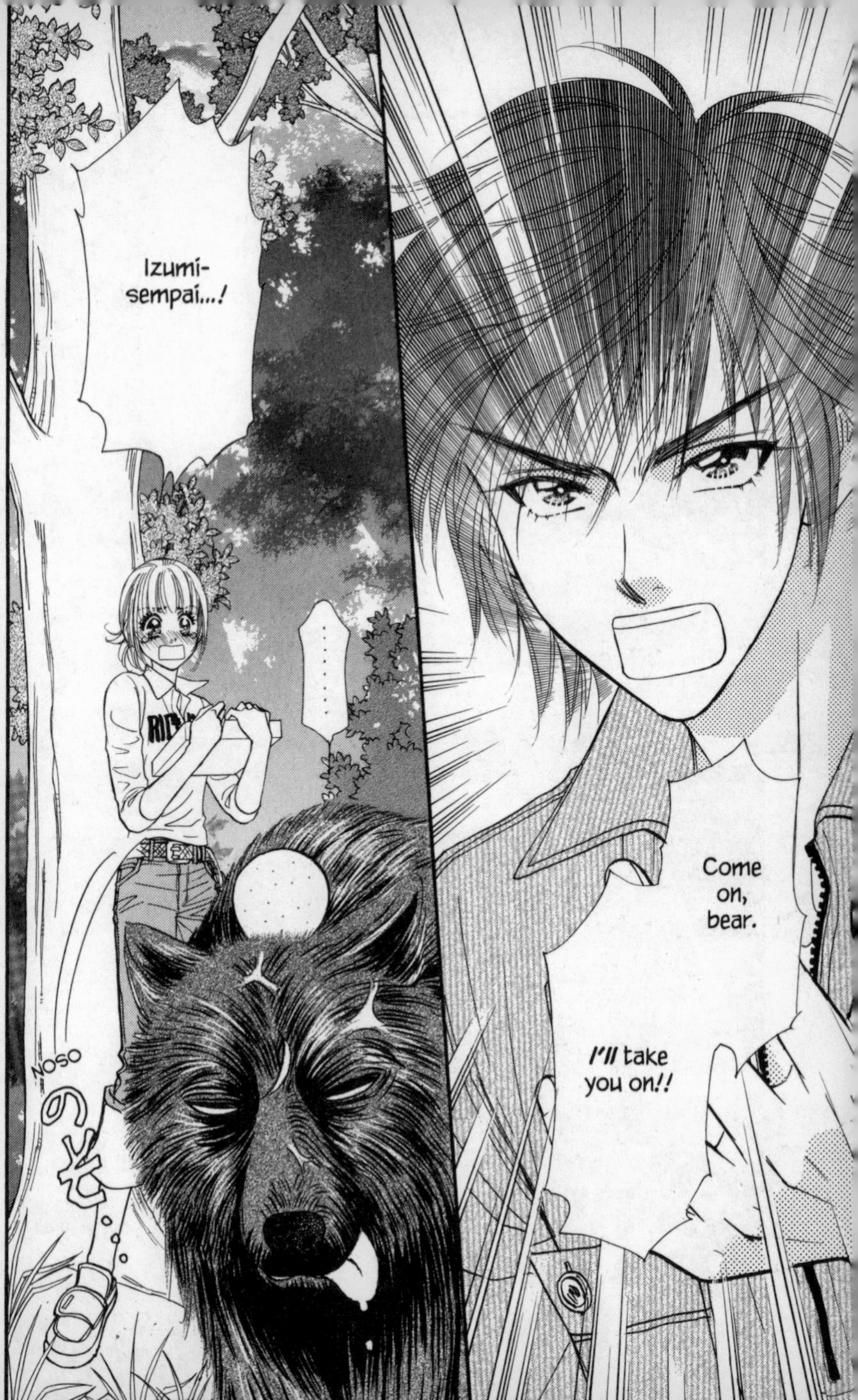
Come on, bear.
I'll take you on!!
Izumi-sempai...!
......
NOSO

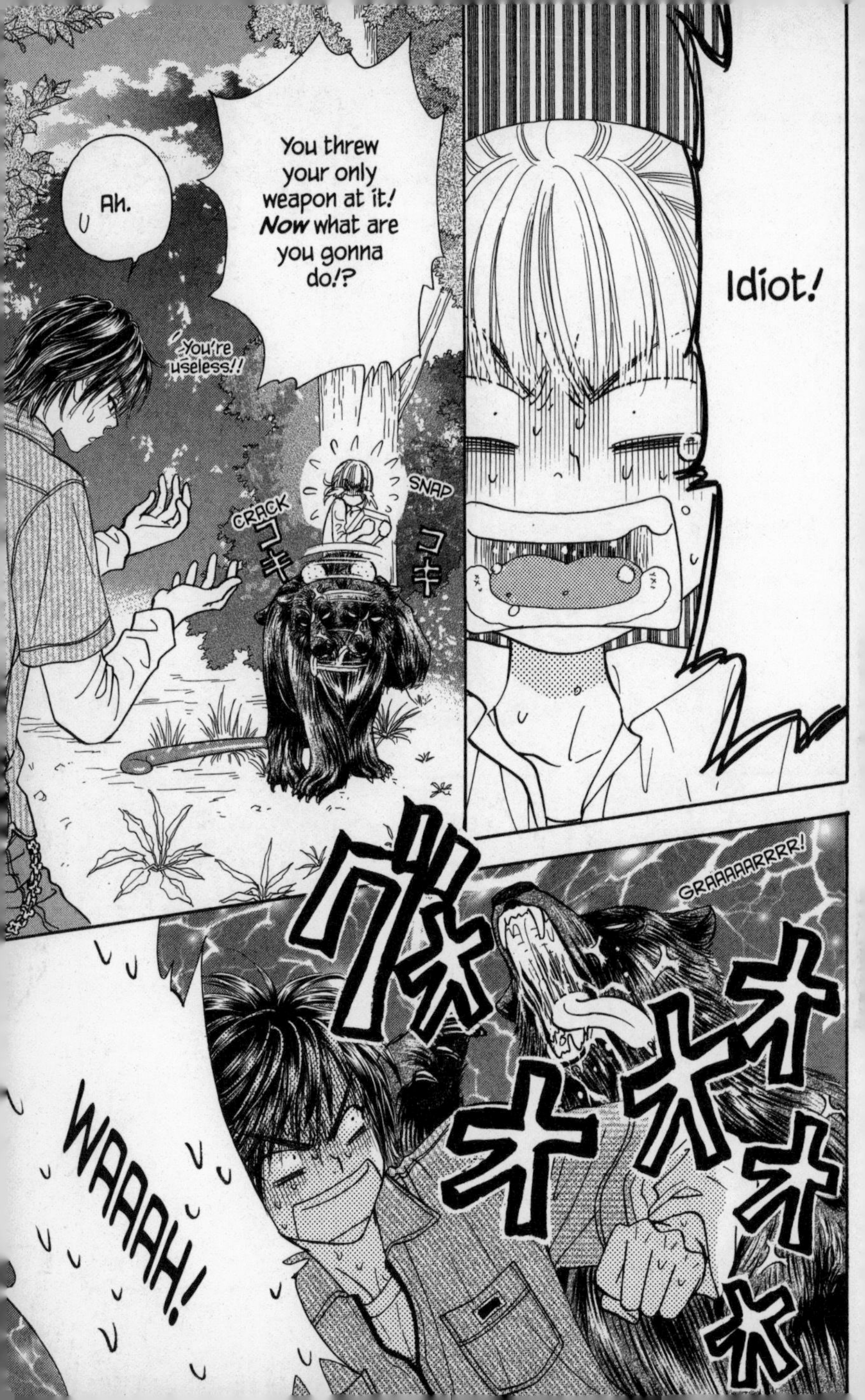
Idiot!
You threw your only weapon at it! *Now* what are you gonna do!?
Ah.
You're useless!!
SNAP
コキ
CRACK
コキ
GRAAAAARRRR!
WAAAH!

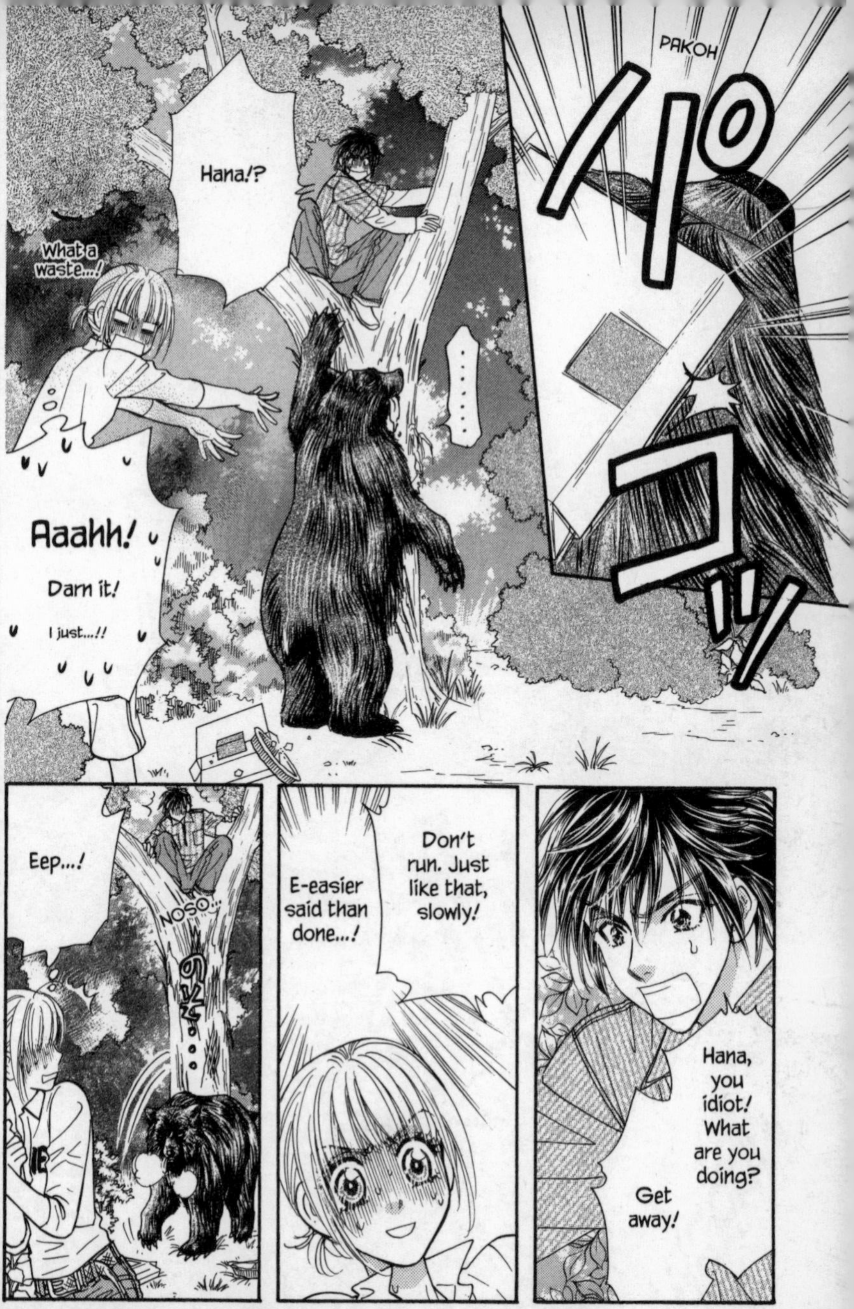
PAKOH
Hana!?
......
What a waste...!
Aaahh!
Darn it!
I just...!!
Hana, you idiot! What are you doing?
Get away!
Don't run. Just like that, slowly!
E-easier said than done...!
Eep...!
NOSO...

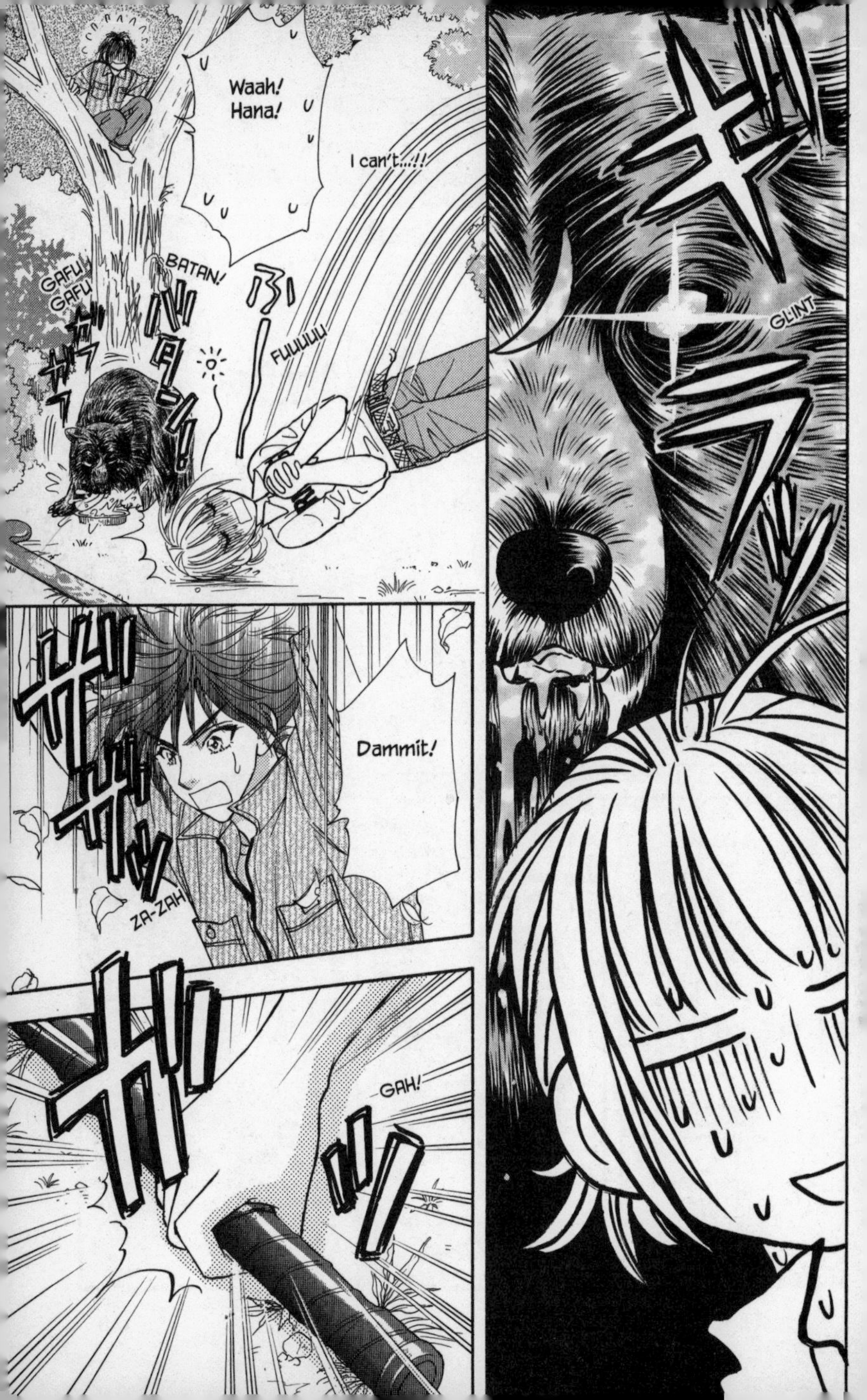
GLINT
Waah! Hana!
I can't...!!
BATAN!
GAFU GAFU
FUUUUU
Dammit!
ZA-ZAH
GAH!

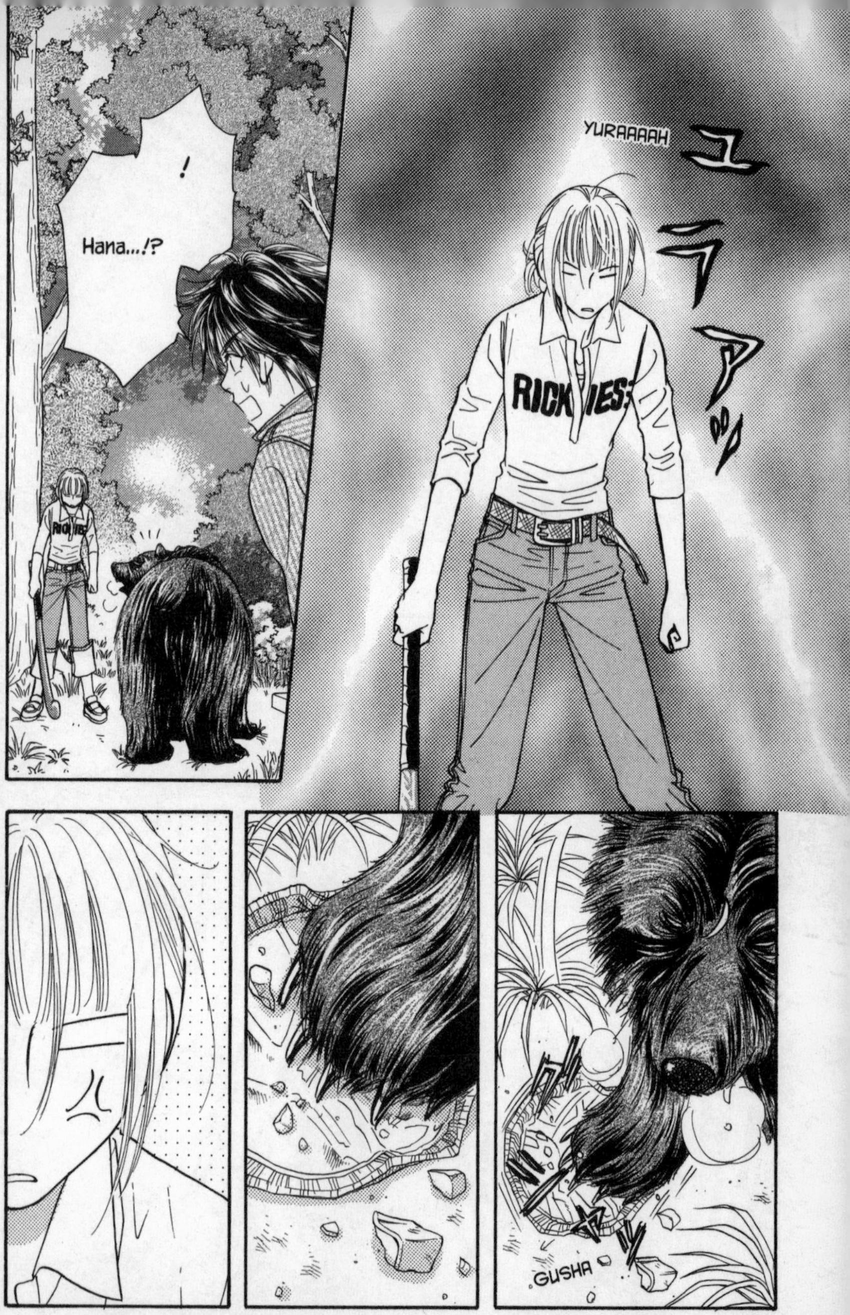
YURAAAAH
!
Hana...!?
GUSHA

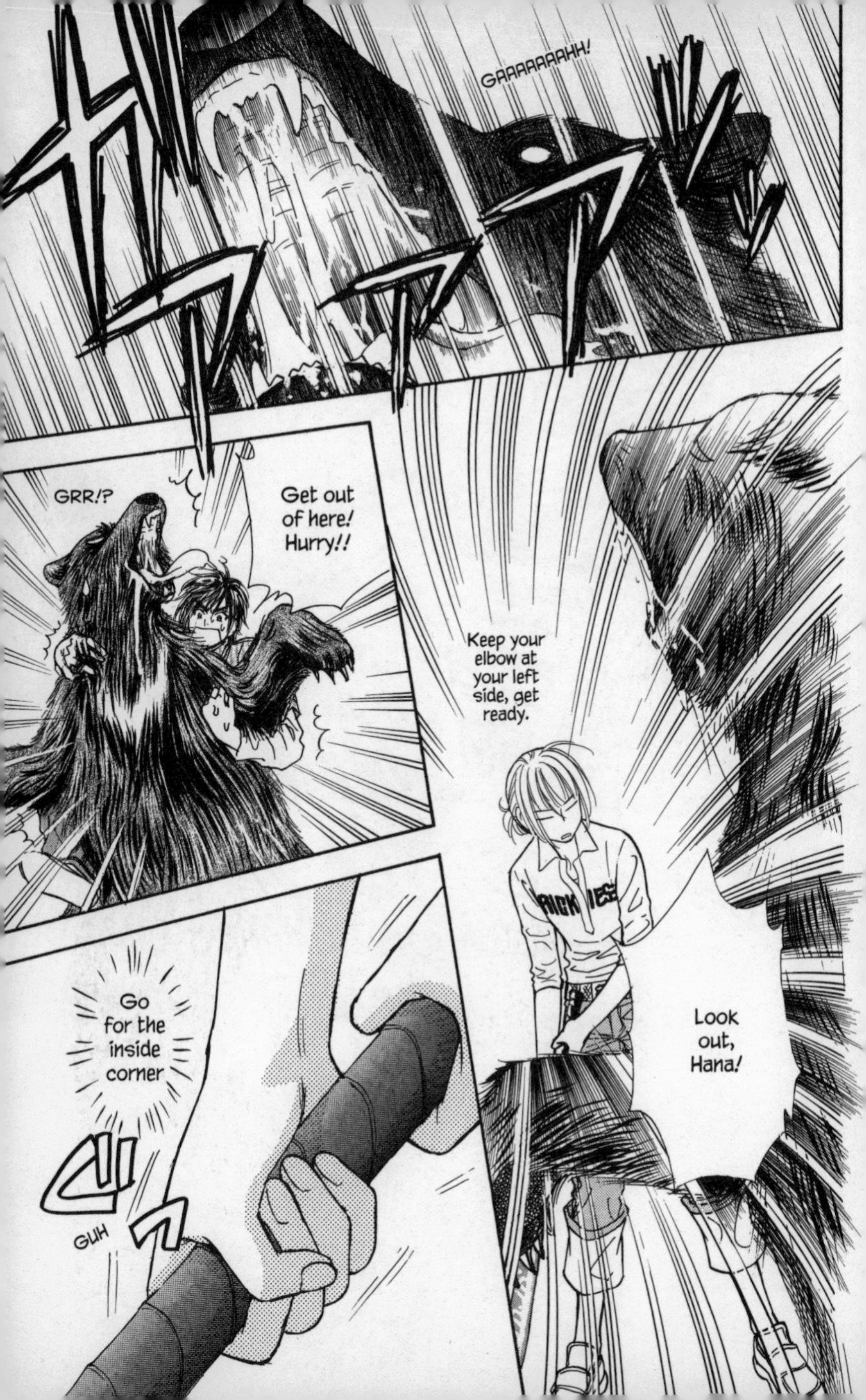
GRAAAAAAHH!
Keep your elbow at your left side, get ready.
Look out, Hana!
GRR!?
Get out of here! Hurry!!
Go for the inside corner
GUH

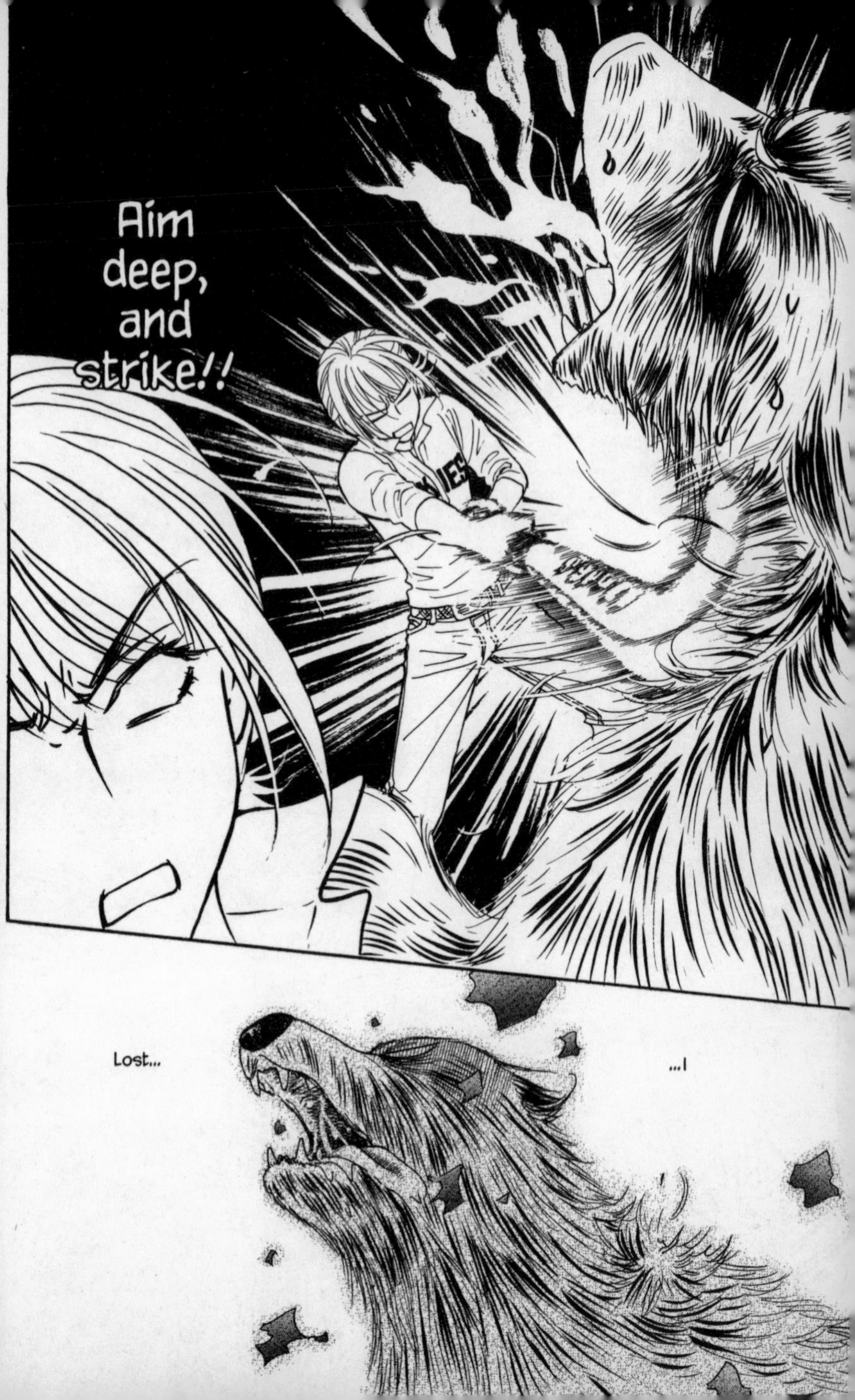
Aim deep, and strike!!
...I
Lost...

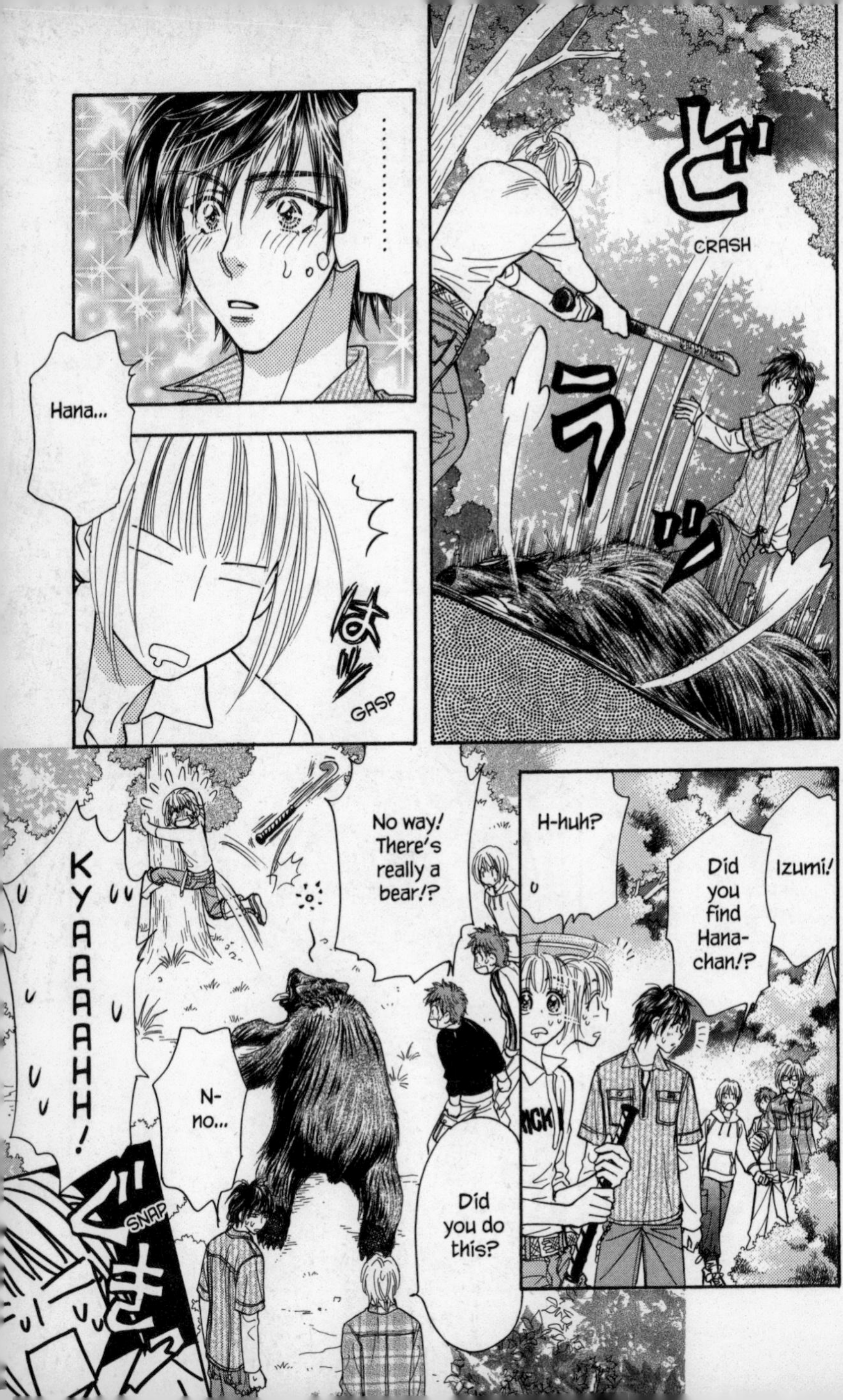

CRASH
......
Hana...
GASP
Izumi!
Did you find Hana-chan!?
H-huh?
No way! There's really a bear!?
KYAAAAAHH!
N-no...
Did you do this?
SNAP

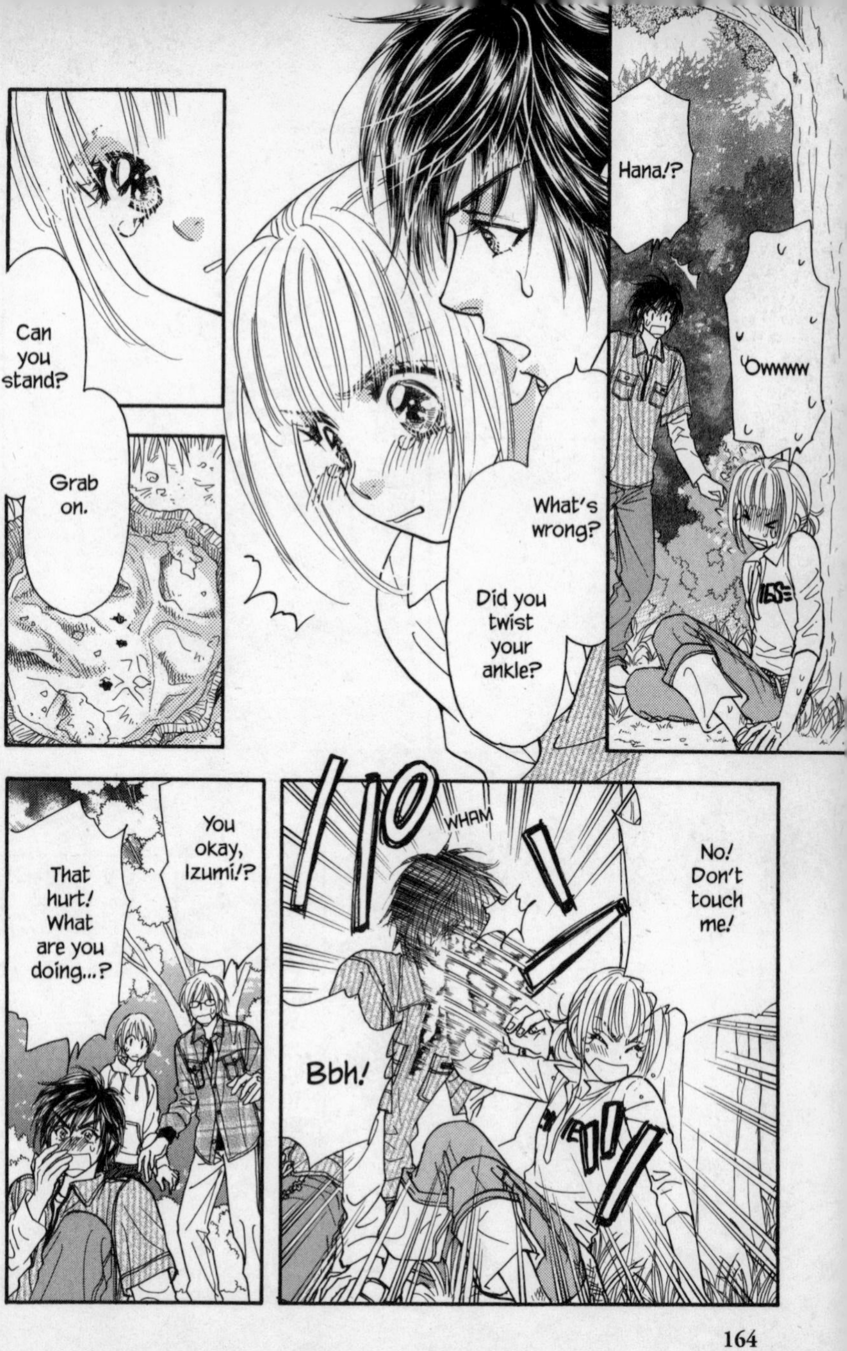
Hana!?
Owwww
What's wrong?
Did you twist your ankle?
Can you stand?
Grab on.
WHAM
No! Don't touch me!
Bbh!
You okay, Izumi!?
That hurt! What are you doing...?

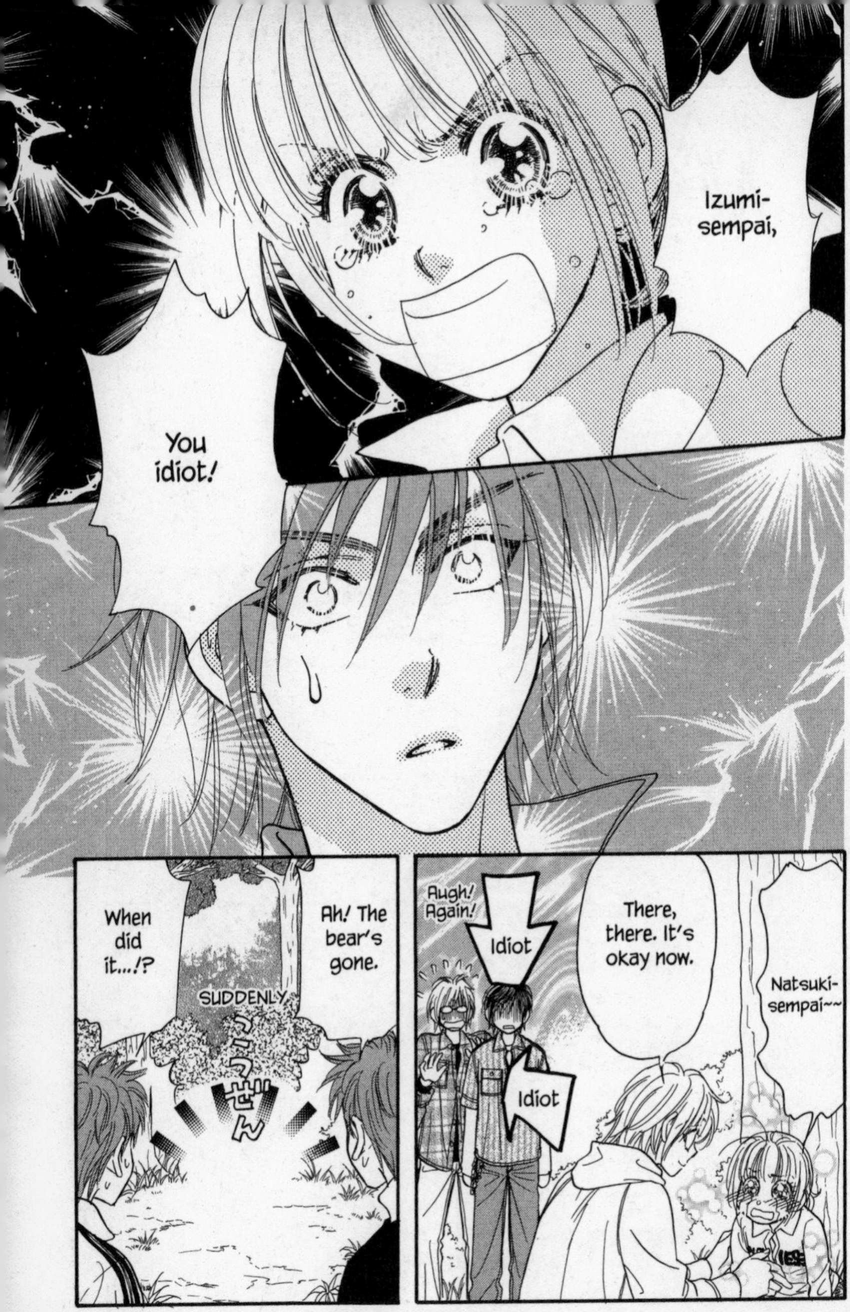
Izumi-sempai,
You idiot!
Natsuki-sempai~~
There, there. It's okay now.
Augh! Again!
Idiot
Idiot
Ah! The bear's gone.
When did it...!?
SUDDENLY
こつぜん

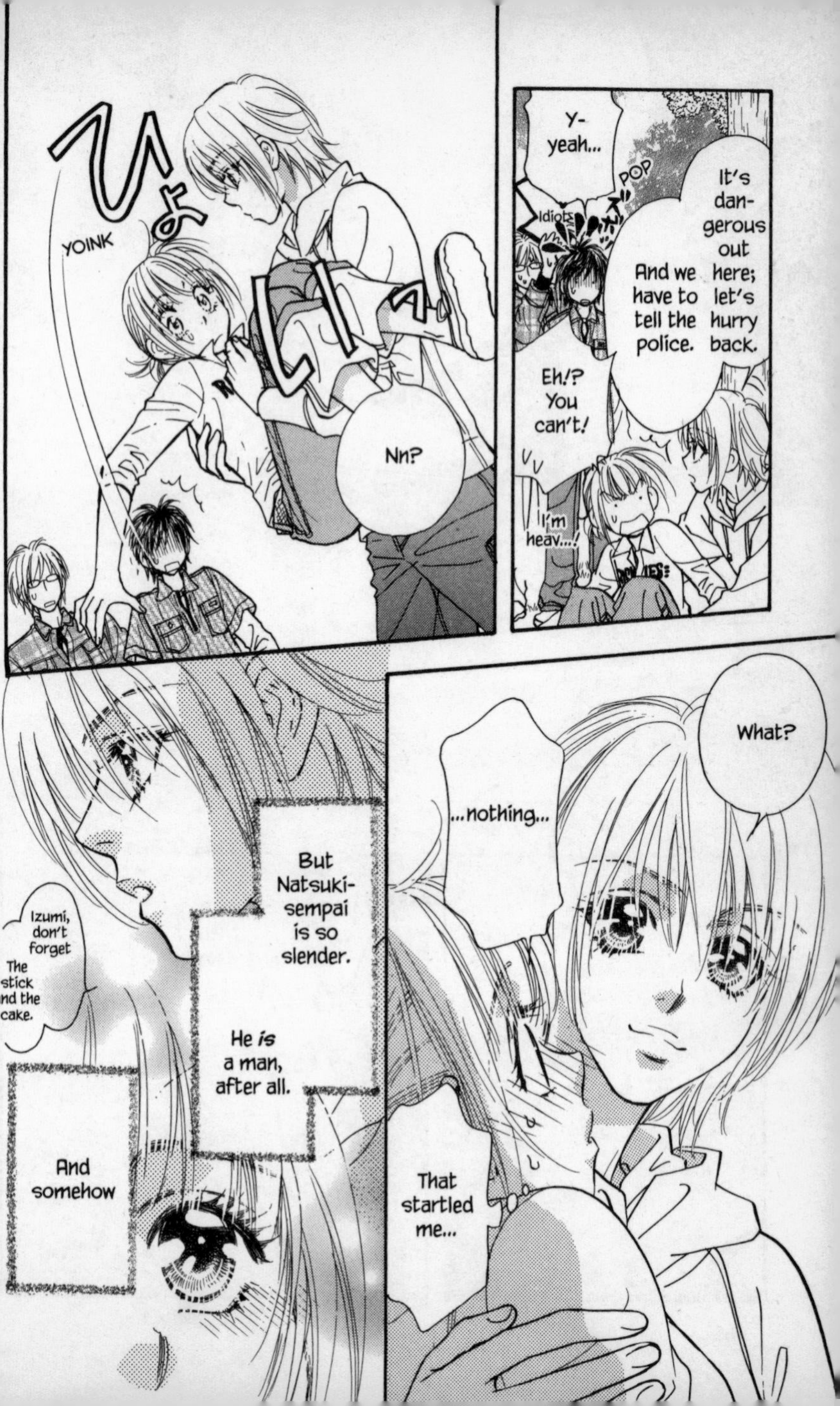
It's dangerous out here; let's hurry back.
And we have to tell the police.
Y-yeah...
POP
Idiots
Eh!? You can't!
I'm heav...!
ひょい
YOINK
Nn?
What?
...nothing...
That startled me...
But Natsuki-sempai is so slender.
He *is* a man, after all.
Izumi, don't forget
The stick and the cake.
And somehow

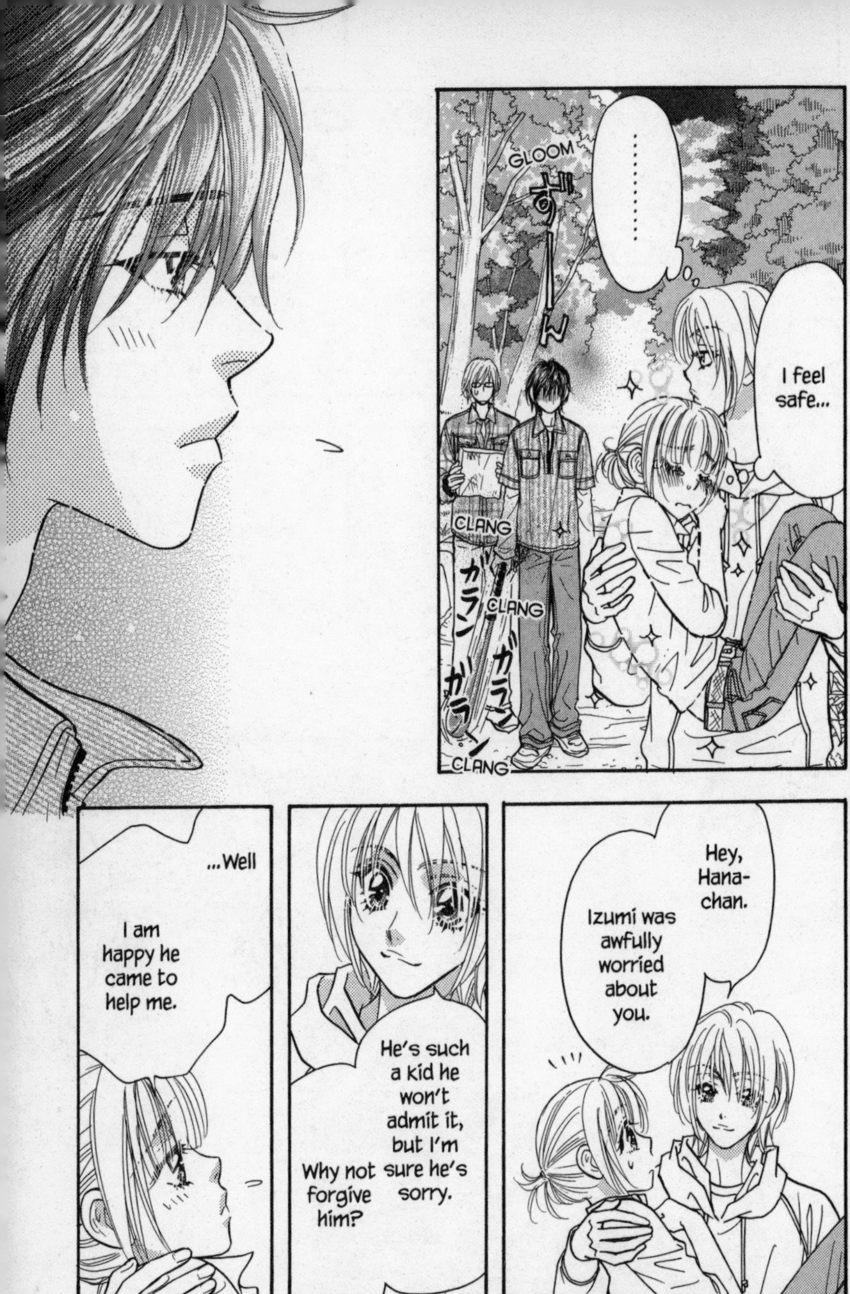

GLOOM
ずーん
......
I feel safe...
CLANG
CLANG
ガラン
ガラン
CLANG
Hey, Hana-chan.
Izumi was awfully worried about you.
He's such a kid he won't admit it, but I'm sure he's sorry.
Why not forgive him?
...Well
I am happy he came to help me.

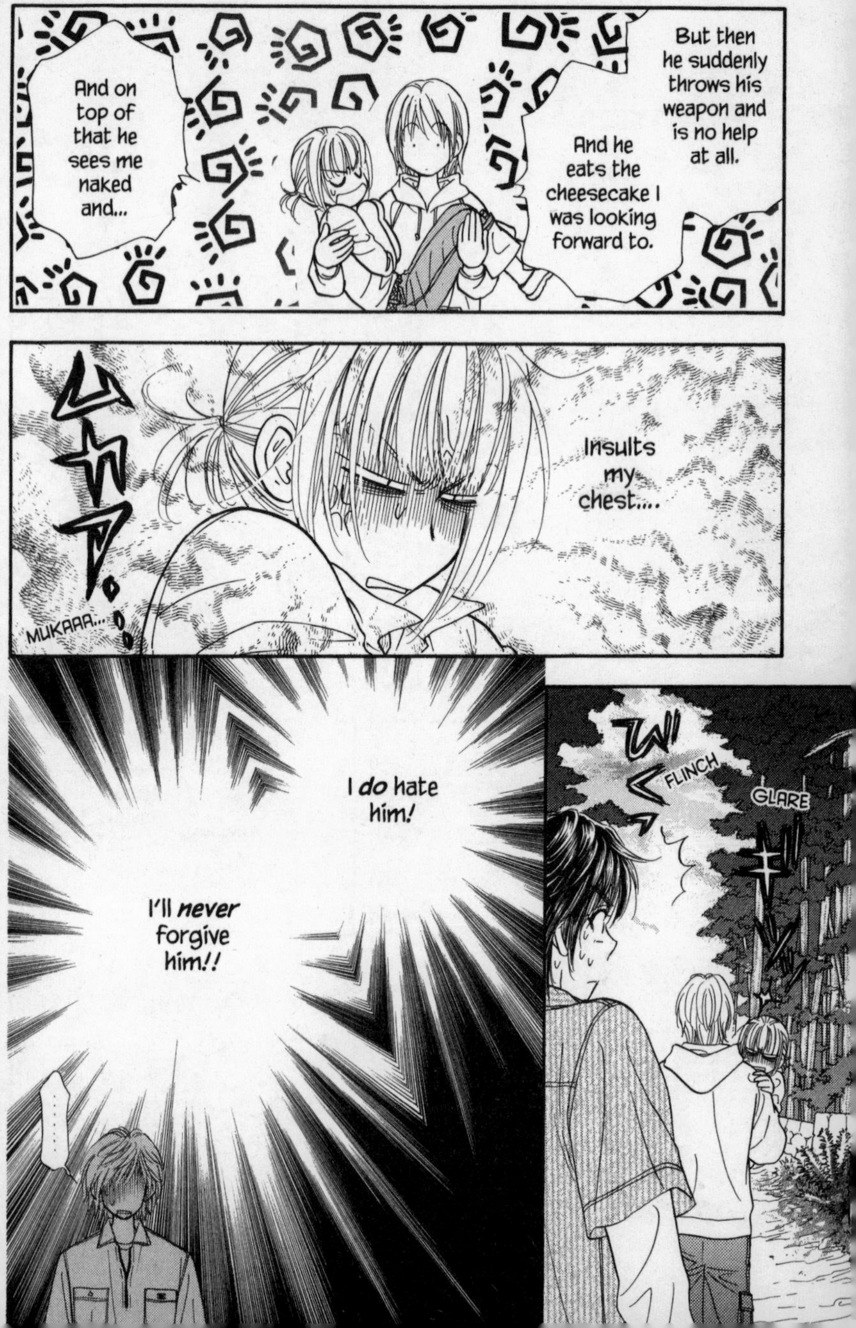
But then he suddenly throws his weapon and is no help at all.
And he eats the cheesecake I was looking forward to.
And on top of that he sees me naked and...
Insults my chest....
MUKAAA...
FLINCH
GLARE
I *do* hate him!
I'll *never* forgive him!!
......

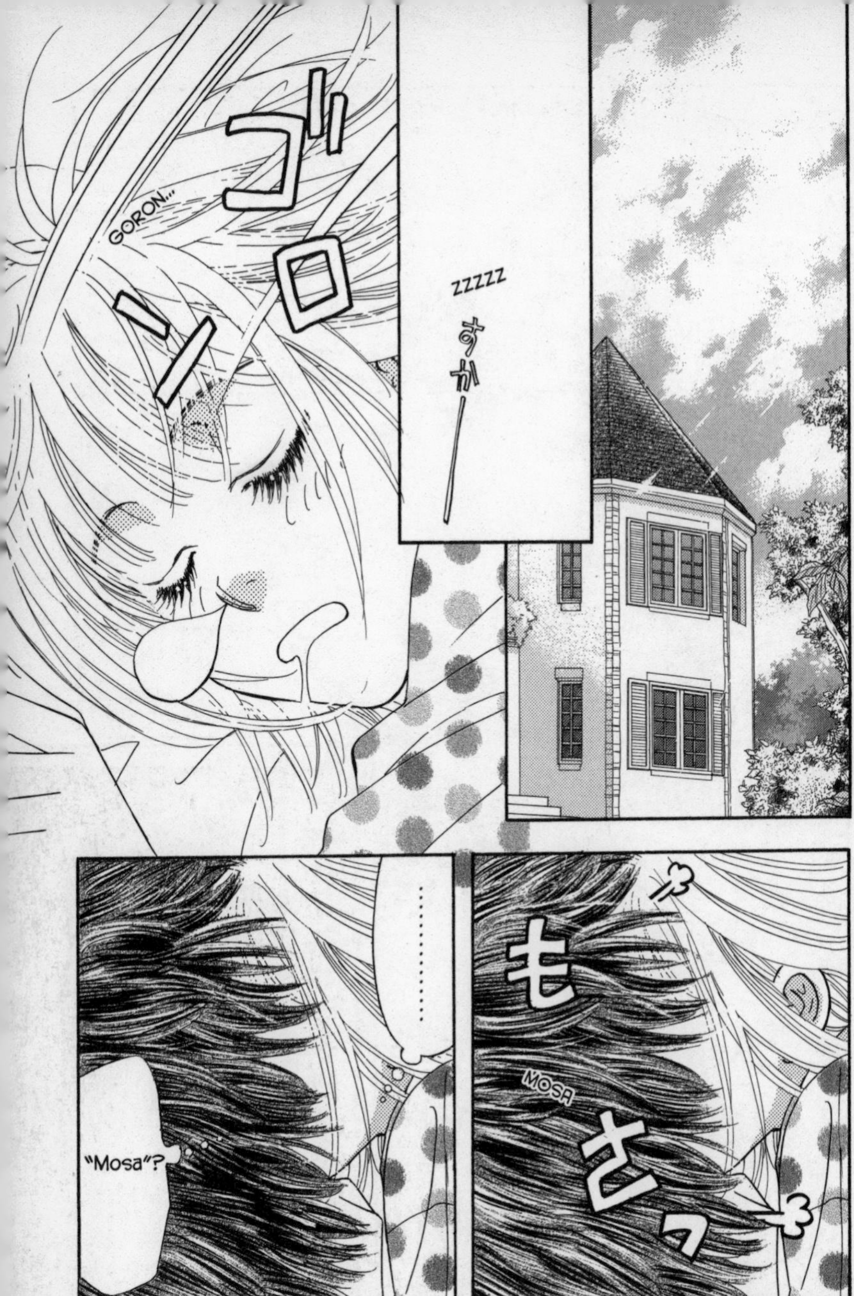
ZZZZZ
すかー
ゴロン
GORON...
もさっ
MOSA
......
"Mosa"?

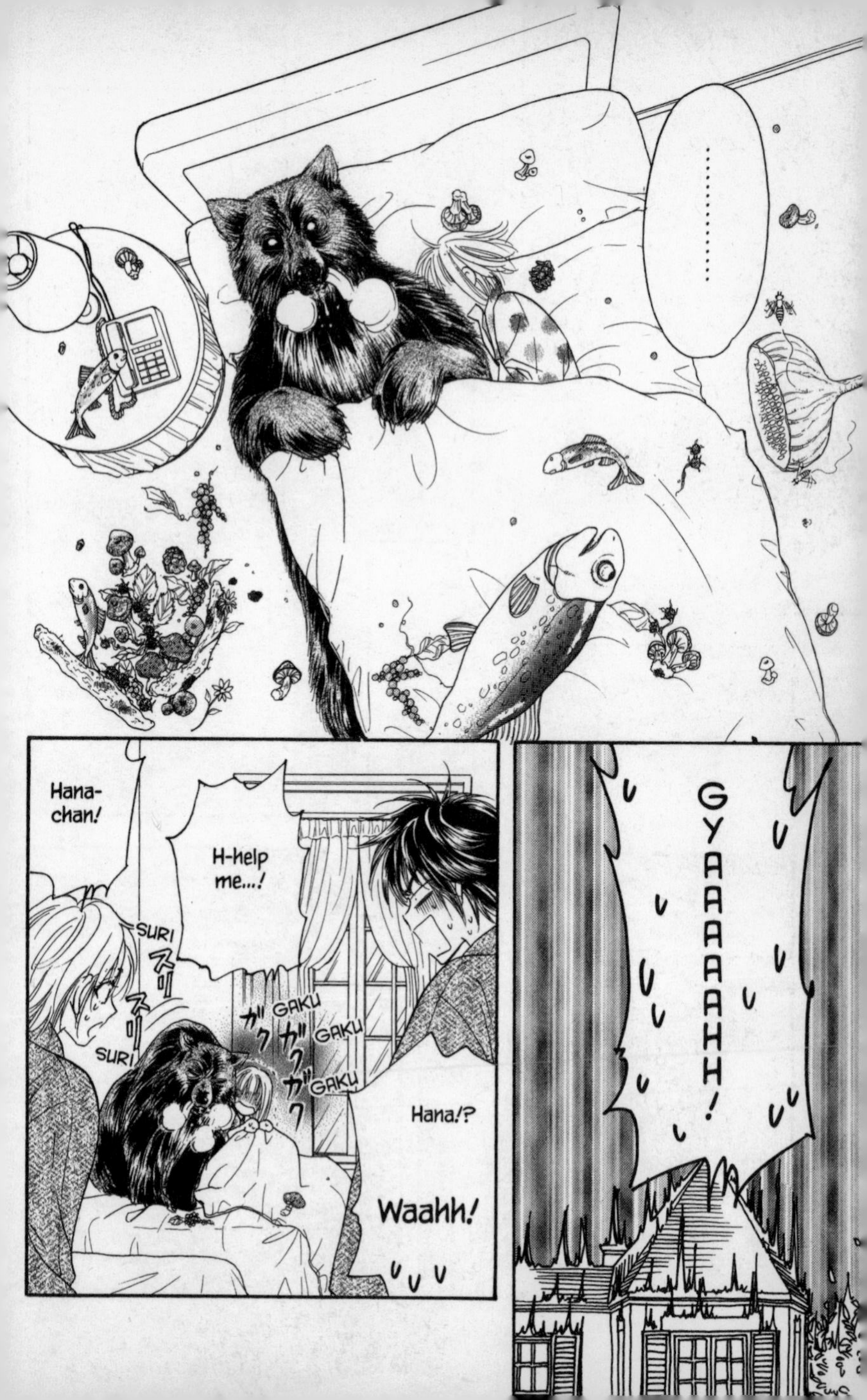
......
GYAAAAAAHH!
H-help me...!
Hana-chan!
GAKU GAKU GAKU
SURI SURI
Hana!?
Waahh!

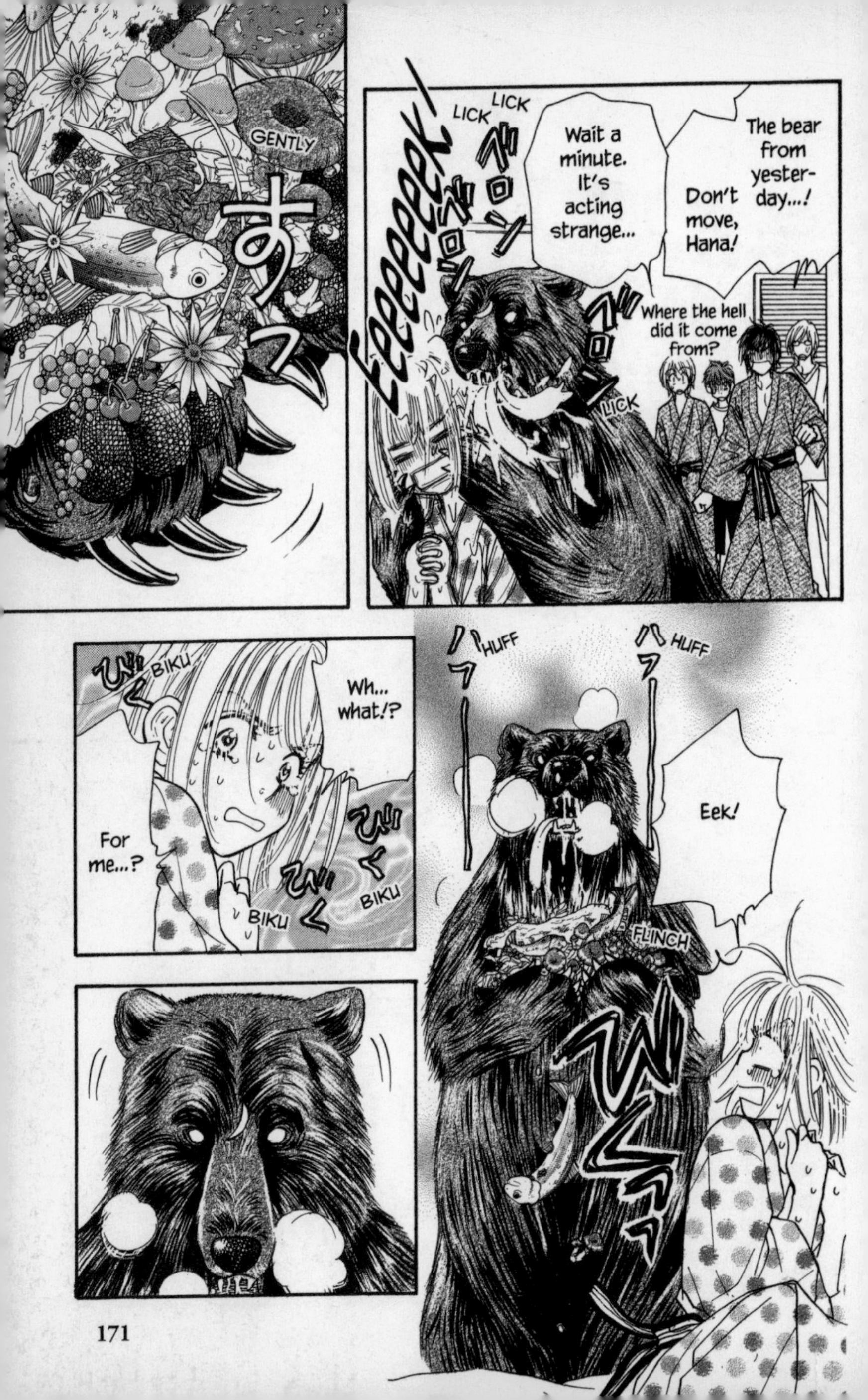
The bear from yesterday...!
Don't move, Hana!
Wait a minute. It's acting strange...
LICK
LICK
EEEEEEEK!
Where the hell did it come from?
LICK
GENTLY
HUFF
HUFF
Eek!
FLINCH
Wh... what!?
BIKU
For me...?
BIKU
BIKU

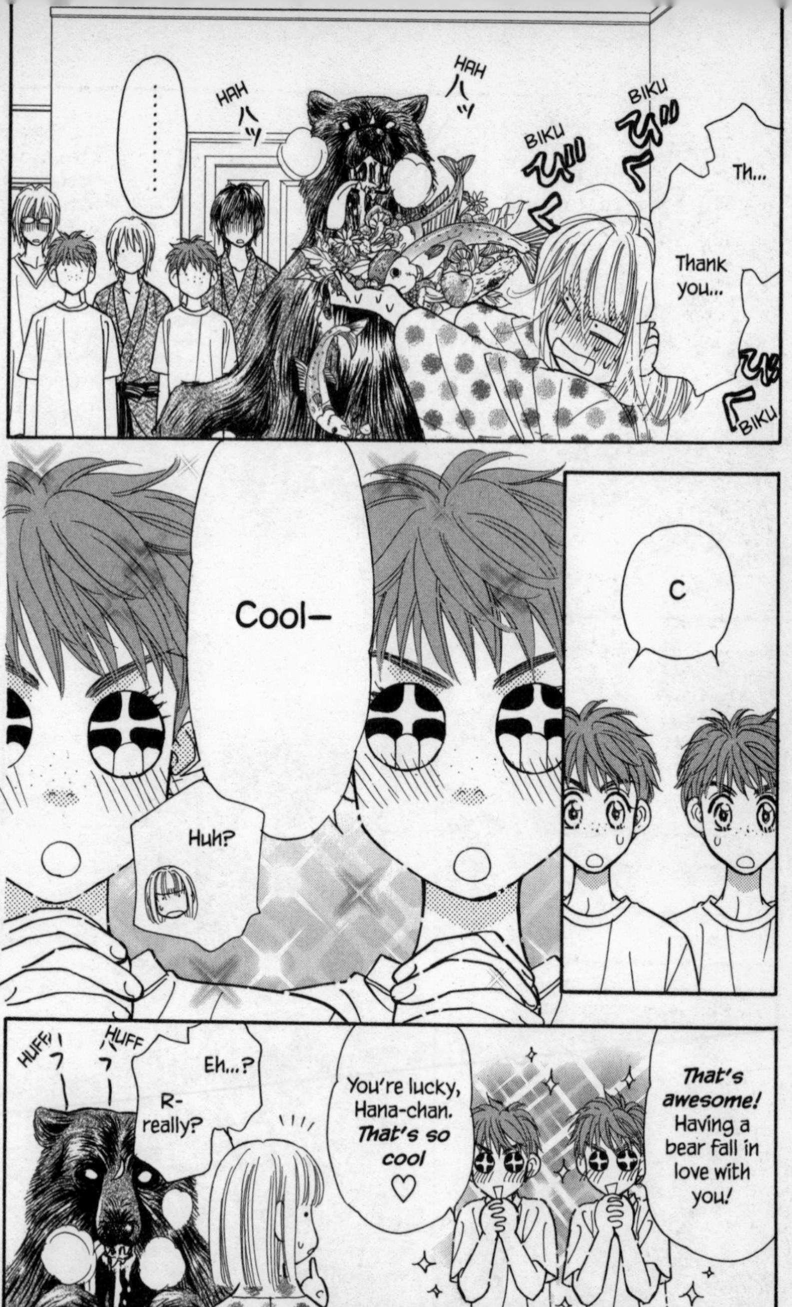

Th...
BIKU
BIKU
Thank you...
BIKU
BIKU
HAH
HAH
......
C
Cool–
Huh?
That's awesome! Having a bear fall in love with you!
You're lucky, Hana-chan. That's so cool ♡
Eh...?
R- really?
HUFF
HUFF

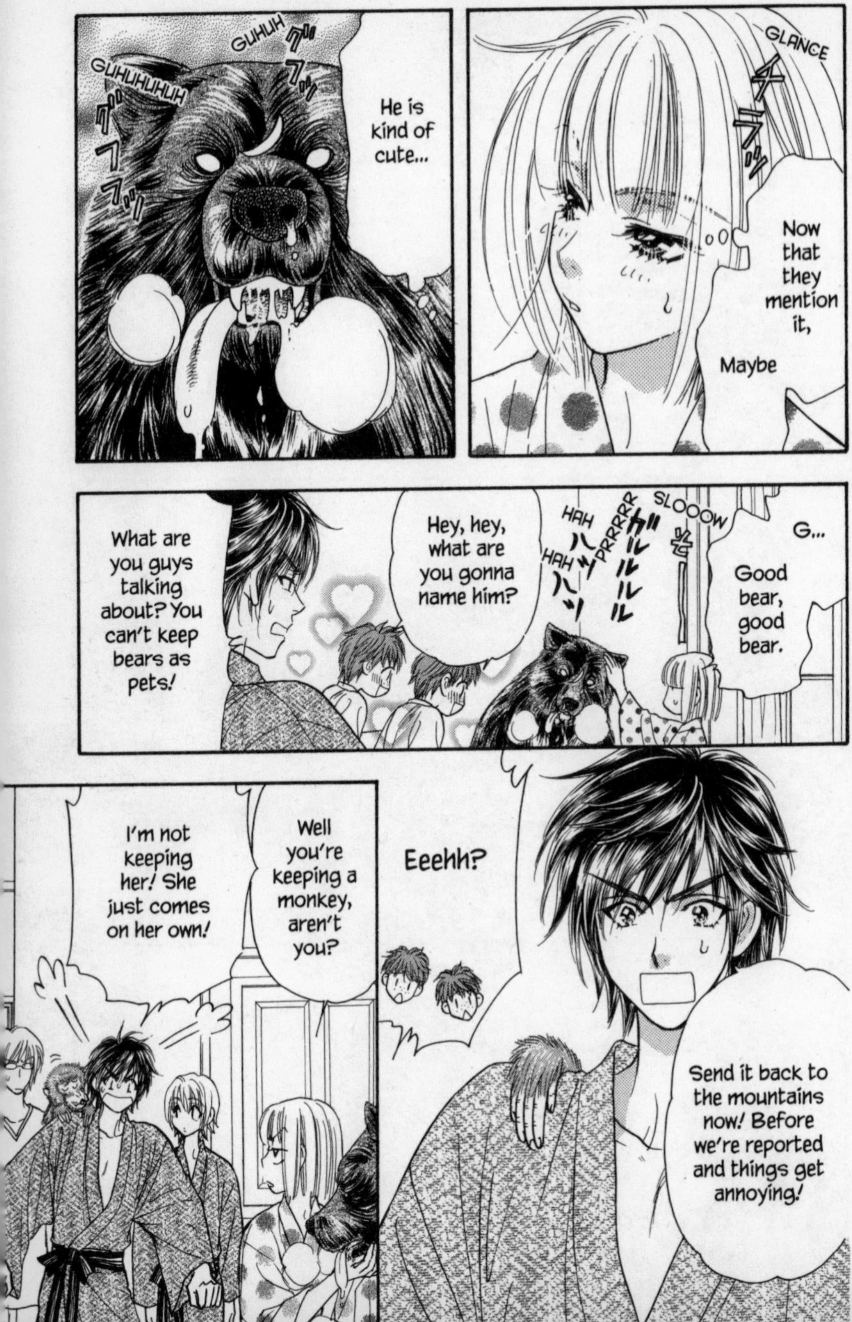
GLANCE
Now that they mention it,
Maybe
He is kind of cute...
GUHUH
GUHUHUHUH
G...
Good bear, good bear.
SLOOOW
PRRRRR
HAH HAH
Hey, hey, what are you gonna name him?
What are you guys talking about? You can't keep bears as pets!
Send it back to the mountains now! Before we're reported and things get annoying!
Eeehh?
Well you're keeping a monkey, aren't you?
I'm not keeping her! She just comes on her own!

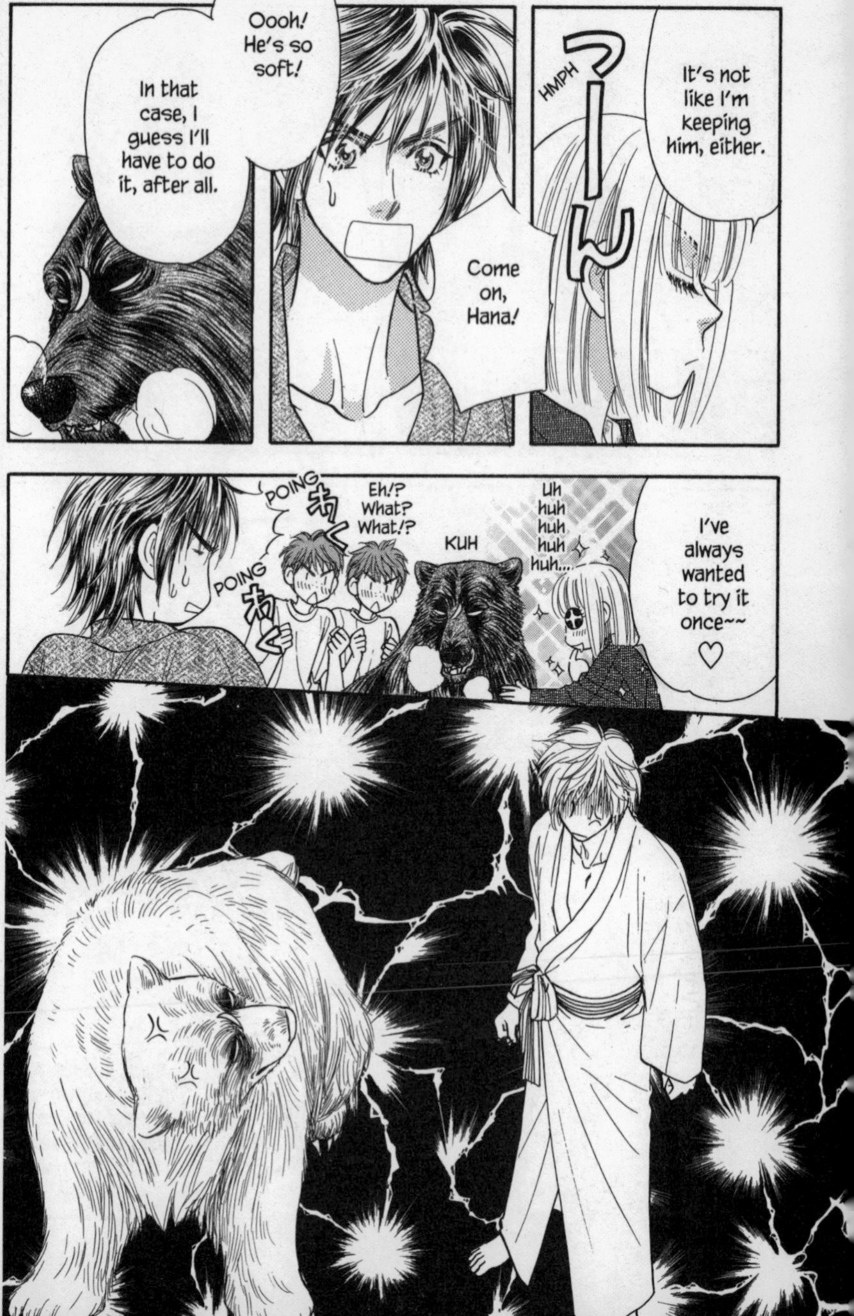
It's not like I'm keeping him, either.
HMPH
Come on, Hana!
In that case, I guess I'll have to do it, after all.
Oooh! He's so soft!
I've always wanted to try it once~~ ♡
Uh huh huh huh huh...
KUH
Eh!? What? What!?
POING
POING

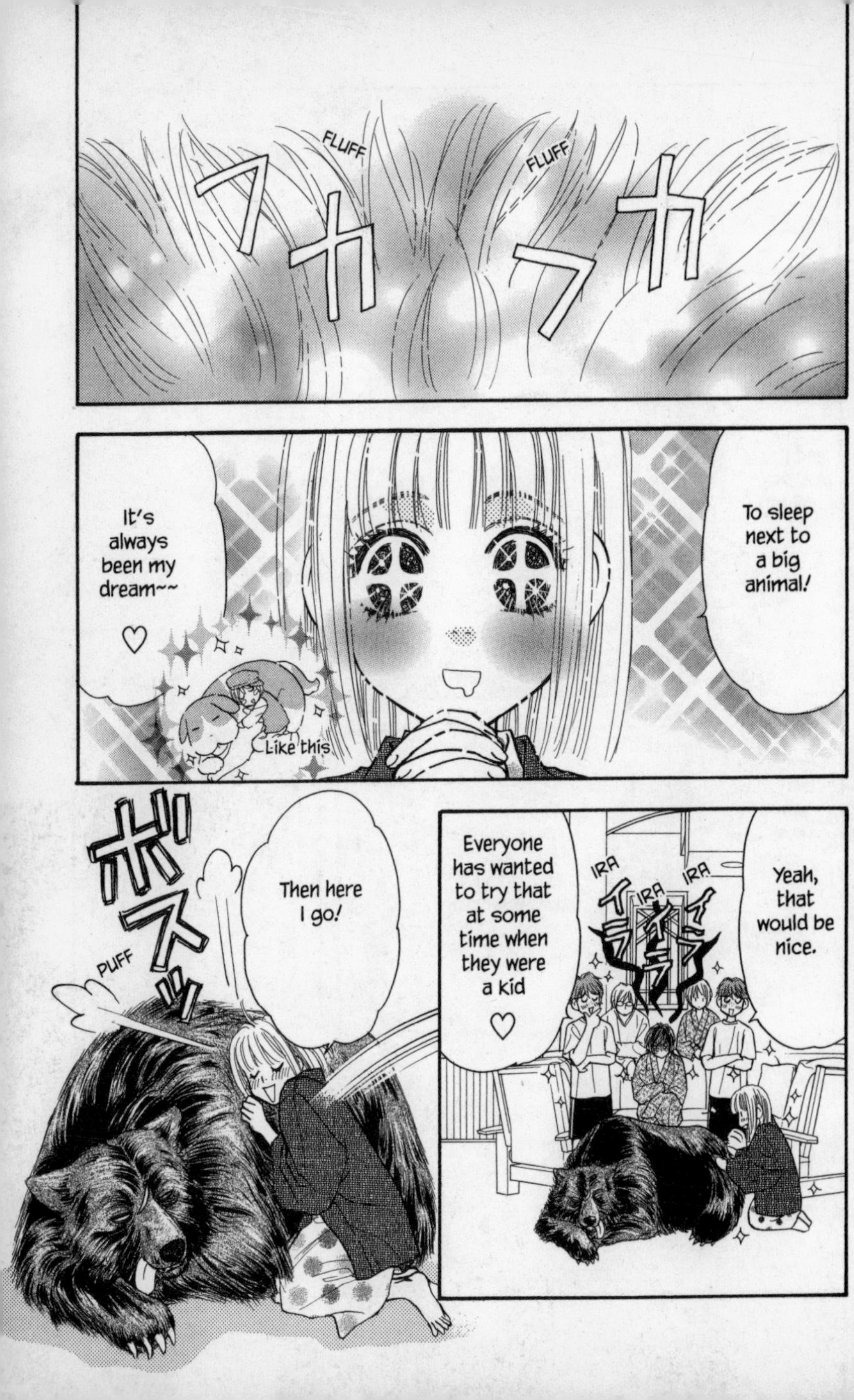
FLUFF
FLUFF
フカフカ
To sleep next to a big animal!
It's always been my dream~~ ♡
Like this
Yeah, that would be nice.
IRA
IRA
IRA
イライラ
Everyone has wanted to try that at some time when they were a kid ♡
Then here I go!
PUFF
ボスッ

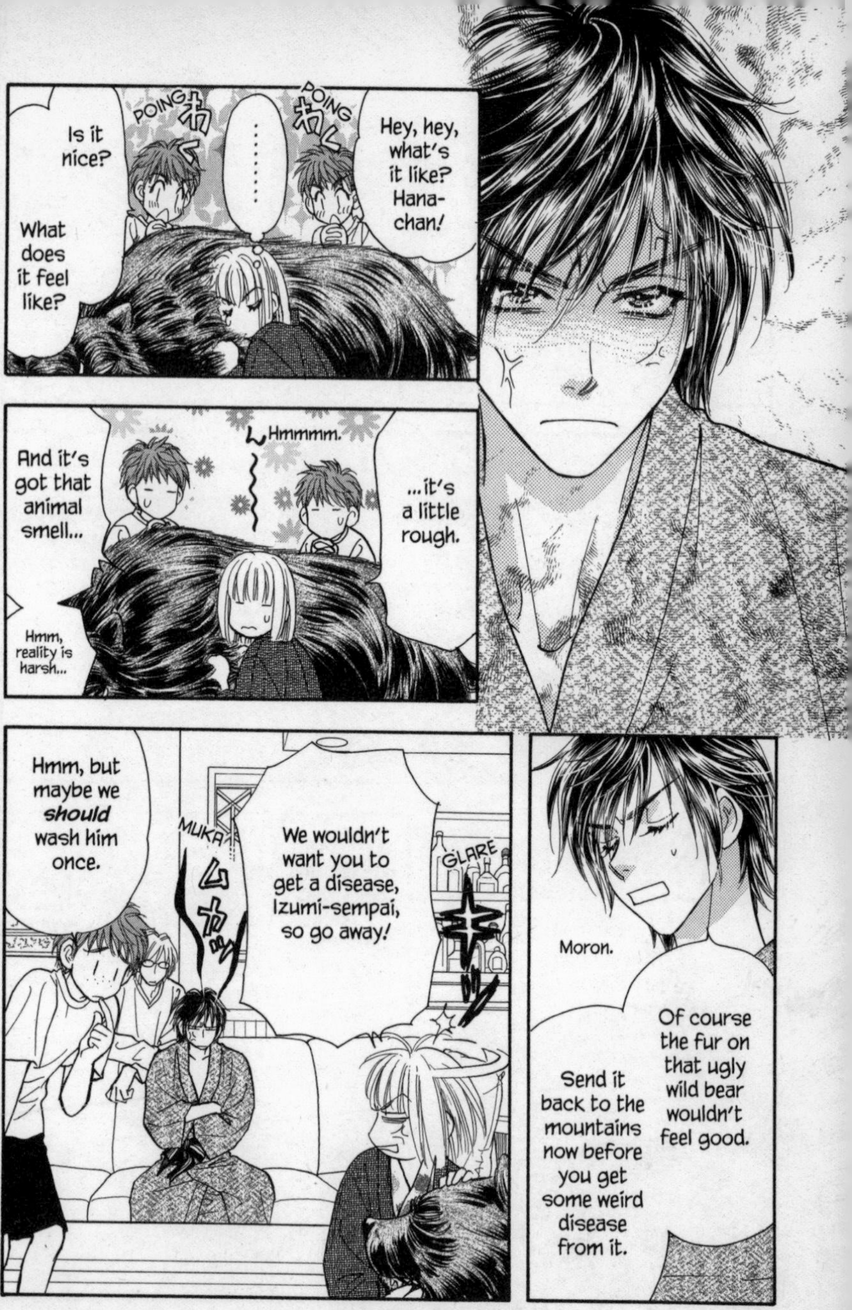

Hey, hey, what's it like? Hana-chan!
POING わく
....
POING わく
Is it nice?
What does it feel like?
...it's a little rough.
ん～～ Hmmmm.
And it's got that animal smell...
Hmm, reality is harsh...
Moron.
Of course the fur on that ugly wild bear wouldn't feel good.
Send it back to the mountains now before you get some weird disease from it.
GLARE
We wouldn't want you to get a disease, Izumi-sempai, so go away!
MUKA ムカッ
Hmm, but maybe we *should* wash him once.

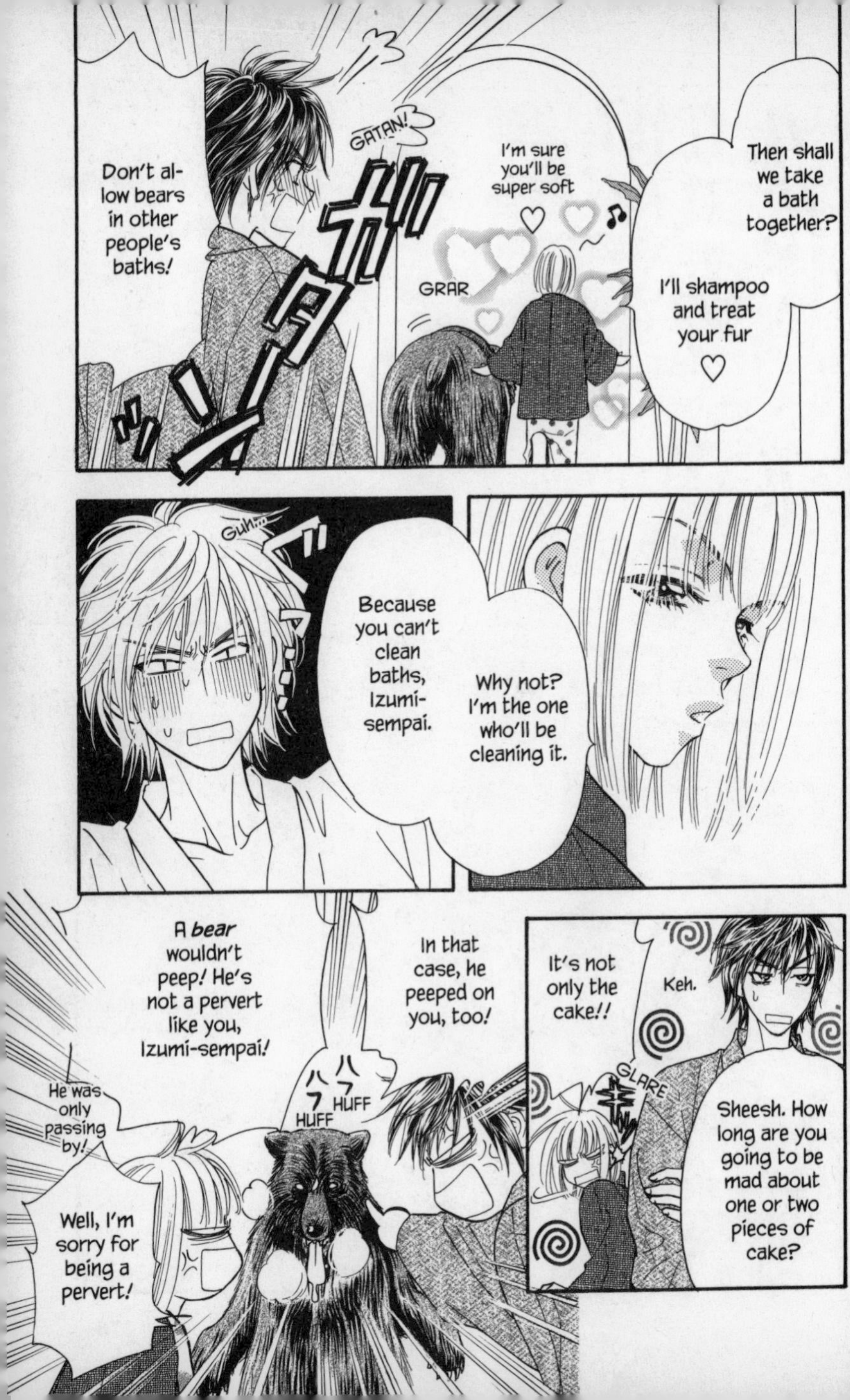
Then shall we take a bath together?
I'll shampoo and treat your fur ♡
I'm sure you'll be super soft ♡
GRAR
GATAN!
Don't al-low bears in other people's baths!
Why not? I'm the one who'll be cleaning it.
Because you can't clean baths, Izumi-sempai.
Guh...
Keh.
It's not only the cake!!
Sheesh. How long are you going to be mad about one or two pieces of cake?
GLARE
In that case, he peeped on you, too!
A *bear* wouldn't peep! He's not a pervert like you, Izumi-sempai!
HUFF
HUFF
He was only passing by!
Well, I'm sorry for being a pervert!

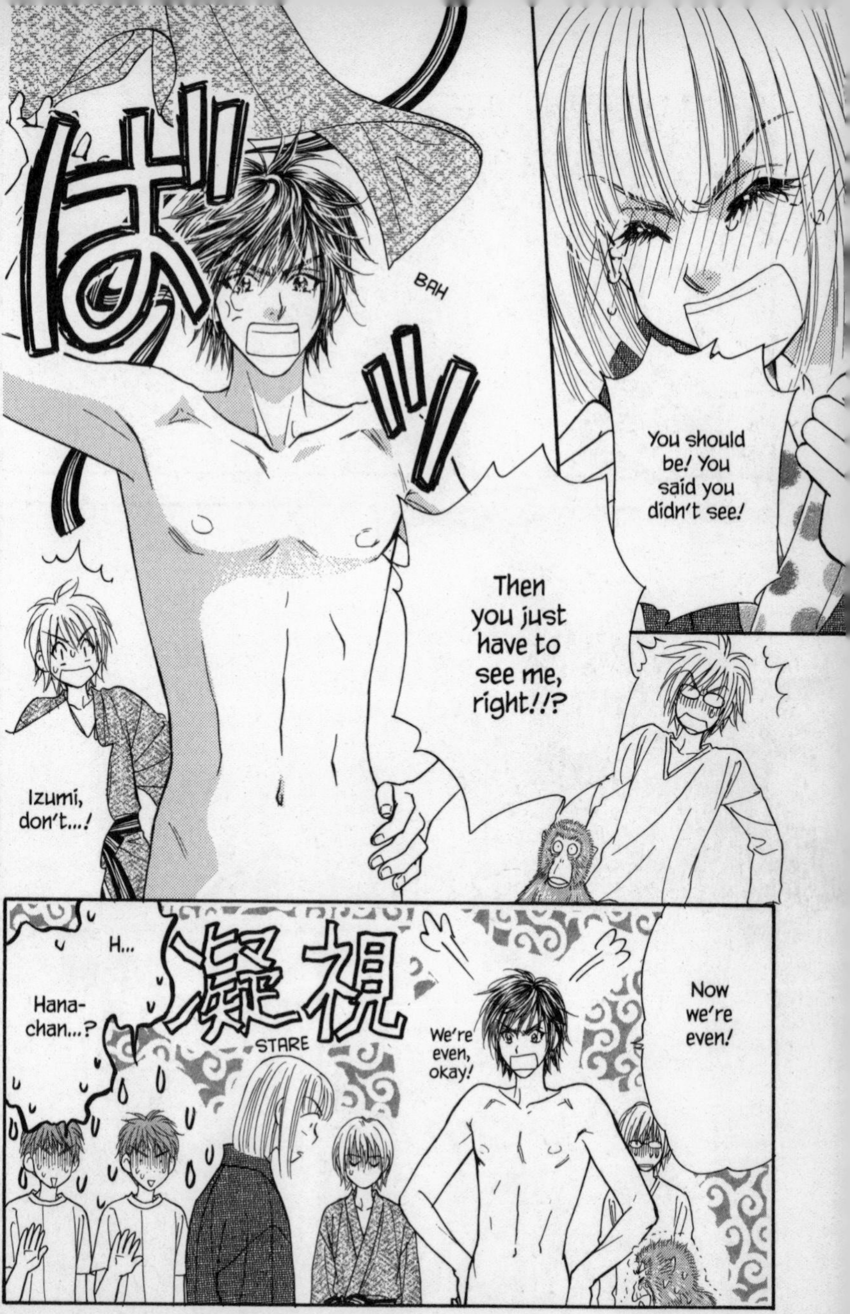
You should be! You said you didn't see!
ばっ
BAH
Then you just have to see me, right!!?
Izumi, don't...!
Now we're even!
We're even, okay!
凝視
STARE
H... Hana-chan...?

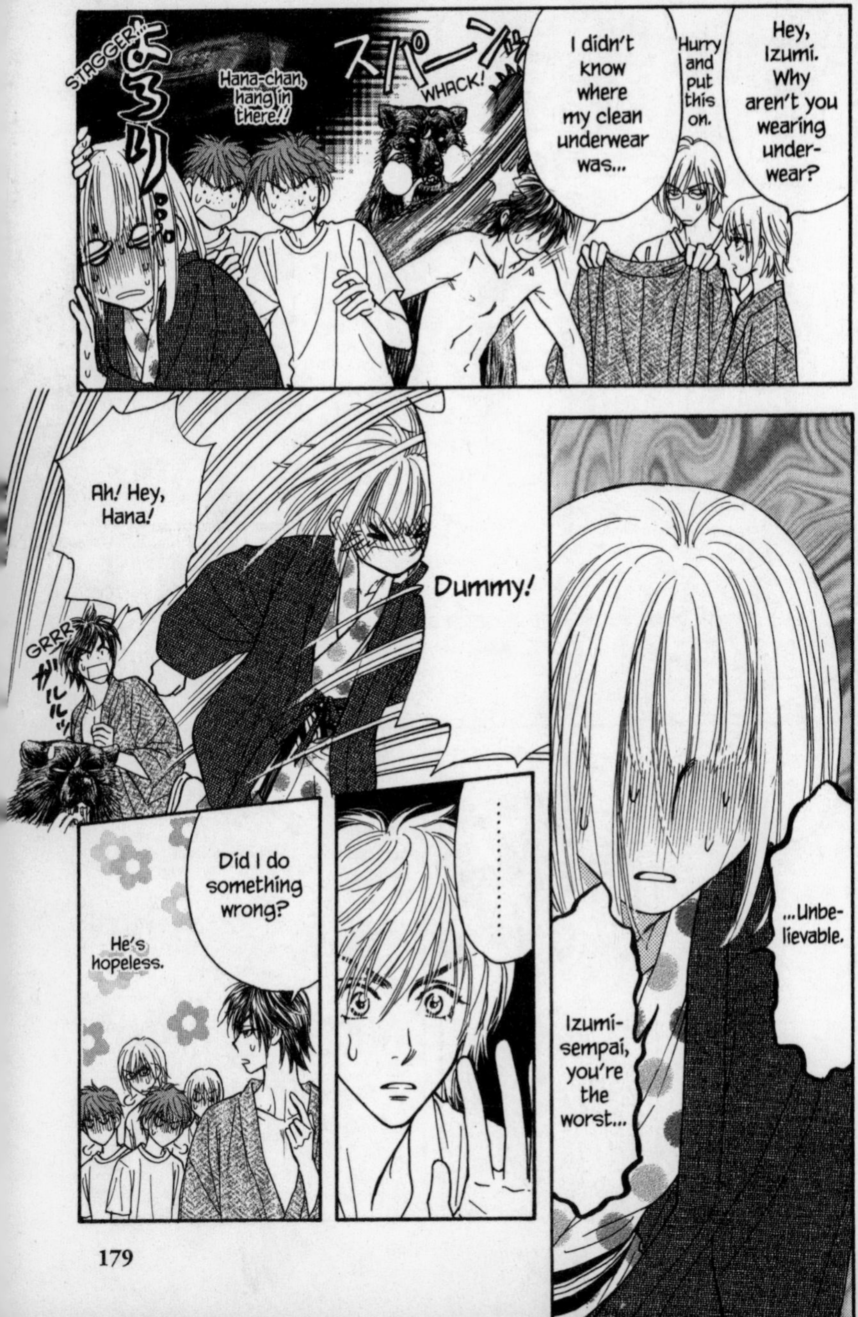

Hey, Izumi. Why aren't you wearing under-wear?
Hurry and put this on.
I didn't know where my clean underwear was...
スパーン
WHACK!
Hana-chan, hang in there!!
よろり
STAGGER...
...Unbe-lievable.
Izumi-sempai, you're the worst...
Dummy!
Ah! Hey, Hana!
ガルルッ
GRRR
......
Did I do something wrong?
He's hopeless.

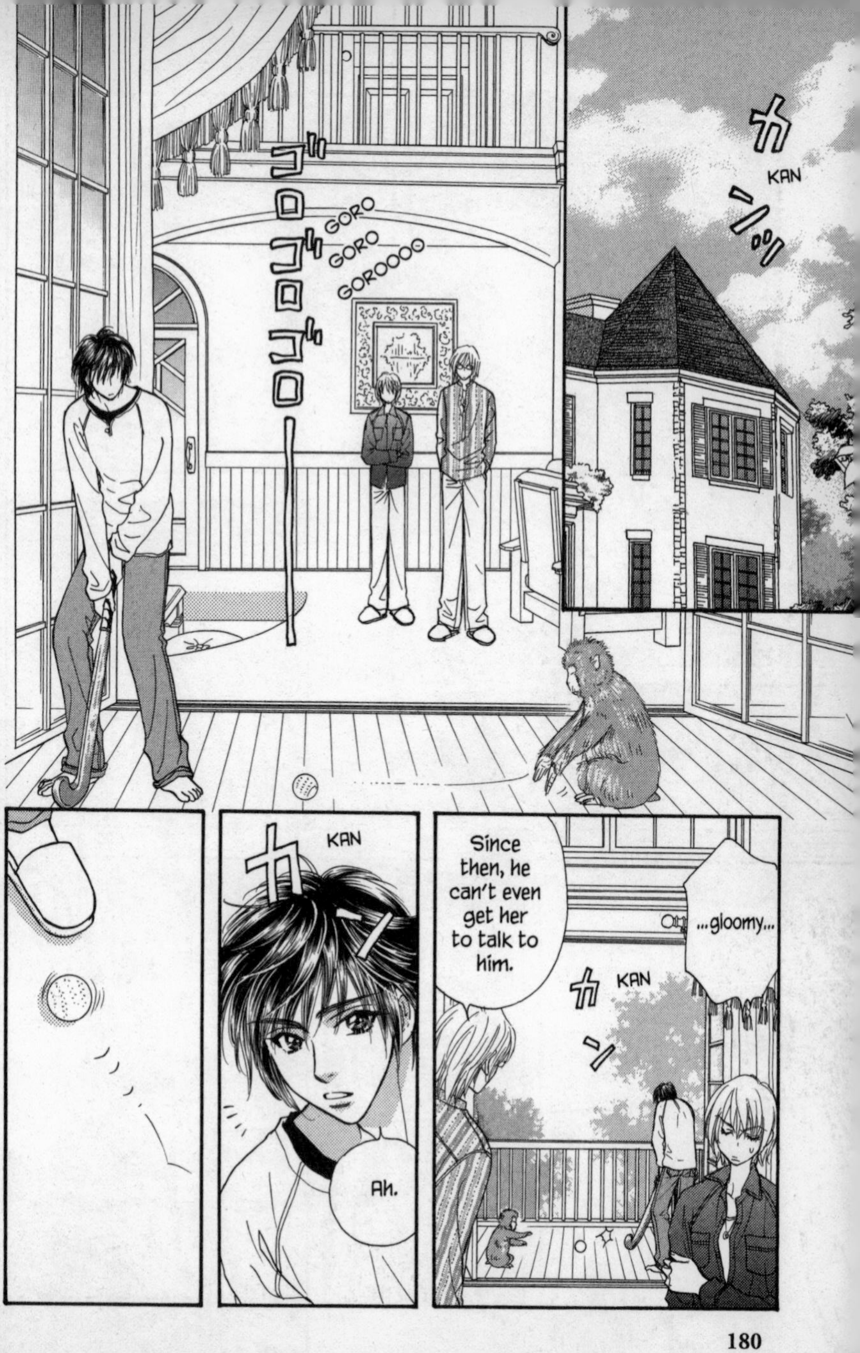
KAN
GORO
GORO
GOROOOO
...gloomy...
Since then, he can't even get her to talk to him.
KAN
KAN
Ah.

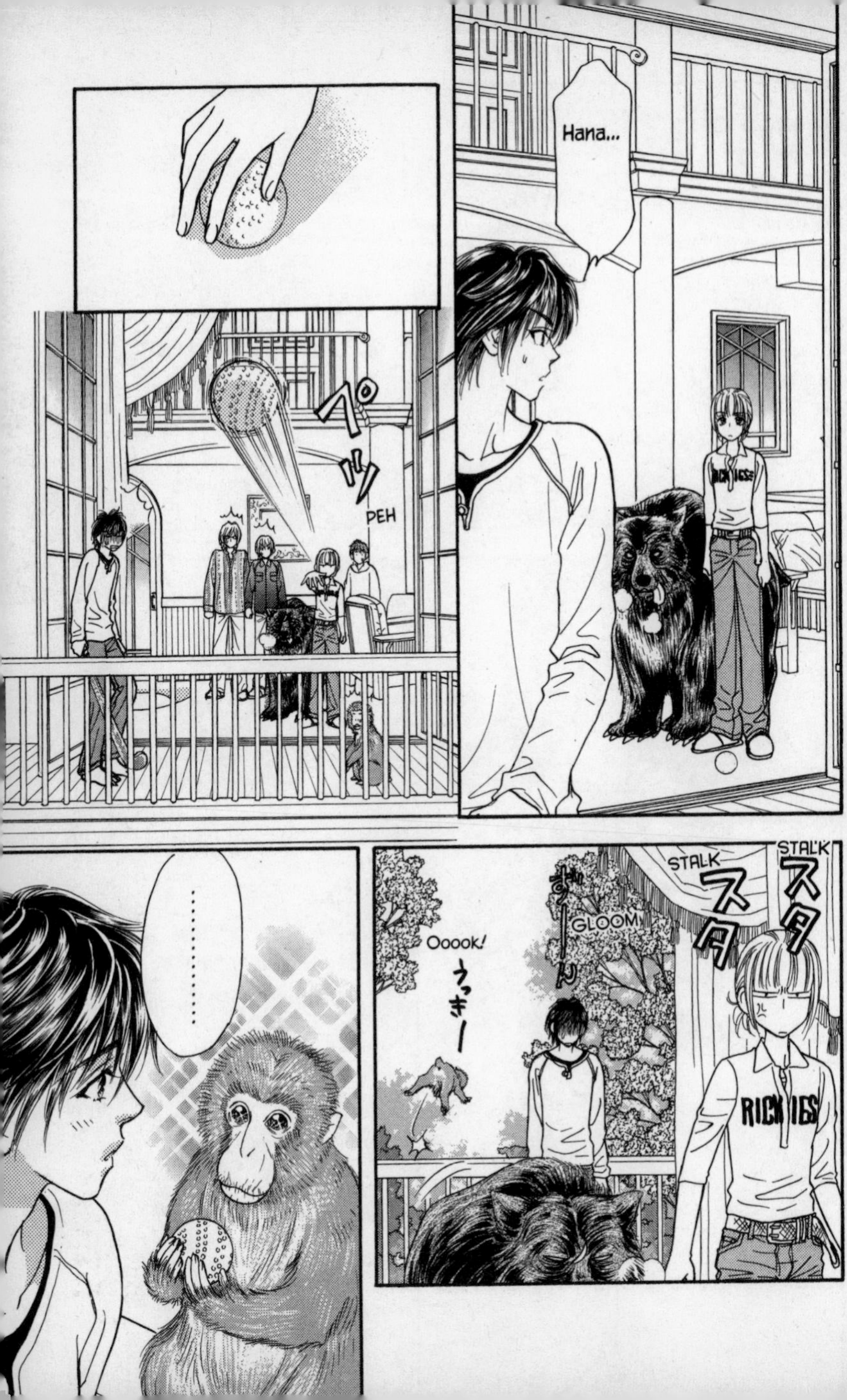

Hana...
ペッ
PEH
スタ
STALK
スタ
STALK
ずーん
GLOOM
うっきー
Ooook!
......

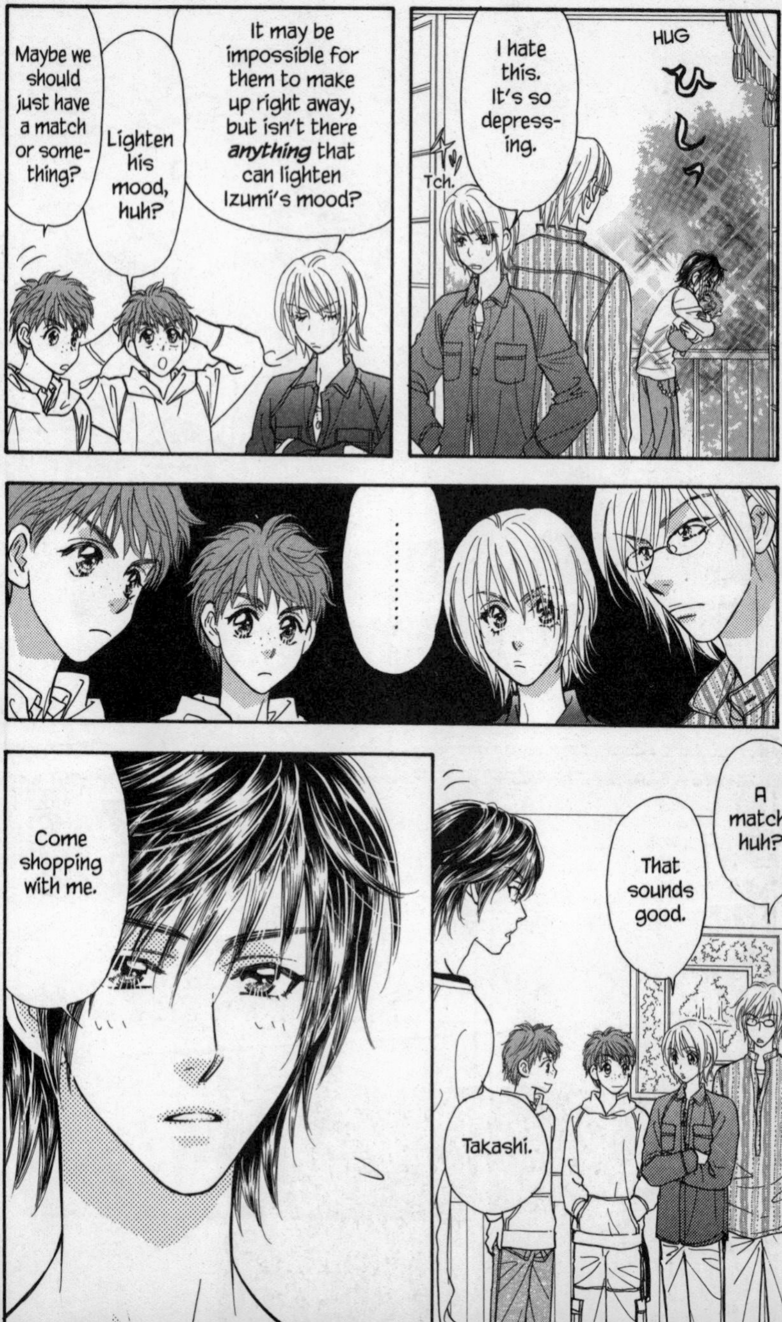
HUG
ひしっ
I hate this. It's so depress-ing.
Tch.
It may be impossible for them to make up right away, but isn't there *anything* that can lighten Izumi's mood?
Lighten his mood, huh?
Maybe we should just have a match or some-thing?
......
A match, huh?
That sounds good.
Takashi.
Come shopping with me.

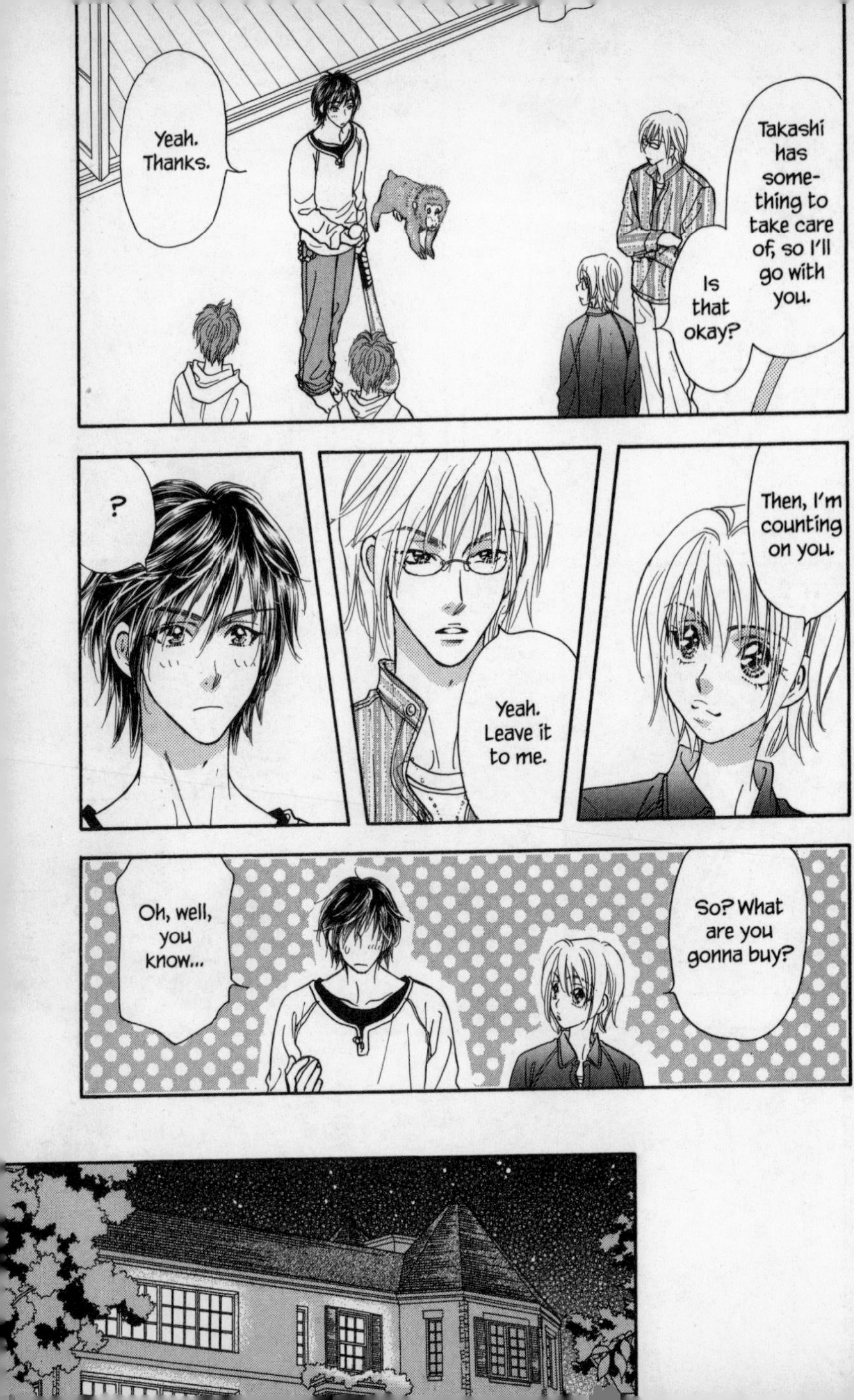
Takashi has something to take care of, so I'll go with you.
Is that okay?
Yeah. Thanks.
Then, I'm counting on you.
Yeah. Leave it to me.
?
So? What are you gonna buy?
Oh, well, you know...

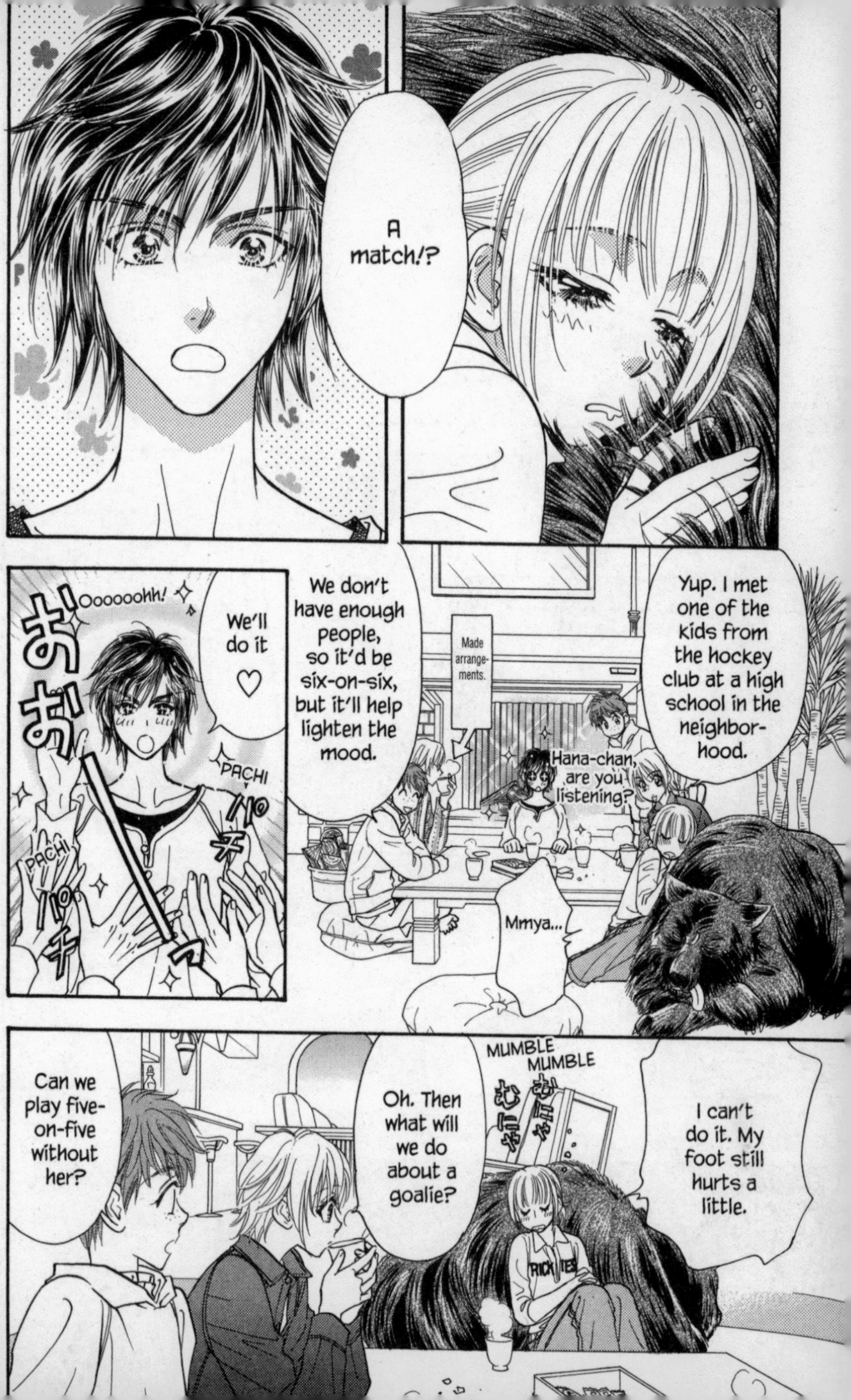
A match!?
Yup. I met one of the kids from the hockey club at a high school in the neighbor-hood.
Made arrange-ments.
We don't have enough people, so it'd be six-on-six, but it'll help lighten the mood.
Hana-chan, are you listening?
Mmya...
Oooooohh!
We'll do it ♡
PACHI
PACHI
I can't do it. My foot still hurts a little.
MUMBLE MUMBLE
Oh. Then what will we do about a goalie?
Can we play five-on-five without her?

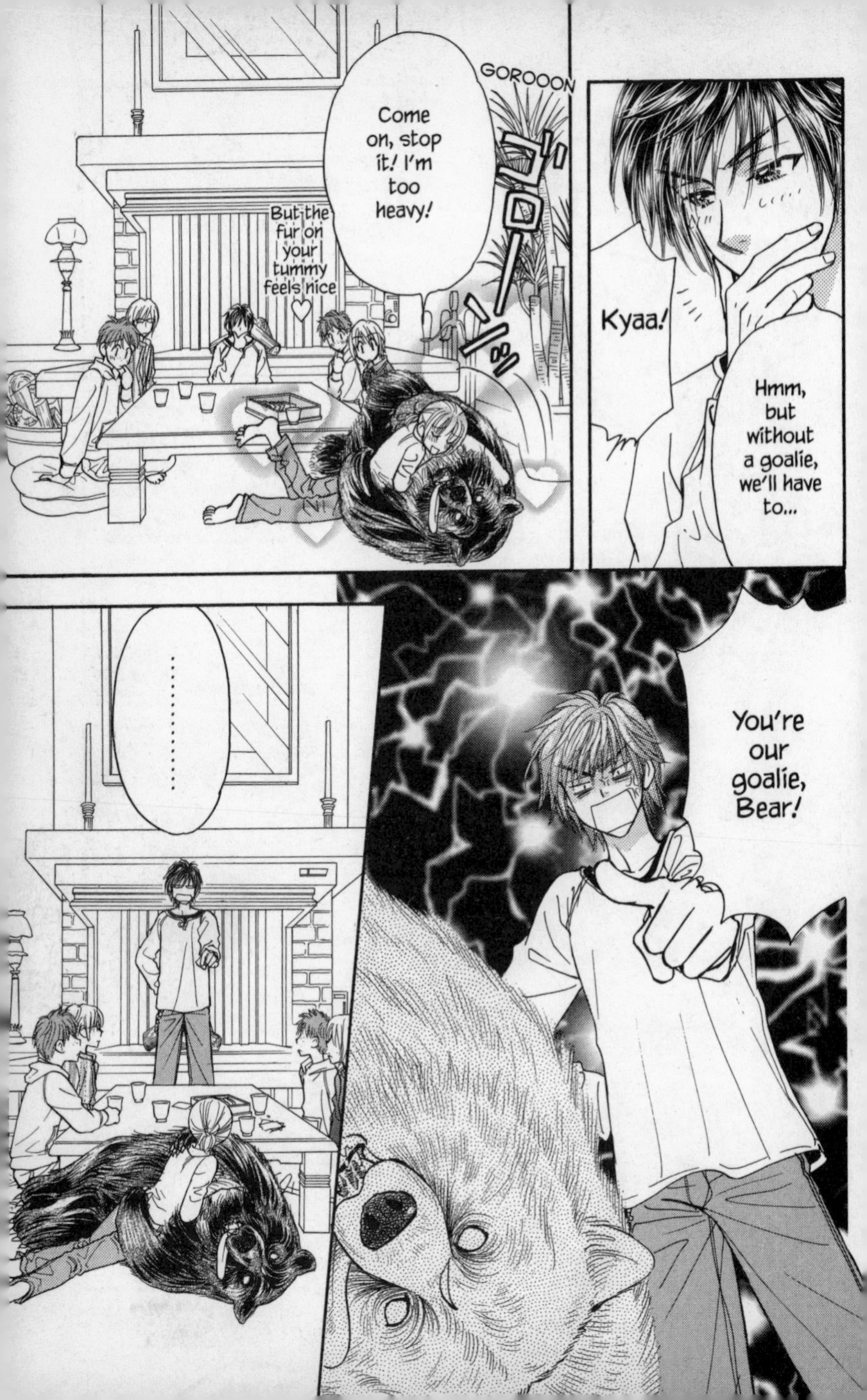
Kyaa!
Hmm, but without a goalie, we'll have to...
GOROOON
Come on, stop it! I'm too heavy!
But the fur on your tummy feels nice
You're our goalie, Bear!
......

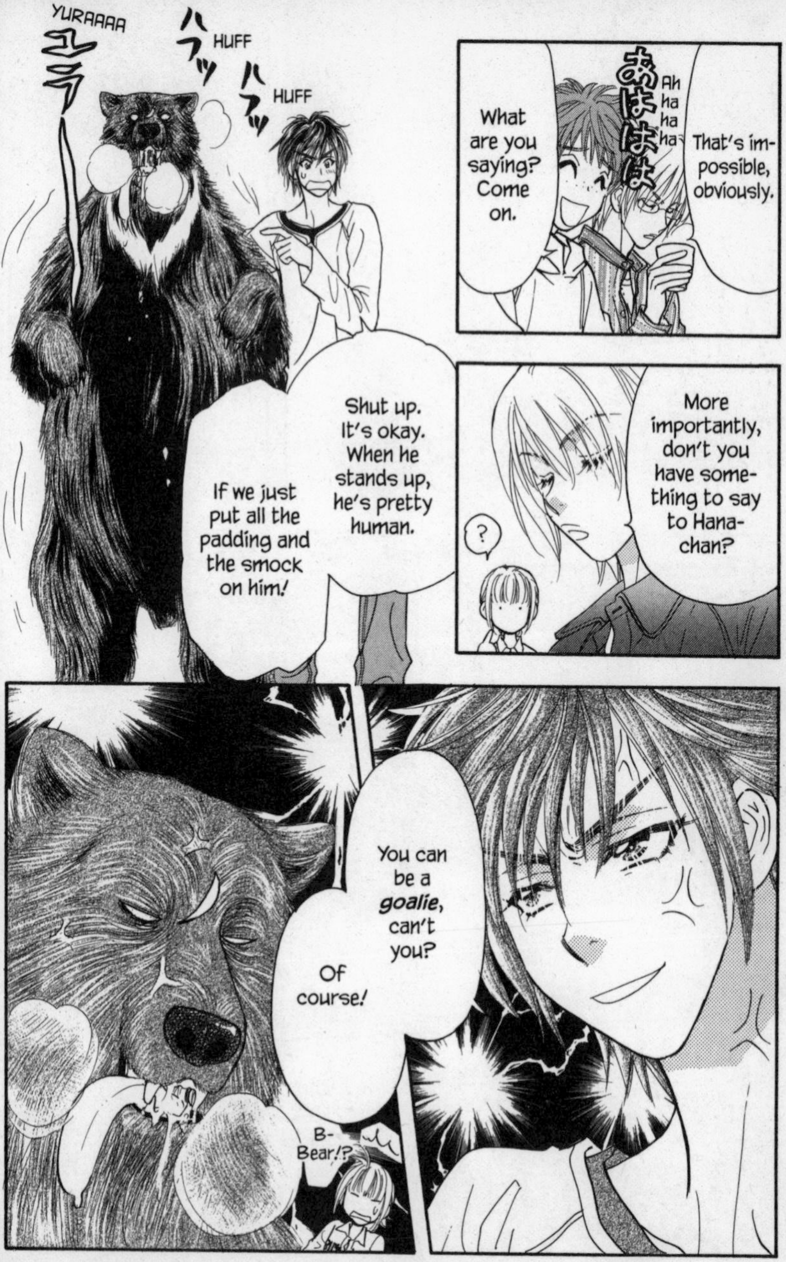
That's impossible, obviously.
あははは
Ah ha ha ha
What are you saying? Come on.
More importantly, don't you have something to say to Hana-chan?
?
ハフッ
HUFF
ハフッ
HUFF
ユラ
YURAAAA
Shut up. It's okay. When he stands up, he's pretty human.
If we just put all the padding and the smock on him!
You can be a *goalie*, can't you?
Of course!
B-Bear!?

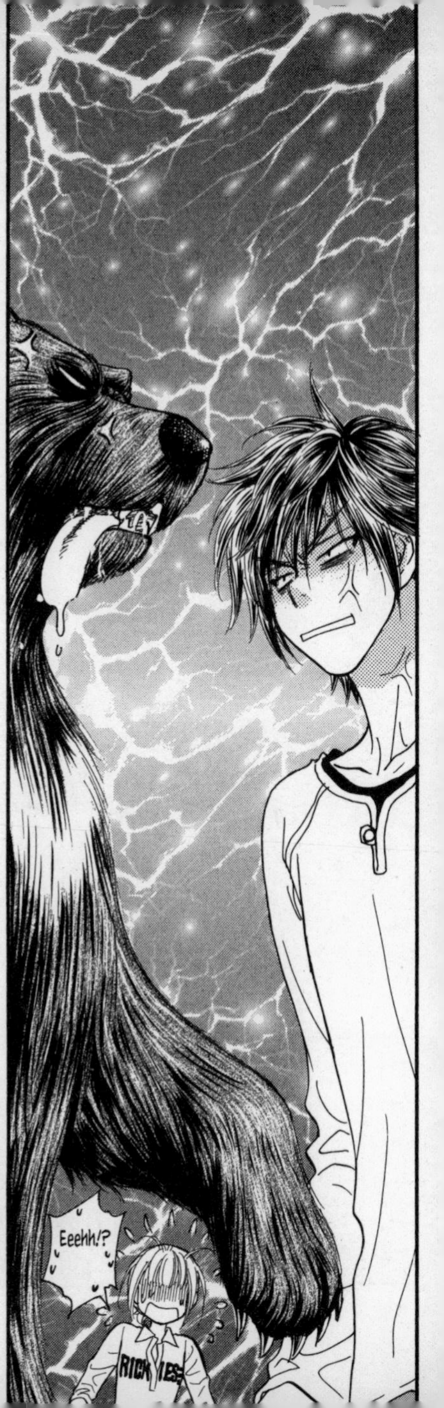
Eeehh!?
RICK IES

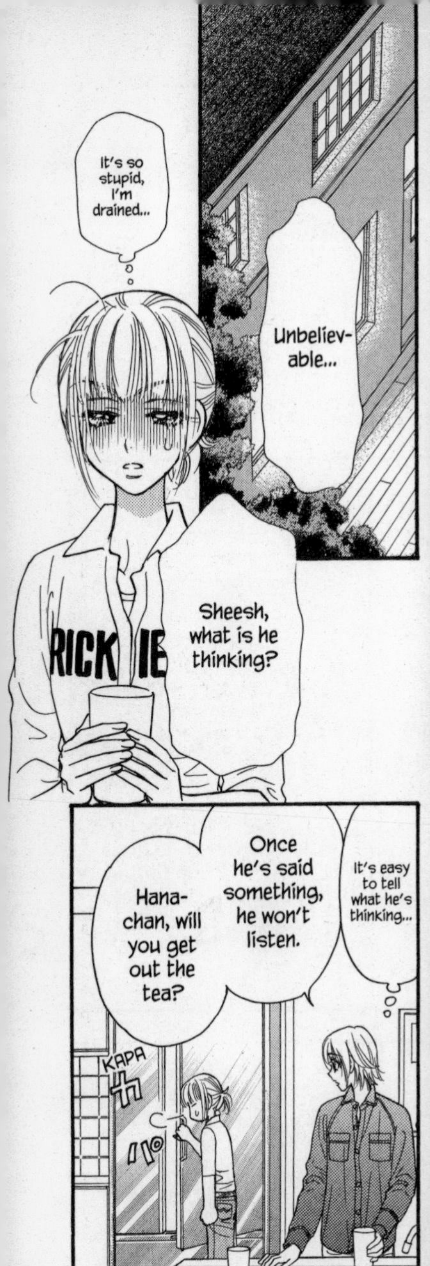
It's so stupid, I'm drained...
Unbelievable...
Sheesh, what is he thinking?
RICK IE
It's easy to tell what he's thinking...
Once he's said something, he won't listen.
Hana-chan, will you get out the tea?
KAPA

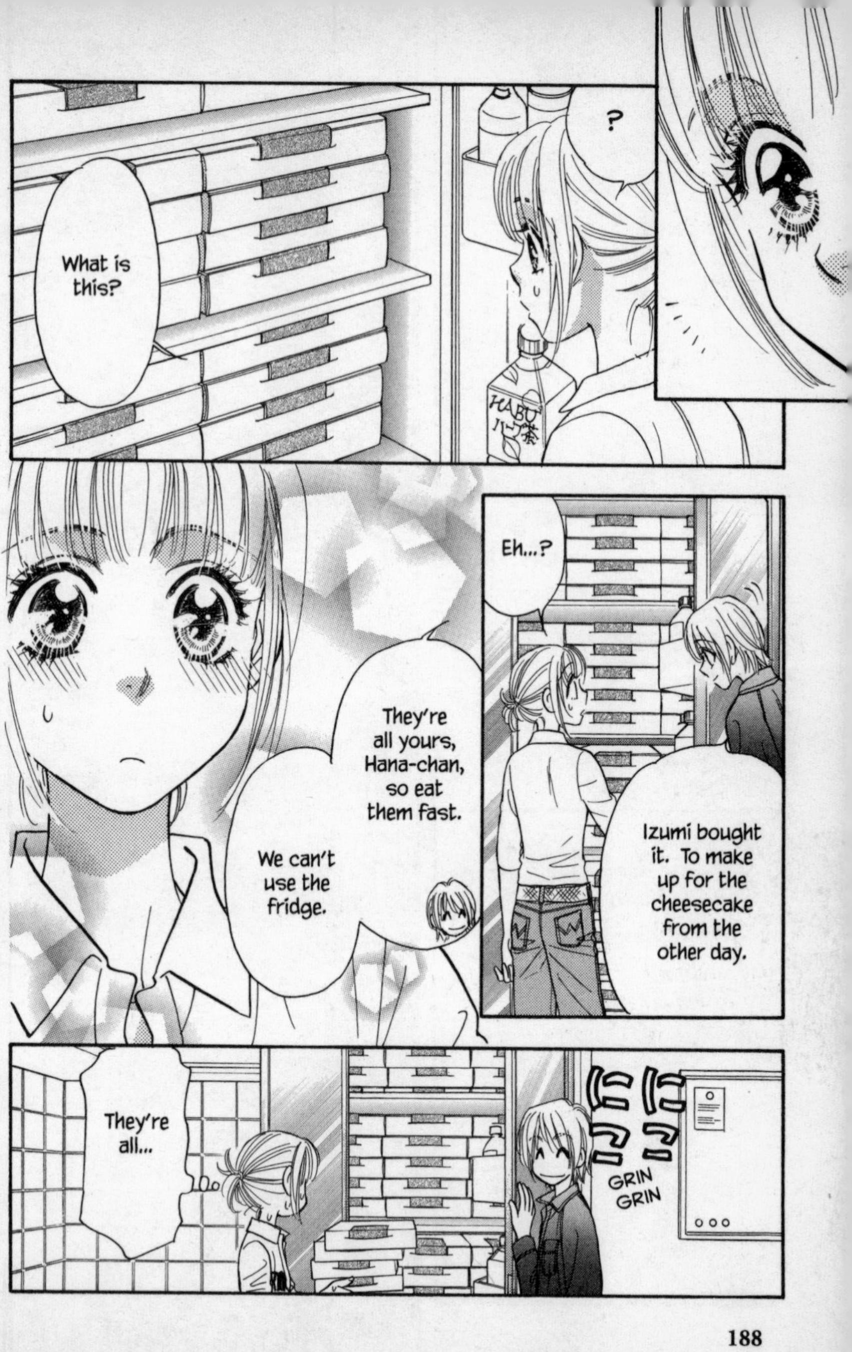
?
What is this?
Eh...?
Izumi bought it. To make up for the cheesecake from the other day.
They're all yours, Hana-chan, so eat them fast.
We can't use the fridge.
にこにこ
GRIN GRIN
They're all...

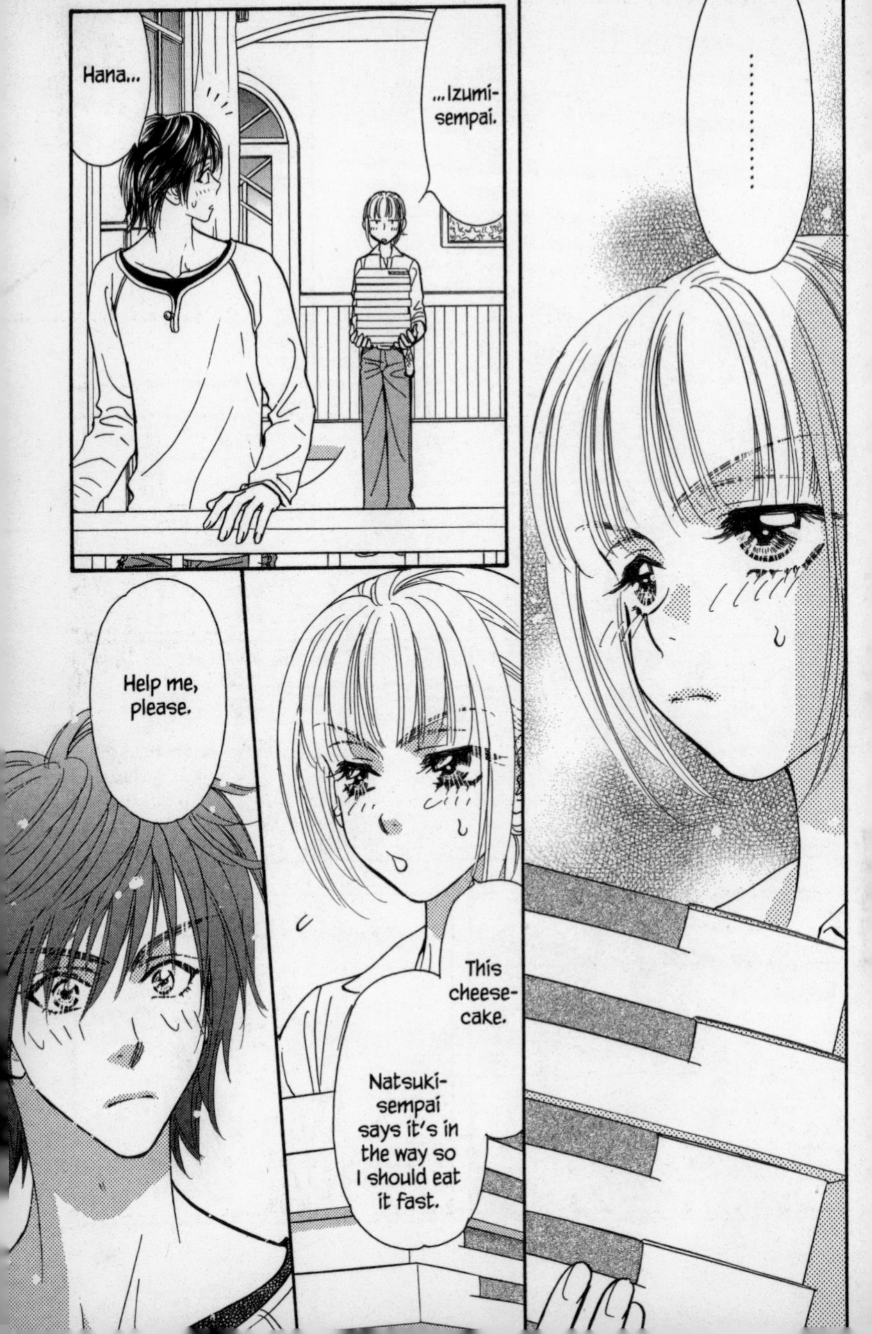
......
...Izumi-sempai.
Hana...
This cheesecake.
Natsuki-sempai says it's in the way so I should eat it fast.
Help me, please.

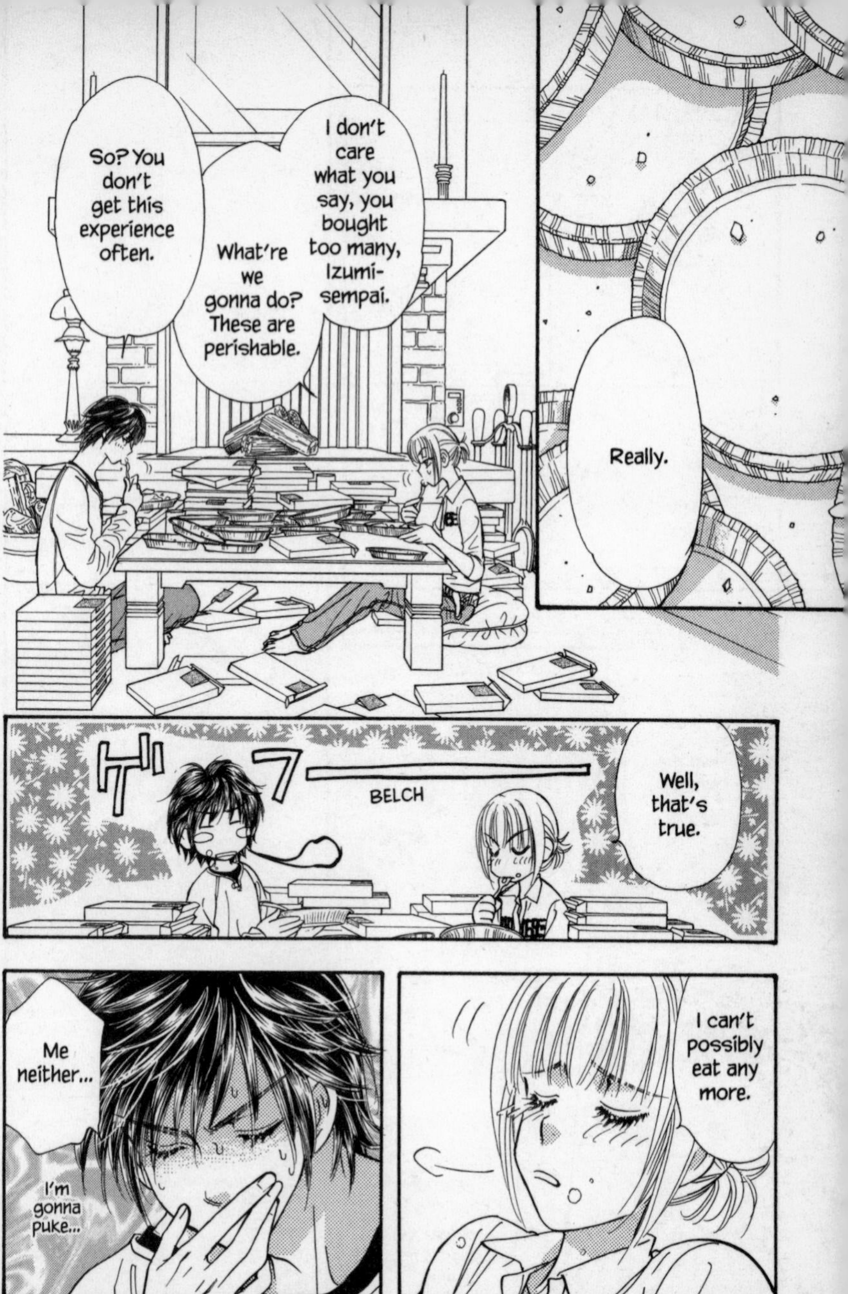
Really.
I don't care what you say, you bought too many, Izumi-sempai.
What're we gonna do? These are perishable.
So? You don't get this experience often.
Well, that's true.
BELCH
I can't possibly eat any more.
Me neither...
I'm gonna puke...

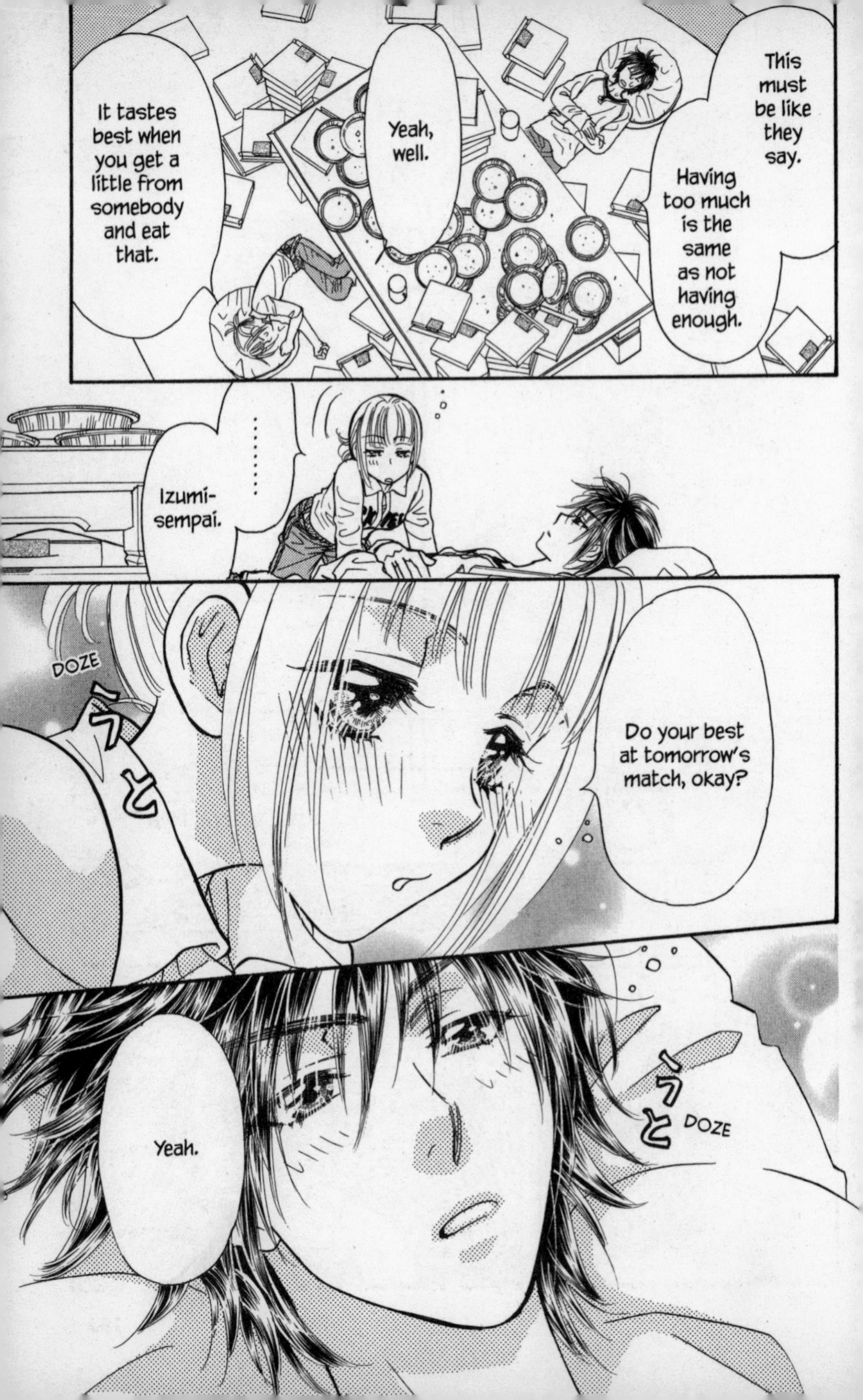
This must be like they say.
Having too much is the same as not having enough.
Yeah, well.
It tastes best when you get a little from somebody and eat that.
......
Izumi-sempai.
Do your best at tomorrow's match, okay?
DOZE
うと
DOZE
うと
Yeah.

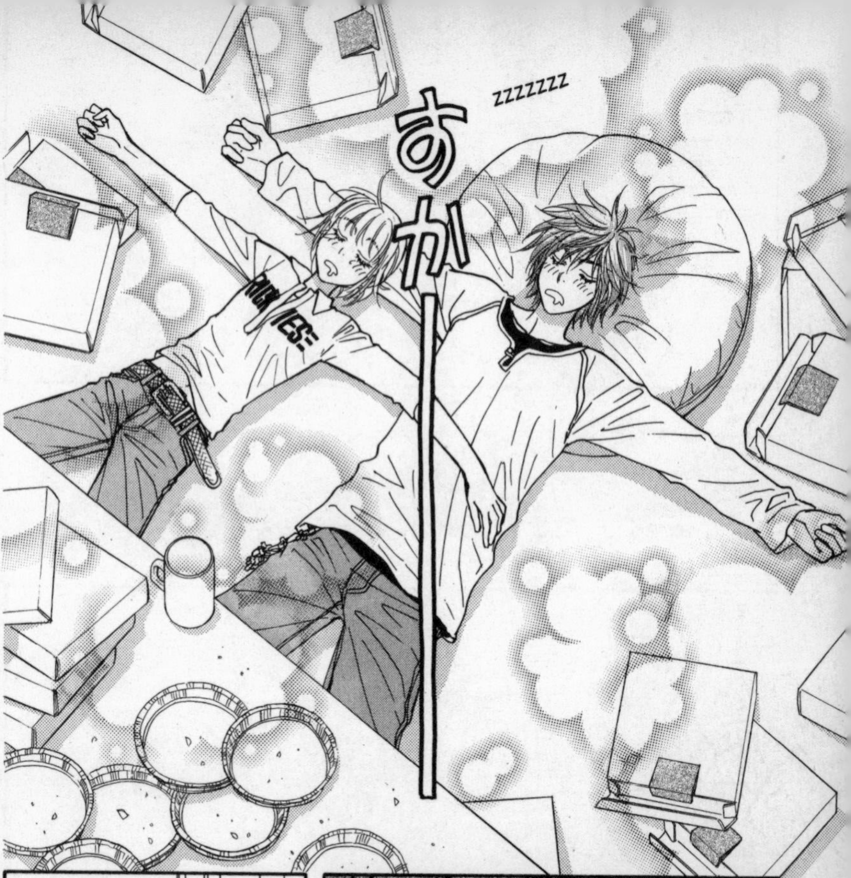
ZZZZZZZ
あか

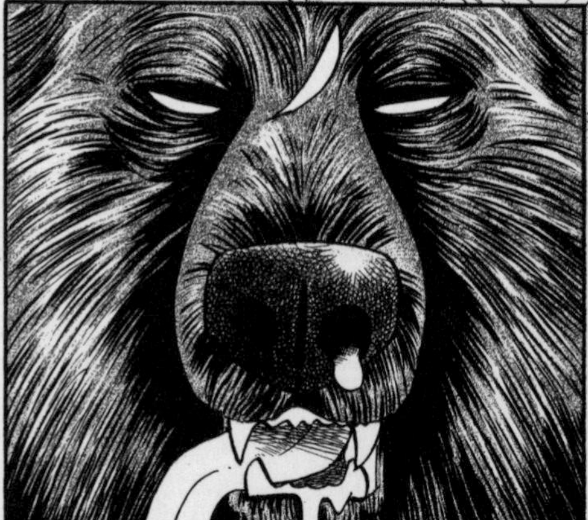

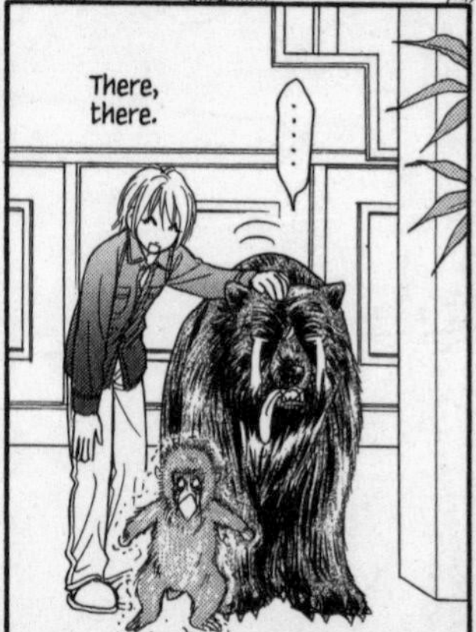
There, there.
……

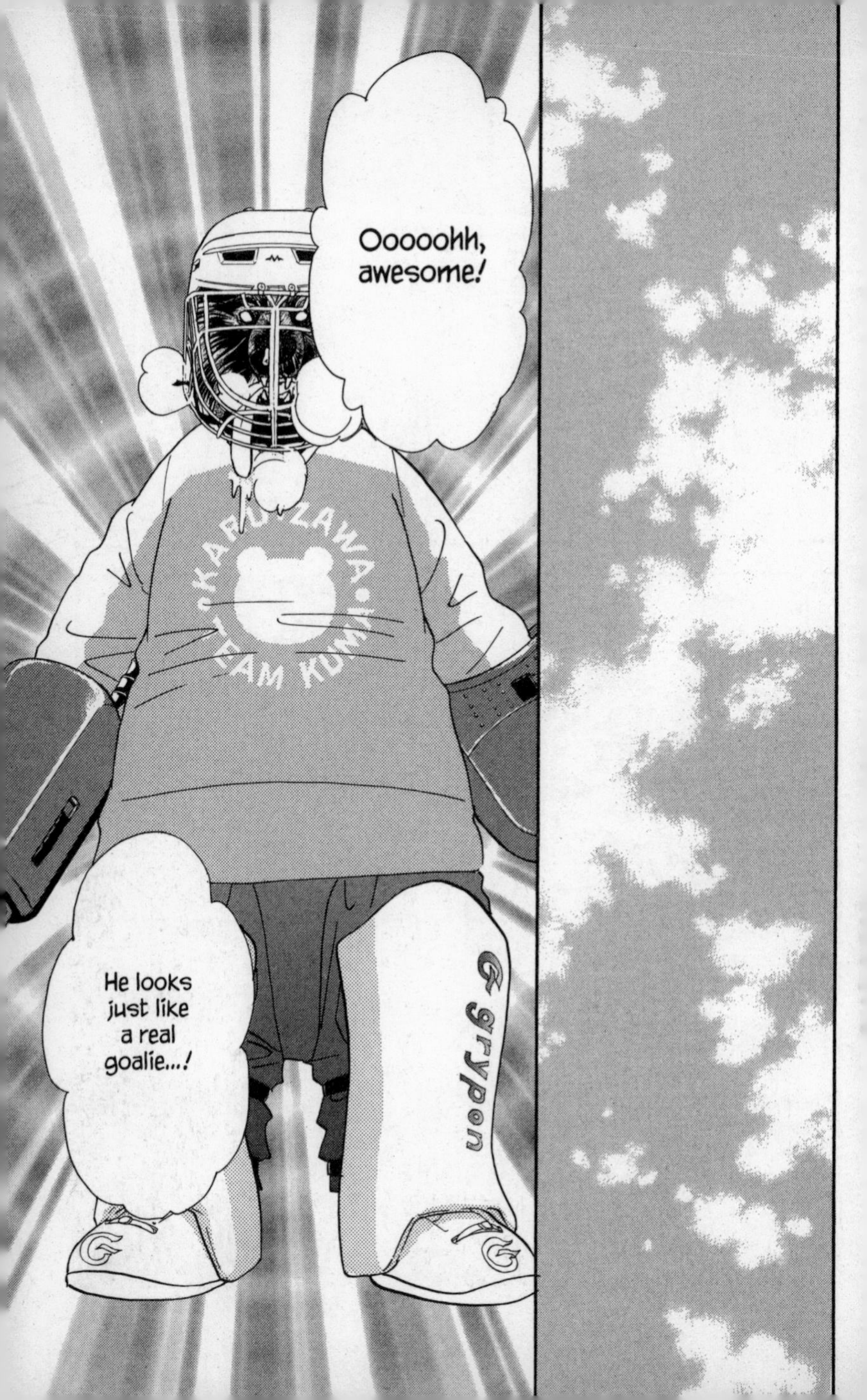
Ooooohh, awesome!
He looks just like a real goalie...!
grypon

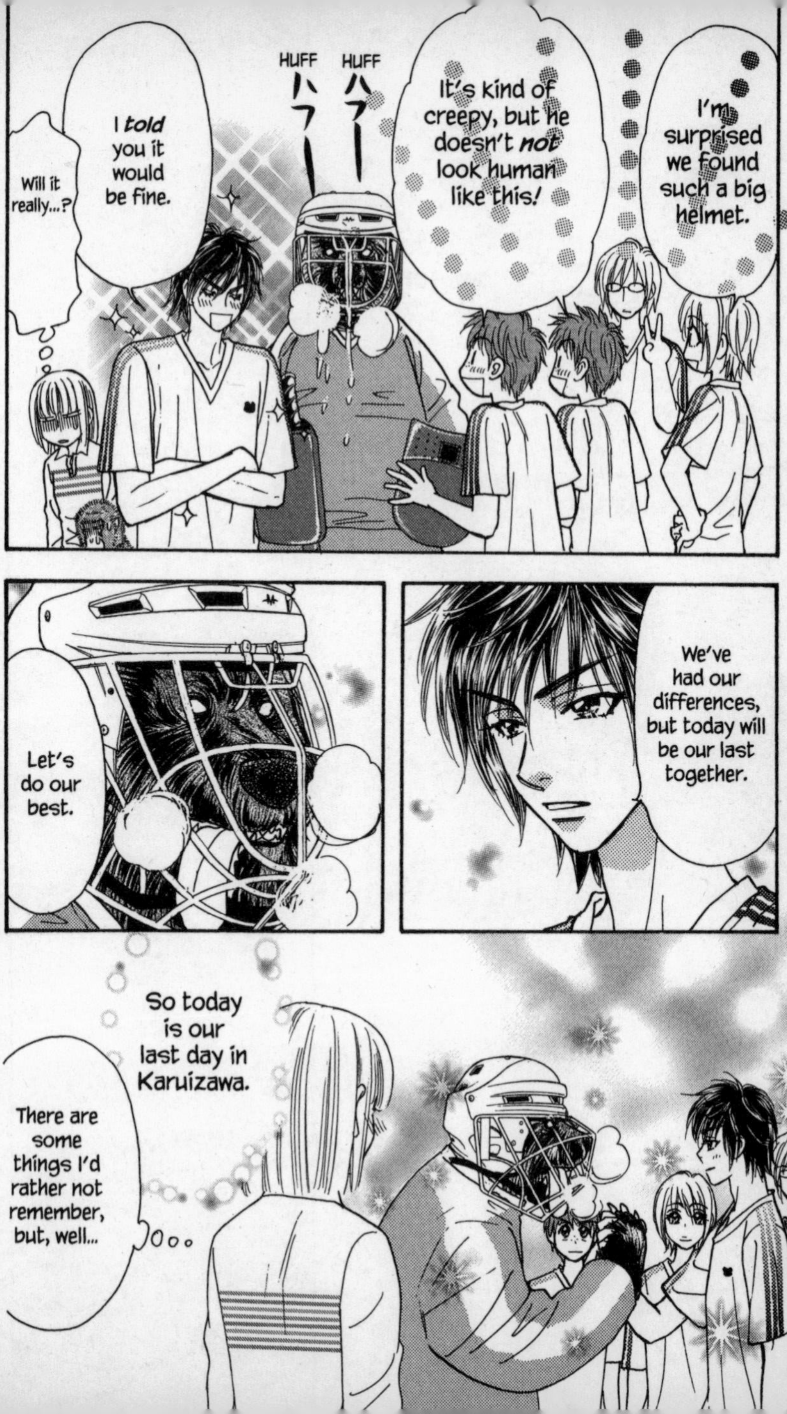
I'm surprised we found such a big helmet.
It's kind of creepy, but he doesn't *not* look human like this!
HUFF ハフー
HUFF ハフー
I *told* you it would be fine.
Will it really...?
We've had our differences, but today will be our last together.
Let's do our best.
So today is our last day in Karuizawa.
There are some things I'd rather not remember, but, well...

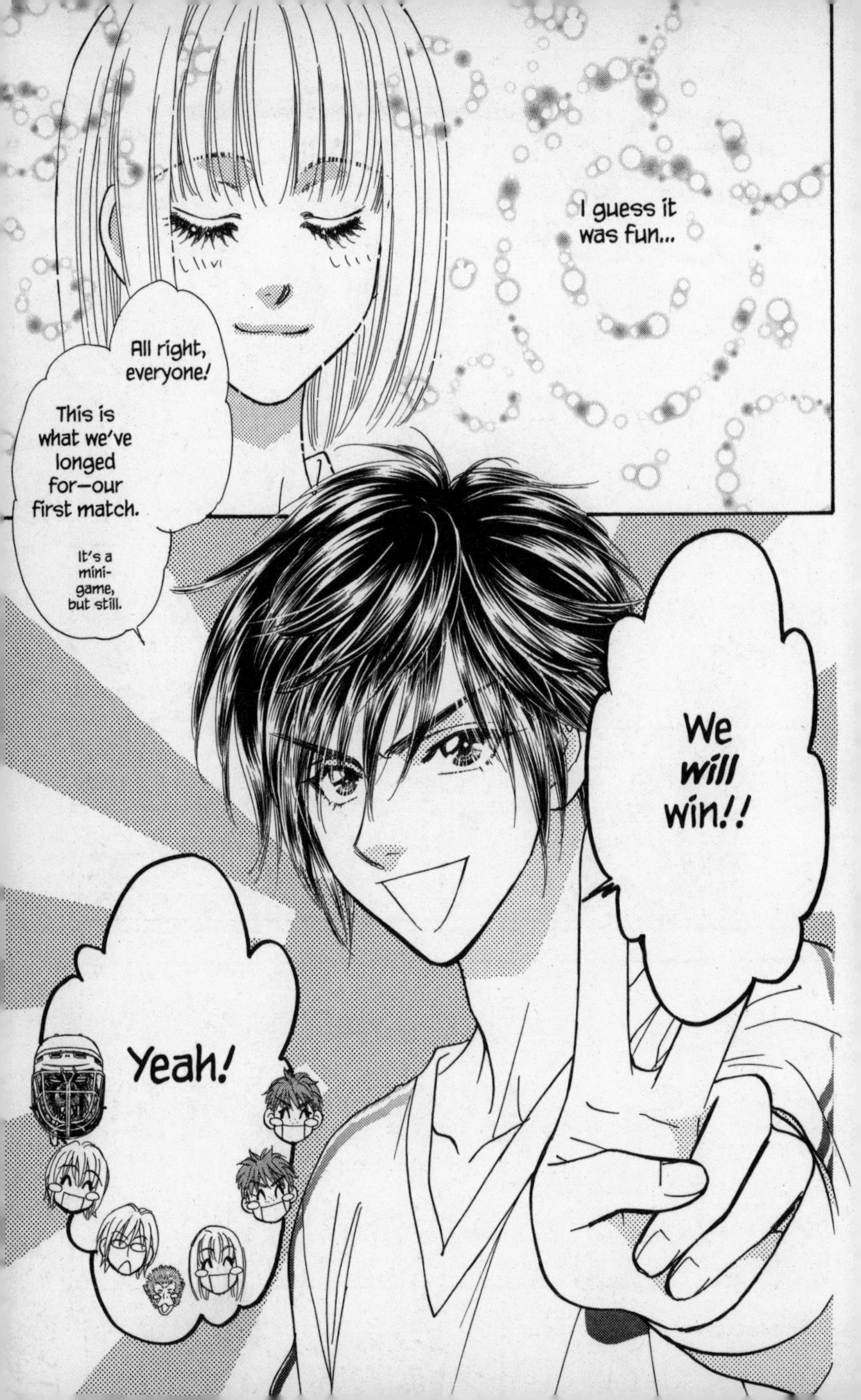
I guess it was fun...
All right, everyone!
This is what we've longed for—our first match.
It's a mini-game, but still.
We *will* win!!
Yeah!

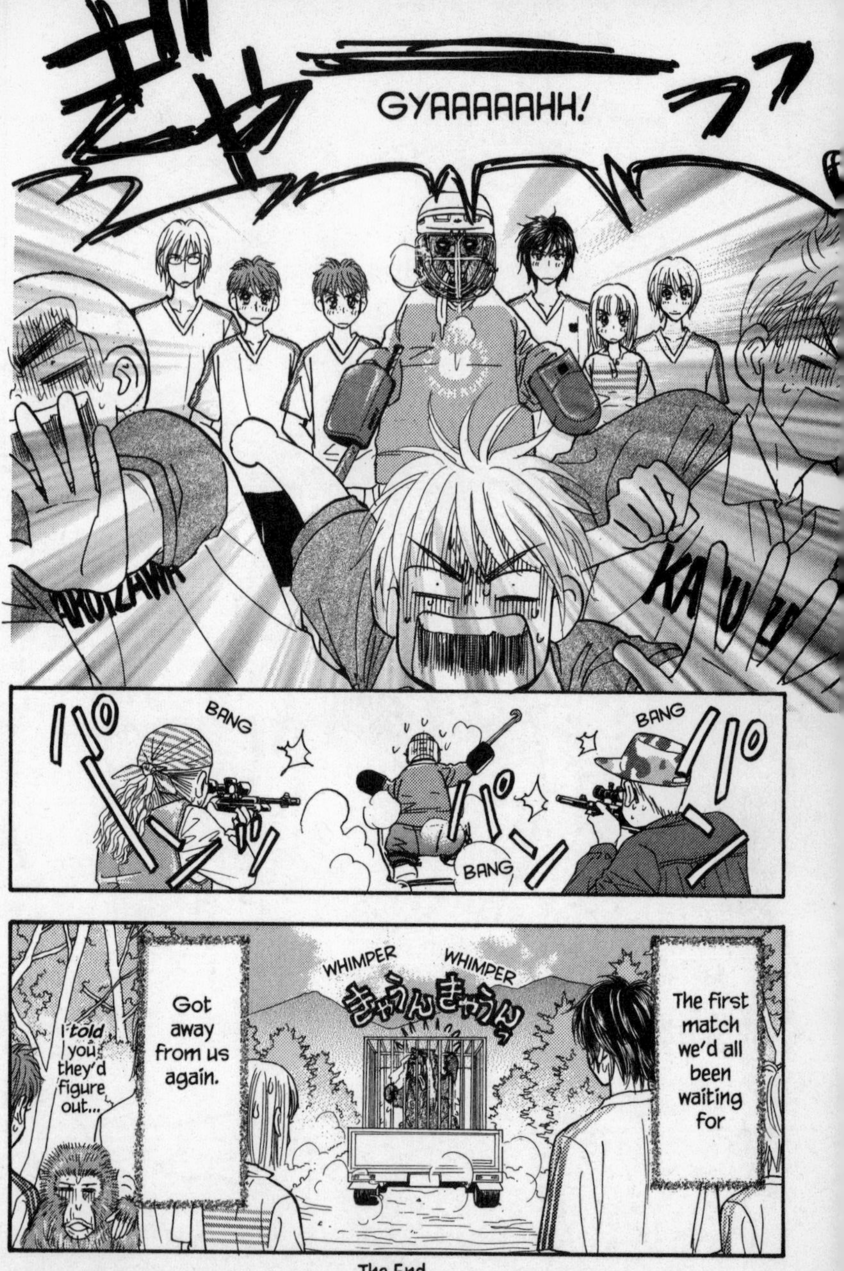
GYAAAAAHH!
BANG
BANG
BANG
The first match we'd all been waiting for
WHIMPER WHIMPER
きゃうんきゃうん
Got away from us again.
I *told* you they'd figure out...

The End

See you in volume 2 ♪

Thank you very much!

Everyone on the field hockey club at
Waseda University Senior High School.

The number of hockey clubs in each
prefecture is fictionalized. I'm sorry~~.
Thank you very much for reading! The
series will go on a little longer, so please
enjoy the next volume, too.

Ai Morinaga

Translation Notes

Japanese is a tricky language for most Westerners, and translation is often more art than science. For your edification and reading pleasure, here are notes on some of the places where we could have gone in a different direction with our translation of the work, or where a Japanese cultural reference is used.

Nebosuke, page 7

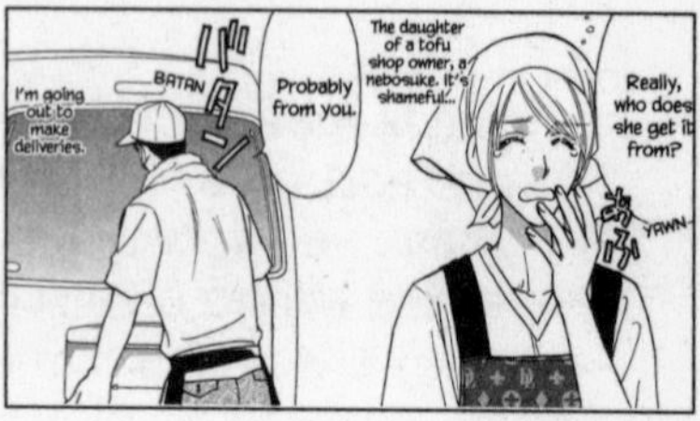
Really, who does she get it from?
The daughter of a tofu shop owner, a nebosuke. It's shameful...
YAWN
Probably from you.
BATAN
I'm going out to make deliveries.

Nebosuke comes from a combination of *nebô*, which means "sleeping late," and *suke*, which is a common ending for male names. So basically Hana's mother is saying that her name may as well be Nebosuke for all the sleeping she does.

Botchama, page 12

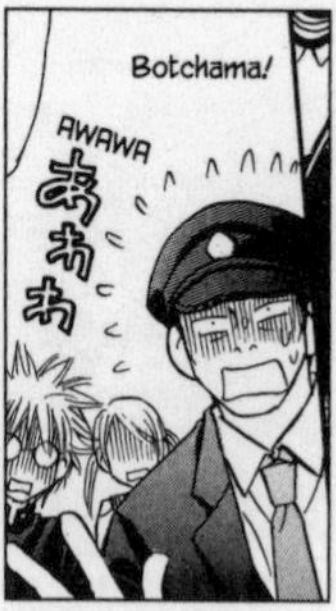
Botchama!
AWAWA

Botchama is a respectful way of addressing someone of a higher social status, but lower age, than your own, especially the son of a family where one works as a maid, butler, etc.

Grand Hockey Club, page 13

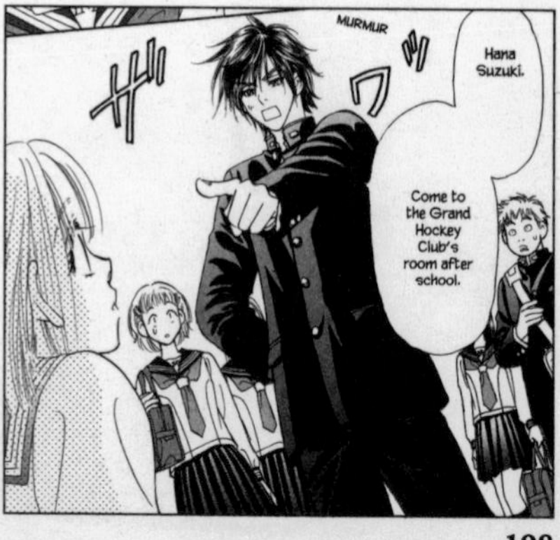
Hana Suzuki.
MURMUR
Come to the Grand Hockey Club's room after school.

The term *gurando* can be the Japanese pronunciation of the English "grand" or "ground." In this case, it probably means both, as the team plays field (or "ground") hockey and Izumi is likely to think of his club as being grand.

Hocke, page 14

Hocke, or *hokke,* is the Japanese name for the type of fish known as the Arabesque greenling, used in sushi. Later on, we find out that Hana still thinks it's a *hocke* club when she sees the club's sign and wonders why there's a "y" at the end!

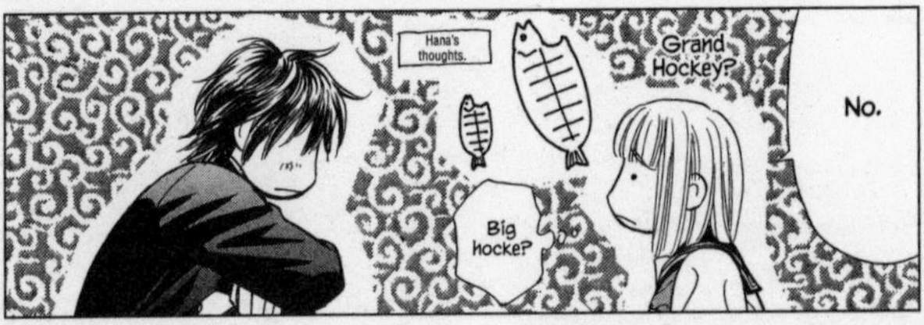
No.
Grand Hockey?
Hana's thoughts.
Big hocke?

Gyûtan, page 24

Sendai, a city in the Miyagi prefecture, is famous for its *gyûtan,* or beef tongue, cooking.

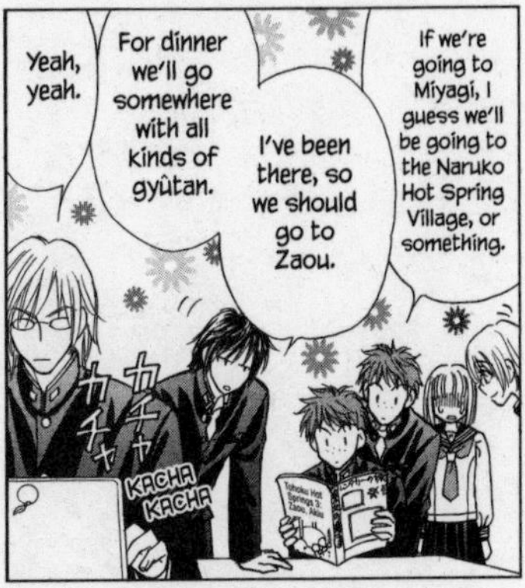
If we're going to Miyagi, I guess we'll be going to the Naruko Hot Spring Village, or something.
I've been there, so we should go to Zaou.
For dinner we'll go somewhere with all kinds of gyûtan.
Yeah, yeah.
KACHA KACHA

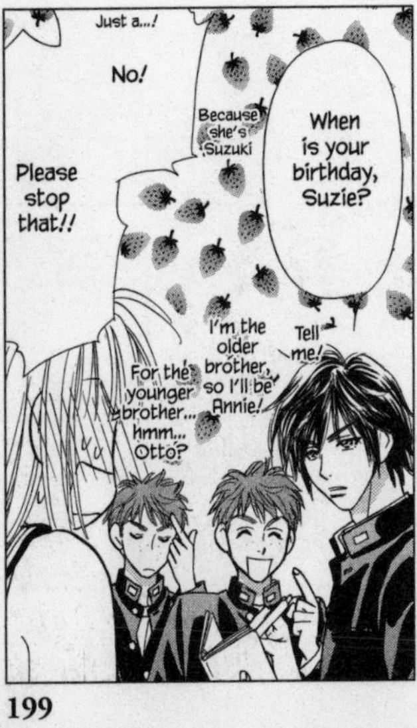
When is your birthday, Suzie?
Because she's Suzuki
No!
Just a...!
Please stop that!!
Tell me!
I'm the older brother, so I'll be Annie!
For the younger brother... hmm... Otto?

Annie & Otto, page 26

The Japanese word for "older brother" is *ani,* and the word for "younger brother" is *otôto.* So for nicknames, the Ayuharas choose Annie and Otto. Apparently, they place little value on their given names.

Jîya, page 32

A *jîya* is an elderly servant, kind of like a nanny, but male. This Ayuhara is saying that Takashi is protective of Izumi.

Well, Itoigawa-sempai has always been Izumi-sempai's jiya.

What are you saying? You're doing sports surrounded by hot guys. Isn't that what youth is all about!?
You're really gonna get it, Hana!
GH is the club every girl in the school is dying to join!
What-ever.

You're really gonna get it, Hana!, page 35

Hana's friend is warning her that if she doesn't appreciate this blessing that she has been given in being allowed to join the hockey club, she will be punished for it sooner or later.

Zunda-mochi, page 47

Zunda-mochi, a type of rice cake, is another famous Sendai food.

Take care! Bring back some gyûtan for your mother ♡
I want zunda-mochi!
I am sleepy.
YAWN
But why are we meeting on the roof of the school?
Not the train station?

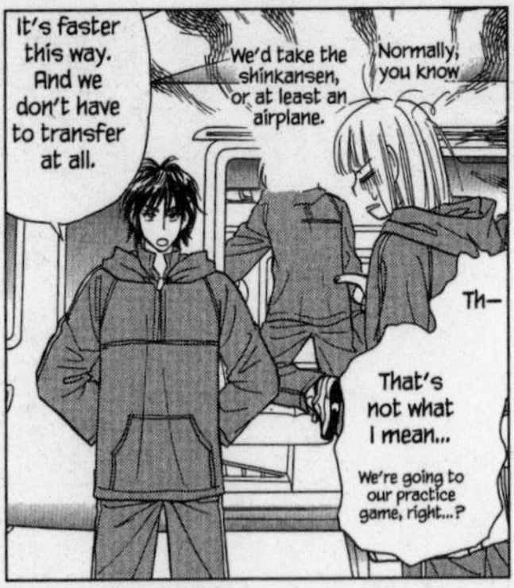
Normally, you know
We'd take the shinkansen, or at least an airplane.
It's faster this way. And we don't have to transfer at all.
Th—
That's not what I mean...
We're going to our practice game, right...?

Shinkansen, page 50

The *shinkansen* is the bullet train.

Ekiben, page 51

Ekiben comes from *eki* (train station) and *bentô* or *obentô* (boxed lunch). In other words, it's a lunch that you buy at the station.

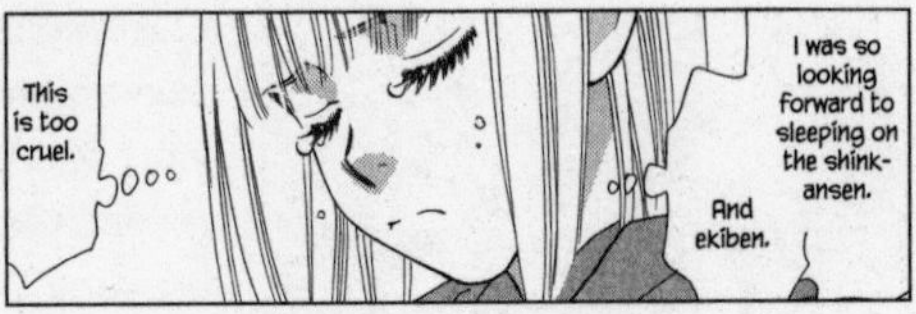
I was so looking forward to sleeping on the shink-ansen.
And ekiben.
This is too cruel.

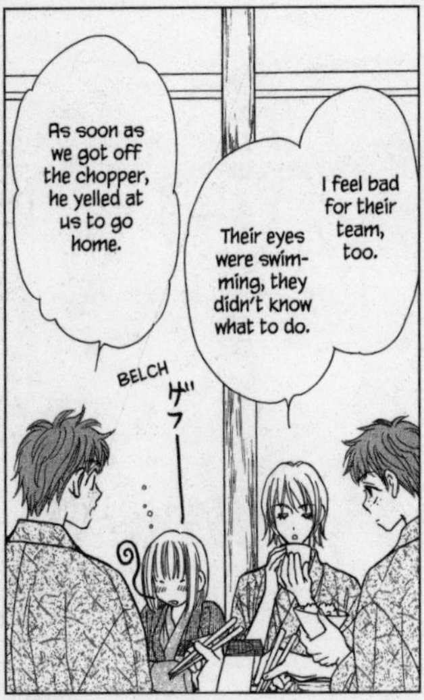
I feel bad for their team, too.
Their eyes were swim-ming, they didn't know what to do.
As soon as we got off the chopper, he yelled at us to go home.
BELCH
ゲフー

Their eyes were swimming, page 59

Because the team didn't know what to do, their eyes darted around, looking for some hint, as if swimming.

Gochisô-sama, page 59

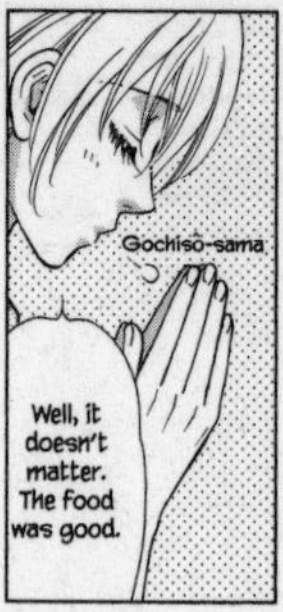
Gochisô-sama
Well, it doesn't matter. The food was good.

Gochisô-sama is a ritual expression used after finishing a meal. A rough equivalent would be, "Thank you for the wonderful meal."

Futon, page 60

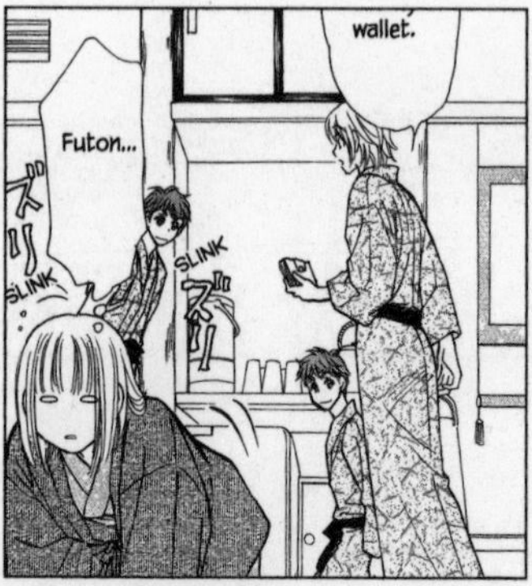
wallet.
SLINK
Futon...
SLINK

Unlike the futons we use in America, a Japanese futon has two parts. The thicker part is laid on the floor and used as a mattress, while the thinner part is used as a blanket. In the morning, it's all rolled up and put away.

Revenge, page 67

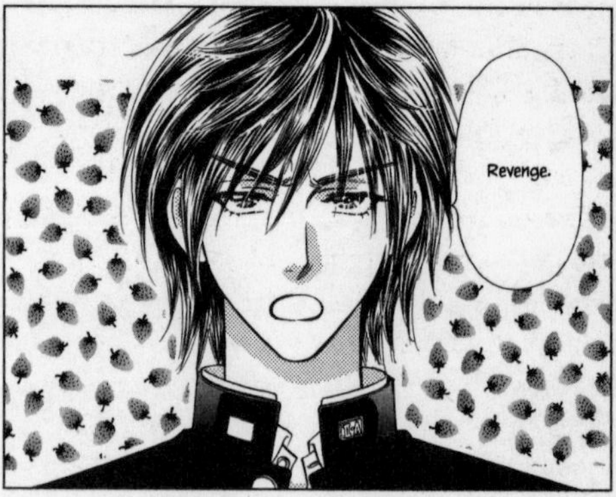
Revenge.

In Japan, the English term "revenge" can refer to revenge, or to the determination of a loser to win their next game or match.

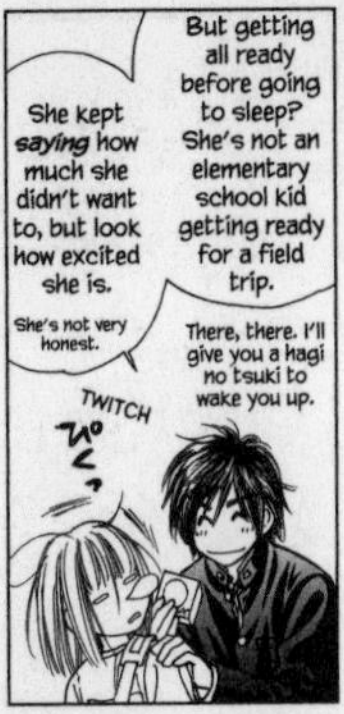
But getting all ready before going to sleep? She's not an elementary school kid getting ready for a field trip.
She kept *saying* how much she didn't want to, but look how excited she is.
There, there. I'll give you a hagi no tsuki to wake you up.
She's not very honest.
TWITCH

Hagi no tsuki, page 73

Hagi no tsuki literally means "bush clover moon," and refers to a treat made in Miyagi Prefecture to resemble the harvest moon.

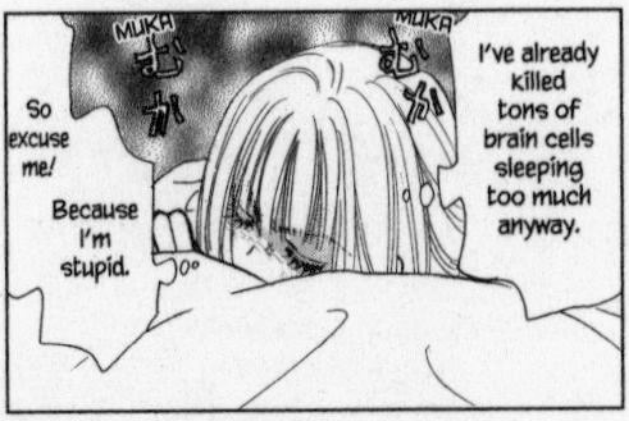
MUKA
MUKA
I've already killed tons of brain cells sleeping too much anyway.
So excuse me!
Because I'm stupid.

Muka, page 89

Muka is the sound of being angry or annoyed.

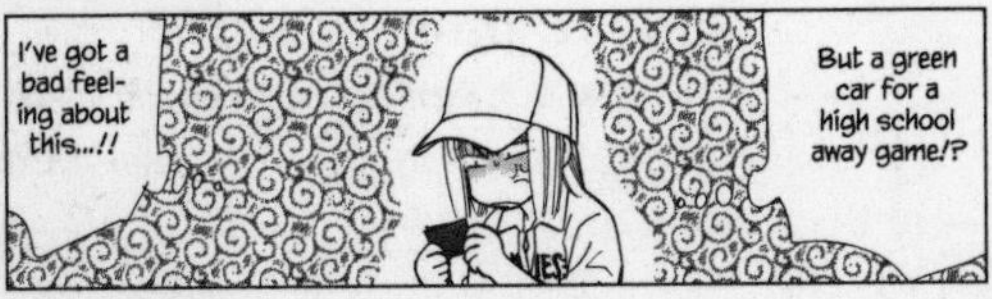
But a green car for a high school away game!?
I've got a bad feeling about this...!!

Green car, page 100

A first-class car.

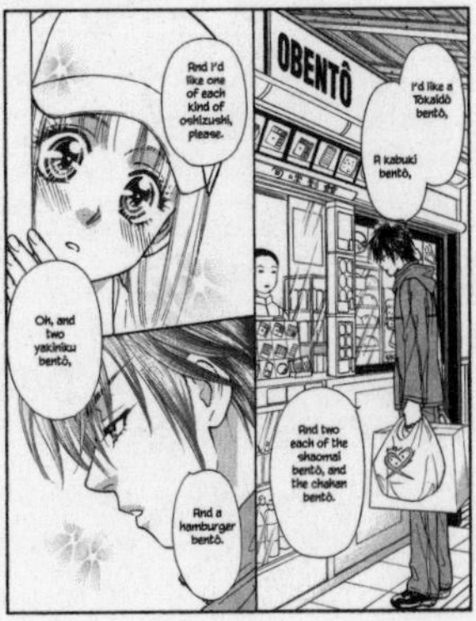
OBENTÔ
I'd like a Tôkaidô bentô,
A kabuki bentô,
And two each of the shaomai bentô, and the chahan bentô.
And I'd like one of each kind of oshizushi, please.
Oh, and two yakiniku bentô,
And a hamburger bentô.

Tôkaidô *bentô, kabuki bentô...*, page 101

The different types of *bentô* Izumi orders refer to the different side dishes that come with the rice in the lunch. One of the highlights of an *ekiben* is that it gives a sampling of the local specialties at the various stops along a train line. A Tôkaidô *bentô* is a sampling of the many cuisines one might find at the stops along the Tôkaidô line. A *kabuki bentô* is the standard *bentô* and includes fish, *tamagoyaki* (fried egg), and vegetables. A *shaomai* or *shumai bentô* features Chinese-style fried dumplings. A *chahan bentô* has Chinese-style fried rice. *Oshizushi* is literally "pressed sushi": sushi rice and other ingredients are pressed together in a box or mold. *Yakiniku bentô* comes with Japanese-style fried meat, and a hamburger *bentô*, of course, is served with a hamburger patty.

Fu mochi, page 107

A type of confection made by wrapping *nama-fu*, a kind of dough made from wheat flour, around some red bean filling.

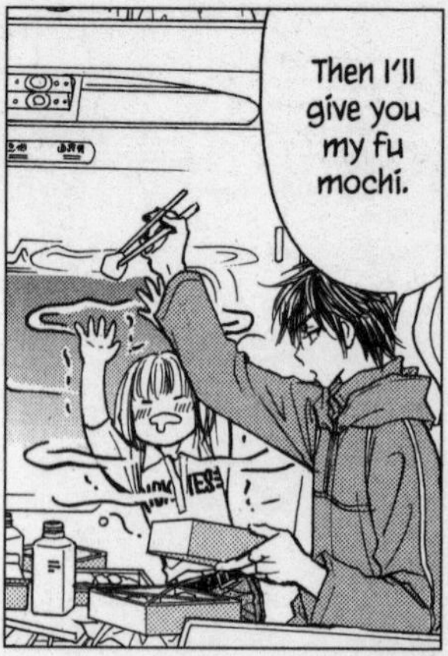
Then I'll give you my fu mochi.

Kansai, page 108

The western region of Japan where famous cities such as Kyoto and Kobe are located.

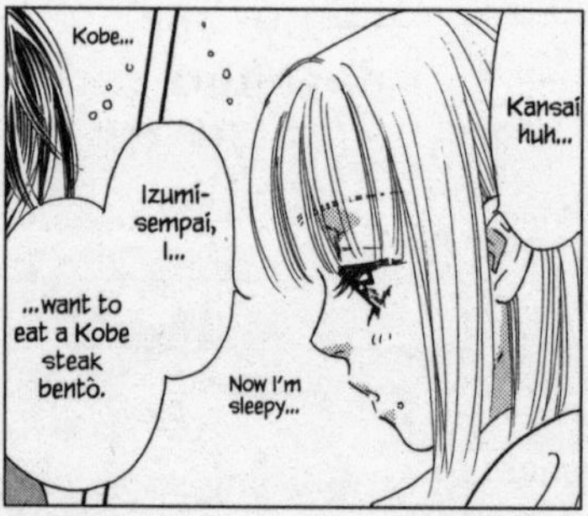
Kansai huh...
Kobe...
Now I'm sleepy...
Izumi-sempai, I...
...want to eat a Kobe steak bentô.

Stupid in kanji, page 115

When Takashi calls Hana stupid, *baka*, or "stupid," is written in kanji, or Chinese characters. Usually it is written in the much simpler Japanese characters, katakana, so Takashi is emphasizing how much smarter he is than Hana by showing off his knowledge of kanji.

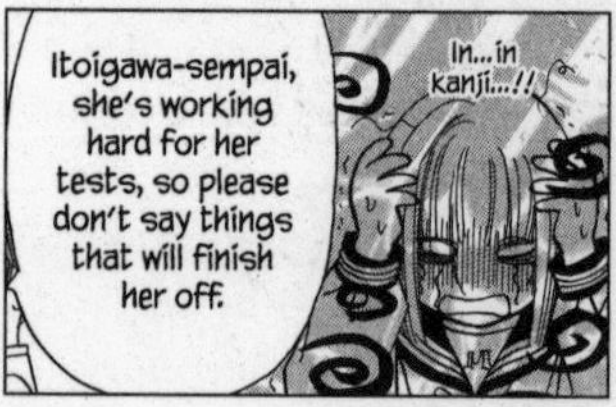
In...in kanji...!!
Itoigawa-sempai, she's working hard for her tests, so please don't say things that will finish her off.

Botan-nabe, page 125

Botan-nabe, also known as "peony hot pot," is a type of *nabemono* or stew, made with wild boar meat.

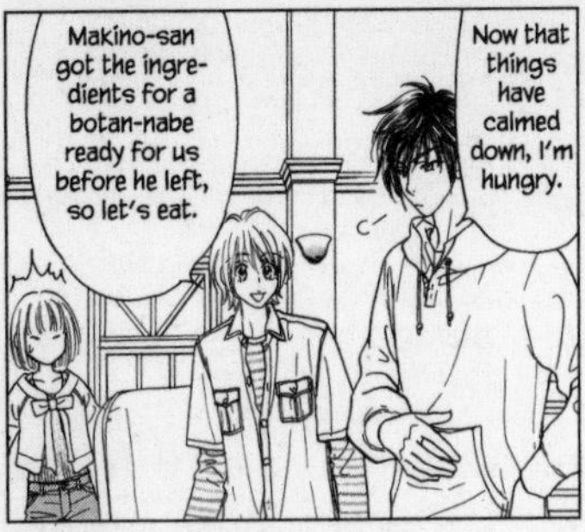
Now that things have calmed down, I'm hungry.
Makino-san got the ingredients for a botan-nabe ready for us before he left, so let's eat.

Yukata, page 136

A *yukata* is an informal summer kimono made of cotton, also used as a bathrobe.

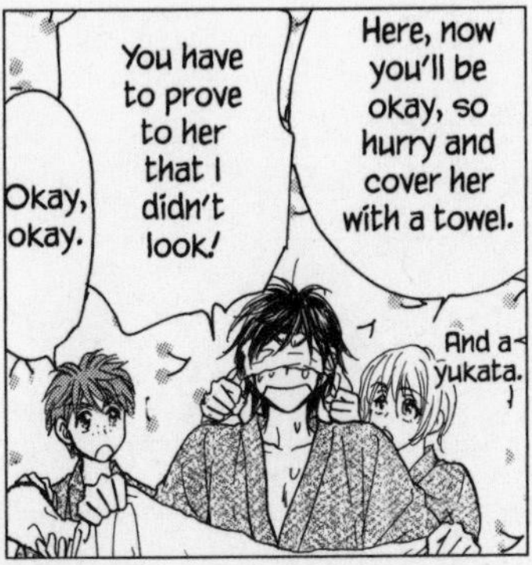
Here, now you'll be okay, so hurry and cover her with a towel.
You have to prove to her that I didn't look!
Okay, okay.
And a yukata.

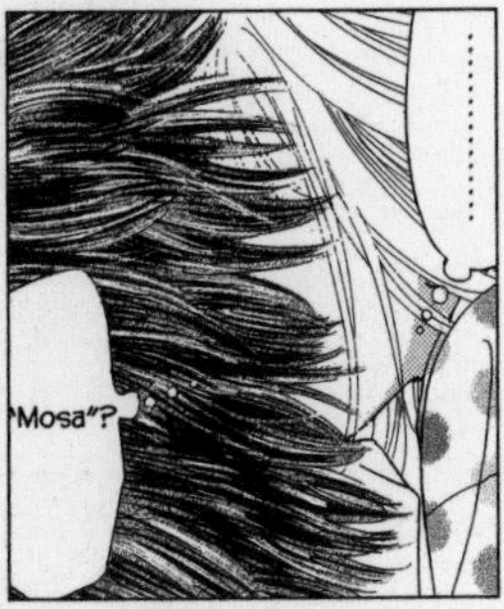
......
"Mosa"?

Mosa, page 169

Mosa is the sound of touching something furry.

Ira, page 175

Ira is the sound of being irritated or impatient.

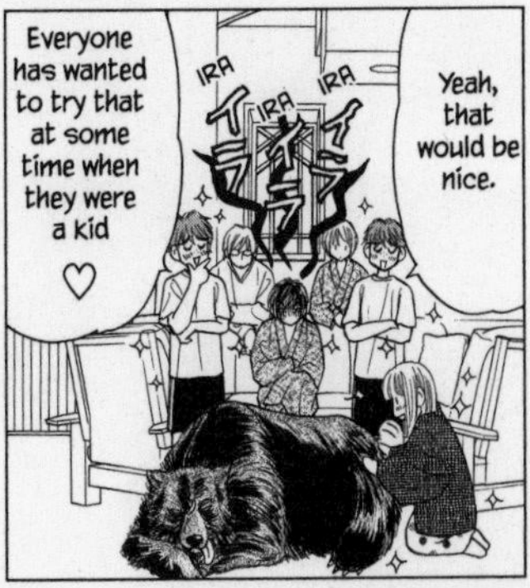
Yeah, that would be nice.
IRA
IRA
IRA
Everyone has wanted to try that at some time when they were a kid ♡

Team Kuma, page 193

Kuma is Japanese for "bear."

Preview of *My Heavenly Hockey Club*, volume 2.

We're pleased to present you a preview from *My Heavenly Hockey Club*, volume 2. This volume will be available in English on August 28, 2007!

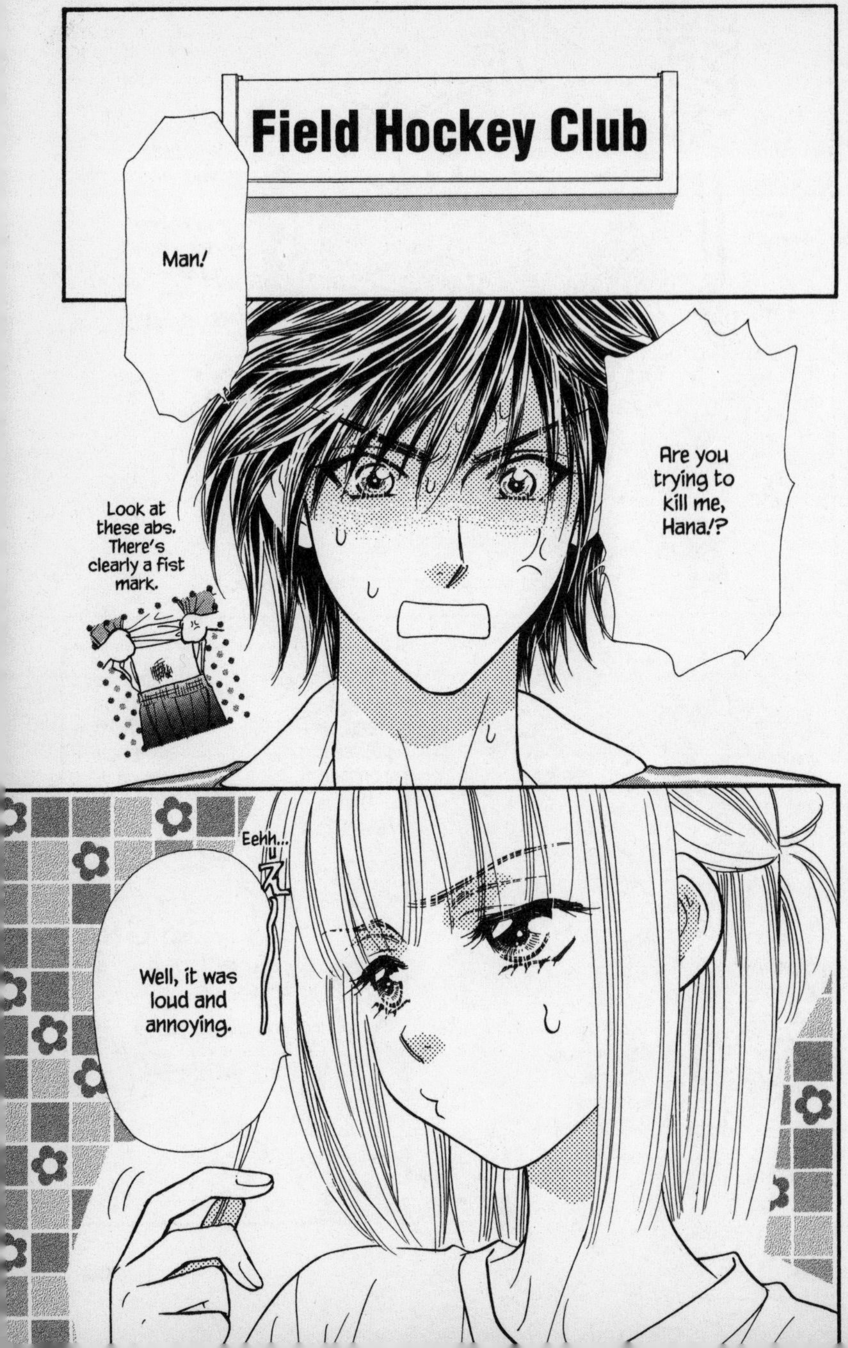
Field Hockey Club
Man!
Are you trying to kill me, Hana!?
Look at these abs. There's clearly a fist mark.
Eehh...
Well, it was loud and annoying.

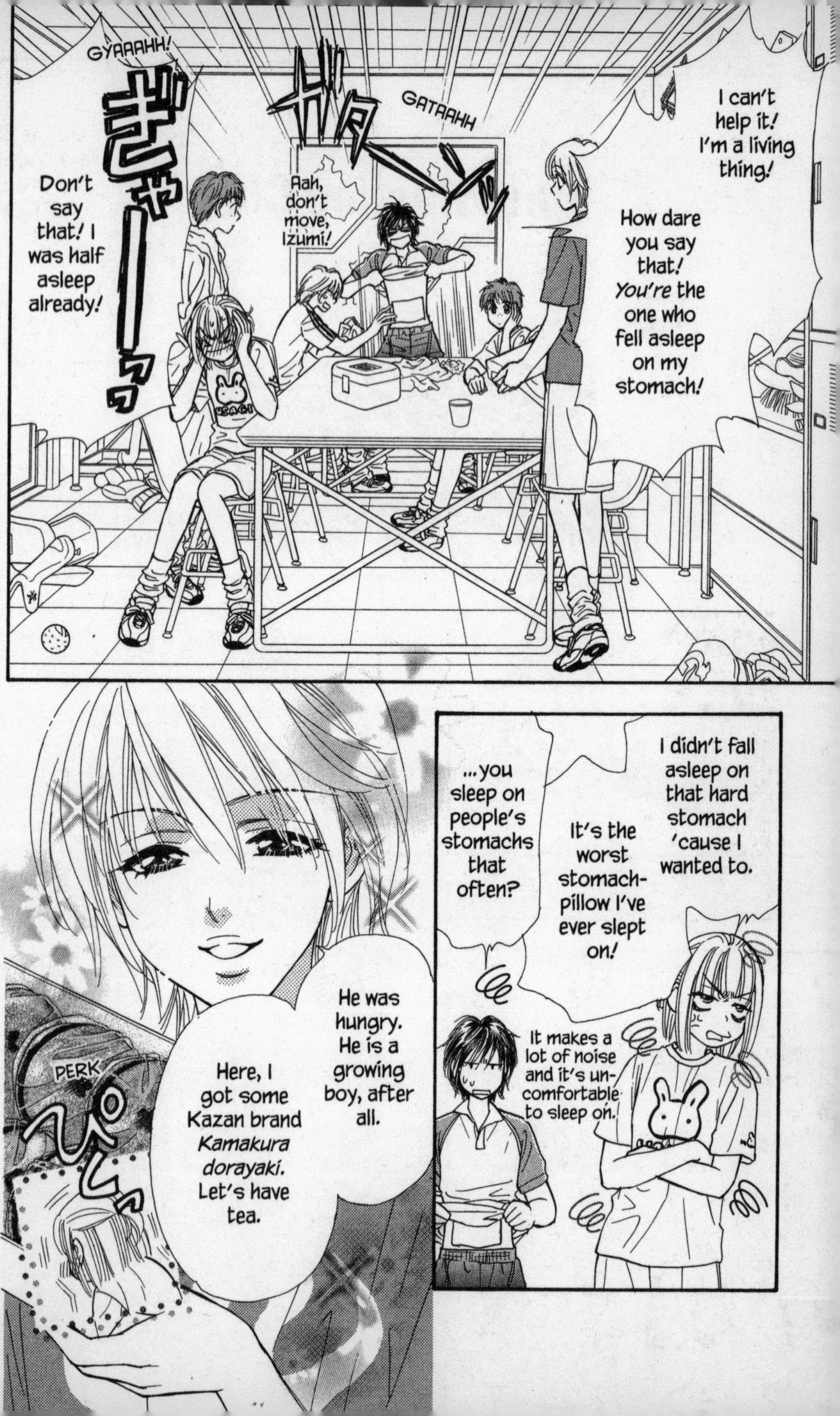

I can't help it! I'm a living thing!
How dare you say that! *You're* the one who fell asleep on my stomach!
GATAAHH
Aah, don't move, Izumi!
GYAAAHH!
Don't say that! I was half asleep already!
I didn't fall asleep on that hard stomach 'cause I wanted to.
It's the worst stomach-pillow I've ever slept on!
...you sleep on people's stomachs that often?
It makes a lot of noise and it's uncomfortable to sleep on.
He was hungry. He is a growing boy, after all.
Here, I got some Kazan brand *Kamakura dorayaki*. Let's have tea.
PERK

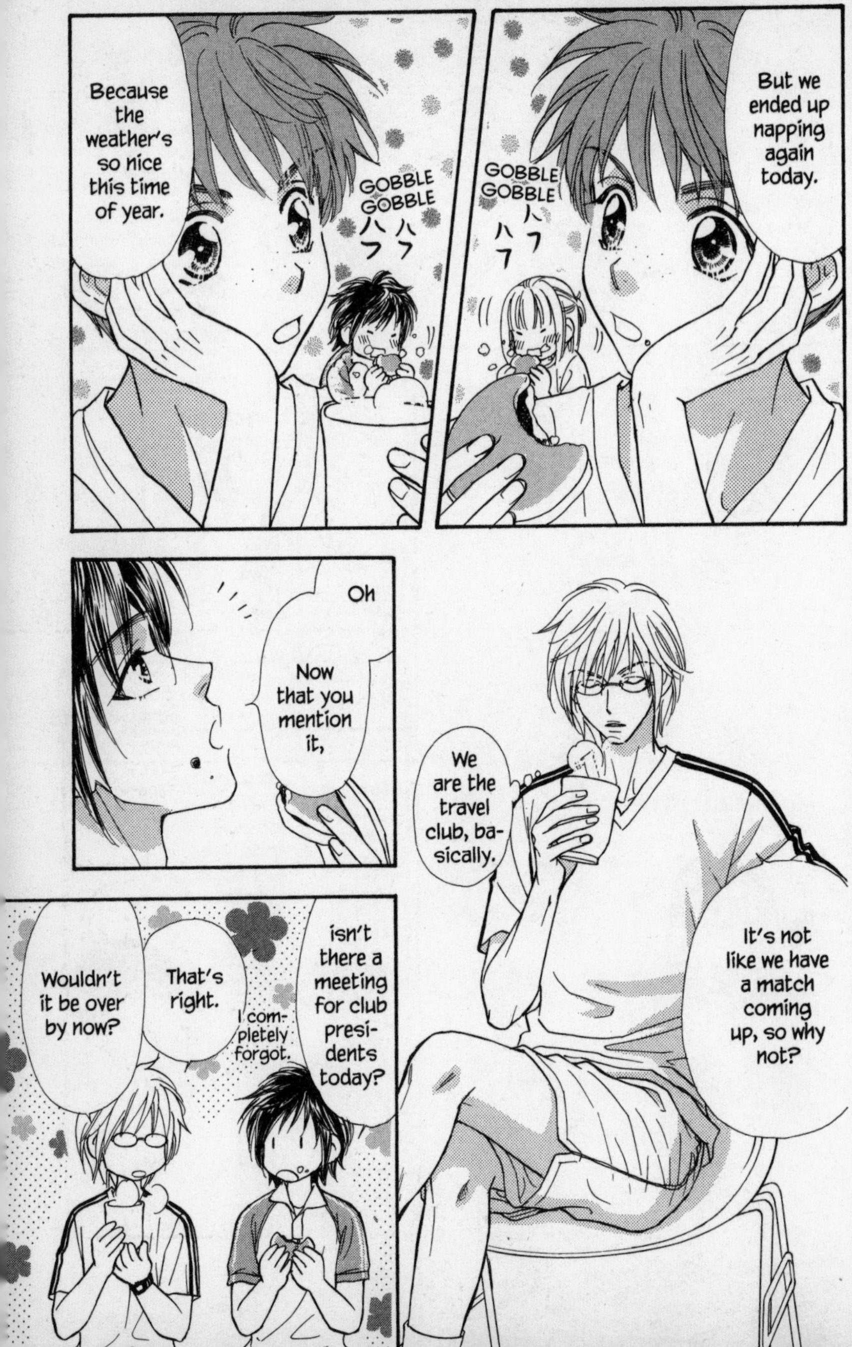
But we ended up napping again today.
GOBBLE GOBBLE
ハフ ハフ
Because the weather's so nice this time of year.
GOBBLE GOBBLE
ハフ ハフ
We are the travel club, basically.
It's not like we have a match coming up, so why not?
Oh
Now that you mention it,
isn't there a meeting for club presidents today?
I completely forgot.
That's right.
Wouldn't it be over by now?

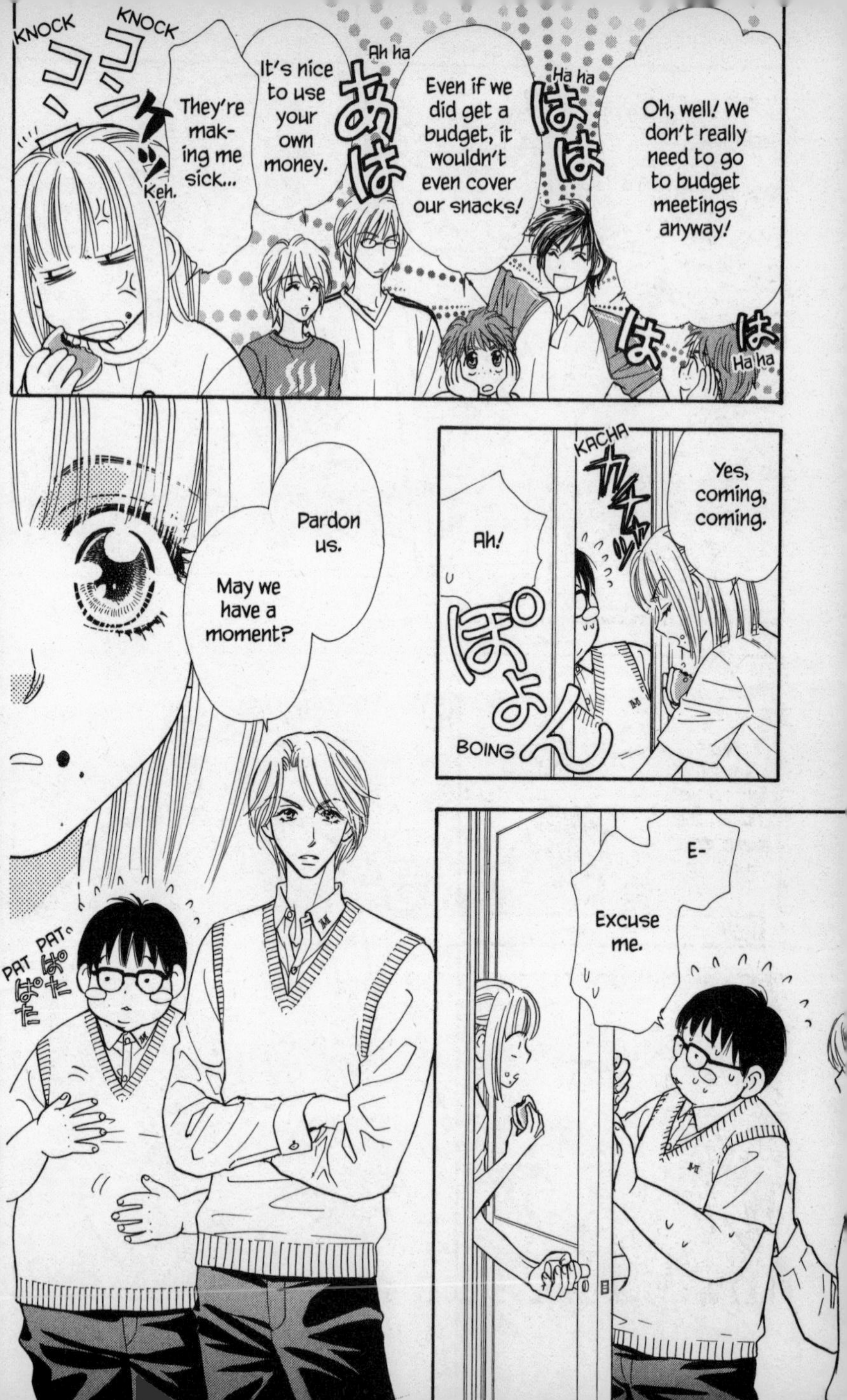
Oh, well! We don't really need to go to budget meetings anyway!
Ha ha
Ha ha
Even if we did get a budget, it wouldn't even cover our snacks!
Ah ha
It's nice to use your own money.
They're mak-ing me sick...
Keh.
KNOCK KNOCK
Yes, coming, coming.
KACHA
Ah!
BOING
E-
Excuse me.
Pardon us.
May we have a moment?
PAT PAT

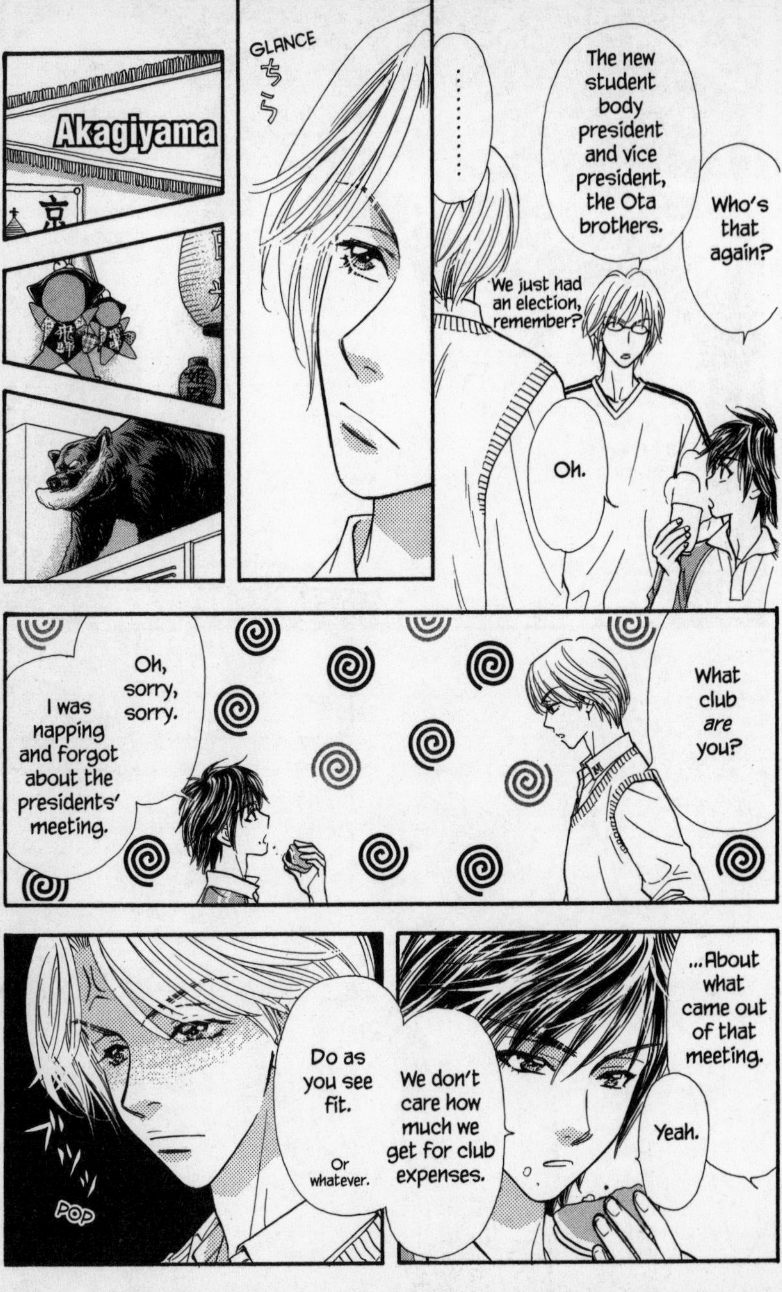
The new student body president and vice president, the Ota brothers.
Who's that again?
We just had an election, remember?
Oh.
......
GLANCE
ちら
Akagiyama
What club *are* you?
Oh, sorry, sorry.
I was napping and forgot about the presidents' meeting.
...About what came out of that meeting.
Yeah.
We don't care how much we get for club expenses.
Do as you see fit.
Or whatever.
POP

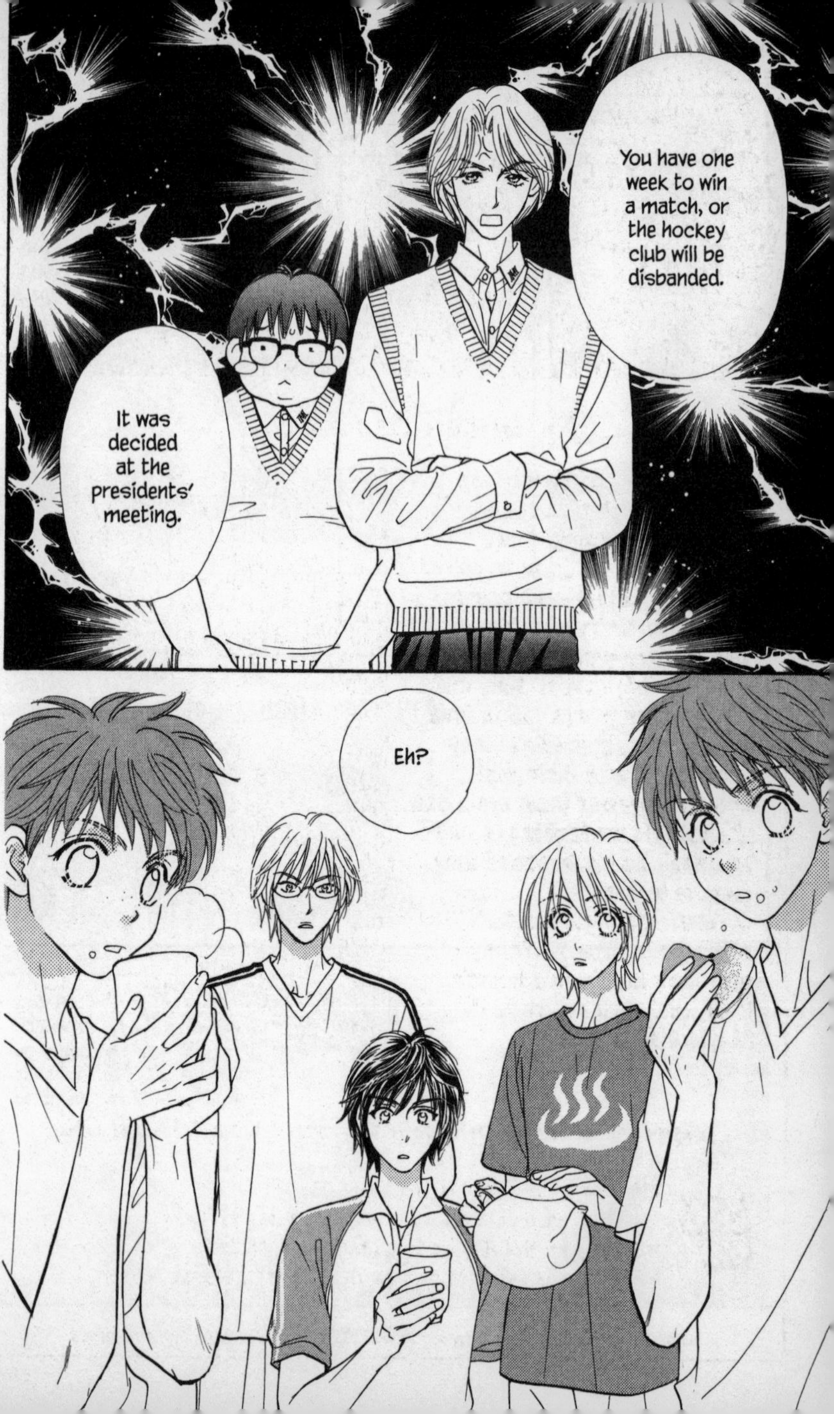
You have one week to win a match, or the hockey club will be disbanded.
It was decided at the presidents' meeting.
Eh?

Sugar Sugar Rune

BY MOYOCO ANNO

QUEEN OF HEARTS

Chocolat and Vanilla are young witch princesses from a magical land. They've come to Earth to compete in a contest—whichever girl captures the most hearts will become queen! While living in a boarding school, they must make as many boys fall in love with them as possible if they want to achieve their goal. Standing against them are a pair of rival princes looking to capture their hearts because they want to be king!

There's danger for the witch-girls, though: If they give their hearts to a human, they may never return to the Magical World....

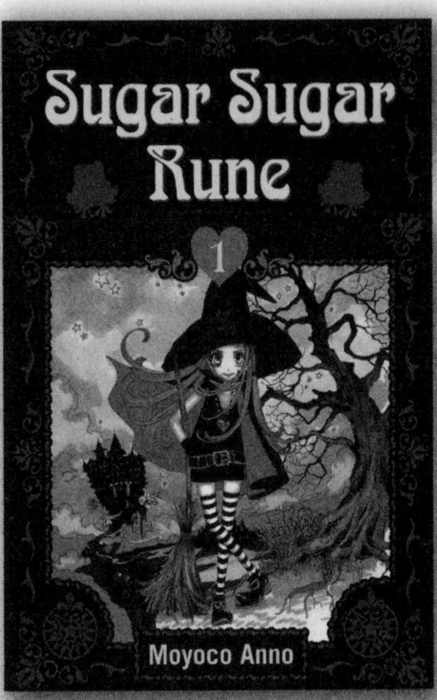
Sugar Sugar Rune
1
Moyoco Anno

Ages: 10 +

Special extras in each volume! Read them all!

DEL REY

VISIT WWW.DELREYMANGA.COM TO:
- View release date calendars for upcoming volumes
- Sign up for Del Rey's free manga e-newsletter
- Find out the latest about new Del Rey Manga series

Pichi Pichi Pitch

MANGA BY PINK HANAMORI
SCENARIO BY MICHIKO YOKOTE

WET AND WONDERFUL!

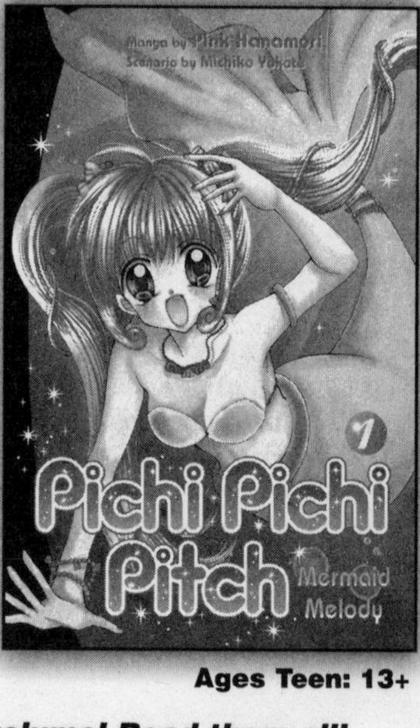
Manga by Pink Hanamori
Scenario by Michiko Yokote
1
Pichi Pichi Pitch
Mermaid Melody

Lucia is the new girl at school. She and her sister run a public bath that's all the rage. When Lucia meets a terrific-looking surfer boy, there's just one little problem: Lucia is a mermaid—not just any mermaid, but a princess on an important mission to save the seven seas from an evil force bent on taking control of the marine world. Such a responsibility doesn't leave much time for romance. But Lucia vows to protect her world and win the heart of handsome Kaito.

Pichi Pichi Pitch is an extremely popular anime in Japan. Now it's the newest craze in the world of magical-girl manga!

Ages Teen: 13+

Special extras in each volume! Read them all!

DEL REY

VISIT WWW.DELREYMANGA.COM TO:
- Read sample pages
- View release date calendars for upcoming volumes
- Sign up for Del Rey's free manga e-newsletter
- Find out the latest about new Del Rey Manga series

KITCHEN PRINCESS

STORY BY MIYUKI KOBAYASHI
MANGA BY NATSUMI ANDO
CREATOR OF ZODIAC P.I.

HUNGRY HEART

Najika is a great cook and likes to make meals for the people she loves. But something is missing from her life. When she was a child, she met a boy who touched her heart—and now Najika is determined to find him. The only clue she has is a silver spoon that leads her to the prestigious Seika Academy.

Attending Seika will be a challenge. Every kid at the school has a special talent, and the girls in Najika's class think she doesn't deserve to be there. But Sora and Daichi, two popular brothers who barely speak to each other, recognize Najika's cooking for what it is—magical. Could one of the boys be Najika's mysterious prince?

Special extras in each volume! Read them all!

VISIT WWW.DELREYMANGA.COM TO:
• Read sample pages
• View release date calendars for upcoming volumes
• Sign up for Del Rey's free manga e-newsletter
• Find out the latest about new Del Rey Manga series

RATING T AGES 13+

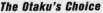

The Otaku's Choice

TOMARE!

You're going the wrong way!

Manga is a completely different type of reading experience.

To start at the beginning, go to the end!

That's right! Authentic manga is read the traditional Japanese way—from right to left. Exactly the opposite of how American books are read. It's easy to follow: Just go to the other end of the book, and read each page—and each panel—from right side to left side, starting at the top right. Now you're experiencing manga as it was meant to be!